UP CLOSE AND PERSONAL

A HISTORY OF LA PORTE COUNTY

by
Arnold Bass

Bloomington, IN   Milton Keynes, UK
authorHOUSE

AuthorHouse™
1663 Liberty Drive, Suite 200
Bloomington, IN 47403
www.authorhouse.com
Phone: 1-800-839-8640

AuthorHouse™ UK Ltd.
500 Avebury Boulevard
Central Milton Keynes, MK9 2BE
www.authorhouse.co.uk
Phone: 08001974150

This book is a work of non-fiction. Unless otherwise noted, the author and the publisher make no explicit guarantees as to the accuracy of the information contained in this book and in some cases, names of people and places have been altered to protect their privacy.

©2006 Arnold Bass. All rights reserved.

No part of this book may be reproduced, stored in a retrieval system, or transmitted by any means without the written permission of the author.

First published by AuthorHouse 5/10/2006

ISBN: 1-4208-3880-6 (sc)

Library of Congress Control Number: 2005902882

Printed in the United States of America
Bloomington, Indiana

This book is printed on acid-free paper.

TABLE OF CONTENTS

PREFACE	VII
WRAF LA PORTE "VOICE OF THE MAPLE CITY"	1
BENJAMIN FRANKLIN: THE FORGOTTEN ONE	11
AVIATION HISTORY IN THE MAKING	13
THE INDIANA TERRITORIAL BOUNDARY	47
A DREAM FULFILLED: THE BUILDING OF THE AFRICAN METHODIST EPISCOPAL CHURCHES IN MICHIGAN CITY & LA PORTE	51
AMAZING WOMEN OF LA PORTE COUNTY	61
THE LIFE AND TIMES OF HENRY "DAD" HEISMAN	71
DISCRIMINATION A PART OF CITY'S HISTORY	81
IN THE BEGINNING: LONG BEACH SCHOOL	84
POTTAWATTOMIE BOY SCOUT CAMP	89
THE SALVATION ARMY: "PENETRATE(S) THE 'DARK CORNERS' IN THE UNCULTIVATED FIELDS OF RELIGIOUS AND RELIEF ENDEAVOR."	97
INDIANA DUNES HIGHWAY	105
THE ADVENTURES OF CAPTAIN EDDY	109
BEACON LIGHTS	117
WHEN THE STAGECOACH RULED THE ROADWAY	171
MICHIGAN CITY'S SPORTY GOLF COURSE	177
THE CENTRAL THEATRE: A VAUDEVILLE, PICTURE AND ROAD SHOW HOUSE	185
CAMP ANDERSON & THE BOYS OF COMPANY A	189
THE PROTESTANT HOSPITAL	197
INTIMATE SKETCHES OF BUSINESS MEN OF MICHIGAN CITY	207
KNIGHTS OF THE KU KLUX KLAN	231
APPENDIX NO. 1	259
APPENDIX NO. 2	261
APPENDIX NO. 3	263
APPENDIX NO. 4	265

APPENDIX NO. 5	267
ENDNOTES	269
INDEX	275

PREFACE

One afternoon in 1967 I was in the Teacher's Lounge of Elston Senior High School with Miss Charlotte Taylor. We were both teachers at the time. We were engaged in conversation, reminiscing about Michigan City and its past history. Miss Taylor (I was never able to call her Charlotte because she was my language arts teacher back in 7th grade at Elston Junior High in 1947) at one point began talking about her recollections as a very young girl watching the Ku Klux Klan parade on Franklin Street. Up until that time I had never given thought to such an event taking place in "my town." The scene of those ghostly figures dressed from head to toe in white bed sheets and pointed hats with masks covering their faces stayed with me. I thought someday that I would document the Klan's activities in La Porte County.

It wasn't until 1996, a year after my retirement from the Michigan City school system that I recalled that conversation with Miss Taylor. My curiosity took me to the libraries in La Porte and Michigan City. As I began reviewing the microfilm of the four major newspapers in the county during the 1920's, I not only found the information about the Ku Klux Klan but also became aware of numerous articles related to the history of La Porte County. My discovery caused me to splinter my efforts into many directions. I was excited over my find of interesting historical material buried in the archives of microfilm. Activities, stories of individuals whose contributions helped to shade and shape the history of our county and events that hadn't seen the light of day for over seventy years attempted to pull me from my original task.

After years of research I wrote a history of the Klan in La Porte County but I also wrote several articles that I hope will capture your interest and excite you as I have been in this process. I have also incorporated in this book unedited reprints of articles that appeared from time to time in the four county newspapers. This book is not an effort to provide the reader with a chronological history of La Porte County. It is my attempt to bring you an UP CLOSE AND

PERSONAL view of some of the people, places and events that have shaped and molded La Porte County.

I would like to thank James Rodgers, Curator of the La Porte County Historical Society Museum for his assistance, keen eye and the many hours he devoted to the editing of the preliminary draft of this book. He spent numerous hours reviewing the manuscript and noteing gramarical errors and the silly mistakes made do to my impatients. Jim, I thank you one more time for your effort to make me look good.

Arnold Bass

"Radio and television, which is ready to step on the stage, represents the greatest possibilities in the field of communication which men had yet wrung from nature."

Editorial, **HERALD-ARGUS**
February 10, 1930

WRAF LA PORTE "VOICE OF THE MAPLE CITY"

Radio station WRAF was one of the oldest stations in the nation. It was established by Charles Middleton the founder and owner of the La Porte Radio Club. The station was located in his home at 1210 Michigan Avenue, where it remained for a year. Middleton, who held a radio operator's license, built the broadcasting equipment. The first successful broadcast of a program over WRAF occurred on April 12, 1923, according to the DAILY HERALD. Middleton read a story from a radio magazine. He asked at the end of the program that those who were able to hear him and "testify to the success of the venture," should call. Several local persons called to say they heard the broadcast.

According to Middleton, WRAF would not attempt to compete with surrounding stations, but would concentrate on programs of interest to the people of La Porte. Future programming was done entirely for testing purposes until a license to operate was obtained. Feature programs as well as news events were initially heard. The following month it was announced that, through special arrangements made between the HERALD and the Radio Club, late big league baseball scores would be broadcast to the local residents. The HERALD would pass on to the station for broadcast scores received too late to appear in the evening paper.

The station, WRAF of the Radio Club, Inc., received a federal license near the end of April to broadcast its programming over a wave length of 224 meters. A formal inauguration was planned that included a local speaker and a concert performed by a local orchestra. Middleton stated that, "These concerts will not be held often, as we do not wish to interfere with the high class concerts broadcast from other stations."

A variety of programming was heard over the next 18 months that included select church services and local talent. In mid-June, the Reverend Paul Eickstaedt of St. John's Lutheran Church, conducted services from the station. A church quartet composed of George and Fred Petering, Charles H. Meier, and Paul Tanger sang before and after the sermon. By February of 1924, "What promised to be the most complete radio program yet to broadcast from station WRAF" on Monday radio, according to the ARGUS, was heard by the citizens of La Porte. Through the cooperation of THE ARGUS and The Radio Club, Inc., semi-weekly concerts included vocals by Hazel Heinbeck, Earl Crowe, John Neilson, and C. D. Chipman. Pianists Mrs. V. Houserand and Earl Crowe performed, as well as violinist Warren Cook. Jack Dresner presented the various artists as well as doing a number of humorous sketches. The station's equipment was also upgraded a week prior to the new programming. The transmitter was completely rebuilt and rewired, resulting in a change in wavelength to 235 meters. Those that experienced difficulty in tuning in the signal previously were assured of better reception.

In less than 2 years of broadcasting, WRAF in partnership with THE HERALD-ARGUS may have begun what was to become a normally expected tradition, the "Play-by-Play Tale of (basketball) Game(s)." That innovative event took place on January 30, 1925. The HERALD-ARGUS had "Leased a telephone wire...at considerable cost..." between La Porte and the Y. M. C. A. in South Bend. THE ARGUS proclaimed that this might very well be the first time in the history of radio that a play-by-play description of a high school basketball game, as it was being played, was brought to home fans. A representative of the paper attended the game in South Bend. He spoke directly by phone to the radio station, describing the game. The radio announcer repeated the information into the microphone. La Porte won the game, 51 to 17. The paper reported that the glass backboards, "a novelty to the visitors was given as the reason for the small score." A letter from a fan in New York State saying he had enjoyed perfect reception of the game indicated that the account of the game received wide circulation. A long tradition of broadcasting La Porte basketball continued.

Another innovation in broadcasting occurred in mid-February, 1925. WRAF aired Sunday school lessons for those unable to attend. The Methodist Fraternal Bible Class provided the lessons. The first teacher was R. N. Smith. The class orchestra provided music.

Three months later the station temporarily closed down in preparation of its move to larger quarters in the Rumely Hotel. In conjunction with the Chamber of Commerce, a committee composed of H. Myron Smith, R. E. Teverbaugh, Charles A. Beal, and Middleton completed arrangements for the move. The Chamber's "Me for La Porte" campaign was the catalyst for close cooperation between it and the station's development and operation. The station was back on the air, May 18, with the completion of the construction of the station's antennae on the roof and the conversion of a room in the basement "...into a first class studio...." The first program upon returning to the air was referred to as a test program. A well-known local singer in amateur dramas along with G. Earl Moss and Clifford Davidson performed. WRAF boasted that the improvements and increased power output of 100 watts made it possible for the programming to be heard all over the United States and far into Canada.

UP CLOSE AND PERSONAL

One of the more popular groups heard by La Porte listeners in 1925, was Fred Berger's Society Synconaders. This local dance band featured Roger Hybner, violin; John Neilson, vocal; Irving Ebert, trumpet; all accompanied and with "incidental refrains by Ethan Franklin Hiley." The E. C. Luedtke Drugstore often sponsored these programs.

Figure 1 The Sod Busters, 1926. Top row l-r Eugene Wright, Bob Montieth, 2nd row-Bob Milles, Paul Smith, Ralph Smith, and Ben L. Griffin. Courtesy of the LaPorte Co. Historical Society.

For those fortunate to own a radio, WRAF aired a New Year's Eve program that lasted well into the wee hours of the morning. The All Men's Bible Class Orchestra under the direction of Miss Marvel Hunt had "...a prominent part in the evening's entertainment. The Sod Buster's orchestra alternated selections, rounding out the instrumental portion of the program. One of the vocalists featured was Verne Watts who was accompanied by his daughter at the piano.

The New Year found the station moved to the basement of the Odd Fellows Building at the corner of Michigan and Jefferson Avenues. By the end of July, a newly remodeled soundproof studio was completed upstairs in the rear of the Radio Club room. Listeners continued to be treated to the sounds of local talent as well as performers from outside the county. The harmonious sounds of the Peterson's Florida Crackers, The Maple City Four, the Conn Holloway's High Tension Orchestra, and the All Men Bible Class Orchestra provided many evenings of entertainment. November 1, 1926, brought a special treat. The La Porte Democratic Committee sponsored the highly sought after Wiedergott Sisters of Knox. The previous summer they had won first prize at the Indiana State contest put on by WLS of Chicago. The second half of the l926-27 basketball season saw Charles Middleton announce a change in policy. The HERALD-ARGUS would no longer be involved in the broadcasting of Slicer basketball. The announcement marked "the passing of the famous combination..." of WRAF, the ARGUS and the former La Porte Telephone Company that inaugurated what was believed to be the first broadcast of a high school basketball game. The ARGUS had paid the telephone and travel expenses, as well as the announcer, during the first year.

The last two games played in January 1927, as well as the remaining contests were underwritten through advertising done by various city firms. Middleton hired an announcer that would be in the school gym. The change resulted from the expenses he incurred by furnishing the power to air the home games. He had told the ARGUS that he could no longer afford the expense "...and that some revenue is necessary to make the broadcasting possible."

Figure 2 The Maple City Four from top to bottom Fritz Meissner, Al Rice, Pat Petterson and Art Janes in a 1930's photo. Rice replaced Bob Meissner an original member of the quartet. They made regular appearances on the WLS Barn Dance for over 25 years. Courtesy of the La Porte County Historical Society.

March brought a cloud that immersed the listeners of station WRAF in despair and anxiety. The passage by Congress of new radio legislation put the fate of the station's continual operations in jeopardy. Middleton applied for a new license. He was optimistic that a new license would be granted since his station had obtained the 36th license in the country, thereby making it one of the oldest. May of 1927 brought good news. The Federal Radio Commission granted WRAF, one of the 69 stations in the Chicago district, a new wave length. The change was an effort to clear up "air-congestion" in the area, particularly from WBBM, Chicago, that "...proved a continual source of annoyance..." for local radio fans.

The next day, May 24, the ARGUS announced the sale of assets, stock, fixtures and accounts of the station to Roy Pagin, president of the Radio Shop, and Paul Bowman. The two, for the previous two years, had owned the shop at 605 Lincoln Way. Their purchase meant a considerable expansion for the business. Charles Middleton was employed to manage the station.

The following month, it appeared as though the sale fell through. It was announced that WRAF might be forced to leave the air on June 15. The cost to upgrade the equipment to meet the new federal standard was more than Middleton or the new owners could afford. The largest expense would be an antenna system that would not allow the station's signal to sway during times of strong winds. The new equipment and antenna system was expected to cost $300. The station's income had been insufficient to support the station and the necessary upgrade.

The ARGUS initiated a fund drive to keep the station on the air. By the end of June, the paper had announced that $231.07 had been raised. Radio fans and boosters had been urged to do their part. The drive ended successfully by the end of the first week in July; $305.32 had been collected. The remodeling and upgrading of equipment to improve the sending qualities began. Floyd Zerber assisted in the renovations. Two wooden towers "...built in the shape of skeleton frameworks..." would hold the aerials more securely and prevent them from swaying in the breeze. The towers were located in the vicinity of Jefferson and Michigan Avenues.

With the upgrading of the equipment the station in conjunction with the Herald-Argus inaugurated the broadcasting of short summaries of sporting events as well as local and national news on a daily basis with the exception of Sundays. The 12:30 afternoon reports began on July 27th and were preceded by a musical program.

Station WRAF, Radio Club, Inc., returned to the airwaves officially on August 1st under the ownership of R. Paul Bowman, J. Roy Pagin, Charles Middleton and John B. Condra. With improved reception, listeners on the next two evening broadcasts were treated to the sounds of La Porteans Marie Henry Danner, pianist; Della Morrow, violinist; Aden Long, cornetist; Marjorie Smith, contralto; as well as Arnold Carter and John Murr Long Beach and Michigan City entertainers headed by Conn R. Holloway "gave a snappy group of guitar selections." Assisting him were Walter Calvert, Floyd Bentley, George Signitz and Charles Van Gisen. The Swift brothers played Hawaiian guitar music. Ben Griffin called and George Reynolds and Elmer Freeland played some lively, hand clapping barn dance music.

WRAF continued on the cutting edge of history. On the 6th of August 1927, Roy Pagin flew over the city of La Porte with Gene Gabbert, of the Dale Seitz Safe and Sane Flying Circus, to test the station's radio reception. Pagin, with a radio and headphones, relayed to Gabbert directions given by Middleton from the ground. A series of maneuvers were performed over the business district of La Porte. The "... plane turned or dived almost as soon as the words were out of the mouth of the announcer...." A large number of downtown shoppers and listeners at home were attracted by the test that Saturday afternoon. The following week another test was scheduled due to the high level of listener interest. This time miniature parachutes were dropped over the city on Middleton's command containing several prizes. Some included a Radiola Receiver, a Brunswick phonograph record and a De Forrest radio tube.

The apparent end of an historic tradition of broadcasting Slicer basketball occurred with the 1927 basketball season. The school board announced that the games would not be broadcast unless all seats to the contest were sold. Due to a losing season the previous year, attendance declined. Middleton cited the financial uncertainty and the hardship surrounding the acquisition of an advertiser with short notice as reasons to end broadcasting. Nine days later, the school board reversed its decision. The editorial support and the unprecedented public outcry and demand saw W. G. Ludlow, principal of the high school, announce the school board's decision to reverse its earlier announcement.

WRAF under Middleton's leadership continued to grow and prosper. As programming became more extensive, Bradley Kincaid of La Porte was hired as its program director. Kincaid had been a featured entertainer for station WLS, Chicago, performing old mountain songs and "Negro" melodies. Over the years, the station had established sub-stations that allowed the broadcasting of news or events from a location other than the main studio. Middleton had constructed a new amplifier that would increase the station's efficiency and capability to provide composite programs from one or more of the other places. The laying of under ground telephone cable and an automatic switch at WRAF made it possible to change programs on the air from other locations with the turn of a dial and no interruption of air time.

By mid-May, 1928, new equipment, consisting of a microphone and amplifier, was installed "...in one of the less noisy corners..." of the HERALD-ARGUS editorial room. The public was able to hear G. R. Parker, managing editor, give "...snappy local, national, (and) foreign news bulletins." In the background could be heard the clicking of telegraph printers and typewriters, adding a little newspaper atmosphere.

The mail at the end of May contained a notice from the Federal Radio Commission of a hearing in Washington D. C. on July 9. The commission was requiring stations to justify their existence by giving proof that they served the "...public interest, convenience or necessity," or stop broadcasting by August 1. This burden was placed largely on the smaller stations. A large-scale campaign to arouse public support was launched. Middleton urged the public to write letters to the commission, Congressman Andrew J. Hickey and Senators Arthur R. Robinson and James E. Watson. The Michigan City Chamber of Commerce added its voice of support by passing a resolution, urging the commission to keep WRAF on the air.

In order to mount a more effective campaign, representatives from 50 small radio stations met at the Stevens Hotel, Chicago, and organized the Independent Broadcasters' association. Middleton and Paul Bowman attended. Middleton was elected to serve as a director of the association. Representatives from the newly formed association attended the Washington hearing to plead their case. Middleton was among them and made strong arguments as to why WRAF and the members of the new organization should be allowed to stay on the air. The stations that argued their case before the commission were notified at the end of July that a 31-day renewal of their operating licenses was granted. The commission stressed that the licenses would expire on September 1, and could not be "...construed as any evidence whatsoever that the continued use of operations of WRAF serves or will serve public interest, convenience or necessity."

Upon receiving the notice of extension, Middleton, on behalf of the Radio Club, mailed a request to the Federal Radio Commission, for permission to increase the power of WRAF from 100 watts to 1000 watts. The "Urgent solicitation of organizations and individuals of the area," the letter stated, prompted the request. Complaints had indicated that the power was insufficient to properly serve the needs of those wishing to hear the station.

In lieu of the station's request for an increase of power, the government assigned WRAF a new wave length to go into effect on November 11, eliminating the need for increased wattage. The station was to share its time with WWAE, Hammond, another 100-watt station. Middleton was optimistic that an arrangement could be reached with WWAE to broadcast at alternate times to avoid either station from interfering with the other. It was believed that if an emergency were to occur requiring an irregular broadcast, it would be easy enough to alter the schedule by contacting the other by phone.

WRAF, at 1:30 AM on that November 10th morning ran a two-hour test over their new wave length. Those results and the Sunday morning broadcasts of the New Methodist Church services and later in the afternoon the Trinity Lutheran Church vespers services demonstrated that the new wave length the two radio stations shared had no negligible effect on the other. Calls came in from throughout the county expressing satisfaction in the reception on the new wave length. Listeners from places where reception was previously almost impossible were now able to hear their favorite programs.

Two weeks before Christmas Middleton announced that he would take over on a full time basis the sole management and operation of the station. He had signed a 5-year lease with the Radio Club. The station was to operate on a business basis, with the sale of advertising to pay for the maintenance of the operation. The club still owned the station. John Condra, one of the members of the club, purchased Middleton's interest in the station.

Arrangements had been made with the Odd Fellows to lease rooms 7 and 8, above the Radio Club. One room was remodeled to accommodate a sound proof broadcast studio. The walls were covered with layers of felt paper and hidden from view by "attractive tapestries." The other room was to serve as a reception area. A window between the two rooms allowed spectators to view the entertainers without interfering with the broadcast. The motor generator and the transmitter were located in the reception room. The cleaning and furnishing of the rooms were done with the help of Mrs. Middleton.

A "high class 'house warming' program" was broadcast later that week. The regular scheduling of programs was kicked off by the "Kessler Hour" that featured the playing of phonograph music. The public had also been invited to inspect the new accommodations the evening of December 18.

The New Year, 1929, saw the popularity of the station grow. Dick Cook and his Footwarmers became part of the "Fairway Hour," sponsored by the Fairway Stores. The ever-popular seven-piece orchestra from Michigan City had toes tapping throughout the county. The first two programs brought over 150 song requests from Michigan City alone.

The success of WRAF under Middleton's watchful eye continued to grow and make a profit. In May he became the sole owner, purchasing the station from the Radio Club. He severed ties with the Club and affiliated the station with the Polk College, but remained the station's owner. Middleton was hired to instruct classes in radio repair at the college. One change in programming had been announced. Evening broadcasts would begin at 9 PM instead of the 6:50 start. The daily 12:15 news bulletins from the HERALD-ARGUS as well as the services from the First Methodist Church and other churches and programs such as the one from the Joseph C. Smith Music Shop were continued.

A broadcast studio was located in Michigan City in the Independent Order of Odd Fellows Hall at 132 W. Tenth Street (*date of opening not found*). On occasion, programming would originate from the satellite studio, as was announced in an advertisement that appeared on November 2, 1929, in the DISPATCH. Deacon Long of Chicago conducted a service heard over WRAF the following Sunday morning.

The popularity of the station, with its expanded programming, continued. At the end of November, WRAF, for the first time in its operations, participated in a nation-wide hook-up. It was the largest hook-up of stations to participate in a single broadcast. Over 100 stations took part. The program originated from station KMOX, St. Louis, Mo. The second section of the Shriner's ceremony received nationwide coverage.

Charles Middleton continued to make improvements to the station. The description of improvements was reported in the January 15, 1930, edition of the ARGUS. New and higher towers that supported a better-insulated antenna were constructed. WRAF's improved signal was evidenced by an increase of phone calls. Nearly one fifth of the calls came from Michigan City listeners and points outside of the county. The station's signal was heard from Nova Scotia to Saskatchewan and as far south as Columbia, N. C. and Natchez, Miss., the paper reported.

The increased support from Michigan City listeners prompted Middleton to expand his operation. The Michigan City NEWS, the last week in January, announced the formation of the Michigan City Broadcasting Company. It would operate independently from the La Porte station. E. A. Keeler was hired to handle the business affairs of the new organization. The production and handling of programs was placed in the hands of William S. Wales. The entire seventh floor of the Warren Hotel was leased to provide facilities for the new studio. Programming began the last week of April 1930, "...due to unforeseen difficulties."

As fate would have it, on the last evening of April, a windstorm toppled one of the 31 feet high antenna towers. The sudden blast of wind sent the tower crashing to the alley behind the Odd Fellows building. Two boys, Martin Wilmeth, 101 Bond Street, and Robert Chlebowski, 514 Brighton Street, were in the alley at the time and barely escaped injury. The falling tower took with it the antenna and "a tangle of wires" that pulled the second tower over, causing it to crash to the roof. Leo Middleton, Bill Wales, and Charles immediately began repairs. A temporary aerial was rigged along the edge of the roof and to the flagpole, allowing the station to return to the air by 6:33. However, the regular schedule of programming could only be heard in the city. By noon of the next day the two towers were rebuilt and the station was back on its regular schedule.

Despite the accommodation made with station WWAE some six months previous, their signals frequently interfered with each other, shortening distance and effectiveness. This prompted the two to divide up their broadcasting time as was earlier ordered by the Federal Radio Commission. Slight changes in each schedule were made.

With the expansion of station WRAF that added a studio in Michigan City, the people of the county were able to enjoy countless programs that enriched their daily lives. The station continued to provide a wide range of programming over the next year. On location remotes from the La Porte Methodist Church, St. John's Lutheran Church, the English Trinity School, the Civic Auditorium and the Joseph C. Smith Music Shop delighted audiences.

Throughout the station's eight years of existence, it was nearly impossible to convince the merchants that radio advertising would improve their profitability. For the most part they considered the money spent was in reality a contribution that would help keep the station operating. "However, the station seldom brought in enough to meet expenses and financial difficulties became worse." Middleton said. New federal regulations handed down from the Commission that "...required precision apparatus..." demanded expenditure of funds he didn't have or could not raise.

As the popularity of radio grew throughout the nation, the value of radio was beginning to become evident. Charles Middleton wrote in a brief history of RADIO IN LA PORTE, which is on file at the La Porte County Historical Society Museum, that "every day brought letters from firms, individuals and chambers of commerce all trying to buy WRAF for more money than I had ever had in my life." He made every effort to keep the station in La Porte but could not find a buyer. Then came the offer from the South Bend TRIBUNE to purchase the broadcast license of WRAF for $15,000. He accepted. On May 31, 1931, the license was transferred and moved to South Bend.

Added to station WSBT, which the TRIBUNE already operated, would be station WFAM. Federal regulations, at that time, restricted the number of on airtime a station could broadcast. With two stations the TRIBUNE would be able to be on the air nearly full-time. The transfer of the license ended the eight-year history of WRAF. A chapter of history was ended. The "voice of the Maple City" signed off the air at 9:15 in the evening for the last time on April 30, 1931. There was, perhaps, a tone of bitterness in Middleton's voice when he explained that he was sorry that the city "...couldn't or wouldn't support the station..." and that he had no alternative but to sell it. He added that he would write the final chapter of WRAF'S history "by pulling the carrier wave, tie it in a knot and throw it in the alley."

Radio brought into the living rooms of the citizens of La Porte County a variety of entertainment as well as church services that administered to their religious needs. Late breaking national and world events kept them on top of the news. In the early days of radio, people sat in front of that little box and listened in amazement to the sound of the spoken word and music materializing out of thin air. As an editorialist wrote in the ARGUS, "Radio and television, which is ready to step on the stage, represents the greatest possibilities in the field of communication which man has yet wrung from nature." Life as many knew it was forever changed. The history of radio in La Porte County continued to grow with the introduction of stations WIMS and WEFM in Michigan City, and WCOE and WLOI in La Porte. The history of those stations is still unfolding and is yet to be told.

"Like the old soldier of the ballad, I now close my military career and just fade away, an old soldier who tried to do his duty as God gave him the light to see that duty".
General Douglas MacArthur
The Columbia Dictionary of Quotations
is licensed from Columbia University Press
Copyright © 1993, 1995 by Columbia University Press.
All rights reserved.

BENJAMIN FRANKLIN: THE FORGOTTEN ONE

There are many approaches to good health. Some enjoy exercising, others running, and some of us enjoy walking. As for me, I am a reluctant walker even though I know the important contribution it makes to good health. Nonetheless we manage to take a walk nearly every day. We walk in La Porte and Michigan City and on occasion in Chesterton.

Our favorite place in City is in Greenwood Cemetery. The numerous roadways and the serenity provide for a safe and enjoyable walk. One cannot help but notice the grave markers with the names and inscriptions. Some of the stones are large and impressive while others humbly mark the final resting place of the vast majority of deceased citizens.

The larger markers and mausoleums are usually of a bygone era of Michigan City. Such names as Ames, Winterbotham, Barker and Krueger stand out. These individuals or families have made their contributions of either their time or resources to make Michigan City a nice place to call home.

It is important, however, not to forget the thousands of men and women that have made contributions to the community and the nation. The height on one's headstone should not be the measure of one's greatness. They may not have been as flamboyant and as conspicuous as some, but nevertheless deserve our admiration.

Arnold Bass

Figure 3 Momument in Greenwood Cemetary honoring the Civil War veterans Photo coutery of Fern Eddy Schultz

Many men and women interred in Greenwood Cemetery fought in the numerous wars to preserve this nation. All of them must be remembered for their contributions. As the years pass, our memories of some dim and fade away.

In researching the old editions of the MICHIGAN CITY NEWS and the EVENING DISPATCH, I came upon the obituaries dated August 2, 1922, of a Civil War veteran buried in Greenwood. His name would be recognized throughout the nation, for it was Benjamin Franklin. This Ben's parents were slaves on a plantation near Nashville, Tennessee. It was said he escaped the bondage of slavery in the early days of the war. He traveled north to Indiana, stopping at Indianapolis in 1863. There he, at the age of 18, enlisted in the Union Army as a member of Company F, 22nd Indiana Volunteers, serving for two years. He settled in Michigan City, Indiana, around 1880. Ben married a Malay Walls of this city in 1897. They owned and operated a 12-acre truck farm east of the city near Grand Beach Road. Later, he also collected garbage as a private scavenger with a horse and wagon for many years.

He and his wife lived at 620 East Second Street at the time of his death. Ben had lived in Michigan City for forty years. The newspaper said he was about 77 years old. The Greenwood Cemetery record lists him as 80 at the time of his death. The exact date of birth was unknown because he was born under the bondage of slavery. Malay and a son Oscar survived him. Oscar Franklin was living in Indianapolis at the time of his father's death.

It is interesting to note that another Benjamin Franklin is buried in Greenwood. He too served in the Civil War. He died during the battle of Chickamauga and was buried October 15, 1863. He is not buried with his comrades, as was the case with many others.

These two ordinary men as well as others that served have a towering monument in Greenwood that recognizes and memorializes their contribution to this nation. At the top of the obelisk is a sculpture of a Civil War Soldier standing guard. When you walk past that granite soldier standing tall atop the monument you might catch him casting his eye of protection over his other comrades.

The city which does not have an airport...will soon be as far behind the times as the city which does not have a railway depot or a bus station."
Earl J. Smith, Stinson Aircraft Corp.
September 11, 1929

AVIATION HISTORY IN THE MAKING

Wright Brothers are credited with making the first successful airplane flight in 1903. Three years later they made a 40-mile non-stop flight. It was not long after that monumental flight that small factories were producing airplanes. Daredevil pilots purchased many of these planes and used them to put on thrilling air shows called "barnstorming."

These barnstormers with their feats of daring, together with World War I, brought about many technical improvements in the airplane. Commercial air travel however, did not begin on a large scale in the United States until about 1925.

LaPorte County has had a long, rich, and colorful love affair with the airplane that was influenced by its close proximity to Chicago and men of vision. The areas around Michigan City and LaPorte seemed to be the centers of aviation activity. Hans Grede, W. J. Waterhouse, Elmer Burlingame in LaPorte and Donald Gregory in Michigan City were experimenting with their designs for heavier than air machines. Unlike the Wright brothers, Grede and Waterhouse focused their attention on the monoplane, a one-wing concept. All three would-be inventors believed that the engine should be placed in front of the pilot as opposed to being located behind him.

Hans Grede, during the same time frame that Gregory was experimenting with flight, was at work in LaPorte. Grede's experimental plane was constructed with long cross pieces of hollow tubes of steel that formed the body of his airplane. Grede's monoplane design was not a popular concept and was among the few built in the United States in 1913, the LaPorte DAILY HERALD reported.

IN LA PORTE

Figure 4 Bill Waterhouse and son "Stub" seated in the cockpit of his airplane. Photo courtesy of the La Porte County Historical Society Museum.

Grede gained "celebrity" status with his successful prototype. However, he was unable to find financial support in the United States. His disappointment caused him to look overseas for backing. The German government was impressed with his monoplane. They accepted his aeronautical theory and design, "...fostering (it) everyway possible...." By 1913, according to the HERALD, Germany's army was using his airplane. A January 1928, issue of the HERALD-ARGUS noted, aviation authorities said Grede actually "beat the Wright brothers in a successful flight of a heavier-than-air flying model."

William J. Waterhouse, deputy in the LaPorte County Surveyor's office in 1913, gained recognition locally. Prior to working in the surveyor's office he worked for International Harvester in Chicago. He became an aviation enthusiast in 1908, when he met Hans Grede. The HERALD, in June of 1913, related that Waterhouse helped Grede "design the machine which proved a winner." Since that time "Curley", as his friends called him, continued to explore the mysteries of flight during holidays and many Sundays.

By the summer of 1913, Waterhouse was ready and unveiled his plans to build his own monoplane, the "LaPorte." The DAILY HERALD carried the report and a drawing of his design. The ship when completed would stand 28 feet long, six feet wide and was expected to weigh about 250 pounds. A 20 horsepower engine would propel the craft. The long cross pieces that made up the body would be fashioned from bamboo, thereby, making it lighter than his former colleague's design. He calculated that the plane would be ready for flight in about one month to six weeks.

A few years later Waterhouse moved to southern California. The government employed him as a pilot and a designer of airplanes. His interests and skills in airplane design and engineering grew. The NEWS reported that it was Waterhouse that designed the plane, the Spirit of St. Louis, in which Charles Lindbergh made his famous non-stop trans-Atlantic flight.

He and another engineer in 1928 collaborated on designing a $250,000 all metal airplane, which was to fly around the world. The plane was to have a 95-foot wingspan, which weighed 72,000 pounds when loaded with cargo. Gasoline tanks with a capacity of 7,500 gallons would provide fuel for five motors.

Elmer Burlingame also found himself in the race to perfect a flying machine. Using his own funds, he designed and built two monoplanes. However, according to a news release in the ARGUS-BULLETIN, May 1910, he had experienced financial difficulties. Over a five-month period he spent $1,500 and had overdrawn his expense account by $500. In order to conserve

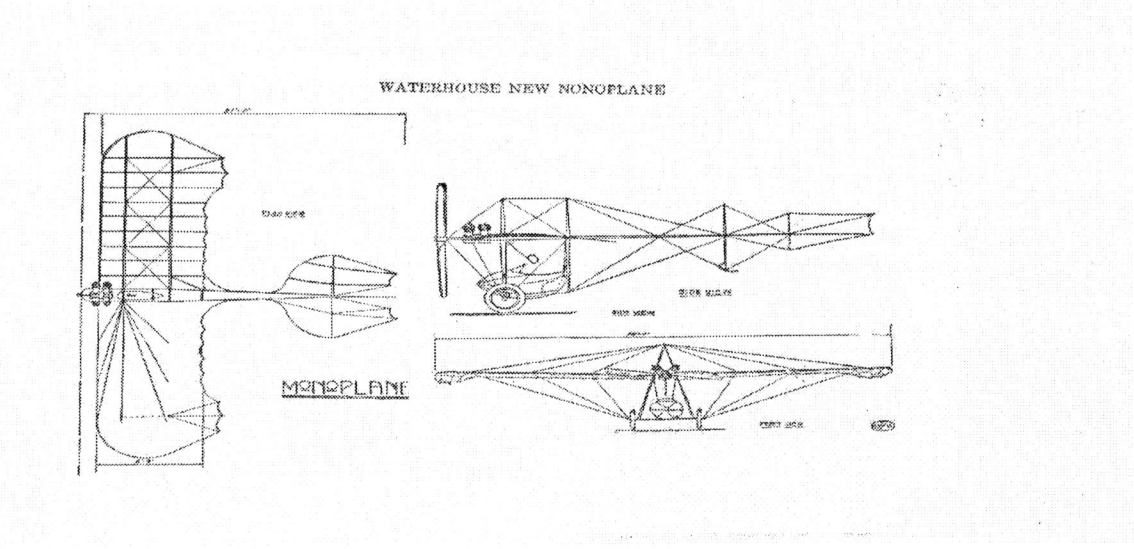

Figure 5 The above diagram of the W. J. Waterhouse monoplane appeared in the Daily Argus on June 16, 1913.

funds, he reduced his work force and moved his operation to "cheaper quarters", thereby saving $65 a month.

Burlingame announced that the mechanical construction of his machine was to be tested in early June. He planned to fly his monoplane from Boston to Providence depending upon the success of that test flight. An incentive for the "aerial jaunt" was offered by local backers "Some local sports have made up a purse of $2,500 for a flight from Boston to Providence, R.I.," he announced in the ARGUS. In the meantime he entered a glider of his design in competition in May 1910, in Waltham, Mass. Burlingame offered a prize of $50.

The HERALD-ARGUS, in 1931, received word that Burlingame had died in San Pedro, California, where he had made his home for a number of years. His obituary stated he gained prominence for his invention and development of "the first telegraph - typewriter, a device by which the printed word is sent over wire."

Aviation technology continued to grow at a rapid pace during the intervening years. The United States government's desire to speed up the delivery of mail was one of the factors that contributed to those advances. Airmail routes were established between major cities. The government purchased landing fields for regular stops or for planes to refuel and pick up mail. They also purchased land along these routes for emergency landings.

Those landing fields were established every 25 miles along the route. A site near the city of LaPorte was selected for such use. It was located between the Chicago to Cleveland route. The mail service's need for such a field may have been prompted by an emergency landing of one of their planes at Pinhook in November of 1923. The plane found a suitable field and landed safely. It remained there several days.

Negotiations between a government mail engineer and Francis Morrison were made public by the DAILY HERALD the following January. The site selected was located on the McCormick farm, about one mile south of LaPorte. Approximately 20 acres would be used "as a trouble landing field." A six foot black and white flag was left with Assistant Postmaster William Gooden for the purpose of officially marking the field.

Arnold Bass

The directors of the LaPorte Chamber of Commerce, at a November 1923 meeting, put into place a plan to develop a "field as a community aviation center." Their field would operate independently of the mail service facility. R. E. Teverbaugh, Secretary of the chamber, announced in February 1924, that the organization signed a lease for a 40-acre tract of land on the Ridgeway farm. The field at the south edge of the city would eventually be developed for aviation purposes.

The government field, in the meantime, located south of the city along I street, was to have its facility upgraded, according to Gooden. He announced that "electric lights will be stationed near the limits of the field " that would supplement the "powerful" beacon presently located in the center. ARGUS reported in August 1924, that with the improved lighting, the mail planes would fly over the field on a regular basis on its route between Chicago and Cleveland.

A week later the DAILY HERALD reported that Walter McLellan of Union Mills and E. D. Beatty of LaPorte would install the lights. Twelve lights spaced every 100 yards would

Figure 6   Pictured is pilot Fred Hoover in 1917 seated in Eddie Nelson's Pusher Bi-plane.
Photo courtesy of the La Porte County Historical Society Museum.

outline the field. Three wet batteries per light powered the small candlepower beacons. It was expected that the batteries would allow the lights to burn 12 hours a night for six months without recharging. Twelve kerosene lanterns posted along the field provided added emergency lighting. Walter McLellan was appointed caretaker of the lights.

Two months later the HERALD reported that the auxiliary landing field had its first use. A dense fog appeared on Thursday, October 16th, about 5:30. According to the report the field lights were off. The pilot flew past the field when the lights were turned on. He returned to the field and landed safely. "The pilot was nearly exhausted when he landed," the paper said.

UP CLOSE AND PERSONAL

He "stumbled to the home of Earl Beatty," who had succeeded McLellan as caretaker of the beacon. The pilot after having "some food and coffee," and with the lifting of the fog was back on his way.

Residents of the county, between the spring and fall of 1924, found on many occasions that their eyes were drawn skyward. One such incident occurred when an airplane flew over the city of LaPorte at a low altitude. This prompted Councilman Thomas Brown to introduce an ordinance that would make flying lower than 5,000 feet over the city unlawful. Adding to the controversy was an alleged remark he had made at a local church accusing Carl Edwin Nelson of being an amateur pilot.

Nelson, in "The Voice of The People" letter to the DAILY HERALD dated May 8, 1924, unleashed a stinging repudiation of Brown's remark, citing his vast flying experience. He went on to say that he had eight years of actual flying experience, including two years of flying for the army. "He also (had) given exhibitions flying in the leading cities and capitals in nine different states, where low flying was required."

In fact, Nelson first tried his "wings" in 1914, at the age of 15. The French Aeronautic Federation granted him pilot license No. 99 that same year. The ARGUS reported that he "was

Figure 7 Photo appeared in the La Porte Herald July 20, 1924 In the corner picture (left to right) are Marvin Headley, aviator; Harwood Call, wing walker; C. Guertine, balloonist; J. H. Stewart, aviator and balloonist, and, H. M. Waterhouse, mechanician, who with Dare Devil Taylor, in the oval, thrilled thousands at the Nelson flying field south of La Porte Sunday. In the lower right corner is Headley's ship, which stood on its nose when a shock absorber broke as he landed. Kenneth Moore of Rolling Prairie, passenger is seen climbing from the plane. Gus Dehne took this remarkable photo a few moments after the accident.

the youngest pilot in the country and retained that honor until the war (W.W.I) broke out." As a member of the Early Birds Flying Club, he was one of 180 members who were flying before the war. He obtained the rank of 2nd lieutenant while serving in the Army Air Service. In 1920 he joined the Decatur Airplane Company. During the next two years he organized the Beloit Air Lines. While there he drafted Wisconsin's state law for licensing pilots. The ARGUS observed that it was the model for the federal law on licensing pilots. Nelson thrilled La Porteans during the summer of 1924, with two flying circuses. The shows were staged at his flying field located one-half mile south of LaPorte on Kingsbury Road, on what was known as State Road No.15 and years later renamed Indiana 35.

Planes and aviators from northern Indiana participated. Among the participants was Marvin Headley of LaCrosse, formerly of LaPorte. He was carrying a passenger Kenneth Moore of Rolling Prairie, when they experienced a mishap while landing. The nose of the airplane dug into the ground, smashing the propeller. Headley and Moore walked away uninjured.

The July, 1924 newspapers said the 4000 to 5000 spectators crowded on the grounds to see the show. Several thousand cars, four abreast, lined the route from the end of Indiana Avenue to the end of the airfield. The article continued, "State highway officials were powerless in attempting to alleviate the congestion."

Marvin Headley, in 1926, developed and patented an educational board game for children. The game incorporated the elements of constructing an airplane and the knowledge of geography. "The object of the game (was) to beat your competitor in a race across the country over the air mail routes." A map of the U. S. and a spinner that told how far each player could move his game piece was included "...in an attractive box." The Headley Luebker Specialty Company, located at 1707 Lincoln Way, produced the game. W .C Luebker was his partner. The game was to be sold locally and in toy departments in other cities.

Four years later Marvin Headley's luck ran out. He died in a plane crash at the age of 32. His Stinson-Detroit monoplane plunged into the Rock River near Rockford, Illinois. The September 7, 1928, Argus carried the story of his death. Mrs. J. Vere Dorland and Mrs. James A. Terry often boasted of being the first ladies of LaPorte to take an airplane ride. Headley and another pilot (Linsley) in 1919 were the pilots. Commercial passenger service was becoming popular. Independent owners and pilots flew their airplanes throughout the nation satisfying the curious as well as popularizing the new and improving technology. The same American spirit of adventure that prompted the early pioneers to push back the western frontier was present in the pilots that were pushing back the frontiers of space. Poor flying conditions and mechanical problems continued to be the pilots' nemesis. Despite the lack of developed landing fields, the sky continued to be filled with airplanes.

In April of 1925, one of Henry Ford's "all metal air freighters was forced down during the morning hours in a field near the northeastern LaPorte city limits" wrote the HERALD ARGUS. The field was located near to and south of the Nickel Plate Railroad crossing on Park Street. The plane was described as a monoplane type of dull gray color with one 400 horsepower motor. Painted on the underside of one wing, in black, was the Ford name. The April 20, and 22, editions of the HERALD ARGUS reported the plane was forced down due to "high gales" and motor trouble. The pilot made minor repairs to the motor, was back in the air, circled the field twice and then headed for Chicago.

The LaPorte Chamber of Commerce, the following month organized an "Auto Booster Tour" of the county and several of the Michigan towns just north of La Porte County. The chamber had hired Eddie Nelson and Frank Kemp to fly over the tour route prior to the auto caravan to drop handbills. The handbills announced the caravan and advertised the merchants in La Porte.

Only Nelson's plane reached Three Oaks. Kemp's plane experienced problems and did not get away. Nelson scattered handbills over Rolling Prairie, New Carlisle, and Union Pier. His plane developed engine problems over Union Pier and had to return to La Porte, the ARGUS reported.

In LaPorte, the government auxiliary emergency field continued to be upgraded. A Delco engine and lighting system was installed over the intervening years that powered a 900-watt beacon. A 50 foot steel tower was erected at the northeastern corner of the field to support the new beacon. The beacon was activated for the first time on the evening of May 1, 1925, to coincide with the beginning of the first regular nightly flights between New York and Chicago. Sixteen landing lights now marked the limits of the field.

Ralph H. Smith, caretaker of the light and field was interview by the HERALD ARGUS in June 1925. His life resembled that of a hermit. He spent all of his time at the light in a dingy 10 x 10 shanty in the shadow of the beacon. The nearest house was about three-fourths of a mile away. A sign painted on the shanty warned visitors to stay away. "About the only things to look forward to was bedtime, mealtimes, and the time to start the beacon," reported the ARGUS.

The city of LaPorte had its share of aviation excitement when Lieutenant A. G. Pearson and Ray Dedrick flew their plane to LaPorte for the purpose of taking up passengers for hire. There was no municipal airport at that time. So they, as others before them, landed their airplane on what was commonly known as Warnecke Field. It was located east of LaPorte, about three blocks east of where the Nickel Plate Railroad crossed Lincoln Way. Robert Coffeen, writing for the TOWN CRIER in August of 1975, reminisced of his first flight with Pearson in August of 1926.

Flying continued to be hazardous due to the primitive navigational instruments and the unpredictable weather of northern Indiana. Another plane, this time a mail plane, was forced to land at La Porte's emergency field just south of the city. The Michigan City NEWS reported in November of that same year that, gale winds of 73 miles per hour, poor visibility due to fog and rain caused the plane to stray from its course and land. The single mail sack was taken to the LaPorte post office and "dispatched with their regular outgoing mail."

The number of flights over LaPorte during the next few years increased. It became apparent, with instances previously described, that the lighting at the airfield had to be improved. This came about in January, of 1927. The existing lights had failed on several nights, due to winter storms. Several airmail flights had been canceled. A relatively new device was installed that would automatically turn the lights on and off. The ARGUS reported, "When a certain amount of light strikes the sun dial device which controls the current the light is shut off and in the evening when it gets dusk the light flashes on." The stringing of electricity to the field ended the need for the Delco plant.

Ralph Smith, who lived on a nearby farm, had been the caretaker for some time. A repairman that regularly visited the light to perform normal maintenance eventually replaced him.

The unpredictability of weather continued to be a problem and played havoc with flying, which was the case on Friday afternoon, October 29, 1927, when a heavy fog blanketed LaPorte. Mr. and Mrs. C. D. Webb enroute from Rochester, N. Y. to their home in Chicago considered landing their "Swallow" plane in the oval at the fair grounds. The dense fog with poor visibility caused them to have second thoughts. Then they saw the airmail light of the government airfield SW. of the city and decided to make an emergency landing. It was an unexpected surprise for their cousin Mrs. A. S. Smiley when she opened the door of her Jefferson street home to find the Webbs. After spending the night they were back on their way home.

Louis McGinn, flying over LaPorte on the evening of November 2nd, 1927, had experienced poor visibility due to rain and low flying clouds. He was unable to see the ground, making it difficult to locate the landing field. Added to this was the malfunction of the plane's engine. Flying extremely low for about an hour, trying to locate the field, alerted La Porteans to the pilot's peril. Hearing the hum of the plane's motor caused many to drive to the field. As he was about to land the rain finally stopped. Aided by the lights from the motorists at the field, he was able to make a safe landing. Three hours later he was back in the air heading east with his precious cargo.

Figure 8 The La Porte beacon in 1925 with Ralph Smith pictured. Courtesy of the La Porte County Historical Society Museum.

McGinn was not a stranger to the LaPorte emergency field at the end of Monroe Street. Three weeks before he was required to make a forced landing. The connecting rod in the plane's engine burned out. He told the newspaper reporter that he was ready to parachute to safety when the "...field loomed up in time to save the situation." He was able to glide his plane to safety.

The business and professional community in LaPorte recognized the need to have a commercial airport. The LaPorte Chamber of Commerce, in May of 1927, appointed a committee to explore the possibilities and suitable sites. Fred R. Liddell, chairman, H. J. Link, L. G. Schumm, Dr. J. M. Siegel, and John B. Dilworth composed the committee. Efforts to enlighten and motivate the community continued over the next several months.

United Airways, Inc. of Detroit in December of 1927 proposed through the Chamber of Commerce of LaPorte that the county seat be placed on an airmail route that included South Bend and Valparaiso. The planes were to fly between Michigan points and Chicago starting June 1, 1928. The carrier qualified its proposal by saying "...these stops would only be made in the event that the amount of mail to be collected would warrant." The city would have to guarantee that five pounds of airmail a day would be sent.

In anticipation of obtaining the airmail stop, the Chamber of Commerce along with the ARGUS promoted the use of airmail by the public and businesses of LaPorte. They recognized the need to have substantial number of letters sent by airmail. In an effort to raise the awareness of the public the Chamber, in mid-July, 1928, had printed about 5,000 "distinctive air mail envelops" that were given away free. In the upper left hand corner was printed, "Bigger and Better LaPorte, Dedicating the 1st Aerial Mail from LaPorte." The envelopes were "flashily decorated" with a red, white and blue border. Letters mailed on the 1st day of service would be stamped with a special seal"...showing that they traveled the route on the opening day." The postal employees placed red, white and blue painted mailboxes on the corner in front of the post office and at the corner in front of the 1st National Bank.

The LaPorte Chamber, in mid-December, invited businessmen and manufacturers to a meeting to garner support for the proposed airmail stop. The meeting was help in the basement of the First National Bank building. The enthusiastic participants authorized Charles A. Beal, president of the chamber, to "...take immediate steps to place the proposition before the postmaster general's office." Congressman A. J. Hickey of La Porte received a copy of the letter. He was to represent the city in the negotiations.

United's plan also called for carrying express and passengers on the mail route. The company hired Eddie Nelson to fly one of the airmail routes. Speculation was that he would fly the Fort Wayne-South Bend, the Chicago-Detroit or the Chicago- Muskegon divisions.

After six months of maneuvering and negotiating, the city of La Porte was placed on the airmail route. The chamber made an effort to establish a courier service using buses to gather the mail from Valparaiso, Michigan City, Knox, and all the smaller towns of La Porte County.

However, United Airways was not selected. Thompson Aeronautical Corporation of Cleveland was awarded the contract to carry the mail between Detroit and Chicago. Air service was to begin on July 17, 1928.

The city's Chamber of Commerce immediately signed a three-year lease for 100 acres with Mrs. Mary A. Andrew. In preparation of the arrival of the air mail planes, a "large area of hay was cut." A large circle of limestone was placed on the field to guide the fliers to the field. The field was a short distance from the city, at the end of Monroe Street and the Yellow River Road, only one and a quarter miles from the post office.

"La Porte's first chapter as a center of aerial transportation was written in a glorious, sunny field just south of the city shortly before 8 o'clock this morning when the wheels of a Stinson-Detroiter monoplane, making its first trip on the Contract Air Mail Route 27, touched La Porte's airport and rolled to stop before a small crowd...," the HERALD-ARGUS wrote.

On hand to greet the plane were J. B. Dilworth, acting chairman of the Chamber of Commerce airport committee; Charles A. Beal, president of the Chamber of Commerce; John Wilk, superintendent of the mails at the local post office; Ira J. Barber, assistant postmaster, and Walter K. Greenebaum, manager of the Chamber of Commerce.

Eleven mail pouches as well as the receipt of one pouch from Chicago were hurriedly transferred from a waiting Garrison Baggage Service truck. After a few quickly taken pictures, along with "a cheery word or two of greetings," the pilot was off again "winging his way toward South Bend."

That evening 8,000 people gathered at the airport to greet the west bound mail plane. It was estimated that 1,500 cars were parked on two sides of the field and that another 500 parked along the highway. The La Porte police department, workers for the highway department and members of the Chamber of Commerce were on hand to direct traffic. The event also brought out the American Legion Hamon Gray Post Drum and Bugle Corps. Parked near the entrance, a refreshment stand did "a land office business," adding to the carnival atmosphere.

Mayor John Line, after congratulating the pilot, gave him a large wooden key to the city. Charles A. Beal, Jr., son of the president of the chamber, presented the pilot a silk American flag. Postmaster P. O. Small, and other chamber and city officials were present. Then came a quick exchange of mail pouches and pilot James L. Rutledge was "winging westward," toward Chicago, on the last lap of the route.

After one week, the novelty of La Porte being an airmail stop wore off. The public and business community's use of airmail dramatically declined. Post office and Chamber of Commerce officials warned; "use it or lose it." They did! By the end of August, Thompson Aeronautics had made a request to the postal service to drop La Porte from the route. The ARGUS had reported that they had opposed La Porte from the very beginning, due to the city being much smaller than the others. The county newspapers announced at the end of the first week in September that La Porte lost its airmail service. The reason given was the Monroe street field was unsafe due to the lack of lighting needed for night landing. It had also been reported that in order to get the airport rated by the U. S. Department of Commerce, it needed to be at least 160 acres. The Monroe St. facility was less than 90 acres. Unwilling to spend the money to meet the government's standards, the Monroe St. airport was abandoned by year-end and the I street airport was considered for future improvements.

The delivery of merchandize by air express was becoming more commonplace. The Radio Club, Inc., a local radio dealer, took the opportunity to have the 100th Majestic radio sold in La Porte delivered by air from South Bend. It was billed as, "The first radio ever transported to LaPorte by airplane." The plane, owned by the St. Joseph Valley Aviation Club of South Bend, landed at the airport on September 6, 1928. Kenneth Clendenen of the Radio Club made the trip from South Bend. The radio was put on the Radio Club truck and delivered to the home of J. E. Jewett, 1902 Michigan Avenue. The club boasted that it took "...just 40 minutes after it had left the store of the South Bend distributor," to be installed and in operation.

The curiosity of the public and its love affair with the airplane continued to be used by business and industry to promote their products. A Texas company, Texaco Petroleum Products, used its all-metal airplane with a 74 ft. wingspan and three Wright Whirlwind motors of 200 horsepower each, to promote the La Porte Independent Oil Company dealers and distributors. It was one of the largest and most modern airplanes to visit the city of La Porte. On Thursday, September 13, 1928, "The Texaco No. 1" arrived. The plane was opened to the public for inspection in an effort to "... aid the growth of aviation and to make the civilian population more air minded." Some of the business and professional men of La Porte were given a ride over the city.

The following week saw the unexpected landing of a National Air Transportation monoplane at the emergency landing field at the corner of 18th streets and I. The mail plane, flying over La Porte, was forced to land during a rainstorm. Irwin L. Bauch, who operated the Mayflower Nursery adjacent to the government emergency field, was on hand to give the pilot assistance as he had many times for other pilots over the intervening years. This time he was rewarded with a free plane trip to Chicago and back. His prophetic remark upon his return, "The view from the air shows very clearly the rapidly growing communities are encroaching on the farm lands."

Although the spirits of the citizens of La Porte were dampened by the news of losing the airmail stop, it didn't deter the sponsors of an "Airplane Meet" with their plans. A twenty-five mile air race and related events took place on October 14, 1928. Approximately 10,000 people clogged the roads leading to the airport to witness the "...maneuvers of airplanes over La Porte. The event caught the attention of some Michigan City residents that drove to La Porte to witness the planes and flyers in action. The parachute jumping and the stunt flying kept the crowd spellbound."

Flying was becoming more commonplace with each passing year. Just the thought of man flying conjured up feelings and visions that excited many people. Especially after watching the daredevil antics of the pilots performing in the air circus. William Wallen, of the East Side Garage, was no exception. He had been instrumental in bringing the air meet to La Porte two weeks before. The word went out toward the end of October that those interested in forming an aviation club were to meet at the Y. M. C. A. Nearly 25 people attended. Wallen was elected temporary president and John B. Condra of the La Porte Radio Club was named temporary secretary and treasurer. The members agreed to buy an airplane. Each would pay a $50 membership fee. It was hoped that the membership would increase to 100. The expectation was that by spring they would have enough money to pay for the plane. A flying instructor was to be hired, with lessons costing $10 an hour.

The following month, the club took in three new members. The twenty-five members present elected permanent officers "to handle the affairs of the club." Wallen was president, George Linnell became vice president, and Condra was elected treasurer. In anticipation of having enough money to pay for an airplane by next spring, an order for a new, two-passenger dual control American Eagle biplane was placed. The plane would be used for flying instruction for club members. The official emblem of the club was adopted at that meeting. Harry Olsen of the La Porte Advertising Service drew the design. The design took the form of an airplane propeller. The inscription read, "Learn to fly. Learn to Maintain. La Porte Aviation Club, Government Field, La Porte, Ind."

Towards the end of November 1928, La Porte was the center of a typical mid-winter storm. Pilots were forced to fly "blind" over the area due to visibility being reduced to nothing by the heavy snow. The evening of November 19th at about 7:45 found a National Air Transport pilot circling over the city a number of times, apparently searching for the landing field, the blinding storm making it impossible to find. The pilot flew in a wide circle over the city in an attempt to find the field. Irwin Bauch, manager of the airport for the U. S. government heard the plane and quickly proceeded to the airport. He turned on the beacon and the field boundary lights as well as lighting some flares.

The HERALD-ARGUS realizing that considerable light would be needed at the field if the pilot were to attempt a landing, phoned Charles Middleton, operator of radio station WRAF. The paper suggested that Middleton ask his listeners with automobiles to drive to the airport and turn their light on the field. His announcement brought instantaneous response. It was estimated that by 8 o'clock, 100 automobiles were at the field. One of the fire trucks equipped with a powerful spotlight was ordered to the airport to assist the pilot in a landing.

With all the added lighting, the field remained obscure due to the continuing snowfall. As it turned out the pilot decided to go on to Chicago where he made a safe landing at 8:30. It was later learned that the heavy snowfall was local and that good flying conditions existed to the east and west of La Porte. However, the next morning found a National Air Transport plane carrying mail was required to land at the municipal airport. After taking on a supply of gasoline, he flew off to Cleveland rather than transferring the mail to a train.

As the technology expanded and improved, business and industry continued to explore ways to adopt the use of the airplane to their best interests. The Reid-Murdoch Company, a manufacturer of numerous grocery products, with a plant in La Porte, was no different. They had announced their innovative use of the airplane at the International Aeronautical Exposition at the Coliseum, Chicago, on December 1, 1928. They unveiled the "first flying grocery". The interior of a huge Ford tri-motored plane, named "The Independent," was lined with shelves and display racks so that the company could display its products. This would allow the company to send salesmen to cover a large territory in a very short time. Salesmen would accompany the "flying grocery" throughout their marketing area and make appointments with grocery buyers. The buyers would meet the plane at the airport, look over the stock, and place their order for future delivery. The "flying grocery" was scheduled to make a stop at La Porte on its way to the exhibit.

The Chamber of Commerce's committee on aviation spent the winter months carefully investigating and analyzing possible sites for an airport. At their April 9, 1929, meeting it was announced that a decision was reached to lease 120 acres of land that adjoined the existing National Air Transport Company's 40-acre emergency landing field. The chamber agreed to pay a rental fee of approximately $1,400 a year and was given an option to purchase the land at any time. Fred R. Liddell, chairman of the chamber aviation committee, appointed a sub-committee to carry forward the work of developing the airport. Named to the committee were M. J. Sallwasser, D. E. Zener, and Lemuel Darrow. The combined area was nearly square in shape and was approachable from every direction. The two parcels, totaling 160 acres, brought the airport into conformity with the federal department of commerce requirement for an airport. It was expected to receive the necessary rating in order to receive federal assistance.

The La Porte Aero Club continued to attract men interested in aviation. A state charter was issued to the club in January of 1929. Members of the corporation were William J. Walker, George Linnell, John Condra, and Claude Lewis. The club met on a weekly basis since its inception. At their April 30th meeting I. A. Jenks, a local licensed airplane mechanic and graduate of one of the country's best schools of aeronautics gave a talk on training schools and piloting. He also answered questions about flying gliders in as much as the club had one under construction. The club voted in two new members, Charles Mainland and Fred Grimberg. Plans were made and a committee formed to "make La Porte one of the first cities to enter the air marking campaign." As soon as a suitable roof would become available, the club planned to advertise the local flying field to pilots passing over the city.

The increased demand to move the long distance mail by air caused the United States government to look for ways to improve the trans-continental routes. The main trans-continental line between New York and Chicago, by May of 1929, was in the process of being rearranged. In as much as the city of La Porte was already undergoing material improvements at its municipal landing field, William Boesch and R. Marshall of the U. S. government lighthouse service spent several days in the city meeting with groups interested in building a partnership with the federal government. It was a recognized fact that the government needed to have emergency airports on all its lines and that cities wanted to establish municipal airports. The economics of combining the two could prove to be less costly to the city and the government.

Boesch and Marshall met with Mayor John Line and city officials as well as the directors of the Chamber of Commerce to discuss the prospects for the La Porte airport. All in attendance recognized the importance of having the government continue to combine resources and maintain its beacon light at the emergency airport. They agreed that a fund be started to raise $1,500 to cover the rental fee for the 160 acre field. Several of those present contributed $10 each. The chamber agreed to lend its support to the project.

Directors of the Chamber of Commerce signed a lease for a 120-acre airport at the end of May.

Figure 9 Photo courtesy of the La Porte County Historical Society

The land was leased from Emma M. Payne, 35 acres, Nettie K. Wier, 80 acres, Louise P. and Howard Cutler, 26.75 acres and Lucille Stevens and the La Porte Loan and Trust Company, 20 acres. Part of the acreage was in crops with the plan to harvest at the end of the summer. Any necessary leveling would be done at that time followed by the sowing of grass seed.

Several days later William Boesch and Charles A. Beckner of the Milwaukee division of the U. S. Lighthouse service at a meeting with Fred Liddell signed over its lease for the 40-acre emergency landing field to the chamber, thereby, creating a 160-acre airport. The government, however, retained a 60 square foot tract on which their present airplane beacon stood. Plans to construct a larger and more modern beacon were in the making. The government was to continue to use the La Porte airport as an emergency field for its mail planes.

It was reported in the ARGUS on June 4, 1929, a small group of local men formed the La Porte Airways, Inc and sub-let the La Porte Municipal Airport. It was later learned that John Condra and Paul Bowman formed the company. The newly formed company began the task of improving the facilities. Their plan called for two diagonal runways, each 500 feet wide and crossing at right angles, with one pointing east-west and the other north-south. The runways were of sod with the grass a different shade from the rest of the field.

An airplane hangar built of wood was constructed at the north end of the field that accommodated six planes comfortably or eight if crowded together. The company charged rent for the use of the hangar. Any individual or company carrying passengers for hire were required to pay a rental fee. Casual visitors landing or taking off from the field as well as the government mail planes were not charged. Nearby a servicing area was located to sell gasoline, oil, repair parts and other related services. Their plan also called for the construction of a road across the entire north end of the field that would pass just to the rear of the hangar.

The following month the La Porte Airways, in conjunction with the Shockley Flying Service of South Bend, began conducting a ground and flight school in La Porte. The ground school classes were held in the Y. M.C. A., meeting twice a week. The first meeting saw about twelve men in attendance. Two days later Ortie Raasche and Stanley Cichon became the first licensed beginning flight students at the I Street airport. Irwin, who was working in La Porte at the time and W. Fedder of Michigan City, were enrolled in the course too in order to accumulate solo flying time hours.

Subsequently John Condra, at the Borgerd and Tritt electrical shop located at 610 Indiana Avenue, where he was employed, conducted ground school classes. This allowed the participants to have hands-on instruction in the "mysteries" of magnetos, dynamos, generators, as well as electricity in general as it related to the airplane motor. Bad weather continued to be the nemeses of pilots. Irwin Bauch, owner of the Mayflower Nursery, contacted the ARGUS, on June 12, that two transport planes enroute from Cleveland to Chicago had been forced down by fog and landed at the I street airport. One was a National Transport mail plane and the other a Universal 3 motor cabin plane with one passenger.

A national campaign to assist pilots in navigating across the country was launched in the mid 1920's. Cities around the nation were marking prominent structures with their city's name that could be seen by pilots flying over. Several factory roofs announced to pilots that they were flying over La Porte. However, in July of 1929, "one of the largest airport signs for the guidance of airplanes in the country," was painted on the roof of the Advance-Rumely warehouse. The building was located at Perry and Lake Streets. The 310 foot long, 30 foot high, bright yellow sign, painted by five La Porte boys, bore the name "La Porte". Clem Luebker designed and supervised the project. The sign was painted with the help of four of his friends: Arthur Giesler, Elmer Freburg, Don Sensow, and Jack Jewett. Two arrows were added; one pointing north with a small "N" at its base and the other pointing to the city airport had a circle and the number 3 by it. The circle signified that the arrow pointed to the landing field that was 3 miles away. Through the efforts of the Chamber of Commerce, rooftop signs were also painted on the Standard Oil Building on East Lincoln Way, on the automobile shed at the U. S. Slicing Machine Company and the Reid-Murdoch plant.

In the tradition of the Wright brothers and early county aviation pioneers, the Reverend David Leo Faurote, pastor of the Sacred Heart Catholic church at Wanatah, designed a vertically rising airplane. He received Canadian and United States patents for his invention, according to reports in the November 1929, county newspapers. The county newspaper referred to it as a radically new type of airplane. Father Faurote claimed that in theory his machine would be able to rise and land vertically, and once in the air would be to able to fly at speeds ranging from 3 miles to 400 miles per hour.

The design of the wings was another "revolutionary feature." The customary wing design had them protruding at right angles from the plane's body. Faurote's design had them attached along the body and parallel to it. He believed that his plane's narrower design would greatly reduce the resistance of wing and struts. In theory, his radical new propeller and wing design would be able to create greater lifting power. A copy of the Patent is in the files of the La Porte County Historical Society Museum.

The city had done very little at the airport and had not made a financial commitment during the five months following the Chamber of Commerce acquisition and subsequent sub-leasing on the municipal airport. Then, on November 26, 1929, the ARGUS reported Mayor John Line's announcement that the city would work with the federal department of commerce "...in putting the municipal airport in shape." "Fences must be removed, Canadian thistle must be destroyed and the field must be smoothed and leveled," the NEWS reported

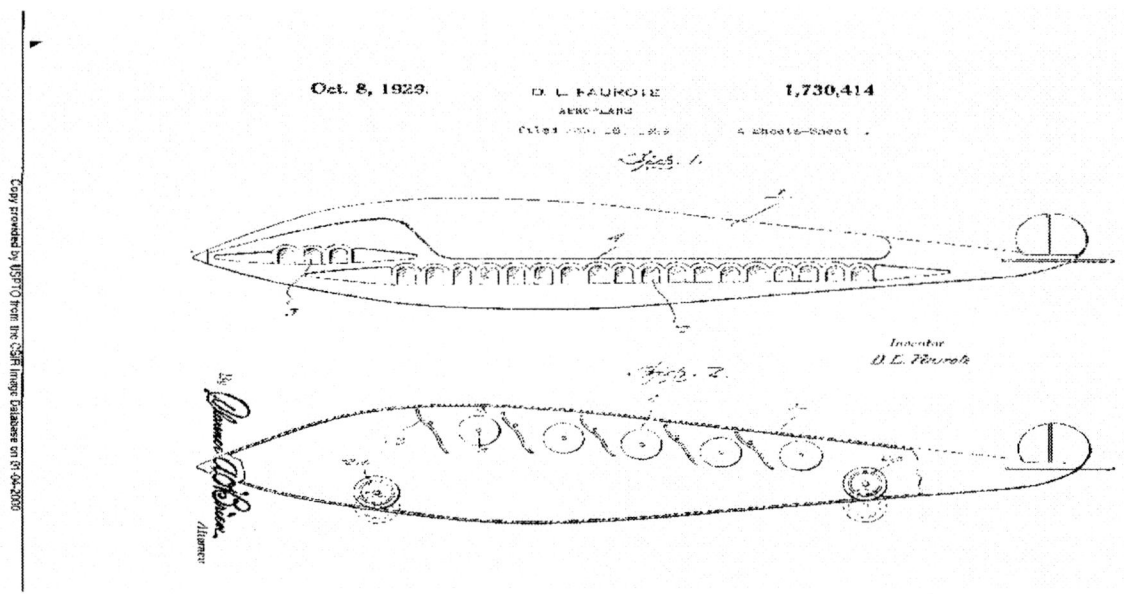

Figure 10 The Reverend David Faurote applied for a patent on his autogiro on February 16, 1929. The United States Patent Office issued the patent on Octaober 8, 1929. The diagram was modified to fit the space. (Figure 1) Side view of aeroplane as seen in flight. (Figure 2) A longitudinal cross section

in mid-December. The city's inaction prompted the Chamber to initiate a campaign to raise $500 in order to get the job done. "...Air-minded people or public-spirited citizen or firms who want to see the airport...." were asked to send their contributions to the HERALD-ARGUS or Chamber of Commerce offices.

The cost of the work was expected to be $20 a day. The names of the initial subscribers to the fund were listed in the ARGUS. They were William G. Meinke, La Porte Aero Club, La Porte Loan & Trust Company, Powell-Rose Lumber Company, G. Elshout and Dr. R. B. Jones, each giving $10. Five dollars each came from Dorland & McGill, Milton H. Low, Hascall Rosenthal, and Judge J. C. Richter. Mrs. S. A. Bagely donated $1. Other contributors were added to the list as the campaign progressed. Mrs. E. E. Weir donated $10 of cinders to be placed on I street road.

The one mile of road that extends from the end of I street pavement to the airport was in "terrible condition." The traffic during the winter weather of November, 1929 made the road almost impassable to motor vehicles "as the bottom has fallen out of the road in several places." This section of road lay in Scipio Township, who had no money available for road construction. Air mail pilots forced to land at the airport and transfer their cargo to the train station in town dreaded the ordeal of traveling the road more the tribulation of making an emergency landing in La Porte.

The task of placing boundary lights around the perimeter of the recently acquired acreage to the municipal airport had been at a standstill. The lighthouse division in charge of air did the work of digging a trench around the perimeter of the airport mail emergency fields. Street Commissioner R. C. Steffenhagen and his men as well as workmen hired by the chamber assisted. The trenching was started at the end of November and completed by mid-December. The last week of December saw the delivery at the railroad freight house of 8 rolls of cable, weighing 1,000 pounds each. They were hauled to the airport by sleds over drifted roads that were impossible for trucks to travel. Representatives of the Department of Commerce, airway division of labor were in the city to oversee the laying of the cable.

The city of La Porte's difficulty in raising funds for airport improvement and the county's reluctance to improve the I street approach along with the increase in the volume of flights over the city prompted the federal government to put pressure on city and chamber officials to sign over the leases to the airport to them. The move was to be temporary and extended to January when the city was to reacquire the leases. However, this action required that the original leases with the land owners be renegotiated, extending the time period to five years, until December of 1934, instead of the two year contract. The HERALD-ARGUS disclosed that Nettie Weir received $8 an acre for one 40 acre tract and $10 an acre for a second, Emma Payne, Lucille Stevens and Louise Culter$8 an acre. The total came to $1,368 per year. The city of La Porte took over the payment on January 1, 1930.

The federal government, holding the leases for the entire airport, was able to proceed with the installation of boundary lights around the 160 acre tract, with the condition that the city pay for the electricity after January 1, 1930. Up until that time only the original 40-acre emergency field was lighted. They also put in place a larger flashing beacon, "making the airport one of the largest and best emergency fields in the middle west." The 1,000,000-candle power beacon rotated six times per minute. The electricity for the beacon was a federal government expense.

Little was accomplished toward making improvements at the airport over the next eleven months. The ARGUS on December 12 reported that Harry Hoelocker, city street commission, directed a group of men as they were making additional improvements at the airport. The Unemployment Relief Organization paid them. The county road department lent their support by sending their caterpillar tractor to assist in pulling hedge along the east and north sides of the field. Horse drawn teams and discs were borrowed from the county farm to disc and level the old fencerows around the original 40-acre emergency landing field. The work was done in preparation of turning on the boundary lights around the 160-acre airport that were installed the previous winter. The lights had not been used because the condition of the field did not meet with the approval of the department of commerce.

The chills and thrills associated with the early history of aviation took many strange twists and turns, much like something one would see in a 1930 movie. On a cold February morning at about 5 A. M., the home of the William Schoffs and their children caught fire. Flying over the area, the pilot of a plane discovered the flames beneath him.

Swooping down over the house, he was unable to see anyone outside of the house. He flew over the burning house as close as possible, circled around the building a second time, with the hope of waking those who might be inside sleeping. Mr. Schoff was in the barn milking at the time. Hearing the roar of the plane's engine, he hurried outside to see the house in flames. He rushed inside to awake his family and led them to safety.

The pilot then flew to other houses nearby. The roar of plane's engine awoke the neighbors who rushed to the aid of Schoff. With his mission of mercy complete, he flew off into the sunrise and "resumed his course and winged out of sight...."

With all of the time, effort and money invested to provide a safe emergency landing field in La Porte and the municipal airport in Michigan City, emergency landing could not always be delayed until a pilot could reach one of them. This was evident the evening of March 7, 1930. On that "inky" dark night at 11 P. M., the residents of Rolling Prairie were startled by brilliant light from a magnesium flare dropped from a plane in distress. The flare landed "a

UP CLOSE AND PERSONAL

few rods" from the William Wehrley home. The engine of the charted Thompson Aeronautical Corporation mail plane "...coughed a bit then died completely," forcing the pilot to land on a hilly field surrounded by trees on the V. E. Huddleston farm, about 6 miles northeast of La Porte. The plane was traveling from Chicago to Kalamazoo. The pilot, Al DeWitt, called the Jones Garage in Rolling Prairie for a car in order to take the 10 pouches of mail to La Porte and place them on a train. The next day the plane was repaired and on its way.

The transition to transfer the ownership of the city's airport from the Chamber of Commerce to the city of La Porte took a step backward. A front-page story in the HERALD-ARGUS on March 3, 1930, announced: "New City Administration Adopts A 'Hands Off' Policy on Airport." The Line administration the previous fall approved a budget that provided for the payment of $1,280 rental of the airport for 1930, as well as committing to take over the lease agreements held by the Chamber. The Board of Works under the recently elected Mayor Miller administration agreed to make the payment to the Chamber but stipulated that the rent was for 1930 only, "with no assurances for the future."

The Miller administration did not want to assume the cost of upkeep to the airport. The actual amount needed to meet the terms of the leases was $80 more than the $1,280 appropriated due to needed upkeep. Had the city taken over the leases, the city would assume the added costs of upkeep. The board's resolution made it clear that the city did not intend to take over the leases from the Chamber of Commerce.

In the midst of the controversy, the airport continued to provide a safe emergency landing field for pilots flying near the city of La Porte due to the latest improvements. The ARGUS, on July 1, 1930, reported that thirteen airplanes made use of the field located on I Street during the month of June. Elmer D. Beatty the government caretaker for the field said that several of the planes landed due to weather conditions or motor trouble. The most distinguished guest to use the facility was Governor Fred Green of Michigan.

The final phase in getting the field lighted hinged on the government's requirement that the landing approach from the south be made safer by moving the telephone poles from the north side of the road to the south side. "The poles were nine and a half feet above the ground and are far enough from the edge to make the approach safe for planes." The La Porte County Telephone Company completed the task at the end of January 1931. The lighting of the entire 160-acre field occurred on the first Saturday of February.

The federal government had long recognized La Porte's strategic location on the airlines to Cleveland, Detroit, and New York City. For that reason, two years previous, the government employed Irvin Bauch and his wife to telephone weather information to the department of agriculture's Chicago headquarters whenever bad weather struck. On some occasions of severe weather Bauch made as many as 15 calls to the Chicago office, the ARGUS reported on April 8, 1931.

Although the Municipal Airport provided a safe landing field for numerous emergency landings over the years, the unthinkable occurred due to a cloudy, rainy Tuesday night on September 15, 1931. A Continental Airways, Washington to Chicago flight, crash-landed. As the Lockheed Orion transport approached the runway to land the motor died. The pilot put the nose of the plane down on the field just north of the airport about 100 feet from a 3 foot hedge fence, plowing through it. The plane came to a stop 100 feet within the airport. The ARGUS reported that the right wheel was doubled up under the wing and the other wheel under carriage was badly damaged, causing the "crippled ship" to nose over, placing the plane's tail at a

45 degree angle. The motor was jammed back into the pilot's cabin. However, the pilot escaped injury.

Irvin Bauch arrived at the scene within minutes. Only one of the six passengers was seriously injured. William J. Froelich, special assistant attorney general of the United States who had aided in the preparation of the case, which resulted in the indictment of Al Capone, received cuts on the face. The other passengers, Assistant District Attorney Dwight E. Green, Ralph Updyke, former congressman from Indianapolis and then connected with the U. S. Bureau of Internal Revenue, as well as three others who refused to give their names, were rushed into La Porte by a passing motorist. Froelich was treated at Holy Family Hospital. Later a police car was dispatched to the scene and brought their baggage to the Rumely Hotel where the men rested before catching the midnight New York Central for Chicago. The next day representatives of the company arrived to dismantle the damaged plane in order to ship it to Chicago.

Additional work of improving La Porte's municipal airport began in late September 1931. The decision was made at a meeting attended by attorney Fred R. Liddell, head of the Chamber of Commerce airport committee and pioneer in the airport development and G. B Maple, manager of the Chamber, that included E. S. Logan, supervisor of government emergency fields for the area, Harry Hoelocker, city street commissioner, and Arthur C. Sheldon, manager of employment for the Unemployment Relief Organization. The task of disking, rolling and seeding took about a week to complete. The government supplied 1,000 pounds of grass seed as well as paying the $15 a day for hiring a roller and operator for six days from the Gross Construction Company.

The last Saturday of September the citizens of La Porte were treated to a close up view of aviation's newest wonder, the autogiro. This version of the "flying windmill" was not the craft patented by the Reverend David Leo Faurote. This version sustained flight with the use of its four 45 foot long rotor blades. The autogiro came to La Porte from South Bend after it made an air tour of Michigan City and Valparaiso. The Beech-Nut Company sponsored the tour that included other cities. The aircraft was the same one that Amelia Earhart used to complete the first trans-continental autogiro round trip of 10,000 miles. Between 200 and 300 people were at the airport to see the landing and witnessed a series of maneuvers that demonstrated the aircraft's versatility in near vertical takeoffs and "especially the coming to an almost complete stop in the air."

The residents on the north side of La Porte, the following month, were treated to the historic landing of the first amphibian airplane on a La Porte lake. U. S. Navy pilot, Lieutenant G. C. Helebrandt, landed his Loening Navy biplane, painted the official navy gray, on Stone Lake. He had stopped off to visit his boyhood friend Lawrence Folk, who lived with his parents, Mr. and Mrs. Joseph Folk, at 223 Pine Lake Avenue. Helebrandt was stationed at the Great Lakes Naval Training Station, Illinois. The ARGUS printed:

> "...(the plane) glided gracefully downward...to the surface of the water and then taxied to the beach. After landing in the water, he (Helebrandt) lowered landing wheels from out of the hull of the ship, enabling him to taxi up on the beach and step from the plane to the shore.... He thanked La Porte for having such a splendid beach, with a firm sand bottom, that made it possible for him to pilot the ship upon the shore."

The final year of the Chamber's lease agreement for the municipal airport began February 15, 1934. The previous three years brought little in the way of improvements. Nonetheless, the facility experienced extensive use. With the final year of the lease in front of them, questions were raised as to which way to go in the matter of airport control and development. Another issue revolved around how much the La Porte City Council would contribute toward the rental of the facility. The council had not included an item for airport rental in the 1934 budget. Through negotiations the matter was settled.

The issue of ownership of the airport remained in limbo for another two years. In February, 1936, La Porte Mayor Alban Smith, G. B. Maple, Chamber manager, and Wilbur Flickinger, Chamber of Commerce airport committee chairman and city councilman reached the decision to approach the department of commerce to determine if the city was eligible to receive government loans or grants. Development at the airport was at a standstill. The hangar constructed by La Porte Airways, Inc. in 1929, no longer existed. The facility was now comprised of 126 acres. This occurred due to dissension on the rental to be paid causing one of the owners to withdraw their 35 acres from the agreement. "...The present situation with the city and the federal government renting land for an airport, is little better than nothing," Mayor Smith said.

The greatest handicap for development proved to be the fact that the city and the government were only renters. The ARGUS pointed out that the government paid $250 a year and the city paid $200 a year toward the rental of the airport. Aviation enthusiasts agreed that it would be next to impossible to construct hangars and service buildings under those circumstances.

IN MICHIGAN CITY

Donald Gregory and his parents moved to Michigan City in 1908 from Battle Creek. At the age of 15, the EVENING NEWS in August of 1915, related that he had told an engineer:

> "That the right principle of flying machines had never been discovered and that it was
> his belief that the tractor principle, that of placing the engine ahead of the aviator, was
> the correct solution of the problem of perfecting flying."

He is credited with building and flying the first airplane ever flown in the "harbor city." He built the plane in 1910, at Marion Carver's Carpentry Shop, according to the recollection of Clem Spychalski, another city resident. The shop was located at the rear of his home at 803 Spring Street.

Elizabeth Munger's, *Michigan City's First Hundred Years*, relates that Gregory hauled the plane through the streets by a car to a golf course that was located just west of Greenwood Cemetery. The airplane managed to get a few feet off the ground before crashing into a grazing cow. Gregory survived the crash.

On another occasion, he took his "airplane minus the engine" to the top of Lake Avenue hill. In his attempt to glide to the bottom, he broke his arm. Then, in March, of 1911, while testing an airplane on its initial flight, he crashed. The plane fell nearly 100 feet on to Belle Island, Detroit, Michigan. Gregory was unhurt.

Two years later, Gregory was contracted to put on a flying demonstration in Michigan City. "Much interest centered...(on) the non-ascension of Donald Gregory, the local aviator, was the biggest disappointment of the day." The report in the 1912 edition of the NEWS related that the propellers were not long enough.

A few days later Gregory took his plane to a field near Greenwood Cemetery for testing. Several thousand people flocked to the site "to see the birdman and his machine." After numerous attempts the airplane "raised off the ground two or three feet and flew a distance of several hundred feet without going up.

Figure 11 Donald Gregory designed and built Michigan City's first airplane. Photo courtesy of the LaPorte County Historical Society Museum

On the fifth of August, at 7 AM, he made another attempt to fly his plane. This time he was successful. One newspaper reported the flight was on the Hotchkiss place at the west end of 10th Street, while the other said it was at the Blair field west of the state prison. He was able to ascend to a height of 65 to 75 feet, and circled the field a couple of times while going through various maneuvers. Gregory's flight was cut short when "his face was besmeared with oil," obscuring his vision.

That evening he attempted another flight, but met with little success. "Mr. Gregory is some ditch jumper," the NEWS exclaimed. The article continued:

"After spinning along on the ground almost the entire length of the Blair farm, the machine started up and at the north end of the field, Succeeded in reaching a height of ten feet. Then the motor slowed down...Just ahead of him was a ditch.... He jumped the ditch...most artistically. Fifty feet ahead was a second ditch.... The machine and Gregory just reached the opposite bank and skidded the distance of ten feet or more."

That chain of events caused damage to the plane's landing gear and propeller. So ended Donald Gregory's attempt at flying in Michigan City! Three years later, news reached the harbor city of Gregory's untimely death. At the age of 22, he crashed from a height of 300 feet in someone else's plane. A University of Michigan faculty member said, "that his death was a distinct loss to American aviation." At the time of his death his parents were living in LaPorte, on Pine Lake.

Moses Moritz of Michigan City was also a visionary. He was the owner and proprietor of a long established clothing store. One of his suppliers, Society Brand Clothes of Chicago had started an airplane express service. He was successful in negotiating with the manufacturer to have a shipment delivered by air. Through his efforts he brought the first commercial airplane to Michigan City.

The plane was to land at the Donnelly sub-division located at the corner of Willard Avenue and west Tenth Street. The EVENING DISPATCH of June 20, 1919 reported that five thousand people were on hand to view this historic event. "When the bird was discovered just above the prison buildings.... Every pair of eyes followed the plane as it cleared the field...." The plane circled the field passing over the chair factory, hugging rather close to the ground, when suddenly the pilot sent it upward and was soon out of sight.

It was learned later that the pilot had concluded the Donnelly site was not large enough to afford a safe landing. The plane finally landed on George Bull's farm, our miles southwest of the city. Bull phoned the DISPATCH office that in turn notified Moses Moritz, relaying the request to send out some gasoline. "Two good-sized bundles of...clothing" and a bundle of Chicago newspapers for the C.E. Meyer store were brought into the city by automobile. "Several thousand persons visited the spot to get their first view of the curious machine." Shortly before one o'clock the plane left the farm, flew over the city, made "a few fancy turns" and flew off.

Across the road from the Bull farm lived the Henry Ziemer family. In an interview conducted by Gladys Bull Nicewarner, in 1985, with Lewis Ziemer and Harry Frey, Ziemer recalled that at the age of 10 or 12, he and his brother Rudy flew back to Chicago on that plane

Michigan City residents during the summer and fall of 1924 had the opportunity to experience the thrill of flying. On a Sunday, late in July, Frank R. Kemp and Walter E. Cains of LaPorte were in the harbor city carrying passengers for hire. The DAILY HERALD reported that just six weeks previous, "Kemp tried to enter a house in South Bend through the roof."

Kemp was quoted as saying "I believe I'm the only aviator that ever escaped death when his ship rammed into a house." Walter F. Behrndt recalled that Kemp, between the years 1920-25 had crashed his planes (he had two) five times and survived them all.

Kemp like Eddie Nelson was an accomplished pilot. He was the first LaPorte citizen to own his own airplane. He learned to fly at the Diggin's Flying School in Chicago, according to information in the LaPorte County Historical Society's Museum's files. Behrndt joined Kemp in 1920 and worked for him until 1925. They along with Cains carried passengers for hire. The going rate throughout the country during the early 1920's was $1.00 a minute or $15 per flight. On a Sunday in October, of 1925, Kemp, assisted by a Chicago flier, performed an air show. The field was located 4 miles east of Michigan City on what was then State Road 25.

WATCH FOR THE CHECKERBOARD PLANE

World's First Aero Express
ARRIVES IN MICHIGAN CITY, INDIANA
Friday Morning, June 20th
At Donnelly's Sub-Division, Willard Ave. & Tenth St.

WITH A SHIPMENT OF
Society Brand Clothes
For **MORITZ & SON**

Watch for the Checkerboard Plane!

Figure 12 This advertisement appeared in the Evening NEWS in June 1919

Stunt flying, wing walking, parachute jumping and formation flying were done with four planes. According to Behrndt, he and Kemp in 1930 were the first to use the field that later became the Michigan City airport. That field is located at the intersection of highways 35 and 212.

In August 1924, the Michigan City NEWS carried an ad announcing that the Echterling brothers were in town for one week. The two brothers were from Hammond. The paper described them as "crack pilots of four years experience, do no stunt flying, and have never had an accident."

Figure 13 Walter F.Behrndt and Frank R. Kemp standing in front of Kemp's JN-4D Curtiss Bi-plane. Photo taken July 4,1920. Courtesy of the La Porte County Historical Society Museum.

They located a temporary operation at a field a mile and a half east of the city along Michigan Street. With two new airplanes, they offered rides for $3.00. Spectators were also treated to a thrilling parachute drop preformed by Edward Derrell of Chicago.

The summer of 1925 brought thousands of Michigan City residents to Washington Park bathing beach. The Lakeview Amusement Company and the concessionaires in the park brought Eddie Nelson's flying thrill show to the city, underwriting the entire expense as a way of demonstrating their appreciation of the public's patronage.

The EVENING DISPATCH, August 1925, related that Ruth Tomlinson made a parachute jump into the waters of Lake Michigan from a height of 2,500 feet. Nelson performed trick aerial acrobatics "at extremely low altitude" over the water. Wing walking and other "death-defying stunts" were also staged. "Playing checkers with death" was the way aviators of the day described these kinds of stunts. "It is the first time that a thrilling exhibition of this kind has ever been staged in Michigan City."

History was made on October 3, 1925, with the inauguration of the first airline in Indiana. C. Edwin Nelson and Robert Mensing of Chicago formed the company known as the Intercity Airline Company. Lieutenant Ernest Moser, a former German pilot, also from Chicago was used to assist in the project. The new service connecting Michigan City, LaPorte, and South Bend was scheduled to operate daily.

An airplane was scheduled to make four round trips to, the three cities each day, two in the morning and two in the afternoon. Arrangements were made with City Manager Albert R. Couden to use the beach near the park for a landing field. The Michigan City NEWS credited Phillip T. Sprague, who worked through the Chamber of Commerce, for the establishment of a local landing field.

The airline service had contracted with the Yellow Cab companies in the respective cities to pick up and deliver passengers and mail to the planes. Upon arrival, the cab company would meet the passengers and pick up the mail for delivery.

On that eventful morning Major George O. Redpath traveled to the city of LaPorte where he met with Eddie Nelson. He returned to the harbor city in a plane flown by Nelson. On board was "express and Mail" from LaPorte. The plane landed on the beach near Washington Park at about 10 that morning.

As scheduled, Nelson took off from the beach for South Bend at 11 o'clock. His plane was filled to capacity with packages and mail. Included were official greetings from City Manager Couden, to the mayor of South Bend, and from Leon Kramer president of the Rotary Club to the South Bend Rotary Officials. W. W. Pepple, president of the city's Chamber of Commerce also sent greetings to his counterpart.

An official ceremony inaugurating the event followed. Major Redpath, a well-known Michigan City resident, acted as master of ceremonies. More than 200 spectators were in attendance, according to the newspaper report. The high school band played several numbers prior to the landing of the plane from South Bend.

Redpath addressed the crowd. Included in his remarks, he said:

"You are standing within a few miles of the spot where the Wright brothers made the first attempt to navigate the air in machines heavier than air. You are assembled here to see the launching of the first Aerial Transportation Company promoted and put for the purpose of carrying mail, freight, express and passengers over the invisible right of way among the clouds."

A number of other dignitaries also gave short talks following his remarks.

The plane from South Bend arrived at 11:29 AM, greeted by cheers from the enthusiastic crowd. Moses Moritz, owner of a long established clothing store was on hand to receive the "first express package" from a South Bend manufacturer. Letters of greeting from Eli Seebirt, Mayor of South Bend, and Rotary and Chamber of Commerce Officials were read.

The leaders of government and business in LaPorte and Michigan City saw this airline service as a boost for their communities. It was expected that the federal government would establish a feeder route for airmail service to other cities. Unfortunately their dreams and expectations were not fulfilled.

Eddie Nelson took a job with Motor Discount Corp. in South Bend. He donated the use of his Curtis bi-plane to the South Bend Police Department. It was to be used in manhunts in rural areas. He trained two police officers to handle the airplane. The plane was kept temporarily on a field in east Mishawaka until one could be found closer to police headquarters. As a volunteer, he was sworn in as a special police officer. The city and his employer bonded him.

The value of the airplane as a means of transportation and the need for adequate terminal facilities became apparent to the business community of Michigan City. The air transportation of mail, express, passengers, and even freight had quickly become the most economical and speediest method. Some believed Michigan City needed a terminal for airplanes because of its location close to the ever-increasing traffic of commercial and mail routes.

Both city newspapers, in May and June of 1925, reported that the directors of the Chamber of Commerce had taken action to establish a permanent landing field in Michigan City. It was felt that such a field would encourage the airmail planes to land "to deposit and pick up such mail as comes within the area of the transcontinental mail route." The fact that 1925, saw "thirty-eight planes land near here in various fields to get gasoline and one thing or another," made it apparent that such a field would provide a place for emergency landings.

The Lakeview Amusement Company brought the William Shelton, Charles Siegonous flying circus to the city the next year. In addition to the exhibition, passengers were taken on a ride "through the clouds by the birdmen." Both men were ex-WWI army aviators. Shelton's father, August lived on south Porter Street, Michigan City, and was employed by the Sullivan Machinery Company, according to the NEWS.

Later in that summer of 1926 the park management brought still another air show to the lakefront. The Mabel Coody Flying Circus held its large audience spellbound with the stunt flying of "ace aviator," Ray Ahearn, and the "intrepid aviatrix, Mabel Coody." The NEWS referred to her as "one of the most nervy women air pilots to hold a stick...."

By 1926, with no apparent progress in developing an airfield, business and community leaders were showing their frustration. They continued to support and push for its development. S. T. Nelson, works manager for the Sullivan machinery plant, in an interview with the EVENING DISPATCH said:

"Corroborating with statements of others, I most heartily endorse the proposed establishment of a permanent aerial landing field near Michigan City, the outcome of which will tend to increase commercial capital to an incomparable extent."

Michigan City officials recognized the necessity of providing the city with an airport where "safe landings" could be accommodated with facilities for "quartering and repair of aircraft." With this in mind the City Plan Commission, directed by Charles E. Arnt, President hired Lawrence V. Sheridan, an Indianapolis consultant. Sheridan include as a part of the 1926 city plan, suggestions for an airport.

The proposed site selected contained approximately 160 acres. It was located one-half mile south of Coolspring Avenue. Its west boundary was Woodland Avenue. U. S. Highway 20, Woodland Avenue, Pahs Road and Roeske Avenue extended border that site as of 1997. It was described as being convenient to the city and would be served by several major thoroughfares and the LaPorte Interurban.

Sheridan also suggested an alternate site might be provided by erecting a platform over the wider portion of the Michigan Central railroad right-of-way. That would provide a landing field at the edge of the central business district. He believed that, unquestionably all of the railroads entering Chicago will be electrified within the next few years," thereby eliminating a hazard from the steam locomotives. He continued:

"Eventually the space over the Michigan Central tracks would make a fine landing field and it seems worth while to point out in this report the advantages of such a possibility."

Needless to say, the city did not follow through on that portion of the city plan. However, business leaders through the Chamber of Commerce continued to discuss and explore the need for an airport.

Michigan City's location on the southern shore of the lake has always had a direct influence on its citizens. On a winter's day in January, 1927, the ARGUS wrote, that three City fishermen, Frank Jentzen, Harvey Freyer, along with their employee Joseph Van Kirk were missing. The 60 foot tug, Imperial, had left the harbor on a Friday morning. The tug was owned by a Chicago firm and chartered to Jentzen and Freyer. The next day the Coast Guard about a mile and a half from shore observed it.

Captain S. R. Johnson, the station commander, and three guardsmen took a launch as far into the lake as the ice pack would allow. Three of the men ventured out across the ice in an attempt to get some food to the stranded fishermen. They were successful but almost paid with their lives. The ice floes began to break away. In order for them to return to their boat they had to leap from floe to floe. In the process all three had fallen into the icy water.

The Coast Guard lost sight of the tug with nightfall. Calls to neighboring cities were made in an effort to obtain the services of an airplane to fly over the area in hopes of locating the missing men. The United States Army took the lead in the search. It was announced that the Ford Airship Corporation at Detroit would send a fleet of planes to assist in the search. Five days after the Imperial left the harbor, H. C. Little, a commercial pilot, located it near New Buffalo, Michigan. He was able to drop food, clothing, and fuel to the stranded fishermen. The next day, the New Jersey, a steel prowed tug reached the stranded boat. The Imperial was lashed to the New Jersey and towed to South Chicago. The crew of the Imperial suffered no ill effects.

The board of directors of the Chamber of Commerce, in February of 1927, decided to appoint a committee to plan and arrange for an airport for Michigan City. They had come to the conclusion that the time was quickly approaching when an airport would be essential to the continued growth and health of the city.

In the meantime, the public's interest and fascination with the airplane continued. Pilots were finding new ways of making flying pay. Planes would fly over cities pulling banners behind them advertising one thing or another. Or as in the case of Schnick brothers, who owned a meat market at 409 Chicago Street, they hired a Detroit pilot to drop 2,000 pennies over Michigan City. The pennies were individually enclosed in specially made cardboard sleeves. Those finding "lucky" numbers would receive a package of Schnick's special sausage or other prizes. The brothers, Henry and Rudolph, used this event to introduce their sausage they made from a recipe received from Germany.

A few days later in June of 1927, the NEWS reported that three navy seaplanes patrolled the thirty-sixth annual Columbia Yacht Club race to Michigan City. This marked the first time in the history of the race that airplanes patrolled the course. "The big water planes" from Great Lakes Naval Training Station (Illinois), circled the city and then landed on the waters of west beach. After refueling the planes, Walter J. Eden, commodore of the Columbia Yacht Club along with Captain S. R. Johnson of the Michigan City Coast Guard Station and a NEWS reporter boarded one of the planes to patrol the course.

The Michigan City Chamber of Commerce continued to spearhead the movement to establish an airport for the city. Lieutenant Robert E. Blick, of the United States naval air force spoke to the August 16th meeting of the chamber board regarding the feasibility for a local landing field for airplanes. He informed them that he would send "complete necessary data regarding such an aviation field," from department headquarters at Washington.

Ten days later the NEWS published an editorial urging the city to stop wasting time and delaying the progress of an airport. It stressed that, "Early action...will place Michigan City more rapidly in the front rank of progress...."

Aviation technology continued to make rapid strides. Airplanes were becoming larger and more powerful. The NEWS carried a release from Hartford, Connecticut, in September of 1927 that announced a "Flying Truck Coming To City." It was publicized as "a pioneer in its field..." The Royal Air Delivery "truck" was described as an all-metal plane, powered with three motors. It had a cruising speed of 100 miles per hour. Its 74-foot wingspan made it the largest commercial airplane in service. Due to the fact that most landing fields were small or for that matter nonexistent in many parts of the United States, the plane was built with a "special trap" in the fuselages where cargo could be dropped by parachute.

The occasion for the event on September 14, 1927, was fostered by the Michigan City NEWS' purchase of three Royal portable typewriters. Since there were no fields in the city large enough to accommodate a landing, the plan was to drop the cargo by parachute. Cushman Acres east of the city was selected W. L. Shafer of the Chamber of Commerce marked the spot of the drop with a white sheet. A fair size crowd gathered to watch.

Precisely at 3:30 PM the large plane bearing the inscription NC800 Royal Typewriter Company "flew listlessly" over the field and dropped its "packet of snowy whiteness." The pilot then "gave her the gun and zoomed away." J. Edwin Purple, city editor of the NEWS received the wooden box and parachute. With treasure in hand, he returned to the NEWS office. The typewriters were placed on display for public inspection. Anyone interested was allowed to try the typewriters, "to prove to their own satisfaction that aerial shipment by plane and landing consignments by parachute is altogether practical and feasible."

The NEWS had boasted that it was the first to receive "a package of aerial freight ever to be consigned to the city." The fact of the matter was that Moses Moritz was the first eight years prior in 1917, and Society Brand Clothes of Chicago was the pioneer in airplane express service.

After the successful parachute drop in Michigan City, the Royal Air "Delivery truck" flew off to LaPorte. It had a delivery of typewriters for the La Porte Supply Company. Flying over the La Porte County Fair Grounds, the plane's crew successfully parachuted its cargo into the waiting hands of company officials.

Earlier that same morning, shortly after the heat of the day began, a monoplane known by the name of "Miss Anderson" roared out of the sky from the south at an altitude of 3,000 feet. The pilots had no difficulty in locating the landing field. They were able to read with ease the immense sign that read "MICHIGAN CITY." The letters were 20 feet long and prepared with white lime. The NEWS reported that, it "gracefully swooped down" at Bon Air, the Coonrod and Kimbill subdivision located four miles east of the city on the Michigan Road.

The plane flying from the city of Anderson, Indiana, brought the first of the thousand delegates and visitors to the fourteenth annual convention of the Indiana Real Estate Association. The Anderson delegation maintained its headquarters at the Red Apple Hotel, high atop of the Warren Building. An entire floor was reserved for them.

One of the most spectacular stunts of the convention occurred the next morning. A representative of the Fort Wayne Real Estate Board flew his plane over the city, "swooped down from the sky" in front of the Oasis Ballroom and dropped two scrolls of parchment which contained greetings from the Fort Wayne Real Estate Board to George B. Johnson, president of the Michigan City board and to C. H. Summers, president of the Indiana Real Estate Association. The plane then circled over the city and dropped about a hundred thousand greeting cards from Fort Wayne.

Michigan City community leaders continued to keep the issue of a local airport before the public. The Rotary Club at one of their March 1928, meetings hosted Thomas Wolfe, Jr., division transportation manager of the National Air Transportation Lines. The company was the largest air transport line in the country at that time. One of the Rotarians suggested at the meeting the city "transform the city park property east of the amusement park and north of Lake Shore drive..." for use as an airport. Wolfe agreed that the site would be good, "for it would be available to water planes, as well as land planes."

The Chamber of Commerce, the next month, took a positive step towards the establishment of an airport. A meeting was held at the Vreeland Hotel. Arthur Wolfe, vice-chairman of the airport committee was named to investigate available or suitable locations for a landing field. The committee was composed of Charles E. Arnt, A. R. Couden, Lee F. Dresser, Theron F. Miller, George O. Redpath, Dr. M. A. Schutt, and Wolfe its chairman.

Several days later the committee, accompanied by William L. Shafer, secretary of the chamber, surveyed the available sites for an airport close to the city. They determined that approximately an 80-acre site would be necessary. It was also suggested "...that it might prove practical to combine the uses of the field...by utilizing it for both an aviation field and the proposed public golf course and recreational center..." the NEWS reported.

Michigan City's drive to have an airport received added impetus on June 1, 1928, with the announcement of the formation of the Michigan City Aviation School. Roy Piotrowski, one of the backers of the enterprise, informed the NEWS that the Kintzele farm located one mile south of the city on Franklin Street had been leased for the "Michigan City Airport." He went on to say, "there has been considerable talk of establishing an airport here, now we have one of sufficient size to accommodate any ship."

Russell Handforth was appointed to operate the school as well as the other activities at the field. He had been an instructor at the Gary airport. The new firm did commercial flying and the carrying of passengers. At the time the field opened they owned one plane with plans to add four more.

Support for a commercial airport in Michigan City picked up momentum in November when the John Franklin Miller American Legion Post appointed Robert Bradley, chairman of a committee to study the Zorn farm located one mile south of the city, as a possible airport site. The committee was composed of Dr. Whitefield Bowers, Richard J. Kruse, Orlando Johnson, Carl Meakins and Walter Timm. One week later Dr. Newton E. Clark, Phil Sprague, Rudolph Keithley and Fred Bartels were added to the committee. Joseph E. Taylor, secretary of the United Business Men's Protective Association, told the NEWS that his organization was aiding the Legion in the task of acquiring an airport.

The property was considered to be an ideal site by the Legion. It was located about one mile from the city in close proximity to the downtown. It was reported that three hundred feet of the 80 acres needed to be plowed and graded and several trees needed to be removed. Bradley believed that the taxpayers of Michigan City would save about $40,000.

Arnold Bass

It became apparent that the task of securing an airport for the city needed to be consolidated. William Shafer, secretary of the Chamber, later in the month, called a joint meeting of the Chamber and Legion's aviation committees. After a luncheon meeting in the LaSalle Cafe, the two committees adjourned to the Chamber of Commerce clubrooms to continue their discussions. Arthur Wolff was chosen to chair the meeting. Following a discussion of possible sites and financing, the group decided to join efforts and continue the task of securing an airport for Michigan City. Their task received an added incentive when Assistant Postmaster General Clover announced that airmail service for Michigan City would begin on December 1, 1928, according to a United Press release that appeared in the EVENING DISPATCH in mid November.

The year, 1929, started with a bang. More accurately put, a crash. Coastguardsmen at the Michigan City station observed a small biplane crash land onto the ice-covered Lake Michigan about a half a mile off Sheridan Beach. The pilot walked away, unhurt, across the ice to the beach. The police and the Coastguard arrived on the scene. Officers Tony Piotrowski and Roscoe Stephenson took the pilot to the police station.

After questioning and an opportunity to warm up the pilot was escorted to the South Shore Railroad station and placed on a train for Chicago where he was to get expert help to bring the plane ashore. He never returned.

Figure 14 Michigan City Coastguardsmen inspecting the wreckage of a biplane that crashed on the ice of Lake Michigan off Sheridan Beach January 31, 1929. Government officials believed the plane was the first used to smuggle liquor into the United States from Canada. Photo courtesy of William Swedenberg.

That evening two boys managed to get to the plane that remained stuck fast to the ice. Due to their youthful inquisitiveness and to their surprise, they discovered, behind the pilot's seat, 10 gunnysacks full with 240 pints of Old Elk Canadian Whiskey. The police and coastguard were notified and retrieved the booze. Many sightseers were seen on the ice later that night and the next day. The Michigan City NEWS speculated they were looking for souvenirs from Canada. After all, "...a long walk across the ice can usually work up a thirst." The hundreds of persons that managed to cross the ice, however, broke parts off the airplane for souvenirs.

The collector of customs of Chicago arrived by car on February 2nd. D. A. Furst, captain of the local United States Coastguard Station, handed over the whiskey. A short time later the customs agent was on his way back to Chicago with the cargo in hand. Government officials surmised that the plane was the first used to smuggle liquor into the United States from Canada. The next day, a south wind carried the crashed plane far out into the lake. That evening the plane sank to the bottom.

By the mid-1920s a national campaign to assist pilots in navigating around the country was launched. Cities around the nation were marking prominent structures with their city's name that could be seen by pilots flying over. With the insistence of the Chamber of Commerce and the cooperation of the Northern Indiana Public Service Company the roof of the tall gas storage tank at the corner of Wabash and Michigan was marked with the city's name. Michigan City, in April 1929, received national recognition for its "air marking." Postmaster M. A. Schutt had received a letter from the Daniel Guggenheim Fund for the Promotion of Aeronautics, Inc., N. Y., recognizing the city's contribution to aeronautics. A certificate was enclosed signed by Col. Charles A. Lindbergh and Harry F. Guggenheim, President.

The thrill and desire to fly continued to capture the imagination of the public. Wilhelmina Schultz was no different. She lived with her grandson, Otto Gruenke, five miles south of Michigan City. At the age of 102, in April of 1929, she claimed to have ridden in everything from an ox-cart to an automobile, but never experienced a ride in an airplane.

Word had reached John Dignan, manager of the Hotel Vincent, and the manager of the soon to be opened Benton Harbor, Michigan, municipal airport, of Mrs. Schultz's wish. Arrangements were made to fly her and her granddaughter August Stick to Benton Harbor for the annual Blossom festival and the official opening of their airport. A Stinson-Detroiter, a soundproof cabin monoplane, was dispatched from Benton Harbor on the morning of May 7th. It landed on a pasture a half-mile south of the Gruenke farm. A crowd of over 100 was there to welcome and inspect the plane.

Her arrival in Benton Harbor gave her the honor of being the first passenger to officially land at the Benton Harbor municipal airport. She also had the distinction of being the oldest person at the time to ever fly.

The constant urging of the Chamber of Commerce for a municipal airport took a strong step forward on July 13, 1929, when William J. Mackenzie, an airport specialist with the U. S. Department of Commerce, came to the city to discuss plans for a development of an airport. Arthur Wolfe, chairman of the chamber's aviation committee called a special meeting to consider and develop plans for an airport. Following the meeting, the committee conducted Mackenzie on a tour of several proposed sites for the purpose of determining their suitability for a landing field.

As mentioned earlier, Lake Michigan has always had a direct affect on the residents of Michigan City. Many Chicago families were building summer residences in Sheridan and Long Beach. They found themselves commuting to Chicago daily to work. The trip around the lake by automobile took in excess of two hours. The trip time could be reduced to a half-hour if an air route connected the two cities directly across the lake.

S. E. Purdy and seven other Chicago men who had summer residences in Sheridan Beach and Long Beach made the first trip in a hydroplane on August 16, 1929. The plane was a tri-motor design capable of carrying eight passengers. They hoped to make it an everyday occurrence. The plane left the Chicago airport that afternoon and landed on the lake in front of the Purdy home, "The Sparrows." Those who made the first trip were Everett Granger, Edward Garrily, John Smale, "Dutch" Ploner, John Tyrell, Sparrow Purdy, W. K. Jones, and Losey Lansford.

What appeared to be a perfect solution to the long driving commutes culminated in a nightmare landing the following week. John Tyrell, William Jones, I. I. Ward, Everitt Michaels, R. O. Langford, E. Ploner, and Sparrow Purdy boarded the hydroplane in Chicago for what they thought would be a short, uneventful flight to their summer retreat in Michigan City. The flight was pleasant enough, and in just 23 minutes the plane was circling over Michigan City preparing to land. To the dismay of the pilot the lake "...stirred up a strong north wind, (and) was rolling up some big ones...." It appeared as though the pilot would not be able to make a safe landing on the turbulent waters of Lake Michigan. The plane circled the lakefront off Long Beach several times, "...dipping now and then into the lake and attempting to run up on the beach...." near the "The Sparrows" cottage, but it was impossible.

The pilot then decided to land near the public bathing beach, but found the lake to be no less understanding. The pilot finally was able to settle the plane into the water near the entrance to the harbor. His attempt to edge the airplane behind the breakwater to let the passengers out on the pier was in vain. "The passengers in the meantime were experiencing all the delightful feelings of seasickness as well as of the thought of sudden drowning in the cold water."

The Coast Guard observing their plight, launched their boat, and came to their rescue. Fifty-five minutes after the plane "...first attempted to perch here," the Coast Guard was able to get a line secured to the hydroplane and tow it into the more serene waters of the protected harbor. "...the passengers began to look happier and take an interest in life again."

"It was some experience," exclaimed S. E. Purdy. With that said, the misadventures of the pilot and passengers on that fateful day led to the demise of the perfect commute between Chicago and Michigan City.

The need of a municipal airport was further underscored during the first week in September. The Los Angeles to Cleveland transcontinental air derby had been completed a few days previous. Frank Copeland of Los Angeles, owner of the winning plane, ordered his pilot to stop off at Michigan City to pick up a friend. The pilot, in his Lockheed Vega monoplane, circled over the city for some time looking for a place to land. Coincidently, Louis Gielow and George Peglow were joy riding in their recently purchase American eagle bi-plane. After a lot of animated gesters and hand signals, Gielow and Peglow landed their plane at the Majot farm, four miles east of the city, with the Lockheed racer just behind. The unnamed pilot contacted Dr. Arnold H. Kegel who lived in Grand Beach. A short time later Dr. Kegel arrived at the field. He climbed into the rear cockpit with the winning trophy and the plane took off for Chicago.

The Chamber of Commerce efforts to establish an airport for Michigan City had been quietly going on over the past several months. The committee, chaired by Arthur Wolff, of the Wolff Service station, along with committee members' attorney Theron Miller, Charles E. Arnt and Victor Coonrad, met at the Spaulding Hotel, at a meeting of twenty citizens. They reported that an option to buy the land cost $46,000. Their report revealed that $17,500 had been subscribed toward the purchase of 212 acres located on the Michigan road southeast of the Michigan City Country Club property. Their plan was to raise an additional $28,000 "...to complete the purchase, (and) form a holding company to own the land." The stock was sold for $100 a share.

The Michigan City Aeronautical Association was organized to develop and operate the airport. Dues of $10 a year was charged for membership. The following men volunteered to work in pairs to make calls on City residents to obtain subscriptions to the stock company: M. C. Murray and Clem Dick; James R. Cullen and Floyd Haviland; John Lass and R. D. Shaw;

UP CLOSE AND PERSONAL

William A. Underwood and Theron Miller; J. H. Lutz and Phillip T. Sprague; Charles Tonn and H. F. Keppen; H. R. Misener and Victor Coonrod; and Arthur Wolff and Nate Rosenberg.

The plan also called for the eventual sale of the land to the city. The October 30, 1929, NEWS editorial went on to say:

> "The largest contributor to the purchase fund is James C. Baine of the Excelsior Cycle Company who subscribed $10,000. Other contributors are Victor Coonrod who owns a section of the land required and who subscribed $3,000; Theron F. Miller, $1,500; J. Henry, Sr. $1,000; Ralph H. Dean, $1,000; R. F. Garrettson, $500, and Judge (Harry B.) Tuthill, $500."

The EVENING DISPATCH expanded on the information, saying that all possible sites within a six-mile radius had been thoroughly studied. William J. Mackenzie, with the U. S. Department of Commerce, had conducted a two-day survey of the tract of land known as Majot's Mill and concluded that it was the best possible site for the airport. The choice was based upon its physical characteristics, "sufficient altitude, rolling ground and good natural advantages--will afford the clearest visibility, of any tract in this vicinity." The Warnke farm on South Franklin Street was the second choice.

Even though the airport was to be a municipal airport, the city's participation was minimal due to the lack of funds. This option route was selected by the chamber in order to protect the city. The plan allowed the city to purchase the land at the original purchase price should the field be unimproved for several years.

Mechanical problems and weather made it necessary for pilots to continue to seek level pastures in and around Michigan City to land their planes safely since a municipal airport was not in operation. The local newspapers, in late November and December of 1929, report the incidences. The Boyd-Garrettson acres provided for a safe landing for two aviators. The pilots in their all red biplane made a perfect landing. However, as they were taxiing along the rough field, they struck a ditch and the plane over turned on its nose smashing the propeller. After the two uninjured pilots righted the plane, they proceeded into town. They contacted a Chicago company and made arrangements to have them send a new propeller. The aviators spent the night in a local hotel. The propeller was replaced early the next morning, and the plane made its departure.

Earl Rose, a La Porte truck driver, while returning to the county seat on the 9th of December, reported an unusual event. As he was passing by the George Warnke farm, four miles southeast of Michigan City, two aviators waved him down. They had made what appeared to be "an entirely successful landing" on Warnke's pasture. They explained that they had been lost in the fog and asked Rose for directions to South Bend. Rose, after pointing them in the right direction, watched them take off in their plane and disappear out of sight.

The last aviation emergency of the year occurred the night before Christmas. A blinding snow storm forced Thomas J. Hill, a mail pilot for the Thompson Aero Corporation of Kalamazoo, Mich., to crash land his plane in a field about four and one half miles south of the city on the Fred Bannwart farm. The airplane struck the ground and somersaulted pinning Hill in the cockpit. The DISPATCH reported his recollection of the accident.

> "I left Chicago at 9:05 P. M. from the municipal airport at Sixty-third and Cicero. When I reached McCool, and Porter counties, I ran into snow which became thicker all the time. The visibility was very poor and the ceiling was low.... I had been flying

about 10 minutes when the air became very rough. I had great difficulty keeping the ship right side up. The air became worse all the time so I pulled a flare (costs $.75) and it either failed to light or I failed to see it. I then pulled the second flare and tried to follow it to the ground, but found it impossible as it blinded me...I cut the motor off and tried to keep the ship slowed down as much as possible and right side up at the same time. The ship nosed into the ground.... The plane turned over on its back and I was knocked unconscious and when I regained consciousness I was in the hospital."

A neighbor walking down the road to his house after a visit with the Bannwarts witnessed the crash. Neighboring farmers were aroused. A team of horses was hitched to a sleigh and was driven to the scene of the wreck. They found the pilot unconscious and "imprisoned" in the wreckage. Their rescue efforts required them to chop away a part of the sides of the plane in order to release Hill from the cockpit.

The police were notified and rushed to the scene, followed by the Carlisle ambulance. Captain George Starke, patrolmen LeRoy Barney, Alex Byksa and the ambulance crew found county line road to be impassable and were forced to leave their vehicles at the Dunes Highway (W. Hwy 12). The last mile and half was made by sleigh. Tom Hill was placed on a stretcher and carried by sleigh back to the awaiting ambulance. Upon his arrival at St. Anthony Hospital, Doctors Warren and Ralph D. Bergen were waiting. The injuries proved not to be fatal.

Seven pouches of mail were retrieved from the wreckage. They were kept at police headquarters until Christmas morning, and then taken to the post office and later placed on an eastbound Michigan Central train.

Two Thompson corporation officials came to the city the following day to interview Hill in order to determine the cause of the crash. After interviewing the pilot, they, accompanied by police officers went to the Bannwart farm. The airplane was dismantled and carried away.

Members of the Chamber of Commerce and the citizens of Michigan City awoke on Christmas morning, 1929, to find in their stocking a contribution of $20,000 toward the purchase of a municipal airport. Mrs. Catherine Barker Spaulding's donation raised the contributions to over $38,000. An editorial that appeared in the NEWS a few days later said, "Like a fairy godmother Mrs. Catherine Barker Spaulding waves her fairy wand and presto some civic project is made possible in Michigan City." Other major contributors not previously named included Joseph Bojewitz, Emil F. Krueger, F. H. Burnham, E. M. McLundie, and C. E. Arnt. The airport committee needed to raise the remaining sum of $7,100.

Arthur A. Wolff's constant promotion of a need for a local airfield bore fruit. On January 18, 1930, a group of civic-minded men and women put Michigan City far ahead of cities its size in the field of aviation. Their vision and determination caused them to form the Michigan City Airport Corporation. Those who held stock, according to the NEWS DISPATCH, were Mrs. Catherine V. Hickox, Emil F. Krueger, Joseph Bojewitz, James C. Baine, Theron F. Miller, Ralph H. Dean, Hugo F. Keppen, A. J. Henry Sr., R. F. Garrettson, Frederic H. Burnham, Simpson and Adamson, Nate Rosenberg, C. E. Arnt, H. R. Misener, H. B. Tuthill, Harvey Rogers, Vincent Milcarek, Evan Roper, E. M. McLundie, and Victor T. Coonrod. The corporation purchased 200 acres of land at U. S. 20 and Indiana 212 at a cost of $42,000. It was their intention to sell the field to the city at cost but the depression put an end to that plan.

The fate of an airport for Michigan City was now cast. The airport provided a safe landing field that attracted visitors to the area. The first woman pilot to use the airport was

Helen May of Chicago. May was a friend of Dr. William Scholl, who had a home in Long Beach. She had contacted Scholl expressing a desire to visit the city. Dr. Scholl asked his friend John Blank to mark the field. A large white sheet was spread on the ground. When the plane appeared, Blank signaled the flyer with an American flag. As the plane circled the field several times before landing, Dr. Scholl took motion pictures.

With May was Major Kenneth K. Griffith, vice president of the Aero Agents Company of Chicago, a prominent aeronautical authority. Griffith was impressed with the location and expressed enthusiasm for its possibilities. He told Scholl and Blank that he would be happy to advise the officials regarding the field if they requested his help. There doesn't appear to be any record to indicate whether his offer was accepted.

Plans to dedicate the Michigan City airport were announced by the aviation committee of the Chamber of Commerce on May 14, 1930. The committee revealed that the Indiana Aircraft Trade Association's second annual tour would coincide with the dedication ceremony on June 18 that would include a stop at the city airport. A representative of the tour committee had visited the airport the previous week to determine if the airport could safely accommodate the

Figure 15 The first official Michigan City Airport at Indiana 212 and U.S. Highway 20 was dedicated on June 18,1930. Photo courtesy of the La Porte County Historical Society.

large number of airplanes expected to participate. "Through the cooperation of Uncle Sam..." the Michigan City Post office issued a Michigan City airport dedication stamp. A total of 649 Airmail letters were bagged and cancelled and were delivered to the airport the day of the dedication. They would be taken to the Chicago Post office, sorted and forwarded by mail planes to their destination.

Four years later, December 26, 1933, the city leased the landing field for $1 per year. The maneuver allowed the city to obtain $50,000 of federal money toput in two runways, one 1,850 feet long and the other 2,500 feet. Other improvements including 5,107 lengths of vitrified tile, 11 catch basins and crushed stone boosted the total value to more than $100,000. The city promptly subleased the field back to the stockholders. Nate Rosenberg was appointed business manager for the corporation to oversee the project. Emil Majot acted as field agent and gave assistance to planes landing. Five years later, in 1935, the field operations were assumed by Victor Lindemann.

As of this writing, La Porte County is blessed with two fine municipal airports that attract business and industry. Improvements and expansion to the La Porte and Michigan City airports continued into the next millennium. However, that portion of the history will be left for another to pursue. They stand as a testimonial to the many people who had a belief and a vision that the airplane would be a tool and the key that would unlock the door through which millions of dollars would flow. Many individuals have followed in their footsteps. They believe that the future success of the county's economy will depend on the continued development and improvement of those facilities. Their tenacity and unrelenting drive has helped to secure La Porte County's economic future.

THE INDIANA TERRITORIAL BOUNDARY

The national government under the Articles of Confederation took title to the land that lay between the Appalachian Mountains on the east and the Mississippi River on the west. Adventurers and pioneers moved on to the land. They looked to Congress for legislation that would safeguard their economical and political rights.

Thomas Jefferson drafted the Land Ordinances of 1784 and 1785, which Congress adopted. They provided for the survey and sale of public domain and established a plan for the admission of new states into the Union.

Two years later the Congress enacted the Northwest Ordinance, which established the precedent followed to this day for admitting new states into the Union. A provision stated that a minimum of three states and a maximum of five states would be created out of the "Northwest Territory."[1] The line, sometimes referred to as the Indian Boundary Line, created by the Ordinance was to serve as the boundary between two tiers of states that were to be created at a later date. However, the Northwest Ordinance of 1787 was based upon erroneous information supplied from Mitchell's map of 1755, which indicated that the mouth of the Detroit River at the north shore of Lake Erie was on an east-west line with the southern shore of Lake Michigan.[2] Ohio protested that boundary line because it claimed a "very prosperous little colony of farmers" located at what later became known as the mouth of the Maumee River. The Northwest Ordinance placed this settlement inside of the Michigan Territory, thereby providing a bone of contention between Michigan and Ohio.

With the admission of Ohio into the Union in 1802, the northern boundary of the Indiana Territory and of Ohio was created. The Enabling Act of 1802, Section 2 established an east-west line "drawn from the southerly extreme of Lake Michigan." The newly formed state of Ohio continued to make its claim and protest known to the United States Congress without relief. The controversy lasted forty years and ultimately involved five states.

This territorial line was further legitimized with the creation of the Michigan Territory in 1805. "Section 1 of the Act provided that it (Michigan Territory) was to consist of all the part of the Indiana Territory which lies north of a line drawn east from the southerly bend or extreme of Lake Michigan.3

Today that Territorial Line passes through the city of La Porte. "It entered the city at North Street, crossed Tipton Street near the New York Central tracks, plunged into Clear Lake near the foot of Detroit Street, crossed the channel between Lilly and Stone Lakes a little north of Weller Avenue, passed about 200 feet south of Soldier's Park club house and baseball diamond, crossed the spot where the school children planted the evergreen tree in 1932, and traversed the channel between Stone and Pine Lakes about 350 feet south of the bridge on Waverly Beach Road, continuing due west to the most southern point of Lake Michigan near Miller's Station."[4] The exact location of the marker would be where the Territorial Line "...cuts diagonally through the north wing of Fairview Hospital (no longer there but in its place in 1999 a KFC restaurant); crosses the driveway and clips the southeast corner of the old tennis court and at this point where it strikes Pine Lake Avenue." [5]

The territorial government of Indiana petitioned Congress for statehood in 1811. After five years of deliberation Congress voted to admit Indiana into the Union with all rights and privileges of the existing states. In its infinite wisdom Congress established the new state's northern boundary to be "drawn from a point ten miles north of the southern extreme of Lake Michigan; on the north by the said east-west line, until the same line shall intersect the first mentioned meridian line which forms the western boundary of the State of Ohio."[6] The territorial government of Michigan did not recognize Indiana's newly established northern boundary.

The Michigan Territorial legislature protested the northern movement of Indiana's boundary, claiming it violated the intent of the "Northwest Ordinance." When Michigan applied for statehood in 1833, they demanded that Congress reestablish the ordinance line as the southern boundary of Michigan. Their effort failed. In 1835 Michigan decided to go ahead and form a state without congressional approval. Their state constitutional convention among other things specified that the Ordinance line was the state's southern boundary. A state government was formed declaring that they were a free and independent state.

The dispute between Ohio and Michigan escalated to the point that both sent armed troops to Toledo to enforce their claim. The issue became a national nightmare. On one hand there was a state petitioning congress to establish a boundary but usurped the right to fix and protect that line itself. On the other hand there was a territory that denied Congress' right to interfere with its right of self-determination. Cooler heads prevailed. The Ohio militia pulled back allowing Michigan to take "possession of the bloodless field," bringing an end to what history refers to as the "Toledo War."

Both now awaited a congressional decision to settle the issue. The following year congress admitted Michigan to statehood. It gave Ohio its present northern boundary and in exchange for its relinquishing its claim to the ten mile strip of land given to Indiana, Michigan received jurisdiction over 9,000 square miles of the upper peninsula.

The compromise gave Indiana a shoreline on Lake Michigan, paving the way for it to have an international lake port at Burns Harbor. Added to the state's economic base are the numerous cities that lie to the north of the Indian Boundary Line. Some of the nation's largest oil refineries and steel producers have been or are in Indiana and not in Michigan. The city of La Porte would have straddled the state line, dividing the population between two states. Michigan City, and the cities in St. Joseph, Elkhart Counties, as well as in the other counties that line up along the northern border with Michigan add to the economic strength of Indiana.

A vivid reminder of the struggle that gripped the nation during its early years can be found on the lawn of the KFC Restaurant on North Pine Lake Avenue in the city of La Porte. The Indiana Historical Bureau and The La Porte County Historical Society, Inc., along with the financial support of the Albert V. Hinton, Jr. family dedicated and unveiled a highway marker on April 29, 1999, that designates the site of the original Indiana Territorial Boundary. A special thank you goes to the Watkins family that owns the KFC franchise for allowing the marker to be placed on their property.

Indiana Territory Boundary Line

Indiana Territory Boundary Line

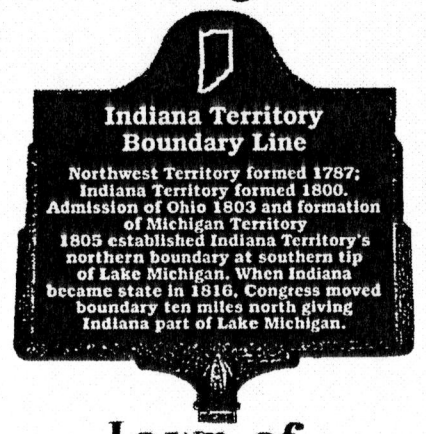

Northwest Territory formed 1787; Indiana Territory formed 1800. Admission of Ohio 1803 and formation of Michigan Territory 1805 established Indiana Territory's northern boundary at southern tip of Lake Michigan. When Indiana became state in 1816, Congress moved boundary ten miles north giving Indiana part of Lake Michigan.

Lawn of
Kentucky Fried Chicken Restaura
Pine Lake Avenue
La Porte, IN

"This work should not be left wholly to the colored people but should be shared cheerfully by all church people and public spirited citizens."
The LA PORTE TIMES

A DREAM FULFILLED: THE BUILDING OF THE AFRICAN METHODIST EPISCOPAL CHURCHES IN MICHIGAN CITY & LA PORTE

The Reverend George Wilber Baber, in 1924, had a dream. It wasn't as grandiose or as immense as the Reverend Dr. Martin Luther King Jr.'s, but to the black community of the city of LaPorte, it was no less important. The Rev. Baber, with the help of Mrs. Frank Keller and the financial support "...and faithful service of Mrs. J. B. Rupel," gave them hope and a new direction. A permanent place to worship and gather for social activities had been nonexistent for a great many years, at the time Pastor Baber arrived in LaPorte, from Flint, Michigan, in 1923.

The black community of the City of LaPorte as early as 1845, established the process for the construction of a meetinghouse. D. G. Oaks, Superintendent of the circuit, called the meeting to order on March 31, 1845, for the purpose of electing trustees for the church. "...A majority of the male brethren of the African (Methodist Protestant) Church..." were present. John Worley, Emanuel Brown, and Berry Banks were duly elected trustees, according to information on file with the LaPorte County Historical Society Museum.

A church and school were established in 1862, with the influx of 27 black families, mostly from Tennessee. They settled on Pulaski Street. A church and school was built on the corner of Washington and Pulaski streets, based on undocumented information from Gene McDonald on file at the museum.

The Rev. T. H. Calhoun, pastor of the A. M. E. Church of LaPorte, in 1932, wrote, "The first house of worship that was confined to colored people was a school house and church combined in a small house on the corner of what is now called "G" Street." The pastor of the church was the Rev. J. Gregory. His son Monroe taught the school. However, the HERALD-ARGUS, reported in a May, 1926, article:

Arnold Bass

"The first negro church was a small building seating 25 persons at Oberreich and Darrow streets. This building was abandoned a year and a half ago and services have been held until (May 16, 1926) in the Rumely Flats."

Figure 17 George Wilbur Baber served as pastor at La Porte 1924-1927 and in Michigan City 1927-1929. He was elected Bishop in Philadelphia in 1944. Photo courtesy of the Bethel A.M.E. Church, Michigan City

The black community by 1888 was on a decline. The property was sold, with the money placed into a trust fund to "be used when the colored people of the community had increased so-as to necessitate a building." Dr. Robert Sampson, Herom Harrison, and Sylvanious Stewart were selected as trustees of the fund. Attempts were made to keep the congregation together. Some meetings were held at the First Methodist Church on Monroe Street, in rooms used by the Men's Bible Class, until 1924.

La Porte for many years had a population of 25 to 30 "colored" people prior to W.W.I., according to the Rev. Baber. The call of the industrial north created demands for labor. Thousands of "Negroes" crossed the Mason Dixon line to find work and make a new life for themselves and their families. With the conclusion of the war, between 240 and 300 "colored people" were living in LaPorte. It was estimated that eighty-five percent of them were permanent citizens. Baber predicted that the industrial growth of the city would bring more, "...with their hopes and fears mingled with a strange delight, into the promised land of the north...."

LaPorte, like many communities, was fraught with the social evil of prejudice and discrimination. The Knights of the Ku Klux Klan had established itself in the county in 1922. Their doctrine of racial and religious intolerance of Catholics, Jews and blacks provided a backdrop in front of which the Reverend Baber and the black community pursued their dream.

In the midst of all this prejudice and discrimination Reverend Baber was able to secure the support of the white community. Numerous individuals and civic organizations as well as the churches were committed to assisting the "colored" community in a drive to build a community center and a place of worship. It was Leonard Henoch, with whom the idea of a community center was first broached. He was largely responsible for instituting the campaign.

The city issued a building permit to Rev. Baber on July 28, 1924, on the property at 114 Brighton Street, formerly owned by Elizabeth Smith, "colored." George W. Allen and Son, local architects, donated their services in the preparation of the plans and specifications for the $15,000 project. Work on the church began on September 3, 1924.

Baber and the church officials gathered at the site to begin the excavation for the new church. They gave "...their spare time to help the cause along." With shovels in hand Samuel Washington, R. B Stokes, Oscar Adams, James Cole, William Meyers, Melvin Starrs, Murray Lyons, Howard Barker, Carry Mitchell, Gus Thomas, Champ Jackson, R. D. Chunn, Audry McCastle, and Clarence Howard were photographed on that historic moment by the DAILY HERALD.

The drive to raise the $15,000 began in earnest on the 2nd of October at a meeting held at the Rumely Hotel. J. J. Farnan, chairman of the executive committee, and F. Glenn Wood, secretary of the drive explained the plan to the more than twenty people in attendance. The task of campaign advertising was assigned to Ralph Moss and his three aides, Russell Smith, Cy Parker and Paul Bell.

Executive committee members were assigned and gave talks at the upcoming Sunday church services. F. Glenn Wood spoke to the congregation of the Presbyterian Church; John B. Dilworth at the Methodist church; Fred R. Liddell at the Baptist Church; C. V. Shields at the Christian Church and M. E. Siljestrom at the Bethany Lutheran Church.

That evening "A monster mass meeting..." was held at the First Baptist Church. Pastor Baber spoke and gave detailed plans for the project. The Harmony Colored Quartet, of South Bend, provided the music for the event.

The Rev. W. F. Bostick, pastor of the First Baptist Church, continued the effort when he spoke to the Kiwanis Club urging them to "give whole-hearted support" to raise funds for the "colored" church.

The momentum of the drive continued on the following Wednesday at a dinner meeting held at the St. John's parish hall. The executive committee and team captain announced that $10.091.25 had been raised. The first voluntary gift in the campaign came from the Elks Club with a $100 pledge. The three team generals, C. V. Shields, Ed Kabelin, and Van Dien Terry, thanked the captains and their workers for a job well done. A special thanks was given to Mrs. J. B. Dilworth who brought in large number of subscriptions to the drive.

A week later the executive committee, made an appeal to anyone that had not had an opportunity to donate to the "colored community church" to send in their contributions to Russell Smith's office. The following statement appeared in part in the DAILY HERALD:

"While the two day intensive drive for the colored community house... ended, there are approximately 2,000 prospects who were not seen or interviewed...and inasmuch as the goal set has not been reached, this communication is directed to the citizens of the community who have not contributed to this worthy cause."

Despite the appeal, contributions slowed to a trickle and the project brought to a standstill. In an effort to revitalize the drive, the fundraising committee was able to convince a world-renowned black woman pianist, Hazel Harrison, to play a concert for the citizens of LaPorte, on June 25, 1925, at the high school auditorium. She brought an air of familiarity to the concert; after all she grew up and attended school in LaPorte. Her father was Herom Harrison. She began to study the piano at an early age. She received an invitation to play at the Royal Theatre in Berlin, Germany, at the age of nine. The Music of Black America, A History, 2nd ed., refers to her as "The first woman pianist to make a stir in the musical world...." She also won critical acclaim as "...the most accomplished pianist of the race for several decades."

Figure 18 The above architectural drawing by George W. Allen and Son appeared in the La Porte Argus on October 4, 1924. The building was designed so that an additional floor could be added later. The design was to provide a 42 X30 feet auditorium with an accordion door that could be used to separate a social room and a ladies parlor.

More than 500 people attended the concert according to the report in the HERALD-ARGUS. Russell Smith made an appeal for funds to complete the "colored" church. Pledges amounting to $250 were received. The net proceeds of the concert amounted to about $400. Smith thanked the Hobart M. Cable tuners, who donated their time, to tune the grand piano. The Kaber Floral Company was thanked for its efforts to raise the necessary funds to complete the project continued. Community interest and support appeared to decline. In the meantime, Rev. Baber and his parishioners, continued with their attempt to raise money to complete the church. They held a chicken dinner fund-raiser on December 11, 1925. The board of the First Methodist Church allowed them the use of the church basement. The Ladies' Aid Society of the church donated the use of their kitchen and cooking utensils. Charles Dunn, a well known caterer in LaPorte, supervised the dinner. Twenty women of the Mizpah class of the Methodist church served the supper.

The dinner proved to be a success. Four hundred attended. Prizes were awarded to the top ticket sellers. Mrs. Champ Jackson won 1st prize and Mrs. Marie Stewart took the 2nd prize. The TIMES reported that the supper and benefit brought in $176. However, with $5,000 needed to complete the project, there was a great deal of disappointment among the black population.

The HERALD-ARGUS and the TIMES, in January attempted to stir the conscience of the community. Editorials promoting the cause made it clear that they supported the drive to build a community center and church for the black community. The two year long drive had only brought in $7,418 and had been paid to the contractor. The congregation needed to raise an additional $3,200 if they were to receive the benefit of a $1,800 trust fund. The TIMES added, " this work should not be left wholly to the colored people but should be shared cheerfully by all church people and public spirited citizens."

The editorials appeared to restore the momentum and enthusiasm that had been exhibited at the start. The fund-raiser executive committee met at the Rumely Hotel the next month. The architect, George Allen, had been consulted, concluding that $4,000 was needed to finish the church. The committee pointed out, "...that its present state of incompletion is a mark against the community that started out to raise the money and build the church for the negro population of LaPorte."

The campaign was renewed and given new life at a meeting held on February 14, of representatives from all of the Protestant churches. They met in the Presbyterian Church. The "packed audience" heard many inspirational remarks for those present. Fred R. Liddell, a member of the committee asked and received from the audience $446.80 in pledges and cash. Several hundred dollars in pledges from other sources were also announced.

Two days later chairman Earl Rowley reported that the colored population of LaPorte had pledged $1,000 toward their cause. Six hundred fifty three dollars of those pledges came from the "colored" employed at the Advance-Rumely foundry. The pledges were to be deducted from their pay envelopes. A list of the men that contributed to the fund were:

Raymond Brooks	Manuel Moss	B. T. Thompson
J. W. Terry	Handy Jones	John Dean
Henry Penn	Samuel Jenning	Warren Metcalf
J. R. Osborn	Maurice Riggs	Albert Yabro
Jeff Dumas	Norman Stephenson	Caroy Mitchell
A. C. Williams	V. Helcide	William Moss
Henry Gill	Pink Casper	Amos Lane
James Bailey	James Robinson	Obie Williams
Joe Rogers	Andrew Brown	Joe Metcalf
Al Brunson	M. Lyons	Taylor Wales
Herman Cox	Charles Welch	Arthur Johnson
W. E. Thomas	Curley Saverson	S. A. Thomas
Henry V. Bailey	C. Bracy	James Cole
John Bever	Clarence Stevens	Joe Shivers
James Broaden	W. E. Barnes	L. Dean
Earl McCallister	Oscar Adams	Elbert Thomas
Louis Jackson	Wesley Huddleston	

Rowley proclaimed that their goal was in sight. He urged the 20 campaign workers to "put on the pressure" and complete their task.

Rowley announced a month later that the $4,000 goal had been reached. A few faithful workers who labored quietly during the interim put the goal over the top. Most of the pledges were obtained from individuals and organizations that gave to the cause in the original drive in the fall of 1924. Subscriptions were to be sent to H. H. Keller at the People's Trust Savings Bank.

The La Porte Library Board, in anticipation of the completion of the church-community center, authorized the establishment of a new branch at that location "for the use by the LaPorte negro population." They voted $100 for the project. The central library sent a collection of 96 books. Reverend Baber was to supervise the branch. The Board also located branches in the junior high school, the high school and Holy Family Hospital.

The task of completing the church got under way. The windows were installed and the interior mostly finished by May 8th. The first service held at the African Methodist Episcopal community church on Brighton was conducted the next day. At least 250 people reportedly attended each service. Dr. J. W. Edghill, district superintendent of the Fort Wayne district of the African church gave the sermon at the morning and evening services. A "Negro" choir from Michigan City sang in the morning and a LaPorte "Negro" choir provided the music in the evening. F. Glenn Wood and Alfred J. Link gave short talks at the morning service. The two were prominent in the campaign to raise funds for the church.

The dedication of the church was conducted on Sunday, May 15, 1926. The public was invited to attend the services. The Rev. J. W. Saunders of the West Detroit district gave the sermon at the regular morning service. That afternoon the dedication service began with songs from the Quin chapel, A. M. E. Church, of Benton Harbor, Michigan. The Rev. M. G. Long, of the First Christian Church, gave the prayer. The Rev. S. A. Stewart, of the Presbyterian Church, read from Scripture. The Rev. J. W. Edghill gave the hymn of dedication. Mayor John Line, of LaPorte welcomed the participants to the city and praised efforts of all that made the building of the church possible. The church was then welcomed on behalf of the Ministerial Association, by the Rev. John W. Moffatt, its president. Bishop W. T. Vernon, formerly bishop to Africa and head of the 15 Episcopal districts of the African Methodist Church gave the sermon.

That evening a unified Protestant service was held at the First Baptist Church. Messrs. Wilkes, Berry, Lee and Hall, of Michigan City, Negro quartet, sang Negro spirituals. Bishop Vernon addressed the group.

The church was a source of pride for the black community. Above the entrance to the building was a mantle of white limestone, with the words African Methodist Episcopal Church chiseled in to it. The red brick building housed an auditorium that could seat 200 persons. Opening the partitions of the adjoining room could double the capacity. When not used as part of the auditorium the individual rooms provided a reading room, a branch of the public library, classrooms and a woman's restroom. The interior was trimmed in golden oak. The pulpit and the rostrum were made from golden oak. The spacious basement was used as a recreation room, which included shower baths and the heating plant.

Several boards were created to ensure that the church would provide for the secular and spiritual needs of the congregation. The trustees of the church were Murray Lyons, Champ Jackson, Leslie Keller, James Cole, William Thomas, William T. Thomas and Eons Thompson. The board of stewards was composed of William Barrens, R. B. Stokes, William Madden, James Cole and William Thomas.

The stewardesses included Matte Ox, Daisy Metcalf, Isabelle Thomas, Berth Kelley and Laura Adams. The Sunday school was directed by Mrs. William Robinson, superintendent, with her assistant Laura Adams. The remaining board members included Mildred Mailey, secretary; L. Stanley, treasurer; Genevieve Hatchell, juvenile department; Miss Adams, intermediate and James Cole, senior.

The African Methodist Episcopal Church of LaPorte served as a monument to the dedication and hard work of the Reverend George W. Baber, his congregation and the numerous individuals and civic organizations of the white community. As Mayor John Line so ably stated in 1926, and written in the ARGUS the church was "a religious and social force in the community."

The community church came alive with activities during the next several months. Every Negro family in LaPorte affiliated with the church according to Baber, even though all the adults were not members. A Thursday Afternoon Sewing circle, with Marie Stewart as president, purchased a piano and a sewing machine. A girl's glee club, guided by Laura Adams, its president, met each week to engage in singing and dramatics. A scout troop for small boys was also organized.

A Community Athletic club to stage athletic programs for young men was formed. Leslie Keller was its president. The other officers were: Melvin Starrs, treasurer; O. B. Williams, secretary; R. W. Warner, Norris Riggs and Joe Osborne rounding out the board of directors.

The land around the building was graded and landscaped by members of the congregation in mid-April of 1927. William Allen donated some of the shrubbery that was planted around the church and parsonage. A new sidewalk was added at that time.

Back in September, 1926, the district meeting of the A. M. E. churches in the Michigan conference assembled in South Bend. The district was composed of all the African churches in Michigan and four cities in Northern Indiana. Information was released stating that Rev. Baber would stay in LaPorte at least one more year. However, added to his responsibilities would be the Michigan City congregation. Although the Michigan City membership was larger than LaPorte, it did not have a church. Baber said it was his intention "...to build a church for his flock..." in the harbor city. With this appointment, he and his family moved to Michigan City.

The Reverend Baber launched his plan in mid-January, 1927, at a meeting of 30 representatives of business and professional men, at the Spaulding Hotel in Michigan City. James J. Farnan, president of the LaPorte Bar Association at that time and the chairman of the LaPorte drive, spoke to the group on the topic, "the Negro and His Place in the Community." Baber, in conjunction with the meeting issued a press release:

> "The negro population of Michigan City has increased from 150 to over 450 in a period of five years. This number is at a low ebb at present, due to our industrial depression. But during periods of prosperity the negro population has been approximately 1,000 men, women and children...These people have come into the north because of labor shortage, prior and during the war. There are certain classes of work for which the colored people are serviceable. Therefore, there is a constant demand for their labor. Hence the negro is here in these increasing numbers not because of his own desires alone, but due to our great industrial demand of the north. He will be together a worthwhile citizen or a liability to any community in proportion to the interest the fair-minded white citizens take in him..."

James Farnan at a follow up meeting again addressed members of the committee at a noon luncheon held at the Spaulding. He outlined the methods used in LaPorte and the results. Nearly every organization in the city endorsed the project, regardless of their affiliation or purpose.

While attempting to get the white citizens involved, Reverend Baber forged ahead with his dream for the black community of Michigan City. A fundraiser was held in April. The theme for the event was the Most Popular Baby contest. Delores Thompson, the nine-month-old daughter of Mr. and Mrs. Enos Thompson, was voted the most popular. Her father was able to

Figure 19 An architectural drawing of the... proposed new A. M. E. church and community house which is expected to be constructed for the colored people of this community...." The Michigan City News, May 24, 1927, p. 6.

collect more than $55. A total of $109 was raised.

The white community accepted Reverend Baber's request for their support. An organizational meeting was held at the Spaulding Hotel that same month. Many prominent men lent their names and ability to the cause. Committees were appointed and general plans for the fund drive was discussed. Members of the committee were: R. C. Fedder, general chairman; Clyde L. Taylor, of the Merchants National Bank, treasurer; Fred Ahlgrim, president of the city school board, secretary; Rev. Donald C. Ford; A. R. Couden, City Manager; Mayor William F. C. Dall; Rev. Robert Hall; J. B. Faulknor; Rev. Joseph Bolka; E. G. Richter; Dr. M. A. Schutt, postmaster; H. R. Misener; Jacob Hahn; Rev. E. J. Egly and Rev. Emil Kemena.

The committee announced the following week its plan to stage a patriot concert on June 2nd, at the Sky Blue Arena. The arena was located on East Dunes Highway (Second Street). The arena was the site for numerous boxing events in which nationally known boxers fought. Edgar H. Lawrence of South Bend donated the use of the arena.

In the days and weeks leading up to the concert numerous activities and meetings were held. The support from the city was enormous. From the office of Mayor, the city manager, public schools, police department, and all down the line, support for the concert was intense. The Michigan City Knights of Columbus, at their regular May meeting endorsed the project. Tickets were distributed to every child in the school system giving them the opportunity to assist in the sale of tickets for the concert. The Ministerial Association of Michigan City also endorsed the concert. Rev. Baber on the last Sunday of May spoke from the pulpit of the First Methodist Church to appeal to that congregation for their support of the project, as did other members of the A. M. E. church in every pulpit in the city.

W. W. Pepple, president of the Chamber of Commerce, also provided encouragement to the movement. In a letter to Rev. Baber he said in part:

UP CLOSE AND PERSONAL

"The effort made by you in behalf of the colored citizens in Michigan City...is very commendable and your efforts in this behalf should be highly encouraged to the end that you may achieve success in your venture. The establishment of this community church is certainly a crying need in our city for people of your Race and is one that should be supported fairly among thinking people."

Monetary contributions from individuals and organizations were received. The EVENING DISPATCH reported Samuel J. Taylor pledged $100. The Michigan City Real Estate Board as well as the boards of the First Congregational Church and members of the police department each contributed $25. R. C. Fedder upon the request of Harriet Lay, executive secretary of the Charity Organization Society, donated 90 tickets to be distributed among the "poor and worthy families...who will be financially unable to attend the super-musical."

"Weather conditions (for the scheduled concert) have been left to Rev. D. C. Ford and he has given a promise to secure the best brand of early summer atmosphere and cloudless skies that is to be obtained," stated the NEWS. Unfortunately it did not happen and the concert was delayed until the following week.

The concert, held on June 7, 1927, proved to be a huge success. Approximately 2000 people attended. R. C. Fedder officiated as master of ceremonies. The Rev. Robert Hall opened the program with a short address. He outlined the need and the explained the purpose of the community church. Then a choir of 2,000 public and parochial students, directed by Cora Mae Nafa, sang "America." The EVENING-DISPATCH observed, "The youngsters put the zest and patriotic fervor necessary in the rendition and every grown-up was inspired."

The combined bands of LaPorte and the Haskell and Barker played several numbers, under the direction of Paul LaResche. Their rendition of "The Stars and Stripes, "caused the DISPATCH to remark, "The American Legion men and boy scouts who were acting as collectors and ushers, couldn't make their feet behave. They wanted to march." The Michigan City Boy's Band, lead by LaResche, played two selections.

The Apollo Male Chorus, under the direction of Henry Warkentine, performed several selections. The DISPATCH quipped, "...that, in the parlance of the big time 'knocked them out of the their seats.' " As a special feature, they were followed by the Reese Solo Sextet, composed of Negro artists from Chicago, singing Negro spirituals. Their performance alone, the NEWS observed, would "...be worth the price of admissions."

With the fund raising goal close at hand, a building permit was issued in August, for the African Methodist Episcopal Church. The permit provided for a one-story brick church to be located on the east side of Michigan Street, between Second and Forth. The value was placed at $12,000.

The directors of the La Porte County Fair were approached and gave permission to have two flower days at the fair to raise funds for the church. Approximately 20 young ladies from Michigan City and LaPorte participated.

Construction of the church had progressed to the point that in September the contractor was ready to lay the corner stone. On the 11th, a dedication ceremony was held. Three hundred persons attended. The DISPATCH reported that all of the Ministers of the city took part. Three local pastors were a part of the formal program. Reverend Donald Ford did the invocation. Reverend F. O. Fraley read selected scripture and Reverend Ralph J. Karney pronounced the benediction. The Reverend Dr. T. H. Wiseman, superintendent of the A. M. E. Detroit District, gave the address. The Michigan City Boys band and a choir composed of the congregation present provided the music. Fifteen members of the Lake Michigan Lodge of the colored A.

F. and A. M preformed the formal ceremony of laying the corner stone and dedicating the building.

Ten days later, Rev. Baber attended the annual church dirsrict conference at St. Stephen's church in Detroit. It was announced that pastor Baber was transferred from LaPorte and would devote his time and engery to the churches in Benton Harbor, Michigan and Michigan City. The Reverend James Arthur Dean was appointed to the LaPorte pastorate.

FIGURE 20 THE BETHEL AFRICAN METHODIST EPISCOPAL CHURCH LOCATED AT 318 E. MICHIGAN ST. AS IT APPEARED IN 1946. ACCORDING TO THE NEWS DISPATCH THE NORWEGIAN EVANGELICAL CHURCH OCCUPIED THIS SITE IN THE 1870'S.

Work on the exterior of the building continued. However, it became apparent that there would not be enough money to complete the project. Baber petitioned the city commission, requesting their permission to conduct a tag day on October 8th. It was hoped that the event would raise enough capital to supply the necessary money to complete the exterior of the building. With permit in hand, Rev. Baber began the task of organizing the event. E. W. David, the vice-president of the People State Bank, was named general chairman of the campaign.   Once again the white community rallied to support the cause. The NEWS wrote, that women from the First M. E., the First Presbyterian, the Calvary Baptist and Christian churches would "...be stationed on the downtown streets...as a sales force to dispose of the tags." "Buy a brick" was their slogan and printed on each tag was the phrase, "I bought a Brick." The campaign was successful and the exterior of the building was completed by late fall.

However, due to a lack of funds, the project came to a standstill. By April additional pledges were received making it possible to resume and complete the work of the interior.

*"Men and women shall
have equal rights throughout
the United States and every place
subject to its jurisdiction."*
Proposed Constitutional amendment, 1926,
introduced by Senator Curtis, Rep., Kan.

AMAZING WOMEN OF LA PORTE COUNTY

From the beginning of time women were treated as second-class citizens. They were to be seen but not heard in public. The early history of the United States shows that women were treated as being inferior to men. There were barriers hindering their pursuit of higher education. Their right to own property was limited. Men dominated business and the professions, denying women equal opportunities. The industrial revolution opened the door for women to take employment outside the home. In the years following World War I, women began to enter almost every kind of business trade, profession, and political office. A major barrier to women's rights came tumbling down in 1920 when the 19th Amendment to the Constitution granting women the right to vote was ratified. Women's suffrage brought with it the desire to enter public office in judicial, legislative, and executive positions. Political freedom fostered and accelerated women's desires for legal and economic equality. Men begrudgingly acquiesced to their demands.

Many women have worked to improve their position in American society. The names of Abigail Adams, Elizabeth Caddie Stanton, and Susan B. Anthony come to mind. Women's organizations were formed to educate, promote their rights and to serve as a guardian for those already achieved. Through their efforts gains in equality for women in the eyes of business and the law have been obtained.

The Business and Professional Women's Club was organized in Michigan City in 1923 to promote the goals and ideals of their members. It had one of the largest memberships of any similar club that had ever been formed in Indiana the EVENING DISPATCH reported. There were over 100 members by the end of the year. The large membership and numerous civic activities enhanced their opportunities to gain prominence and respect. Their tenacity and visibility assured success.

"Men and women shall have equal rights throughout the United States and every place subject to its jurisdiction," said Senator Curtis, a Republican from Kansas. His proposed Constitutional Amendment was introduced in 1926. Thirty-six states approved the amendment, but thirty-eight were needed. Ten years and two months after its original passage by Congress the Amendment failed to be adopted. It wasn't until 1972 that Congress approved the Equal Rights Amendment.

Today women hold many positions once the sole domain of men. Women now enjoy a higher level of political and economic equality. Their struggle continues to this day.

———◆———

LINIA (DUTTON) BOECKLNG

Such was the case in the spring of 1888. The economic Panic of 1888 had its grip on the nation. However, it did not deter Linia Dutton, who later became Mrs. Frank Boeckling, from embarking on an adventure "full of hazardous perils in an uncharted sea." She was one of the first women in Michigan City to own and operate a shop, becoming one of "...two of the city's first successful businesswomen," a DISPATCH reporter wrote. It was located at 406 Franklin Street. According to Linia, "...there were no business houses located south of Sixth street." She had sent "...neatly engraved cards, decorated with rosebuds and bluebirds..." to announce the spring opening of her Bon Ton Millinery room.

The card read:

"Spring Opening. Fine Millinery. Your attention is called to the elegant assortment of fine millinery at the Bon Ton Millinery rooms. The latest ideas in patterns and novelties in millinery. You are cordially invited to call. Linia Dutton."

The Bon Ton was an immediate success. In those days hat styles were called "Romance," "Hyacinth," and "Hugenot." She said that women didn't buy a hat just because they liked it. Women expected them to "wear for ages." Reminiscing with a reporter in the late 1920's, she said that what she liked best about the business was trimming. She would go into Gages in Chicago to get new suggestions and ideas from the latest styles, as well as copy hats. Within the first year Linia was able to pay all of her creditors. Six years later she sold her successful business to Mrs. E. S. McGlinsey.

Mrs. Louis Ganschow was the other "captain to sail this choppy sea." The newspaper stated she was one of the first stenographers in Michigan City. She had told a reporter that in 1888, there were only four typewriters in town. One stenographer could type enough in one day to accommodate fifteen lawyers.

She went on to describe the typical business office of those days:

"The offices were equipped with discarded things from home. In the room where I worked we had a table for my typewriter, a file filled with a million things—and two desks. My typewriter was a Smith Premier and I used the Pittman revised system of shorthand. I worked for William A. Bray, who had a real estate, insurance and customs office. All of Michigan City's lumber was brought in by boat then.

"Shirt waists and skirts, much longer than they are now, were the vogus (sic) for business girls. We wore low heels and didn't know what makeup was!"

———◆———

ANNA A. & ELIZABETH L. HOPKINS

The Hopkins sisters, Anna and Elizabeth, were the children of Hazard and Anna. Their parents married in Michigan City in 1858. The family played a prominent roll in the early history of the city. Hazard was active in the business community and owned several valuable properties in the city. The Hopkins building occupied the northwest corner of Franklin and Michigan Streets. Annie and Lizzy spent nearly all of their adult life living together and in business together.

One of the interesting avocations adopted by women was the circulation of daily and Sunday newspapers. Anna and Elizabeth opened a book and stationery store in Michigan City in 1887. The Franklin St. operation by 1902 was one of the best-appointed and equipped news stores in Indiana, a Chicago Herald newsman wrote. He went on to say "in the matter of real grit pushed it on a scale attempted by few of the sterner sex." At a time when Michigan City was unable to get early delivery of the Chicago Sunday papers, these "plucky sisters" arranged to have a special messenger bring them from La Porte and they were in the hands of the subscribers by breakfast time. On occasion when the boys failed to deliver the papers, neither sister was above delivering a route herself and this was done in all kinds of weather.

Figure 21 Anna Hopkins in front of her store at 426 Franklin St. The sign reads NEWS DEPOT, BOOKS & SUBSCRIPTIONS, THE SISTERS HOPKINS

It was this kind of passion that made their business in 1902 "one of the best newspaper businesses in Indiana," according to the Chicago Herald. They were handling upward of 1,000 Sunday Chicago papers in March of 1902. Their successful bookstore continued to operate for another fifteen years or so. Around the year 1919 the sisters returned to the business world with the opening of a children's clothing store at 908 Franklin Street. This endeavor, however, lasted about three years. In November of 1926, and through the mid-1930's, Annie was active in politics,

Arnold Bass

serving as Michigan township assessor. She was among the first woman in the county to hold a public office. Her victory over Rudolph Weiler, a Democrat, made her the first woman assessor of the township.

———◆———

HANNA'S DARLINGS OF THE DIAMOND

The LaPorte County town of Hanna had the distinction of a woman's baseball team that played real baseball in 1905, according to the M.C. News. The members of this unique organization were, "Pretty HOOSIER girls that had intimate knowledge of the art of playing ball." According to the Michigan City NEWS: "they didn't hide in the back yards and play town ball, or sneak into the country and play with other girls, they played against the boys and sometimes they won." Their costume was appropriate for the playing of the game, according to the News and they can run bases that put to shame many a young man. They never asked for special favors of anybody and they were open to all challenges.

The pitcher of the girls' team was Dorothy Swihart, and what she didn't know about the "spit" ball was not worth knowing, stated the news. The catcher, Flora Clark, was exceptional, and could catch anything that her partner sent over the plate. The NEWS described all the girls as pretty and athletic. They enjoyed having fun, and it could be seen by the way the played.

The rest of the lineup of the team included: Lillian Wells, shortstop, Miss Iva Rosenbaum, 1st base, Hattie Osborne, 2nd base, Miss Minnie Gibson, 3rd base, Miss Laura Davis left field, Miss Libbie Terrey, center field, and Miss Martha Keel right field.

Speaking about the team, one of the young ladies said she couldn't understand why people made such a fuss out of girls playing ball. Fifty years ago, she said, "There were only two avocations in life open for women. Now (in 1905), a woman has a place In 500 professions, many of which she has chased men out of. Why should not women become the future athletes of America?"

———◆———

MARY P. NORTON

Mrs. Mary P. Norton, of rural La Porte County raised championship Italian greyhounds. She had entered them in the American Kennel Club, Fort Wayne show in 1924. At that show a giant German police dog named Ajax Von Luzenberg displayed its talent as a guard dog in a demonstration that roughed-up its trainer. The dog's owner offered to pay anyone $1 a minute to enter the exhibition ring with the dog. Evidently the other exhibitors had been frightened out. None of the showmen accepted the challenge due to the previous demonstration. Finally Mary donned the padded suit and headgear to show how the giant German police dogs guard and attack their prisoners. She wrestled the dog for several minutes and was none the worse for the encounter. The DAILY HERALD boasted, " LA PORTE WOMAN PROVES METTLE AT DOG SHOW." This was the first time in the history of the American Kennel Club that a woman had been used for that act. Incidentally, her two entries in the show Colonel's Laddie and Roma took firsts.

DR. MARENA L. (BROMBERG) DRESCHER

Dr. Marena L. (Bromberg) Drescher was an early pioneer in her chosen profession. She was born on a farm near Charlotte, Michigan in 1866. Marena enrolled in the Woman's Medical College of the Northwestern University of Chicago in 1887 following a brief career teaching in Eaton County, Michigan. Her marriage to C. N. Drescher brought her to Michigan City. She had been one of the prominent physicians for a number of years in Michigan City, at a time when men were dominant. She announced her retirement from the practice of medicine in 1910. Her obituary that appeared in the NEWS, October 9, 1933, stated that she "... was conscientious in her professional duties and had the goodwill of many people.... (and) was held in high esteem...." She and her husband Charles lived at 2002 East Michigan Street at the time of her death.

Figure 22 Marena Drescher, Photo appeared in the MICHIGAN CITY ILLUSTRATED, 1900

———◆———

CLARA M. HESS

Clara M. Hess resided in Westville with her husband Colonel C. D. Hess in 1907. She possessed the reputation of being bright, trustworthy and honorable. She had demonstrated those traits when she served as the state president of the Women's Relief Corps. When a vacancy occurred in New Durham Township for a justice of the peace, fifty citizens of the township filed a petition at the county auditor's office requesting that the County Commissioners appoint Mrs. Hess.

The "novelty" of the proposal bewildered the commissioners. "Cultured Evanston," Illinois, may have been the only place in the nation that had a lady justice of the peace, according to the News. The commissioners were willing but wanted to be sure that there were no obstacles in the way. The issue was deferred to County Attorney Truesdell to research. There was nothing in the state statutes of Indiana that prohibited such an appointment. That being the case, the commissioners appointed Mrs. Hess a justice of the peace for New Durham Township.

Assistant Secretary of State, Frank I. Grubbs "was up against a dilemma," when word of the appointment reached his office, the Evening Dispatch reported. He was not aware of any women ever appointed to such a position. He searched and could not find any record of a woman appointed as a justice of the peace in Indiana. Grubbs conferred with Governor Hanly who said, "I see no reason why a woman should not serve as a justice of the peace. There is no law to prohibit a woman from serving in the capacity." Thus Clara M. Hess was the first justice of the peace in the state of Indiana to wear a skirt.

———♦———

LAURA. B. SCHARFENBURG

Laura came to Michigan City from Ohio. She was the wife of George Scharfenburg. Their home was at 109 Hancock "avenue." At one time she operated a confectionery store on Willard Avenue.

In the city election held in November of 1921 she was appointed inspector, having "full charge" of the election in the second precinct of the third ward while Mrs. Ella Simmerman was appointed sheriff. According to the EVENING NEWS, they were the first women in the history of Michigan City to hold those offices, "acquitting themselves with full credit." The newspaper went on to say that the voting place was handled in a business-like way and with "less friction" than in many others.

The League of Women Voters organized a chapter in Michigan City in the 1920's. One of the early causes they promoted was the appointment of a policewoman for the city. THE EVENING NEWS reported that at a meeting of nearly 100 members, the League went on record as favoring such an appointment. They presented their request to the city administration. The League gave the following reasons why the women of Michigan City think a policewoman was needed:

> "For the protection of girls, safeguarding their welfare and morals, helping them to avoid indiscretions, which later in life they might regret.
> To serve as matron at the jail when women are incarcerated therein.
> To visit public dance halls and cooperate with their managers and matrons.
> To get in friendly touch with runaway or self-willed girls and advise them with a spirit of true helpfulness.
> To lend a hand to any girl who is In need of protection.
> To be a friend and advisor of the young people of Michigan City, While striving to secure their cooperation in an endeavor to better conditions at the park, bathing beach, dance halls and all places of amusement frequented by them."

The City Commissioners finally acquiesced and appointed Mrs. Laura. B. Scharfenburg to the police force in March of 1922. Prior to her appointment to the police department, she was "a prominent and active club woman." It was expected that as policewoman, she would also act as matron at the city jail. The NEWS stated that, "Mrs. Scharfenburg is well equipped, in physique, mentally and ideals for the position." She spent several days in South Bend getting an insight into the work from their policewoman. She stayed for a little more than a year.

THE MICHIGAN CITY NEWS reported her initial arrest. Four men came to the city with the Pullman excursionists. She found them gambling in Washington Park. "She directed them to go with her to the police station and they obeyed."

She died in May of 1943. Her obituary did not speak of her accomplishments or contributions to the community. It said nothing about her role in the women's rights movement. She might not have led rallies or gave speeches for the cause, but in her quiet way she was one of those that opened new job opportunities for women. She died as humbly as she lived

———◆———

HAZEL HARRISON

On a hot, late June 1925 evening in the La Porte High School Auditorium over 500 people from the community attended a piano concert presented by Miss Hazel Harrison. The applause that greeted her was earsplitting. And why shouldn't it be, for she had played in the most exclusive circles of Europe and America. After all, she was "the first woman pianist to make a stir in the musical world."[8] She played for the cream of German society in 1904 at the Royal Theatre in Berlin. Her career took her to Chicago in 1919 and New York in 1922 where she gave debut recitals. Her concert tour took her to many cities in the United States and back to Germany.[9]

What some might consider unusual about this concert was while the majority of the audience was

Figure 23 Hazel Harrison. Photo courtesy of the La Porte County Historical Society

composed of prominent white citizens there were a izeable number of blacks in attendance. All of this attention and enthusiasm was directed toward a hometown woman. Hazel was born in 1883. Her father, Hi Harrison was among the first rural mail carriers in La Porte around 1895-96.[10] As fortune would have it Hazel took to the piano. Her skills sharpened. Long before jazz orchestras were on the scene many La Porteans learned the art of dance from many instructors with Hazel at the piano. Later she played at parties and dances at Lay Hall "when a piano and a pianist were an orchestra."[11] Every Friday night at Weller's Grove on Stone Lake the New Church of Reverends Daniel and Mercer sponsored a dance. Most of the time Hazel Harrison was the orchestra.

At some point she left La Porte and began her formal study of the piano that took her to Germany and back. She won critical acclaim at home and abroad for her masterful technique and interpretations. She was able to successfully combine performing and teaching later in her vocation.

Her teaching career began at Tuskegee Institute in Alabama in 1931. Howard University was her next stop where she taught from 1934 to 1959 and then on to Alabama State College until her touring often required that she take leaves of absence, some for as much as a year.

What is inspiring about Hazel Harrison was that she was an African-American that was invited by the black and white community of La Porte in 1925 to play a benefit concert in order to raise funds for the construction of an African Methodist Episcopal Church that was built on Brighton Street during a period of history when the Knights of the Ku Klux Klan dominated the hearts and minds of many La Porte County citizens. Her long career brought "critical acclaim from both the white and black press and was the most accomplished pianist of the race for several decades."[12]

———◆———

LIZZIE E. OHMING

A committee of prominent women that same year pressed the city commissioners to appoint a woman to the board of education. They suggested that there were some things a mother would prefer to take to a woman board member.

City Attorney Walter C. Williams acted as spokesman for the commission. The NEWS reported that the commission was of the "opinion that it was doubtful any woman can be found who possesses the necessary business qualifications." It was expressed that although a woman could successfully conduct her home that didn't mean she could act efficiently as a member of the school board. Attorney Williams suggested the "women were led into their request by sentimental reasons. They do not recognize the importance of choosing a school board member and the requirements the appointee must have."

After a half-hour of sometimes heated arguments the women left with no assurances. The NEWS said the committee would anxiously await the commissioners' choice, wondering who possessed the "remarkable qualifications that cannot be found in a woman."

The following month the commission appointed someone with those remarkable qualifications. Her name was Lizzie E. Ohming. The NEWS stated she was the first woman to be selected to fill a position on a Michigan City school board. In a statement to the NEWS she said, "The appointment came as a great surprise as I did not solicit the position. Now that I have been elected to the position I will fill it to the best of my ability."

In the years following her appointment she rose rapidly within the Democratic Party. She served as district vice chairman of the central committee. In 1932 she was appointed manager of the auto license bureau in Michigan City, serving until 1938. The NEWS stated she was the first woman in Indiana to be granted a notary public license.

Following the death of her husband William, she took over his insurance and real estate business. She also for a time managed the Dreamland Theater.

———◆———

KATE VALENTINE

It could be said that on September 17, 1928, the citizens of Michigan City celebrated Valentine's Day. It wasn't the traditional day we all know and remember. It was on this day that Miss Kate Valentine resigned her position in the public schools. For over 30 years she "unquestionably affect(ed) for good the lives of all those with whom you have come in touch," the Junior High School teachers resolved in a public statement of appreciation of her years of "worthy achievement as a teacher." She wore many hats during her tenure. Most of her years of service to the children of the city were in the classroom, beginning her career in the Elston grammar grade building. She then served several years as the Principal of Garfield School. She returned to the classroom where she completed her career as teacher and dean of girls in Central School and then to the junior high to head the literature department as well as dean of girls.

Figure 24 KATHERN (VALENTINE) ENSLIN, one of the original Trustees and Incorporators of the Michigan City Historical Society, Inc. Photo from the 50th Anniversary Brochure.

Kate introduced the concept of the Parent-Teacher Association in Michigan City and helped to organize the first parent teacher club in the city. She also was one of the "active spirits" in forming the first teacher's council.

ALTA PETERS WAYBRIGHT

The Michigan City NEWS in 1925 heralded that for the first time in the city's history "FEMININITY... TO GRACE CITY CLERK'S OFFICE." Mrs. Alta Peters Waybright was appointed Acting City Clerk while Edward Heise was taking his annual vacation. Mrs. Waybright had been Heise's secretary for some time and was thoroughly familiar with the work of the city clerk. She had promised to "appear as city clerk regularly every morning and follow in the footsteps of her chief."

———◆———

DIANA L. ALINSKY, PAMELA S. KRAUSE, THAIS ANN BRONNER

The Michigan City Bar Association elected new officers at its January 27, 1997, annual meeting. The election was believed to have established an historic first for Michigan City. Elected to fill all of the executive office positions were women, making it the first bar association in Indiana to do so.

Diana L. Alinsky was elected president. She had graduated from Valparaiso University School of Law in 1981. She served as a trust officer, starting in 1984 to the time of her election, with the First Citizens Bank. When the bank formed the IMS Investment Management subsidiary, she was made an account executive.

Pamela S. Krause was elected to fill the vice president and president-elect position. She too was a Valpo University graduate, 1992. She was on the staff of the La Porte County Prosecutor's office. Her private practice was located at 831 Washington Street.

The office of secretary and treasurer of the Michigan City Bar Association went to Thais Ann Bronner. Immediately after graduating from the Indiana University School of Law in 1994, she joined the law firm of Sweeney, Dabagia, Donoghue, Thorne, Janes & Pagos. She was engaged in general practice as an associate attorney with the firm.

As a member of the Business and Professional Women's Club, Lizzie Ohming and her contemporaries as well as future generations of women, with thought, words, and deeds established the ground work and paved the way for women to become and excel in what was once considered a man's world.

THE LIFE AND TIMES OF HENRY "DAD" HEISMAN

This biographical sketch of Henry "Dad" Heisman was prepared by using the numerous newspaper articles written about the man throughout his life time and recollections of the family. It is a tribute to "Dad" and his family. Due to his tenacity and hard work, he and his family have blessed Michigan City by ensuring it would always have one of the finest boating harbors on Lake Michigan.

Standing on the dock on the north side of the Port Authority office on a summer day, one would be overwhelmed by the view. Millions of dollars of pleasure crafts line the docks of the yacht basin. There is no doubt that Michigan City is a recreation and a boater's paradise.

It was a common occurrence any time of the year for visitors to the city's lakefront during the 1940's to see this slightly built, weather beaten man, "with his body thrust forward into the wind, patrolling the pier and docks." For those who believe in ghosts or apparitions all one would have to do is close his eyes and he would conjure up the image of

Figure 25 "Dad" Heisman, born September 26, 1862, died 1952. Painting by Roger Wilcox

Arnold Bass

"Dad" Heisman hovering over the yacht basin keeping a watchful, protective eye on the legacy he and later his sons left to Michigan City.

The Michigan City NEWS on the occasion of his 70th birthday in 1932 said: "If it were not for this quiet and retiring little man who is always busy and striving to beautify his premises and promote general lake interest, little attention would be directed to boating and fishing sports such as has been realized in recent years."

As a weather prophet, Henry was not to be excelled, according to family and friends. "One squint at the sky will tell if there is going to be a squall, a hard blow or a perfect calm for boating." The fishermen looked to him for weather information. If he told them the day would be profitable, they would return with their largest catches.

Curiously enough the history and development of the lakefront is closely interwoven with the life of Henry and his family. Due to his legacy, Michigan City has materially profited over the years by the expansion, progress and playground activities related to the lakefront.

Henry was born near Bremen, Germany, September 26, 1862. Like many young boys raised near the seashore or where great ships were built, he was eager to see the world and learn of its wonders.

At the age of 13, he answered the call of the sea. His adventure began when he signed on a Dutch windjammer as a cabin boy. His experiences on the high seas were filled with drama, excitement and adventure that parallel any seafaring tale found in a novel.

On the occasion of his 70th birthday, Heisman related some of his adventures to a Michigan City NEWS reporter. His travels took him to numerous ports in Europe, and North and South America. He had served on numerous ships, all of which were vessels driven by steam power." He said he just wouldn't feel at home on one of them. Practically all were wooden ships. He had often boasted, "I've never boarded a steam powered vessel."

The ensuing years saw him advance from cabin boy to first mate on barques, brigs and schooners. He realized the dream of sailing from New York to San Francisco, skirting Cape Horn at the southern tip of South America. At that time it took several months to make the trip. For the weather-beaten seamen it was just another routine voyage, nothing extraordinary. In fact, he claimed that a good storm now and then broke the monotony by providing a diversion to the daily routine.

He had sailed out of San Francisco on a salmon fishing expedition that lasted several months. "Dude" Calvert, a local historian, interviewed "Dad" Heisman for the NEWS-DISPATCH: "We sailed out of San Francisco to the Bering Sea.... Took 38 days. A strong tide rushes through the Bering Straits and we usually had a short wait until the tide shifted and was favorable so we could ride it through." Besides a large crew of fishermen there were "...99 Chinamen aboard who made the cans, boiled the fish and packed them for shipment to all parts of Europe."

"Dad" continued:

"Aboard the Electra we had three watches of 45 men before the mast. At the first sign of the salmon run we took to our boats, two men to a boat. These boats were small Norwegian double enders that were pointed at both ends and equipped with only oars and sail. There were no gasoline motors in those days. Many times these small boats

UP CLOSE AND PERSONAL

with the two men were lost and never found. We were paid $75 for the round trip and a percentage of the catch. I have made as high as $500 for one trip."

Figure 26 The Heisman family portrait taken in 1925 in front of their home at the lakefront. (l to r, front row) Olga, Hulda, Irene, Henry, Lilia, Madelan. Back row—Herman "Ham," Amalia "Molly," Rudolph, Welhelmina "Min," Harry.

From that time on Henry wasn't able to look at a can of salmon let alone smell ts contents.

The threat of stormy seas was always a factor seamen had to live with. He related two other incidents when King Neptune reminded the seafarers who was in charge. On a voyage from New York to Antwerp, Belgium, his ship, with a cargo of kerosene, was seriously damaged by the time she finally reached port. Nothing remained but her bulwarks.

What was expected to be a month's journey lasted four. On that occasion his vessel left Charleston, South Carolina, bound for New York with a cargo of rice, cotton and rosin. Off the coast of Virginia heavy seas and two hard blows destroyed sails and rigging, swept off masts and dumped precious reserved barrels of drinking water into the sea. The ship drifted far off her course with the current taking them to the Bermudas. After weeks of repairs they were back at sea.

Heisman also shipped on a square-rigger that set a record sailing speed across the Atlantic. With heavy winds at her back, the ship covered the distance between New York and Europe in 14 days.

Henry's last adventure on the high-seas, as fate would have it, brought him to the fresh water port of Michigan City. It started around 1880, with Henry at the helm, enroute from Rio de Janeiro, Brazil, to New Orleans, on a vessel with a cargo of coffee. The Caribbean and Gulf waters were plagued by Yellow Fever. The ship was placed in quarantine upon its arrival. Henry and another shipmate rather than lay in quarantine for months, decided to leave the ship. They took a train destined for New York by way of Chicago.

The docks of Chicago were a friendly site to Henry. With the encouragement of local sailors and paychecks that nearly doubled those paid to seamen on the Atlantic coast, Henry decided to pursue a job on the Great Lakes. The city of Chicago became his homeport for the next several years. It was during this time that he made the decision to become a citizen of the United States. The Cook County Superior Court of Illinois certified that he was granted "...rights, privileges and immunities of a Naturalized Citizen," on October 28, 1884.

Heisman hired on the Charles Foster, the largest sailing vessel on the lakes at that time. He later served on other lake cargo ships in subsequent years. He spent the winter months on ships sailing out of New York and New Orleans, while the intervening summers were spent on the Great Lakes. He had visited the port of Michigan City on several occasions cultivating a liking for the place and decided to make it his future home.

Shortly after the 1893 Chicago World's Fair, at the age of 31, Henry settled in Michigan City. He rented a room in the Union Hotel, located on north Franklin Street, adjacent to the Michigan Central right of way. Joe Smith, a reporter for the NEWS-DISPATCH wrote on the occasion of his 85th birthday, that at the time of his settling in Michigan City, he "...already had lived a fabulous life packed with more adventure than most men experience in twice the time."

Michigan City's port on Trail Creek in 1893 was a busy place. It was the destination point for many vessels carrying their cargoes of lumber, manufactured goods and raw materials that would be later transported to the heartland of Indiana. The port also provided the means of shipping the state's agricultural products to Chicago and the eastern markets. It was easy to see why Henry Heisman found Michigan City an attractive, familiar place to plant his roots.

Like most busy ports, a United States Life Saving Station was in operation. Henry signed on shortly after his arrival in Michigan City and participated in numerous life saving incidents. One of the more notable events occurred when he helped to rescue a crew from the wreck of the Horace A. Tuttle, a freighter destined for Buffalo, New York, out of Chicago. A major storm in the fall of 1898 drove the ship southward causing it to flounder near the mouth of Trail Creek.

The men from the Life Saving Station manned their boats and successfully saved the Tuttle's crew. One of the Tuttle's crew was a woman who served as cook. "Like all true heroes Henry strove to save the woman first, and came near losing his own life because of her size and fighting strength." With the crew safe, surfman Heisman volunteered to go back on board the sinking ship and retrieve the personal effects of the Tuttle's Captain, according to the station's official log. He managed to save some trunks before the "...whole cabin went off of her, with one big sea." Heisman had to be ordered back into the boat. Today, a portion of the wreckage of the Tuttle is forever entombed beneath the Port Authority's offices at the basin's edge.

While in the Life Saving Service he met Hulda Rehbein. They were married at St. Paul Lutheran Church on December 2, 1899. She too had been born in Germany. Over the years nine children were born to their union [Harry, Rudolph, Wilhelmina (Niles), Herman, Amalie (Ladd), Olga (Snyder), Lila (Stib), Madelon (Berry), Irene (Deneau)]. Their daughter Olga may have been the first and only child born on the navigable waters of Michigan City. The family was living on the dredging scow, the Marian, tied up at the city dock at Trail Creek, while their new lakefront home was being built in 1911. Doctor J. B. Rogers was the attending physician.

Their home was located on what is now the parking area adjacent to the Michigan City Yacht Club and the United States Coast Guard Station. The Heisman's purchased the property in 1905. At the time a one story wood frame house provide a comfortable place to live. By 1911, they out grew their home and construction was begun on a large two-story home. Henry purchased a small wood frame building from the H. A. Root Lumber Company on the opposite side of the mouth of Trail Creek. He moved it across the creek on a scow and placed it next to their home. The office building was incorporated into the new construction, becoming their kitchen.

"Peg Leg" Nolan owned the only other private home in the area. Several years later the Board of Directors of the newly formed Yacht Club purchased it. With some remodeling it became their clubhouse and continues to provide a gathering place for their members.

THE HEISMAN FAMILY LEGACY

"Dad" Heisman, in 1906, decided to leave the Life Saving Service. The family was growing and the related responsibilities required a more subdued life style. Thus was born the family business centered on the shores of Lake Michigan at the southern edge of the outer harbor. He began mining gravel from the shallows or by scraping it up from the shores of Lake Michigan and sold it to local contractors. A motorized scow, christened the "News Boy" by his seven-year-old daughter Minne, was added to the business in 1911. The scow was used to haul sand, gravel, fruit, potatoes, timber, as well as other ventures. A three-man crew that included George Seibert, John Love, and someone only remembered as "Curly," plus "Dad" Heisman operated the craft.

Figure 27 The first Heisman home on the lakefront is at the right. It was constructed in 1888 or 89. Behind it is the second home built to accommodate the seven children they had. The building on the right is the present day yacht club. The U. S. Life Saving Station is in the center.

Arnold Bass

The spring storms of 1913 caused the Wabash River to go on a rampage, flooding the city of Peru, Indiana. Henry and his young son Rudy as well as other volunteers went to their aid. Henry reminisced in a 1932 interview, that stranded victims were taken by boat from second story windows to safety. The second floor of the old courthouse building became a temporary headquarters where "the boys rested their timbers" to dry their socks.

The business steadily grew. By the summer of 1914 it was apparent that there was a need for another boat. Henry began construction of a fishing tug that would be named the "Sea Gull". The following spring the boat was put into service. It was used for towing and fishing. A year or so later the "Sea Gull" was converted to an excursion boat. A ticket booth and mooring was constructed on the creek at the present site of the Naval Armory. Some of the Heisman girls manned the booth selling the tickets for twenty-five cents.

Power driven boats were becoming the vogue when World War I broke out. Reporter Smith wrote that Henry followed suit. He had just completed construction of a motor launch when the military saw it. They liked it and bought it. It was used out of Chicago, with Henry as captain, throughout the war, to patrol the southwestern area of the lake for evidence of sabotage.

"Dad" Heisman's business continued to flourish. He purchased a fishing boat and converted it into an excursion boat, christening it the Champion. His sons Rudy and Harry, in 1922, on a part time basis joined their father in the business. Four pleasure boats were moored in the basin at that time. More boaters came to use their services as word spread. Gasoline, oils, fishing tackle, and bait were made available for sale. A marine railway, which consisted of a section of railroad track extended into the water with a wheeled carriage, was in place, in order to remove boats from the water and place them in dry-dock during the winter. Boats were floated on to the carriage and rolled on to shore by use of a winch.

Figure 28 The SEA GULL was built by "Dad" Heisman (standing at the back). His son Harry is standing on the deck in the center.

The Heisman "White Fleet," as it was commonly known, continued to grow. The "Comber," the "Surf" and the "Whitecap" were added. A fleet of small rowboats and skiffs were

76

also a part of the fleet, available to take tourists and park visitors through the harbor. A shuttle service to the breakwater (referred to by the locals as the government pier) for fishermen was started as well.

Then the unthinkable occurred in 1926. The city began to fill in the eastern end of the "park basin or small boat harbor ...with rubbish and floating material," according to correspondence addressed to Henry, on file at the Michigan City Historical Society. E. G. " Babe" Browne, in an interview with Henry Lange of the NEWS-DISPATCH said, "I remember standing down there one day when Dad Heisman pointed out toward the dump and said in his German accent 'let's do something about that.' " They solicited the signatures of the other 19 boat owners and petitioned the War Department, United States Engineer Office located at Chicago, in October, protesting the city's filling in of the park basin. The South Shore Power Boat Club of Chicago lent their support.

The District Engineer informed Henry that his office sympathized with the small boat owners in their desire to maintain a harbor for boats at Michigan City. He also acknowledged that a letter had been sent to the City Manager of Michigan City requesting that steps be taken to stop the dumping. The city was requested to stop dumping and remove from the basin all rubbish and floating material. The city was told that it must apply for a War Department permit if it had a plan for a lake front park that would encroach further on the basin. It appeared that the city continued "...dumping all kinds of garbage, barrels and paper in the basin." The city, in November of 1927, was again ordered to stop the dumping. W. W. Swasick, the city Harbor Master responded, saying that the city had stopped nearly a year ago and had gone "to the trouble of having No Dumping" signs placed at the harbor.

Harry left the business several years later. Rudy began working at the marina full time, about 1930. Improvements and additions to the boatyard continued. At the close of the Chicago World's Fair, Rudy purchased two speedboats from Fair officials. They were named Miss Michigan City and Miss Indiana. On many a hot summer's day tourists treated themselves to the thrills and cool, refreshing spray as they zipped along the shores of the lake chauffeured by Rudy.

The spring of 1932 saw the city complete a new drive along the shore of the basin. The drive lead past the Heisman home, separating it from the boatyard and marina.

Figure 29 The Miss Indiana and Miss Michigan City speedboats tied up to the Heisman fuel dock.

It was Henry's contention that he owned the land on which the drive was constructed as well as the land his boatyard occupied. Henry and the city clashed over this issue. Rumors also surfaced that the Heisman's didn't own the land on which their home was situated. The city claimed title to the land by virtue of a sheriff's deed executed in 1917. The property was sold at a sheriff's sale to foreclose on certain dock improvements.

An amicable settlement was reached that fall after several months of negotiations. The city dropped its claim to the property on which their home was located. A five-year lease granted Henry an exclusive monopoly to operate the pier and boat service in the basin with the provision that the contract would be renewed for a similar period in 1937. Henry, by the terms of the agreement, acknowledged the city's ownership and title to the land that lay east of the Coast Guard property along the shore of the basin and immediately north of their home.

With the dispute settled, Heisman and Son's were back to business as usual. A long pier extending into the basin provided berthing space for the privately owned motorboats, cruisers and smaller craft. A large scaffold was constructed at the edge of the basin in 1932, to facilitate the dry docking operation. The derrick made it easier to get the boats out of the water. The marine track was used to draw the boats from the water to land and then the derrick would raise the hull off the track and load it on to whatever device boat owners used.

The derrick was built on a Saturday by "Ham" and Rudy. The newspaper reported that, " 'Ham' wielded the spade and made all the 'home runs' to speed up the work." Noted among the crew were Joseph E. Karris, Gwalter "Dude" Calvert, and Ted Van Giesen, who did the "high walk" toe nailing the beams to the side supports. As the crew expressed it, "He did the dizzy work." The completed scaffold was painted white and rigged with signs to advertise the excursion, fishing and minnow business.

The crew never questioned the decision to start that project on a Saturday. They knew that Henry believed that there were certain "jinxes" which should be acknowledged. His wife Hulda, years before had experienced certain misfortunes on the day Friday. She had warned "the old salt" the he should never start anything on that day.

Hulda had first noticed the jinx upon applying for a job at a well-known boarding house in Michigan City shortly after arriving from Germany. The other employees suggested that they doubted the length of her stay there, because she had come on a Friday. She hadn't thought much about the incident until she had resigned giving rise to the thought that there maybe something to the jinx after all.

She could cite many instances to prove her point. In an interview with a NEWS-DISPATCH reporter, she told the following story of the passenger ship "The United States." It was launched on a Friday, making frequent trips into the local docks during the summer.

> "In connection with this she brought in the story of the new one. Work started on Friday, and the bridge was let down for use on the same day of the week. "The United States" came in one Friday, and in having difficulty in turning around, ran into the new bridge, and sank the tug which was turning it around. Later, on another occasion, the vessel hit the end of the government pier and tore a piece off the pier. The entire back railing of the ship was damaged. Several months later, while leaving the Chicago harbor, she hit the end of that pier, and was again laid up for repairs...."The United States" was later sold....It wasn't long after...that word was received that she had sunk, after catching fire."

Henry, for several years, "pooh-pooed" the idea and said there could not be anything to it. That notion changed shortly after the completion of the scow "Newsboy." He had been working on the engine and had the cover up over his hand. Without warning the cover, "...

sharpened to the potency of a good razor," fell and cut off his finger. The "Friday Jinx" had Henry "in its tow".

Henry retired from the business in 1936. Herman ("Ham") the youngest of Henry's sons joined the business on a full time basis. The following year he and Rudy became partners in the business. Two years later in 1938, "Ham" and "Dad" Heisman built the "Quickstep." It was used to ferry fishermen to the government pier. Although "Dad" was retired, he was always seen walking the docks or sitting on his front porch keeping an eye on things. When not walking or sitting, he had a paint brush in hand or was seen in hip boots, working around the boat track in the basin "...to have everything in applepie order."

The outbreak of World War II caused "Ham" to temporarily leave the business to serve in the United States Navy. He returned to the marina at the conclusion of the war. In the late 1940's they leased out a building and the live bait and concession portion of the business to Assom and Sam Ankony. The Heisman brothers sold the business in October of 1950. Matt Gorge and partner John Dreske purchased the operation, equipment and service facilities.

Herman put his naval experience to use after the sale of the business. He joined the U. S. Corps of Army Engineers. For the next 14 years he captained the tug "Moore." The tug operated in the Michigan City harbor during those years on several dredging projects. Years later, after "Ham" had retired, the tug sank, was raised, and donated to the Michigan City Sea Scouts. They renamed her the "S. S. T. V. Little Murphy."

The original four-room home and the eleven-room home were sold to the city in 1959. A few years later the city demolished the buildings and replaced them with a parking lot. The city during the decade of the 1990's decided to honor the family's contribution to the quality of life for its citizens. The city named the drive that passed in front of the old homestead the Heisman Harbor Road. This was the same road that put Henry on a collision course with the city.

The remaining Heisman sisters reflect back with a sense of pride on the legacy their family has provided the people of Michigan City.

"...laws and court decisions...cannot wipe away centuries of oppression and injustice—however much we might desire it. "
Hubert H. Humphrey [13]

DISCRIMINATION A PART OF CITY'S HISTORY

World War I and the post war years provided the impetus of industrial development in urban areas. Michigan City was no exception. It offered a concentration of able workers for the growing number of industries. This industrial growth and expansion added to the prosperity and the good life of a large segment of the town's citizenry.

Life in Michigan City during the 1920's was on the fast track. Franklin Street saw revitalization with the construction of numerous businesses. The Spaulding Hotel and the Warren buildings changed the skyline.

Many moved into the city to find work in the rapidly expanding economy. The influx of population provided a demand for more housing. Available homes were at a premium. The city expanded its boundaries. Several subdivisions were developed throughout the community to address the problem.

Among those migrating into the city were large numbers of African-Americans. The Haskell and Barker car factory was the magnet that drew them. Once in Michigan City, housing for them was an issue. The Michigan City EVENING DISPATCH in May of 1922 reported that "Some of the colored men who toil in the shops during the day are compelled to sleep in the city jail at night because there is not a place for them to rest their heads."

The newspaper related that "there were a number of good-sized buildings in the desert...." The area referred to was just west of the Michigan Central tracks and in the Hoosier Slide district. The NIPSCO generating station now stands at that location.

Arnold Bass

    The management of the car factory negotiated "to let colored folks to use the homes" in what had been referred to as Snarltown. The report continued by expressing hope that the negotiations would come to a satisfactory conclusion "thus giving the strangers a home sweet home so much desired by one and all."

    All of this was being played out in front of a backdrop of prejudice and intolerance. The Knights of the Ku Klux Klan dominated and controlled Indiana's government. The Klan was visible and invisible in its exertion of influence on Michigan City as well. The community had its share of cross burnings and parades of Kluxers in white robes and pointed masked hoods marching on Franklin Street.

    The Reverend Frederick Hopkins, pastor of the Presbyterian Church, speaking from the pulpit called the attention of his audience to the fact that "a large proportion of the population

Figure 31 The Elston School located on the corner of 4th and Pine Streets, c 1910.
Courtesy of the La Porte County Historical Society

of Michigan City were foragers, people who have come here from other lands and have become citizens, bought property and given their best to make this country a better place to live in." The EVENING- DISPATCH continued its report by saying that Dr. Hopkins emphasized, "prejudice never got people anywhere and that it never will."

    There appeared to be no verifiable violence or intimidation attributed to the Klan. The absence of reports of Klan violence in either of the community's newspapers was startling and surprising.

UP CLOSE AND PERSONAL

The influx of African-Americans into Michigan City continued. Their children were impacting the schools. The board of school trustees in December 1923, considered the idea of segregating the pupils in the public schools. The DISPATCH revealed that the school board had evaluated two locations for a possible site "...where all the colored boys and girls of the city could gather under one roof and obtain an education." The NEWS, the other newspaper, declared, "It was very evident...that such a school is very necessary in the city."

Residents living near the Wabash and Michigan Street location and on East Michigan Street, between Fifth and Sixth streets, strongly objected to establishing such a school in their district. This prompted the school board to announce in August of 1925 that two rooms at Elston would be "for the exclusive use of colored children...."

The black community also voiced their objections to the move to provide their children with a segregated education. Dr. Gordon R. Thomas, the first colored dentist in Michigan City, in a letter to the "Voice of the People" that appeared in the DISPATCH summarized the colored community's position. Separation "...creates distrust and prejudice in the minds of all concerned," he wrote.

Thomas pointed out that what ever their qualifications it would be impossible for two teachers to "thoroughly or even passably teach several different subjects in six different grades."

With the opening of school in September of 1925, the board of school trustees announced that the black children would attend Elston School at Fourth and Pine streets. "Special rooms and teachers will be provided," according to the board minutes.

Frances Thomas was hired to teach third through fourth and Erma E. Ingram first through third. Thomas was the first black woman to teach in Michigan City. She resigned in 1928. Mattie B. King was hired to take her place. She left the school system in 1930 and was replaced with Georgia Beatty. The board minutes specified she was hired for the "colored room Elston." Martha Burnett was hired for the "colored room at Elston" in August of 1931. Two years later she and several other non-tenure teacher's contracts were not renewed.

A review of the school board minutes for the next several years gives no indication of a replacement for Miss. Burnett. No other entries were found that suggested that segregation of the colored children continued.

Dr. Thomas throughout his education attended non-segregated schools that included college and professional schools. His experience and insight caused him to say, "that the foundation for future understanding is laid in the school room."

Arnold Bass

IN THE BEGINNING: LONG BEACH SCHOOL

Figure 32 Long Beach School---1997. Photo courtesy of the Michigan City Area Schools

The date was June 12, 1997, the time 3:30 PM. The halls of Long Beach Elementary School were void of students. The sounds of voices and laughter of the children will no longer be heard throughout the halls. Teachers were seen taking their personal belongings to be transferred to their new school for the coming school year.

UP CLOSE AND PERSONAL

That day was unlike any other day in the school's 69-year history. The school was concluding its last day of hosting the students of the town of Long Beach. The Michigan City board of School Trustees at their April meeting voted to close the school along with Eastport Elementary. Budgeting concerns, declining enrollment and the age of the buildings were given as reasons for the closures.

The school served the town of Long Beach well. It stood as a monument to the community's resolve to provide their children with an exemplary education. The Long Beach school board composed of James H. Orr, George T. Vail, and Clarence Mathias hired John Lloyd Wright, in 1927, to design the facility.

The plans called for a one story brick and stone structure, having "...adequate natural lighting, and will be the last word in sanitation...." The first unit constructed was 60 x 100 feet in size providing 48,000 square feet of floor space and a basement. The facility housed three 24 x 48 foot classrooms and a Kindergarten department.

The completed plans were submitted to the state for approval. The school board in August of 1927 advertised a bond issue to raise $20,000. Soon after, bids were advertised with the anticipation of occupying the new school on January 1, 1928.

The Long Beach Company during the second week of September deeded the grounds for the site of the school to the school district, making the property a separate part of the holdings controlled by the town of Long Beach. The new school would be located just to the east of the Roman Plunge, a nationally renowned swimming pool where Johnny Weissmuller, an Olympic champion and the star of Tarzan movies, often visited. The school would be built at the intersections of Oriole and Belle Plaine Trails.

Anxious to start school in September of 1927, school officials arranged with W. L. Robertson to use his home, the Bob-White cottage on Hermoine Trail, to open its first school. Long Beach town officials had announced that doors of their "cottage school" would open on September 19th.

Two weeks prior to the opening, the three school board members were in Chicago to purchase "...the most up-to date school equipment they thought best to provide." The following week seats, desks, and other "paraphernalia" to equip the classrooms in the cottage were installed. With the installation complete, the temporary school was "...fit(ted) up into a modern and commodious place for beginners to receive the first rudiments of their educational training."

School officials announced that the Long Beach school system would be conducted on exactly the same principle as Michigan City's public schools. "Advanced pupils, who are ready for their department work and high school," would continue to attend the Michigan City schools. The town of Long Beach would pay the tuition tax.

The Long Beach Board of School Trustees appointed Mrs. M. L. Knapp as its first teacher. Her husband was the principal of the Isaac C. Elston High School. The board, it was reported, had congratulated itself "...on its good fortune in being able to secure the services of so competent an instructor...." Beryl Knapp, prior to being hired had ten years experience as a primary teacher. She attended Indiana University and went to Columbia University where she received her degree. She had taught in Martinsville and LaPorte, "and is thoroughly experienced in directing the course of study now taught in the first four grades of public school."

Figure 33 The Long Beach School as it appeared in 1927.
Photo courtesy of the Michigan City Area Schools.

On the morning of September 19, 1927, the school bell rang, marking the opening of the first public school in the town of Long Beach. Fourteen children were enrolled into the first four grades that day. Shortly there after three more children enrolled. Mrs. Knapp was "in charge" and in the beginning the only teacher. The roster included: Freddie and Dick Schaeffer, Bill Shipley, Russell Berry, Walter and Rolf Illsley, Esther Blair, Betty Wolff, Evelyn Krueger, Florence and Charles Keene, Dorothy Jean and Jimmy Mathias, Milda and John Sinkus, Junior Rudolph and Frank Sprague. At the close of the school year one more child had enrolled.

Plans for the construction of the permanent school continued to progress. By mid-January Long Beach residents began to see the project take shape. William Holstein, a Wheaton, Illinois contractor had been awarded the contract, according to the EVENING DISPATCH. A temporary office building was erected at the site. The property was staked off and construction began.

The Michigan City NEWS in September of 1928 reported that Tonn and Blank was the contractor. Simpson and Adamson, a local firm, installed the heating system. Craig and Moenkhouse did the grading and paving.

As an "economy measure," the original plan to construct a brick and stone structure was revised. The new plan was for a frame building with brick veneer.

Newspaper reports referred to the school as "a model on construction." At a cost of $25,000, the school incorporated many innovations which made it, what many considered to be, the most modern and up to date school building in the area and "possibly over a much wider range of territory."

The school included four large and "commodious" class rooms all on one floor, "thus eliminating any stair climbing for the young folks." The kindergarten room was "more like an immense sun parlor" than a schoolroom. One entire side of the room was glass, "thus affording direct outside light from every angle." A large fireplace was reportedly incorporated into the kindergarten room.

The room was designed primarily for the use of very young people. It contained sand boxes and toys of all descriptions. Special attention was given to the children who made use of the "conveniences." Each child was to have an "individual training table or bench." The primary grade classrooms had an individual table and chair for each child.

Most of the equipment was purchased from Royal Metal Manufacturing Company in Michigan City. Every room was furnished with a complete reference library. The old style common wardrobe had been eliminated and replaced by the installation of a built into the wall unit for each room. A highly improved Kawneer lighting system, manufactured in Niles, Michigan, "readily adjustable to meet every condition," was installed. A special ventilation system was installed, which drew fresh air drawn over the radiators, thereby heating it as it entered the room.

Mr. Wright had incorporated into his design a completely equipped room to be especially used for physical training purposes. It included a utility room furnished with a "sink of large dimensions," a refrigerator, stove and all the articles necessary to permit the use of the school building for community gatherings.

The NEWS reported, "The school was up to date in every manner. Among interesting features will be the icebox provided for children to carry their lunches. Through the kindness of Storm and Sloan Music Shop, a Baldwin piano has been secured for the school."

Construction had progressed, near the end of April, to the point that the cornerstone of the new school was set in place. There was no ceremony in connection with the laying of the stone. The plan was to wait until after the opening of the facility when all of the furnishings and equipment would be installed. Several items of interest were sealed into the cornerstone. Among them was a photograph taken in front of the first school of all the students enrolled with the exception of Frank Sprague, who was not present when the picture was taken, along with their teacher Mrs. Beryl Knapp. The photograph was taken in front of what was the present schoolhouse, the Bob White cottage.

September 4, 1928, was a proud day in the history of Long Beach. They opened one of the finest state-of-the-art school buildings in the Town of Long Beach. Miss Knapp was appointed principal and taught the first, second and third grades. Her future husband Cecil F. Humphrey was principal of the Michigan City junior high school. The kindergarten and pre-school work was in the hands of Miss Mary Louise Oppermann, who had just graduated from college. She was the daughter of Mr. and Mrs. Charles H. Oppermann of Michigan City.

The first day of school was devoted largely to the organization of classes and the distribution of lists of textbooks and other articles needed. The school board expected about thirty children to enroll for the winter semester. The final tally listed fifty.

The school day was divided into morning and afternoon sessions. The kindergarten was dismissed daily at 11:00, the primary grades at 11:15 and the others at 11:30. The afternoon classes began at 1:00. The primary grades were dismissed at 3:15 with the others at 3:30.

So, as it was in the beginning, so it was at the end! The children and their teachers were filled with excitement, celebration and anxiety.

*"Camp Pottawattomie presented
the appearance of a young city
springing up during the days
of the '49 gold rush',"*
The Michigan City NEWS

POTTAWATTOMIE BOY SCOUT CAMP

Figure 34 Above is shown two views of the cabins at the camp on Pottawattomie Lake near Rolling Prairie. One photo shows a cabin open and fully equipped for the use of two scouts. The other shows a cabin closed protecting the scouts during inclement weather.   Photo The Michigan City News, April 18, 1927.

Scouting in LaPorte county has enjoyed a rich and long history. Many dedicated individuals and organizations over the years have and continue to provide leadership and resources.

The Pottawattomie Council of Boy Scouts serving LaPorte and Porter counties embarked on a program to provide the local scouts with one of the best summer camps in the state. A site leased in November 1926, about five or six miles north of Rolling Prairie had been selected. It was situated on the eastern shore of Beament Lake providing a suitable bathing beach.

The council camping committee composed of A. R. Couden, Michigan City; J. B. Dilworth, LaPorte; and Earl Smith of Valparaiso chose a 40 acre wooded tract, which was part of the Andrew Dudeck farm. There were numerous large trees in the woods. The ground was "... quite rolling with a number of natural amphitheaters suitable for the usual campfire programs," the NEWS reported.

Two cabins were constructed at the camp in early spring. H. I. Ziegler and the Michigan City Lions Club donated the first cabin, made from milled lumber. Ralph Tuthill and one carpenter built the cabin. The second cabin was built with native lumber donated by C. C. Quale. He and his two sons had been involved in scouting. Quale lived on a farm adjoining the camp. To access the camp from county road 900, the council leased a right-of-way for a road from Herman Wokersin.

Work at the camp started in earnest in March of 1927. Initially eleven Adirondack style cabins were built. The work was done and donated by F. W. Brown of Three Oaks, Michigan. The cabins were eight foot square, built of native lumber. The outside was covered with rustic bark slabs and tuck pointed with wood pulp. They had a sloped roof, six feet high in the front and five feet in the rear. A drop hinged door canopy at the front could be lowered to provide shelter in bad weather.

Each cabin was equipped with two steel cots purchased through the YMCA from a firm in South Bend. A twelfth cabin known as cabin A was donated by Brown. Different from the others, it was built of poles with a gabled roof. A small front porch was added. This cabin was reserved for guests, adult leaders, or members of the camp staff.

Judge John C. Richter, of LaPorte, donated a 16 x 32 foot rustic style lodge. The outside was slabbed with bark. The building had a screened-in porch and a large boulder fireplace. It served as an office for the scout executive as well as providing him with sleeping quarters. George Griewank, a LaPorte building contractor and a member of the Trinity Lutheran Church, supervised the construction. The Rustic Hickory Furniture Company of LaPorte supplied the furniture.

The foundation and flooring for a 50 by 24 foot dining hall and kitchen was completed by mid April. A large brick fireplace at one end of the building was completed shortly thereafter. Two weeks later, early on a Sunday morning in May, Earl Smith of Valparaiso with about 25 carpenters arrived at the camp intent on completing the cabin by the end of the day. The entire building had been completed by 3:45 with the exception of a few windows and doors. "Camp Pottawattomie presented the appearance of a young city springing up during the days of the 49 gold rush," the NEWS reported.

A large gravity tank was erected next to the dining hall. It was equipped with a force pump and gasoline motor that furnished well water to the kitchen. A sink and drain board were installed for "...the convenience of the chef." The Hunt Brothers of Rolling Prairie drilled the well. "A 14-foot stream of water (had) been struck at a depth of 53 feet," the NEWS reported.

F. W. Brown, in mid-May, began the completion of the remaining cabins. The Michigan City Lions Club sponsored the construction of a larger cabin. Tonn and Blank, a City contractor, along with members of the Lions furnished the labor.

The last weekend of May, The LaPorte County Bar Association held a picnic at the camp. The attorneys were so impressed with the camp that they showed their enthusiasm by voting to build at their expense two "distinctive" cabins. A committee consisting of J. E. Winn, C. V. Shields, J. B. Dilworth, and K. D. Osborn were selected "to look after construction." The ARGUS also reported that Congressman A. J. Hickey would attempt to obtain a small cannon from the government for use at the camp to fire salutes.

The Buck-House Co., LaPorte, donated fifty chairs for use in the dining hall. A refrigerator manufacturing company of Ligonier Indiana donated an icebox. Fred Henock of LaPorte, through his brother was able to secure the donation.

Prior to the camp opening, seventeen cabins had been completed. The goal was to erect 25 cabins. Several organizations throughout the area had expressed a willingness to contribute one cabin each. That goal, plus one, was reached by mid-July. Twenty-one cabins, one staff cabin, one camp director's cabin, one dining hall and kitchen, one supply building and cook's cabin were in use, a total investment of approximately $5,000. The Michigan City NEWS said, "...each cabin bears a plate with the name of the individual, organization or club, sponsoring it."

The list of donors was impressive. Among those not previously mentioned were: Valparaiso Rotary and Kiwanis Clubs, Smith Bros., LaPorte American Legion, LaPorte Rotary, Mrs. W. W. Vail, Dr. Henry Brooks, and parents of scouts in Michigan City.

Michigan City firms donated building materials and supplies: Gotto-Mathias, Seeling and Schumacher, Northern Indiana Brick Co, Michigan City Lumber Co., and Central Coal Co. Other contributors were Haviland Storage Co., Reading and Boss, Arndt Brothers and the Michigan City Street Department donated the movement of material, supplies and equipment.

Other facilities were added after the camp council ring was constructed during the first of Cub Patrol camp, adding to the evening campfire ceremonies. The LaPorte Bar Association erected a 10 x 16 cabin to be used as a staff headquarters. The Izaak Walton League of LaPorte also built a cabin.

Four additional cabins were erected in the fall of 1927, and donated to the council, by the B'nai B'rith of Michigan City, A. R. Putman of Valparaiso and by a backer of scouting from LaPorte who wished to remain anonymous.

Beament's Lake, renamed Pottawattomie Lake, provided the scouts the opportunity for recreation and instruction in Red Cross water safety. R. F. Garrettson donated 2 of the boats used on the lake. One hundred feet of pier had been constructed by mid-April of 1927. A large steel tank raft was built and in place by early July. The following year Tonn and Blank added an additional 150 ft. of pier and developed a sandy bottom beach. Mrs. Frank R. Warren of Michigan City, helping to insure that the waterfront would be one of the more popular areas of the camp, donated several steel airtight compartment boats.

Final preparation for the official opening of camp on June 13, 1927, were made by the members of the camping and finance committees and the chairmen of the Michigan City, LaPorte and Valparaiso District councils. They met in the hotel Rumely, LaPorte, to outline the summer activity program.

Scout Executive Walter B. Brown was named Camp Director. Henry M. Screen was hired as camp cook. He was the chef of Phi Delta Phi fraternity house at the University of Michigan, Ann Arbor. His four assistants were Richard White, troop 6 of Valparaiso; Caryl Walker, troop 18, Michigan City; and Francis Crowley, troop 9, and Fred Cory, troop 5, of LaPorte.

Figure 35 Mr. Dudeck and Arnold Bass standing on the dock on April 13, 1999 looking t submerged remnants of the original dock constructed on Pottawattomie Lake.

The personnel of the junior staff were named. James Root assistant scoutmaster of troop 8, Methodist church of Michigan City, was in charge of the junior staff in the capacity of director of activities. Eagle Scout Victor Johnson, troop 6, Methodist church, Valparaiso, served as camp clerk; Russell Sadenwater, troop 3, Trinity church, Michigan City, as camp quartermaster; while Eagle Scout George Flowers of the same troop was in charge of the waterfront activities.

The formal dedication of Camp Pottawattomie was held on Sunday, June 12, 1927. Over 500 people of LaPorte and Porter counties found their way to the camp that day. The route was well marked with large steel signs mounted on 10 foot steel poles. Warden Daly of the Indiana State Prison donated the signs.

The signs with their orange backgrounds, black letters and an arrow pointing to the scout camp would have been difficult to miss. A sign was erected 1 1/2 miles west of Rolling Prairie with another at the half-mile point. Visitors found a sign at every turn of the gravel road north of Rolling Prairie that directed them into the camp. The South Shore Line, with the cooperation of Ben Smith, installed electric stoplights at the only crossing entering the camp.

All parents of scouts and the general public had been invited to visit the camp for the dedication. They were encouraged to bring their own lunch and participate in the picnic supper in the late afternoon. At 2:30 in the afternoon, the bugler sounded assembly to start the ceremony. Rev. Wharton of Valparaiso offered the prayer. Joseph B. Bisbee, commissioner, Michigan City, gave the opening address, followed by several members of the executive committee. C. V. Shields, executive of the LaPorte council and W. B. Brown, spoke to the crowd.

At the close of Brown's speech, the "Stars and Stripes" were raised over Camp Pottawattomie for the first time. "All heads were uncovered," the NEWS reported. The flag was a gift from Phil Sprague, of the Hays Corporation. Dr. J. B. Rogers, area president, poured a bottle of spring water at the foot of the flagpole.

The camp was open to the boys of LaPorte and Porter counties. The registration fee was either $5 or $6, which included everything. For those scouts that used the stamp savings plan the cost was $5. The boys were able to purchase stamps from their scoutmaster at a cost of 25 cents each. The Council redeemed the stamps at the rate of 30 cents. The stamps were to be pasted in a book. Each book held enough stamps to pay for two weeks of camp. The scouts that did not take advantage of the savings plan, Girl Scouts and Campfire Girls were required to pay $6.

UP CLOSE AND PERSONAL

On June 13, the camp opened for boys under the scouting age. The Cub Patrol camp extended to June 20. K. D. Osborn, a LaPorte commissioner, took care of registration in that city. Each boy was furnished with "...his own bedding, consisting of blankets, comforts, pillows, etc." The following eight weeks were reserved for the regular scouts and extended through August 15th.

The day was alive with Cubs learning and practicing the skills of scouting. A nature area with a reptile cage containing black snakes, water moccasins, garter snakes, puff adders and blue racers, "...frightened and delighted its young audience." Thomas Bayer of Chicago, upon visiting the camp, was so impressed with the collection of snakes in the cement tank that he presented a 4-foot alligator to the collection, "...for the amusement of the Scouts." As many as twelve reptiles were in the snake pit. Near the end of July the number had been cut in half as a number of them had climbed over the huge fence and "...headed for points unknown." With the close of the season, all of the "pets" were turned over to the zoo in Michigan City.

The activities continued throughout the summer. Archery equipment and a marksmanship rifle range were added near the end of June. Evening campfire ceremonies performed in the firelight added to the spirit of Camp Pottawattomie.

A "ranger camp" was constructed in July, to take care of an overflow and served as an over-night camp as well. The South Shore Line, the following year, contributed a 30-foot steel signal tower with an eight-foot platform on top. The "ranger camp" was located several hundred yards west of the camp on a hill overlooking the surrounding country. The plan was to have each camper to spend at least one night sleeping in pup tents, cooking his own meals and spend an evening around individual patrol campfires.

Each Sunday found large numbers of visitors in camp. The DISPATCH advised "...those planning to take meals in camp to make reservations in advance." The dining hall had proved to be a popular place each Sunday, "...with the call for extra meals."

The Girl Scouts and Campfire Girls of LaPorte and Porter counties were given use of the camp from August 15 to the 29th. They were required to pay $6 per week per girl. Mrs. C. V. Shields, Mrs. Carl Loetz and Miss Marjorie Littleton of LaPorte served as leaders for the first week with 41 girls in camp. The final week saw 39 girls participate. The leader of that period was Miss Ina White of Michigan City and Lois Higley and Mrs. Everette Ruess of Valparaiso.

The girls participated in numerous camp activities, hikes and an "auto trip" to the Three Oaks Museum. Meals were taken in the camp dining hall. The NEWS reported that the girls were so impressed with the meals served, "...that they presented Mr. Screen, the chef, with a box of cigars and an honorary membership in the girl's organization." The Girl Scouts presented a hand made American flag to the camp. It was hung in a place of honor in the dining hall.

Camp Pottawattomie, during its first summer of operation, attracted considerable attention throughout the state. The camp gained the reputation of being one of the outstanding camps of Region 7. At least 3,000 visitors from five different states came to view the camp, said the NEWS. Numerous scouting officials have "...pronounced (it) the, neatest, most sanitary and best arranged camp in this section of the state if not the region...."

A portion of the official report published in the local newspapers in September of 1927 provided a concise financial analysis of the construction and operating income as well as the expense for the first summer of camp in order to give the community an understanding of the cost involved in the maintenance and operation of Camp Pottawattomie.

Arnold Bass

RECEIPTS:

Tuition fee received at $5.00 and $6.00 per week (including boys and girls)	$1,596.00
Income from meals served in camp to 531, @ .25 and .50 per plate	256.90
Counsel budget for camping	2,500.00
Contributions received for 21 cabins	<u>720.55</u>
	$5,073.45

EXPENDITURES:

Actual food expense:

Groceries	$ 564.11
Meat	272.50
Ice	38.27
Milk	138.40
Vegetables	<u>20.33</u>
	$1,033.61

Cook's salary at $35.00 per week	$ 396.60
Building	2,544.36
Camp supplies	297.27
Kitchen equipment	205.11
Graveling road	162.40
Pier	97.88
Raft and boats	86.18
Cabin and road signs	34.75
Freight and expenses	21.71
Labor and miscellaneous	54.95
Phone	<u>15.35</u>
	$3,609.96
Rental on campsite	150.00
Refund on camp applications	<u>94.25</u>
Total expenditures	$5,284.25

    Seventy-two years later on April 13, 1999, Lowell Foster, of Buchanan, Michigan, and I walked through the greater part of the 40 acres that once was Camp Pottawattomie. Lowell had arranged to have Norman Dudeck, a grandson of Andrew, meet with and take us to the campsite. Lowell's family had lived near the Dudecks. He had fond memories of hiking through the camp and swimming in the lake.

    I had hoped with excited anticipation to find visible signs of the ruins of the cabins, the cement snake pit, and the amphitheater. The reality of it all was that after nearly sixty years after

UP CLOSE AND PERSONAL

the close of the camp, Mother Nature had worked her magic returning the area to a natural state. A young forest now occupies the entire area. Signs were posted warning intruders that this was now a classified forest and a nature refuge. The open grassy areas of the camp no longer exist. What was once transformed into a beautifully sandy swimming area is now overgrown with weeds. Just beneath the water's surface can be seen the remnants of about thirty feet of wooden pier extending from the north shore of the lake towards its center. It was easy to conjure up a picture of scouts splashing in the water, screaming and yelling with the joy of excitement and pleasure.

Figure 36 Remnant of the concrete hearth of one of the cabins. Photo taken by Lowell Foster

As Lowell and I continued to explore the area we came upon the original well that provided the camp with water. The iron pressure pump, now orange-red with rust, was a silent reminder of the human activity that filled that place during the summers of the late 1920's and 30's. I took hold of the handle and began to raise it up and down, half hoping to have water gush up from the deep, dark well; nothing! There was a cement slab covering the top of the well. The access opening to the valves was concealed by a 12 inch, round iron cover. As visible as the day it was put in place is the molded inscription that reads, MADE BY THE J. BIES FOUNDRY CO. MICHIGAN CITY IND.

A stone and cement fireplace hearth, about five feet from the well, provided more evidence the area was once inhabited. It appeared to be about five feet by six feet in size and was raised up about two feet from the ground. Several bricks were strewn next to the hearth that gave rise to the thought that they could have been part of the chimney to a cabin.

Exploring the area to the west of that was the main part of the camp, we saw on the top of a hill the silhouette of what appeared to be the capital letter "T". Our view was somewhat obstructed by the young stand of trees that filled the hillside. Lowell and I followed what were clearly the remnants of the original path to the top of the hill. It was overgrown with vegetation. The thousands of feet that trudged up the hill left a visible recess. As we moved closer, I was able to determine it was a steel observation tower. My body filled with excitement when I realized that this was the tower the South Shore Railroad Company constructed seventy-one years ago.

Upon close inspection, I found it to be in magnificent condition. The cement footing seemed to be solid even though the corners had crumbled with age. The iron rail ladder to the top was still in place. The ladder's side supports were rusted off at the bottom but were held solidly in place by steel arms extended from the tower in three places. I cautiously placed one foot on the bottom rung and shifted my weight on to it. To my surprise, it held my weight. I then began to slowly climb the ladder. With each step I became exhilarated with excitement as I moved upward towards the top. At the top, I stood on the ladder inspecting what was left of the platform. There were no more than a half dozen short planks remaining. I carefully stepped onto the metal superstructure. A pipe railing provided an element of safety. As I looked out over the once proud Boy Scout camp I couldn't help thinking about the thousands of boys and girls that communed with nature, learning how to preserve and enjoy the wonders that God provided.

Figure 37 The observation tower as it appeared on April 13, 1999. Photo taken by Lowell Foster.

FIGURE 38 CAMP PATCH: BLACK ILLUSTRATION ON GOLD FELT BACKGROUND. ARNOLD BASS COLLECTION

*"...a well-regulated program
in caring for the city's 'needy'
is one of the greatest assets
any town can boast....*
Charles E. Arnt, President
Salvation Army Board, 1928"

THE SALVATION ARMY: "PENETRATE(S) THE 'DARK CORNERS' IN THE UNCULTIVATED FIELDS OF RELIGIOUS AND RELIEF ENDEAVOR."

The Salvation Army has had a long and illustrious history in Michigan City. They have served and attended to the financial needs of those that have fallen on hard times as well as to their spiritual well being. Their early vanguards entered the city in 1895 and established a headquarters at 128 Franklin Street in what was later to become the Lakeview Hotel. The first commander of the Michigan City unit was Captain Duffy. (A list of succeeding commanders, up through 1930, is found at the end of the article.) They are there "...serving the 'dark corners' of our city, willingly and effectively...according to Charles E. Arnt, President of the Salvation advisory board in 1928. Dr. Rogers, that same year declared, "They go about their work without dramatics, and little is said of their results, but day in and day out 365 days and 365 nights a year they carry on tirelessly to make the entire city cleaner, happier, healthier, more prosperous, and a better city for all of us to live in."

The Army, since its initial appearance in Michigan City, has registered numerous success stories. None are any more remarkable than the conversion of Mr. Gordon. He and his wife were among the first converts to the Salvation Army. The NEWS reported that he was a man in his 50's and a "hopeless drunkard." "Following his conversion, he lived 30 years and never again touched liquor."

As was the case in other communities throughout the world, the local corps experienced much persecution. Edwin White, a local carpenter in 1930, had the distinction of having the longest active membership in the local corps up until that time. He had served as a "soldier in the ranks" for more than 28 years. He had recalled that during the early days when the Army was establishing its presence in the city, Jim McNeil had been commissioned as a police officer to keep order in the hall. It was common to see him forcibly eject those intent on disrupting the service.

In 1924 an advisory board made up of businessmen was formed. The Army recognized the need to gain community support as well as the benefit of their expertise. Four years later, Charles Arnt was President. Others serving were Dr. J. B. Rogers, Clyde L. Taylor, Hugo F. Keppen, W. W. Vail, Charles J. Robb, E. G. Richter, Judge Harry B. Tuthill, and George T. Vail. At a routine board meeting, in June of 1928, the subject of the Army paying rent for their facility came to light. Arnt was quoted:

> "...without the proper tools with which to function, and when business men advisors were told that the Army has been paying rent for many years, a halt was called and preliminary steps have been made to conduct an appeal for $36,000 with which to construct a Salvation Army community center and to maintain it for one year."

An ambitious plan was set into motion. The site selected was a vacant lot at 210 East Fifth Street, one-half block east of the post office. The Advisory Board purchased the land from Frank Wolfe. The building planned would provide for a business office and public restrooms as well as living quarters for the officer in charge and his family. Facilities to house "stranded or unfortunate women and girls" and homeless men were included. A section would be maintained for emergency and disaster relief where women's, children's and men's clothing would be stored. An auditorium that would seat 300 persons was planned. A "home league room" where "needy" women could go and use sewing machines and other materials was incorporated into the facility. The building was to also provide living quarters for the officer in charge of the local corps and his wife, according to a July story in the EVENING DISPATCH.

The Chamber of Commerce lent its support. Campaign headquarters for the fund drive was set up in their offices. E. G. Richter was selected as general chairman and Dr. J. B. Rogers was named associate general chairman for the building and maintenance appeal. Richter owned and operated the Central Cigar Store and Dr. Rogers was founder of the Clinic Hospital. They mounted what could be viewed as a full military assault on the city. They methodically divided up the city into numerous sectors. Several professional and business people were added to form an executive committee to head up the many pronged campaign. They included E. W. Tilt, fraternal chairman; C. E. Arnt, advanced gifts; Russell H. Kramer, downtown chairman; E. M. McLundie, factory solicitation chairman; George R. Hill, publicity; L. E. Kunkel, speaker's chairman, and associate chairwomen for residential giving, Helen Albright and Hazel Tasker, representing the Business and Professional Women's Club.

The fund drive got underway in early July, 1928, with a great deal of enthusiasm and energy when volunteers manned numerous Franklin Street corners to solicit donations. Cloth signs, mounted on wooden frames, identified them. To bring attention to their cause "five or six airplane cut out wall box-boards" that would show the progress of the drive were set out a few days in advance of the campaign.

There appeared to be overwhelming widespread support and enthusiasm for the crusade that caused the leaders of the campaign to expect to have the largest volunteer army ever assembled for a cause in Michigan City. One of the things that made this campaign different than the others that preceded it was that, contrary to custom, many of the large industrial plants and wholesale houses allowed for solicitation to be made among their employees. The plan was to have every home, office, store, and factory solicited. Prominent business and professional leaders volunteered and were commissioned temporary "captains" to command an "army, which will endeavor to capture dollars rather than trenches." Over 250 volunteer workers were recruited in the Salvation Army drive for funds.

E. G. Richter, named today as general campaign chairman for the $36,000 building and maintenance appeal to be conducted by the Salvation Army here. Above, architect's drawing of proposed new home to be built for the army.

Figure 39 The above drawing appeared in the Michigan City News, June 28, 1928. The final plan was downsized due to financial considerations.

The downtown business district was divided into square block sections. The captains recruited a team of four workers who called on the businesses in their section. Helen Albright commanded a large volunteer army of women to take the crusade into every home in Michigan City during the five-day campaign. Chairwomen assisting with the residential campaign were Elizabeth Van Ouse, Mrs. Dennis Donahue, Lena Miller and Emma Roderbeck.

The second Monday in July saw 75 people in attendance at the kick-off dinner and rally held at the Y. M. C. A. The principal speaker at the dinner was Edwin Clayton of Grand Rapids, Michigan. He was the divisional commander of the western Michigan and northern Indiana territory for the Salvation Army. Giving impetus to the kick-off was the announcement that the Indiana Stone and Supply Company was the first plant to go "over the top" with 100 per cent of their employees subscribing to the fund.

Many of the large pledges were made on the condition that the campaign reach the full amount required for the project. Among those was the $15,000 pledge from Mrs. Howard H. Spaulding. In addition she agreed to give $1,500 annually for the maintenance and upkeep of the new Salvation Army home.

Even though the community seemed to totally embrace the campaign to build a new home for the Salvation Army, a snag developed a few days after the campaign began. The DISPATCH reported that a prominent resident on East Fifth Street notified them that several members of the Army Advisory Board had been told to select a different site. In the event they would proceed with their plan to construct the building, the residents of the area promised to take the matter to court. It was believed that the Protestant Hospital Association and the Clinic Hospital staff were also supporting the move to block the construction on the East Fifth Street site. Ironically Dr. Rogers, vice-chairman of the drive, was in favor of the location.

It was said that the hospital opposed the location because the proposed Salvation Army building was only 150 feet away "and that the band music will disturb the patients." The area residents complained that if the Army were to build at the proposed site, the area would become "an undesirable neighborhood" because it would "draw a number of undesirable people." They also echoed the noise issue.

In an attempt to lessen the concerns, Major Edwin Clayton responded by saying that for over 60 years, regulations have prevented officers and soldiers from playing drums and instruments while marching past churches or hospitals. He went on to say that "the Army does not intend to be used as a 'bum's roost'." The Army's advisory board added "a city which can plan, to her everlasting credit, the erection of over $500,000 worth of churches, could fail to heed the modest call of the mighty little 'church of the unchurched,' this sturdy band of religious workers who reach down for souls where other churches are unable to go," reported the NEWS. Added to their chorus was an editorial in the NEWS (July 19, 1928) that eloquently supported the choice of location and praised the work of the Salvation Army.

That same day the DISPATCH ran a story that indicated that they had erroneously reported that the staff of the Clinic and the hospital had supported efforts to block the construction of the Salvation Army at the East Fifth Street location. The newspaper elaborated by saying that the residents in opposition included the name of the Clinic in its lists of those in opposition. The article also stated with authority that even though the land in question was already purchased, every assurance was given that consideration would be given to other sites in order to avoid objections to the building of a home for the Army.

Even though the reports in the newspapers indicate continued progress was being made toward the successful completion of the fund drive, there were indications that the ultimate goal of raising $36,000 by the end of July would not be reached. As of the 26th of July more than $9,000 was needed if they were to realize the $15,000 gift promised by Mrs. Howard H. Spaulding, Jr. The house-to-house campaign had not gone as planned due to "Various things, vacations, and some other duties..." that left some areas neglected. Numerous volunteers agreed to contribute additional time to the drive.

The campaign committee held out hope that when the final reports were received in August the drive would meet its goal. During the 2nd week in August the committee reported that 855 subscriptions had been received. The employees of Tonn and Blank and the Indiana Stone & Supply Companies had a 100 per cent subscription. Reports from numerous other companies were received. However, an even greater number had not reported.

The drive lost its momentum by October. The goal had not been reached. Added to the situation was the untimely death of E. G. Richter. The advisory board decided to resume the drive the following spring, since many of the larger pledges were contingent upon the full amount being raised. They also decided to change the location of the Army community center. A lot in another area would be purchased.

The campaign to raise funds for a new home for the Salvation Army started anew in May 1929. A. C. Heitschmidt replaced E. G. Richter, to co-chair the drive with Dr. Rogers. Several team captains and workers from the previous year were replaced due to death or leaving the city. Over the winter a decision was made to locate the facility closer to the business district and therefore, would not be as objectionable to surrounding property owners. Negotiations were concluded with Mr. M. A. Cushman, a local Realtor, for a lot at 113 East Fourth Street. The price was $250 more than the $3,750 option on the East Fifth Street lot. Part of the funds came from contributions acquired the previous fall and the rest came out of the Spaulding contribution.

As August approached, it was announced that the campaign had met with a reasonable amount of success. However, their goal had not been reached. Efforts continued. A tag day was held on Saturday, August 10th, in an effort to acquire the necessary funds to assure construction of the new Army facility by the end of the year. Scattered throughout the business district, thirty-six young ladies affiliated with various city organizations volunteered to solicit funds. "Something over $200" was collected. This volunteer army of "taggers" included:

Florence Shepherd	Marjorie Murray	Ruth Shindell	Mrs. T. Brown
Gertrude Layman	Katherine Jaske	Florence Ricks	Marie Crawford
Genevieve Hansen	Elois Wilson	Eleanor Neulieb	Mrs. Haug
Charlotte Jurgensen	Virginia Will	Mildred Cubbine	Esther Hinkle
Margaret DeMass	Dorothy Lange	Virginia Abele	Helen Wedow
Martha Jurgensen	Mrs. L. Clifford	Loretta Goede	June Bader
Evelyn Cubbine	Anna Ulrich	Marie Hein	Vivian Black
Geraldine Brown	Julia Kachur	Ona Collins	Evelyn Vincent
Bethel McGinnis	Olive Carr	Ruth Gordon	

As was previously stated this effort to raise funds to construct a new home for the Salvation Army was a community-wide effort. The respect that the community had for the Army was evident in its response. That respect also carried over into the Indiana State Prison. As a result of the service rendered to the men at the prison, the inmates collected and donated $191.50 to the fund. However, it wasn't enough and the campaign was continued into the next year.

For those that doubted that a need existed for a new Salvation Army Community Center, those doubts were surely erased after they read the following account that appeared in the NEWS in March of 1930.

The 1930 membership roll showed that the local contingent listed 60 senior and junior members. Adjutant and Mrs. S. Hutchings were now in command and serving the needs of their flock. Their records of the previous year indicated that 250 "air services" were held, which attracted 4,848 "grown folk" while 5,972 attended young people's services. They had a Sunday school enrollment of 102. The Salvation Army during the 1929-30 winter months had assisted 100 families in various ways, the article continued. Homeless men passing through the city found comfort with a hot meal and a bed on many a winter's night.

The Advisory Board in 1930, according to the NEWS, included Charles Arnt, President; Dr. Rogers, Vice-president; Clyde Taylor, Treasurer; Hugo Keppen, Judge H. B. Tuthill, E. B.

Figure 40 Commandant Emma Westbrook was one of the seven original Salvation Army "Lassies" that came to the United States in 1880 along with Commissioner George Scott Railton to establish the Salvation Army in America. Emma served in Michigan City from December 1901-May, 1902. Photo courtesy of the Michigan City Salvation Army.

Stover, E. M. McLundie, and Mr. De Witt. Into their hands was passed the task of building a new home for the Salvation Army. With the goal in sight, E. M. McLundie, Chairman of the building committee announced on the 12th of June 1930, that construction on the new Salvation Army home had begun. The red brick and trimmed with Bedford limestone building was to cost $15,000. The building committee composed of C. E. Arnt, Dr. J. B. Rogers, A. C. Heitschmidt, Clyde Taylor and Mayor H. B. Tuthill signed a contract with the Carl Ahlgrim Contracting Company to do the construction.

Sufficient progress in the construction of the building provided for the opportunity to conduct a dedication ceremony and the laying of the cornerstone on Sunday, July 13, 1930. Although threatening weather in the morning dampened spirits, by 2:30 the weather cleared. On the platform were Brigadier Edwin Clayton and his wife, Adjutant and Mrs. Hutchings, the Rev. Robert Hall of the First Congregational Church and C. E. Arnt, President, Clyde L. Taylor, W. W. Witt, A. C. Heitschmidt and Hugo F. Keppen of the advisory board.

The program opened with the 20-piece Salvation Army band from Benton Harbor, Michigan playing "Onward Christian Soldiers." Following prayer and speeches from the dignitaries, the cornerstone was laid by Brigadier Clayton who "declared the stone to be truly laid," the DISPATCH reported. The newspaper reported that sealed within the cornerstone were photographs of Brigadier and Mrs. Clayton and Adjutant Sidney and Mrs. Hutchings, advisory members, Mrs. Charles Hickox and toys repaired by city firemen the previous Christmas. Also placed in the box were lists of city officials, current issues of The WAR CRY and YOUNG SOLDIER, copies of the NEWS and THE EVENING DISPATCH and several coins.

The Salvation Army "citadel" was formally opened on September 28, 1930. Colonel Arthur T. Brewer paid tribute to the memories of the late Charles J. Robb and E. G. Richter, who had both served as members of the advisory board. Several other speakers took the opportunity to thank the many individuals that made the building possible. Among those singled out were Mrs. Catherine Barker Hickox, the Honorable Martin T. Krueger who donated the cost of laying the sidewalks, W. R. Stockwell, Josam Manufacturing Company, Bastian-Morley Company of La Porte, J. P. Morley and the Kroening Coal Company, all of whom had donated special gifts.

Mayor Tuthill remarked that the crowd at the opening was the largest gathering of the Army he had ever attended in Michigan City, recalling that he had attended the first meeting in 1881.

Colonel Arthur T. Brewer, in his keynote address, prophesied that the Army's new home "would mark a change in the lives of men, that it would be as a lighthouse to people who walk in darkness, it would be a place to care for the uncared for." So it was and so it is today.

A great deal of time and energy was expended to provide the needy citizens of Michigan City a facility that brought comfort for their soul and relief for their financial burden. What makes this undertaking so miraculous is the fact that at the time the nation was in the grips of the Great Depression. Many were without jobs and income. The soup kitchens were visible throughout the country. Many lost their homes and businesses. This being said, the citizens of Michigan City rallied together to raise the funds necessary to construct a new home for the Salvation Army.

**Captain Duffy was followed by: Captain Jones, Captain Cotton, Captain Erickson, Ensign Watkins, Captain Mehan, Adjutant Emma Westbrook, pioneer officer to the United States; Captain Ellsworth, Captain Putman, Captain Davis Captain Woodward, Captain Lalone, Captain Weaver, Captain Council, Captain Barrett, Captain Atkinson, Captain Hinshaw, Captain Bouters, Captain Cobb, Captain Sands, Captain Bonnell, Captain Auld, Captain Lowry, Captain Monsell, Captain Day, Captain McDarby, Captain Smith, Ensign A. Scheinfeldt, Captain Bowie, Captain Conway, Adjutant Murdock, Adjutant Hart, Adjutant Reese, and Captain E. Johnson.

"...solid stretch of blacktop whose history, gritty and distinctively American, is intrinsically linked with the development of Michigan City."
Anthony Lambre, The Michigan City
News Dispatch, *August 3, 2003, p. C1*

INDIANA DUNES HIGHWAY

The April article in the NEWS DISPATCH reporting the proposed rerouting of the Dunes Highway at the County road triggered memories of my childhood. My family moved to Michigan City from Chicago in 1940. That move prompted numerous trips over the Dunes Highway to visit relatives in Chicago. Little did I know as a boy of 6 or 7 years old of the historic and environmental treasures that existed on the other side of our car windows. The EVENING DISPATCH of 1925 referred to the landscape as "...an ever changing panorama of irresistible charm-it passes through a region that is a veritable symphony of water, sand, flowers and foliage."

The Indiana Dunes Highway is approximately 25 miles long and is almost an "airline" route between Gary and Michigan City. The new road completed in 1923 reduced the driving distance between Michigan City and Gary by seven miles and eliminated nine railroad crossings.

It had been long regarded as one of the most important highways in northern Indiana. It was more than that, as a City of Gary official stated at the dedication banquet held at the Spaulding Hotel. He went on to say that it provided a shorter and safer road between Gary and Michigan City. He also pointed out that it was destined to provide the nation with a shorter route from the Atlantic to the Pacific Coast.

The impact on the growth and development of Michigan City was also apparent to its citizenry in the 1920's. Harry M. Miles, a Michigan City resident and civil engineer was acknowledged by Walter Greenebaum, at the dedication banquet, as being the first to envision the Dunes Highway. His conversations with the secretary and manager of the Chamber of Commerce planted the thought. The idea grew and materialized into realization through

Greenebaum's energy and skill in promoting the highway to state and national leaders. " Whatever our dream may be for this city and this region, an important path to the realization is the Dunes Highway." The city stood on the shore of Lake Michigan. It was Indiana's harbor. Industrially it was an integral part of "The Workshop of America." Its recreational facilities made it "The Playground of the Middle-west." As someone proudly boasted "Business and pleasure dwell together in Michigan City."

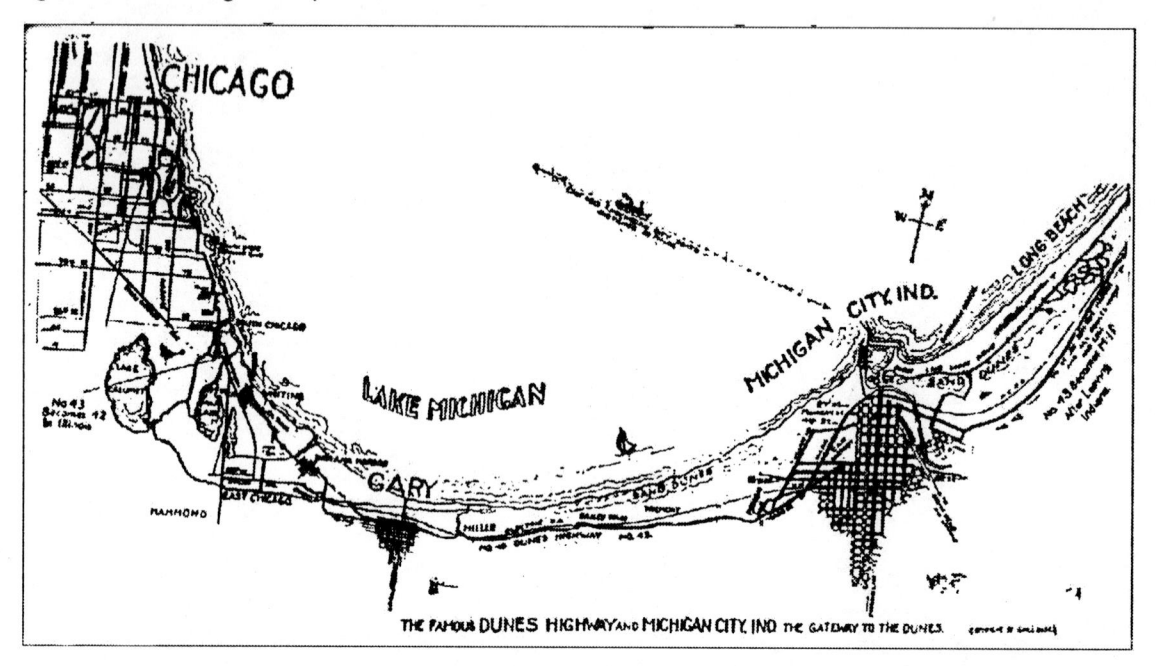

Figure 41 The map was prepared and drawn by George Leusch of Michigan City for the purpose of advertising the city and adjacent summer resorts. The map was included in a brochure to attract tourist in hopes of having them stop in Michigan City. Picturesque descriptions of the area and the city painted a lasting impression of the area.

The Dunes Highway evolved from a narrow mud and corduroy road to an "impossible" stone and gravel road and finally to a twenty-five foot concrete road. It connected Michigan City with Gary following the route the Indians and possibly their predecessors, the Mound builders, and descendants of the Eskimos used to travel across the Dunes country. Adventurers, trappers, missionaries, soldiers, merchants and settlers traveled this trail. Later the old Detroit to Chicago stage carried passengers and mail along the same southern route around the end of Lake Michigan.

From the announced start of construction in January of 1921 numerous delays plagued its completion. Some sections exceeded engineering estimates. East of the town of Miller the road grade had to be raised 18 inches above the contracted grade and were heavily reinforced with steel due to a large three-mile swamp. Difficulties in obtaining materials and right of ways were also experienced. The EVENING DISPATCH proclaimed, "New York Central Rd and Several Farmers Playing "Dog-In-Manger" Act On State." Although the Consumers' Company and Inland Steel Company donated the right of way through their property, the New York Central Railroad Company, according to the Chesterton TRIBUNE, refused to grant a right of way through their property west of Baileytown. Three or four farmers in the same vicinity also had refused to grant right of ways unless the "state pay an exorbitant price" for their property.

UP CLOSE AND PERSONAL

Nineteen months after the start of construction, the last bucketful of concrete was poured. The route between Gary and Michigan City with the completion of the concrete work was opened with the exception of a detour of 2000 ft at Baileytown. Messages were flashed to Indianapolis announcing the completion. The president of General Construction Company, Ingwald Moe, wired Governor Warren McCray: "Hallelujah! Dunes Highway concrete is finished."

The celebration and dedication marking the opening of the Dunes Highway was a spectacular event worthy of a Hollywood production. "Fill up your tank with gas and join the parade," proclaimed the Michigan City NEWS. Some 200 cars created about a 2-mile parade when it left Gary to drive to Michigan City. The procession was led by "a band of music" carried on a decorated truck donated by Armour and Company of Gary. The caravan stopped at Baileytown to place a "suitable marker...with appropriate ceremony." A bronze tablet specified the Dunes Highway would always be "the shortest route between the Atlantic and the Pacific." The procession then continued through Michigan City and on to the Michigan state line.

An unforeseen incident that added to the drama of the event occurred when a barricade halted the procession across the highway. A contractor with his employees, all armed, refused to permit the procession to travel over the highway because the concrete had not sufficient time to season. The work had not been accepted by the state and the contractor vowed "he was not going to have his unseasoned highway destroyed by traffic over it." The celebrants were angry and a "riot was promised." Finally the contractor, with his gun on his hip and his hand on the gun was persuaded to conference with the officials of the parade. Someone in the crowd pantomimed pulling a gun from his hip and "gave the contractor a shot." The point was made. The contractor waved and shouted to his employees, "All right boys, open the road." At the dedication banquet it was revealed that the incident was a stunt that added excitement to the parade.

The Hoosier State Automobile Association took up the task of financing and marking the highway. Businessmen and individuals throughout the entire length of the highway financially supported the project. The DISPATCH reported that most of the businessmen of Michigan City with an $11 membership joined the association to help defray the expense of "blazing" the Dunes Highway.

The markers were octagon shaped, about 18 x 22 inches, made of high-grade steel. Printed on the sign was "State Road 43." In the center was an eight-inch circle with "Dunes Hiway" in large letters around the outside. Within the circle were pictured two "highly colored" sand dunes. "Hoosier State Automobile Association" was printed at the bottom of the shield.

The DISPATCH commented, "These shields carry all the dignity one could expect and represent the official design marking the Dunes Highway. .... no expense has been spared to make the marking of the Dunes Highway a national comment."

*"...one man in Michigan City was
present for the birth of the television age—
Captain William (Bill) Eddy, U.S. Navy, Retired"*
THE NEWS-DISPATCH, *MARCH 25, 1985*

THE ADVENTURES OF CAPTAIN EDDY

The material for this biography was written using material from the series of articles Henry Lange wrote as a resulted of several interviews he and Elwin Greening conducted and tape-recorded.

There are some among us that would call William Eddy the Michael Angelo of our time. However, he would tell the people he met to just call me Bill. In his big white house on the corner of Michigan Boulevard and Roeske Avenue, he could on any given day be found sculpting, oil painting, woodcarving or writing. When he wasn't enjoying leisure time activities he could be found in his basement laboratory experimenting and developing electronic gadgets that revolutionized modern technology.

Bill's life began in Saratoga Springs, New York in 1902. His mother Ethyl and father William D. were prominent citizens of the community.

Figure 42 William Eddy at his desk.
Photo courtesy of William Swedenberg

Bill's father served four terms as a Republican elected Mayor. Later two more sons, Tom and John were added to the family.

The development of radio caught Bill's attention. Intrigued by its mystery he tinkered with it and at the age of 14 made his first crystal receiving set. With that mastered he made several that were sold to his neighbors. Bill's young, inquisitive mind continued to grow and absorb the new technology of the changing world he was living in. "I was Peck's bad boy in school," Bill admitted. His prankish school behavior caused his parents to enroll him in a military school. Following his graduation from military school he worked various jobs around Saratoga Springs. He came to the decision to attend the United States Naval Academy at Annapolis when he realized his life wasn't taking him anywhere. Getting an appointment was another thing.

Governor Franklin Roosevelt of New York was a formidable roadblock to his ambition. Roosevelt wasn't about to give an appointment to the son of a prominent Republican. Not deterred Bill managed to land on the alternative list of U. S. Senator Hamilton Fish. As luck would have it, those on the list ahead of him failed the entrance test, thereby insuring his appointment to Annapolis. Bill's two brothers also went to the Academy. They rose to the rank of admiral. "At one time, there was an Eddy on each ocean, and the Navy Department kept rotating us as a precaution against another Eddy buildup."

Bill's escapades at the academy brought on by his sense of humor and adventure caused his name to be on the demerit list repeatedly. His senior year was a continuation of his usual self-created problems that resulted in his receiving the maximum number of demerits. Not to be deterred, Bill came upon a scheme to use his brother's name when his demerits became dangerously high. His brother was more regulation oriented so a few unearned demerits had little effect on his record.

Eddy's extra-curricular activities while at the academy weren't solely directed toward frivolous endeavors. He made major contributions to academy and professional publications. He also designed the academy's 1926 class ring.

Upon graduation in 1926 he was assigned to the USS Cincinnati as assistant fire control officer. In less than three weeks the Cincinnati was dispatched to Nicaragua to assist in quelling the unrest. Bill's career next took him to Honolulu where he met his future wife. As the clouds of war began to gather over the horizon of China in 1927, the United States government dispatched a regiment of Marines along with the navy to protect America's interests. That included the Cincinnati and Bill Eddy. Bill and Christine Woolridge's paths crossed once again. A short time later they married on July 11, 1927. They lived in China for a time learning the language and culture.

Not long after he transferred into the submarine service. This move didn't dampen his impish behavior. The uninhibited world of submarines provided a backdrop that allowed his ingenuity to expand and advance his career. Bill told the story of how he lashed a flush toilet to the gun mount of his submarine in Subic Bay. Philippinos transported it to his home 3,000 miles to Tsingtao where it became a status symbol. He credits himself with having the first flush toilet in North China.

Throughout his naval career Bill knew he was partially deaf and slowly getting worse. His ability to read lips was his salvation and enabled him to pass the physicals. What some considered a handicap was the opposite for Bill. When he transferred to submarine duty his first assignment was sound officer. Enemy ships were tracked by listening through an extended stethoscope device. The sound officer needed good evenly balanced ears to determine the direction and position of the enemy ship. The sound of the ships propellers coming into both ears at the same time with equal volume meant that the ship was directly in front of them allowing the firing of torpedoes without surfacing. Bill and many of his shipmates couldn't do it.

Bill related a tale while on maneuvers off the Philippines. One evening during war games a seagull decided that the sub's periscope was a perfect perch. The gull consistently sat on the periscope and "did what seagulls do." Bill grabbed a flare gun and shot it at the gull. The fleet took that as a signal to send it into battle stations. "The submarines dived, cruisers ran in circles and all hell broke loose." This being said, Bill Eddy became one of two officers in the Navy qualified to command a submarine without graduating from sub school at New London, Conn. Incidentally, Bill submitted his design of the submarine dolphins when the Navy decided that the Submarine Service should have its own insignia. His design was adopted and he was given the first insignia struck. He was also first in his class to wear them when he qualified for command.

A few years later he was transferred to New London to complete his formal training. Bill recalled his duty as sound officer while at New London and decided to develop a device that would more accurately track a ship. He connected some inexpensive tubes he purchased at Kresge's Five and Dime Store with wire on a breadboard to two microphones. He was able to translate the sound to a meter. The target vessel's position was identified when the needle reached zero. Navy officials in Washington were quick to label the $12 "Eddy Amplifier" a product of a disturbed mind. Their conclusion was it wouldn't work. However, those subs that used his amplifier recorded more success than not. Through the urging of Bill's skipper the Navy began intensive research that demonstrated that the dime store tubes were more effective than the high priced equipment used. The result was that the technology of the "Eddy Amplifier" was placed on the fleet's submarines.

Bill's ingenuity brought other new technology to the Navy. His achievements include "a radio antenna that permitted transmissions under the ocean, a device to measure the speed of a ship by propeller beats and a submarine "ouija board" that utilized a mathematical formula for predicting the zigzag patterns enemy ships would take to avoid a submarine, and thus allow a sub to go directly to an interception point."

Bill's hearing loss finally caught up with him in 1934 when he was issued a medical disability discharge. As a civilian in the midst of the Great Depression he had difficulty finding work. A discharged serviceman by law was not allowed to work for a company that supplied the Navy. This precluded the majority of technical jobs, forcing him to take a job as a radio operator in Alaska. However, he didn't relish the idea. He started out for Alaska by way of Washington. He stopped in Philadelphia on a cold winter's day in 1936 due to deteriorating weather conditions. As luck would have it he met and talked with Philo Farnsworth who was working on developing electronically transmitted television; and he didn't have a Navy contract. Farnsworth had recently moved his shop from California to the East Coast.

Eddy recalled that "He didn't have any money, and I didn't want to go to Alaska, so I agreed to stay with him and started work at $35 a week." Bill's family settled on a rented farm outside Philadelphia. There were times that Farnsworth didn't have the money so he gave Bill a share of stock in the company. Bill supplemented his income by cartooning and writing a weekly television column for the New York Sun, using the pen name of Ken Strong.

Bill's cartooning ability developed into a profitable avocation. One evening in 1937 as he was heading home on the train, Bill was sorting through some cartoons the Saturday

Evening Post had rejected. The person next to him saw and liked them. As fate would have it he happened to be the advertising manager for Brown Instrument, a Division of Honeywell. Bill was hired to do a series of cartoons for the company's yearly calendar that became a classic over a 35-year period.

During the two years Bill worked for Farnsworth he developed the commercial television application of the multifactor techniques necessary , as well as developing the format for lighting and miniature set-staging techniques. He was also charged with coming up with commercial uses for television and studio programming.

During this period of time all of the giants in communication—CBS, NBC, RCA and Dumont—were working to develop an effective and reliable system to convert optical pictures to an electronic image that could be transmitted over radio waves to an electronic receiver. Farnsworth won the race with a team of unknowns that didn't have the credentials of their competitors. Bill reminisced that Farnsworth wasn't as well educated as his counterparts but had the basic ingenuity to think out of the box, "…to think ahead of what was possible, even if it appeared to be improbable at the moment." Besides Bill Eddy, Farnsworth's staff was composed of Arch Brolly, his chief engineer, and a self-taught glassblower who made the tubes, a mechanic and a carpenter.

After a short period of success the Crocker National Bank decided to back out of its financial support of Farnsworth's enterprise. Farnsworth joined a Fort. Wayne firm and Bill went to RCA's National Broadcasting Company. Eddy had written a number of articles on lighting and special effects that appeared in the Theater Arts magazine and took this expertise with him. His innovative approach and experimentation led to 34 patents for RCA.

One of his most unique inventions was the projection kaleidoscope that had the ability to never duplicate patterns. It was used to keep an active image on the TV screen when regular programming wasn't on. The New York Times wrote that according to the Encyclopedia Britannica it was an optical impossibility. Bill's response was "I didn't have enough background in optics to know that it was impossible." He invented it and was issued a patent.

Eddy's reputation for creativity and innovation had spread across the continent by 1939, falling on the ears of Barney Balaban, President of Paramount Pictures. Paramount's subsidiary, Balaban and Katz had plans to build Chicago's first television station. Bill was approached and asked to take on the job. Loving and enjoying life and boating on Long Island, he "set a price I knew they couldn't and wouldn't meet." Much to Eddy's surprise they agreed.

Paramount arranged for the family to move to Kenilworth, north of Chicago along the shore of Lake Michigan. North Shore living did not appeal to the Eddy family. One day the family got into their car and started driving south around the lake and discovered Michigan City with its outstanding boat harbor. The family took up residence in a large old home on Michigan Boulevard.

Bill was now able to concentrate on the task at hand. Paramount obtained a license for the experimental television station W9XBK. The top floor of the 12-story State and Lake Building in downtown Chicago would become the studio. Work to construct a 60-foot windmill tower on the roof began in earnest. A secondhand police radio was installed. Bill invested $1,500 to build a mobile unit, whereas NBC spent $500,000 for its New York unit. The station was up and running with a bunch of kids out of the training schools in March of 1941 at a cost of $60,000 compared to the normal cost of $1,500,000 required to build a station.

The expansion of the station proved to be difficult. Germany was a threat to the stability and sovereignty of the nations of Europe. Japan was threatening the security of Asia. The emerging television industry with the danger of war on the horizon made it difficult to find equipment. After all it was not a priority. At that time there were no network facilities or cables. Everything they televised was originated in their studio resulting from constant experimentation. There were only 50 to 100 television sets in all Chicago, Eddy estimated, that could receive their fuzzy black and white transmission. Nobody was willing to pay for advertising. According to Bill, they asked Marshall Field's and Commonwealth Edison to allow them to use their names on the air. The idea was to impress people that they had a viable new medium that had great potential in the near future.

A source of programming came from the headliners that performed at the Balaban and Katz Theater. Bill would go backstage and convince the stars to appear on television. He would emcee and talk with them on the air. He brought Orson Wells and Tommy Bartlett before the camera. He claimed that Sally Rand was the best talker and that he put Danny Thomas on television for the first time.

With the outbreak of World War II, "Bill Eddy again felt the call of duty." He realized that he had a staff of television engineers that had the expertise necessary to train men in the relatively new field of radar. The Navy knew his reputation in the development of electronic technology. His offer not only to do the training but to do it at the Balaban and Katz Chicago facilities at no cost to the government was enthusiastically accepted. Although Paramount Pictures and Balaban and Katz were unaware of the arrangement, they quickly agreed to Eddy's proposal and approved it without consulting with their board of directors.

"In order to screen the many applicants, I devised the Eddy Test. Anybody who passed it was admitted to the radar school in Chicago or here in Michigan City," said Bill. As late as 1985 his pioneer aptitude test lived on. The large demand for trained radar technicians saw the program eventually expand to the point where it was not only taught at the Naval Armories in Michigan City and Chicago but also at four Chicago area high school campuses as well as Wright Junior College, Crane Tech and Hertzel College.

Eddy's unorthodox methods caused him to bump heads with the Navy. It was inevitable that he was called to Washington to meet with Secretary of the Navy Frank Knox. When asked by the Secretary why he was out of uniform, Bill responded that he retired with eleven physical defects. He recalled, "…my medical records were pushed aside and in one fell swoop I was back in Uniform." At retirement he was a lieutenant junior grade but was elevated to a senior grade lieutenant his second time around. Throughout the war years when Bill Eddy was in uniform WBKB was staffed by an all female staff called the Watts-Women's Auxiliary Technical Television Staff. Bill Eddy's contributions to the technology of radar during his second tour of duty brought him several commendations as well as being awarded the Navy's Legion of Merit. His second retirement from the Navy came with his rank of Captain. Bill returned to WBKB.

The Zoo Parade was one of the early shows televised from WBKB. Marlin Perkins, Director of the Lincoln Park Zoo would bring into the studio snakes and "crazy animals" and discuss their traits and behavior in a talk show format. As the popularity of the show grew, Perkins tried to get Eddy to provide more airtime. The conventional ways didn't work. Perkins resorted to bringing his creatures "and let them loose in my office, trying to scare me into more airtime," Bill related. It must have worked because a short time later remote broadcasts from the zoo were seen in numerous homes throughout the Chicagoland area.

Eddy continued to solicit advertisers for his programming. He went after all the companies that the station did business with. The station's biggest supplier was RCA. Bill turned up the pressure by threatening to cancel the station's order for camera tubes. Finally a representative from RCA called saying they wanted to see the program Bill had been bragging about. There was no show. As it happened Fran Allison was in Eddy's office at the time of the call looking for a job on TV. Bill offered her a job to do five one-hour shows a week and paid her $35. Then he called Burr Tillstrom who had been performing a hand puppet show at the New York World's Fair. Bill remembered seeing the show and used that arrangement for the program format. The RCA representatives were impressed and agreed to sponsor the show. Kukla, Fran and Ollie became one of the most watched and remembered shows emanating from Chicago. Bill recalled that the show had no script; "it was all ad lib."

Today there are millions of TV sets in American homes. All of us take for granted the technology. In the early days few people could afford the luxury. The dilemma was where to begin: with the programming or the sale of TV's. NBC experienced success by targeting the community of Newburg, N.Y. Eddy needed to demonstrate to prospective advertisers that people would buy TV sets and that WBKB had the potential for commercial development.

To that end Eddy devised a scheme that made Michigan City the focal point of his plan. Bill constructed a small wooden tower on the roof of his home. With highly tuned receivers in place he had the station's transmitting antennas turned and focused on Michigan City. The Eddy's would invite people to their home every evening to watch television. "With a captive audience in place, we'd then start calling the local bar," Bill remembered. They would ask if they had a TV set. If the answer was no, they would send a salesman over. This tactic was used on numerous bars, commenting that the other place already had one. Bill said, "By the time our

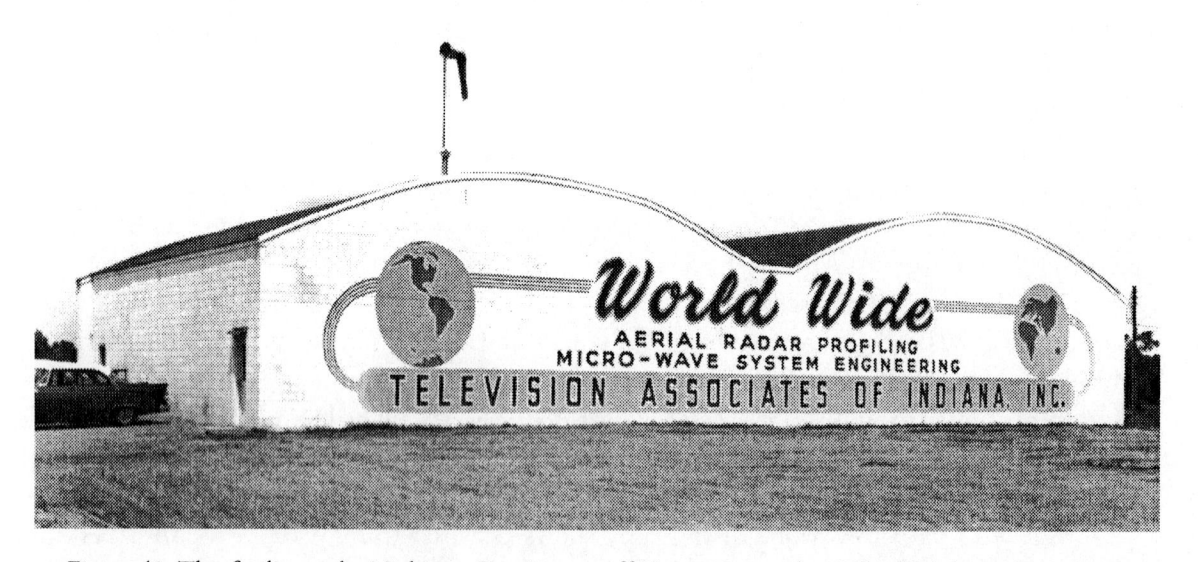

Figure 43 This facility at the Michigan City Airport off Hwy 212 served as Bill Eddy's base of operation.
Photo courtesy of William Swedenberg

salesman arrived, we were assured of a ready sale." According to Eddy the television audience in Michigan City was well above the U. S. average.

Michigan City continued to play a part in the commercial development of Chicago television. With dwindling interest of televised boxing in Chicago, Bill secured the support and assistance of boxer Tony Zale and William "Tex" Nunnally, a Michigan City boxing promoter and brought professional boxing to Michigan City. With the added cooperation of the city's mayor, Russell Hileman and school officials he proceeded to erect a war surplus microwave relay and began to broadcast to Chicago boxing bouts from Elston High School.

Eddy realized early on that the future of television and sports would eternally be intertwined, so he devised a plan to broadcast Notre Dame football to the Chicago audience. His plan called for the construction of microwave transmission towers at Rolling Prairie and at his home in Michigan City, becoming one of the first commercial microwave networks in America.

This successful endeavor turned Bill's attention to Chicago baseball. He was able to get the rights to broadcast the Cub's home baseball games. Televising baseball at that time had no precedent to follow so Bill wrote a how to pamphlet. In the beginning they had one camera baseball with it being positioned on the first base line. According to Bill, Joe Wilson and Jack Brickhouse were two of his best sports announcers.

Eddy's interest in commercial television diminished shortly after returning to WBKB following his stint in the navy. The excitement and glamour related to the early days of pioneering diminished. It was time for Bill to seek new challenges. He was released from his contract with Balaban and Katz in 1947 with five years remaining. Not long after the Meredith Publishing Co. hired Bill to construct what Time magazine heralded as "a marvel of the age." In 21 days Eddy built station WHEN TV in Syracuse, N.Y.

Television Associates had been incorporated years before to manage his patents. Now it would be used to start a new business. TA was transformed into a holding company with subsidiaries in Indiana, the Middle East and Saudi Arabia. His earlier experience with microwave transmission gave him the idea to survey vast regions economically by bouncing radar off the ground from an airplane. A topographical profile of the land could be created and used to design a network. His innovative idea cut the time and cost associated with conventional surveys.

Eddy's new business venture thrived. He was hired to survey the prospective routes for the Indiana and Illinois toll roads. Other projects included oil pipelines, power lines and numerous assignments. These early ventures enabled Bill the time to fine-tune his newly developed technology before taking on overseas operations.

This revolutionary technology took Bill to President Batista's Cuba where he provided the survey for a complex communications network. His biggest job was surveying a 3,000-mile route over mountains and deserts through Turkey, Iran, Iraq and Pakistan for a new communications system that eventually replaced a 1902 German built telephone line. His booming business also took him to Europe, South America and the Far East. Bill was logging a minimum of 100,000 miles a year of flying time.

In the meantime, back in Michigan City, Television Associates had developed into a manufacturing facility that employed 200 employees with sales of $5,000,000 a year. Most of their work took the form of adapting television equipment and motion picture projectors as well as a 24-hour tape recorder that would monitor a central battle station for the U.S. Navy. They were also doing sub-contracting for the Bendix and Allison Company of South Bend, manufacturing the guidance system for the Talos Missile.

Bill's talents and busy innovative mind never seemed to rest. At home in his workshop amidst his major projects he would play around with the numerous visions floating around within his head. His constant commuting too provided the inspiration that led to his inventing and patenting of the Turnpike Pacer. He beat Ford and others who had also been working on what we know to be cruise control.

Eddy soon discovered that while government contracts could be lucrative their speed of payment was appalling. Pentagon red tape, paper shuffling and delays place a harsh financial burden on the company and on Eddy's personal finances. The solution was a merger with Westinghouse Air Brake who was also involved in similar work in Syrian and Egyptian communications. Operations continued in Michigan City for a time but eventually were moved to Falls Church, Va. under the new company name of Melpar Inc.

Eddy's role in the newly formed company seemed to be focused on consulting and development which allowed him to stay in Michigan City. With time on his hands he returned to television when he was contracted to provide his consulting expertise to WFLD, channel 32 and WTTW, channel 11 as well as other communication outlets.

With retirement Bill Eddy devoted his time to the arts, be it ceramics, oil and watercolor painting, woodcarving or creating three-dimensional stained glasswork. When he wasn't reading from his library about the history and culture of China or taking a correspondence course to learn to read Chinese from the University of Minnesota he was sailing from the Washington Park Marina on his genuine Chinese Junk that was brought around the world to Michigan City.

Captain William C. Eddy, United States Navy Retired, passed away on September 16, 1989. Although he no longer graces us with his physical presence his legacy lives on. Bill Eddy was truly a remarkable man that helped to expand the outer limits of technology.

The following character studies referred to as "BEACON LIGHTS" is reproduced as they appeared the the news paper. The grammar and spelling was not changed in order to preserve the integrity of the published descriptions.

BEACON LIGHTS

A PRELUDE.

"In some far off day a student of Michigan City history searching diligently through public records, biographies and dry statistics for a better understanding of our customs and manners, will we hope welcome this series of sketches. We hope they will be to him, struggling to interpret in the darkness of the era of 1833-1933 as a beacon light to the aviator. We hope they aid him in fixing the place of men of Michigan City in the history of Michigan City, through this present day interpretation of them.

These sketches, in no way exhaust, we will, however, as all biographies should, seek to display the men of Michigan City as we have known them yesterday, or know them today and in their most favorable light.

How valueless the biography of 2,OOO A. D. describing "Pep", Fred C., the Judge, "Doc" or Martin, or the many others in these sketches as—Born 18... died 19..., offices, records, etc., following in a dull, tiring list. Something more is needed to explain these breathing personalities for us and something more to reveal their traits and the relation of these men to the trend of our times. They have made Michigan City and been made by Michigan City. The future history of that remote student estimating and fixing these men may receive some aid from our own estimates of them in "Beacon Lights." In that possibility, we allow our admiration for the subjects of these sketches to overweigh our own timidity."

THE EVENING DISPATCH, MARCH 2, 1929

"SNUFF" (OTTO) AICHER.

"Many a nest he has feathered" in many successful years in the furniture business in Michigan City, operated under the name of Otto Aicher. From apprenticeship to proprietor in unbroken progress, and now well to principles able to enjoy the inevitable fruits of constant application and of a devotion assuring success in business.

His nickname is most peculiar and its origin seems lost in the dim pages of the Sitters and Stayers era of our social history, but somehow connected with his pals Dude and Herman.

He is an ever-genial man enjoying old friends and always acquiring new. He not only sells good furniture, but knows how to make it because of an apprenticeship we no longer enjoy in industry.

He relishes an easy saunter down Franklin Street and, incidentally, makes a sure appraisal of window displays that he passes. His bridge is as good as his golf.

THE EVENING DISPATCH, JULY 10, 1929

———◆———

CHARLES E. ARNT.

From farm to large city, back to small city and helping us grow to bigness. Clerk, teller, cashier, president, also all civic honors easily his. A real Hoosier, and yet in carriage, poise and stature there is something different about him. In Paris, in Berlin or in Chicago he would seem to belong in palace, castle or mansion.

He acquired and faithfully followed a systematic training course in physical and mental education. He inspires confidence and deserves it—plays, works or studies with intensity. Makes a splendid appearance on horseback and yet no one is more ready to kneel in garden or on green. Can lead boys in singing, men in business and citizens in civic affairs. Probably our wealthiest citizen in appreciation and full enjoyment of life. Will some day be able to stand on high point overlooking eternal lake and hear breezes sing "There is a fit man and a worthy man."

THE EVENING DISPATCH, MAY 6, 1929

———◆———

GEORGE BAKER.

The kind of a banker that revels in analyses and for relaxation will enjoy the study of a bridge diagram. A faculty for stocks and bonds and trends of the market. Understands a financial sheet or statement.

UP CLOSE AND PERSONAL

Cool, steadied and unblushing. A nervous man on a horse, but mighty cool in his banking chair. A life time in one bank explains his command of the subject.

Will take a chance, will contribute and will work well in any civic campaign. Golfs indifferently and just for exercise.

From collector to Vice-president in a neat, orderly progress marked by great care, exactness and reliability. His opinion on the market widely sought.

THE EVENING DISPATCH, APRIL 9, 1929

―――◆―――

BILL BIEDERSTAEDT.

An odd composite of homely philosophy. Assessment valuations, way back when, as retired farmer, ex-public official and clubman. He can swap stories with Martin or with Feallock within the same hour and that means versatility.

He farmed in the days when farmers must first clear their land and labor-saving devices were unknown.

He will assess with accurate facility and confidence a vacant lot or a city water-works system. A Democratic war-horse, a never-failing attendant at lodge meeting.

Gray hair, bulky, capable hands, bronze complexion, alert mentally and physically. Dependable, generous, and moderate in all things. An honest, trustworthy public official. Politician, honoring the name, a citizen realizing and discharging well his civic duties.

Friendly and fair, hale and hearty. Watch him some day doff drab black suit for gray and Panama, and why not? He is young as the youngest Beacon Light, if old as the oldest.

THE EVENING DISPATCH, JULY 13, 1929

―――◆―――

DR. E. G. BLINKS.

Our most enthusiastic equestrian, greatly responsible for our revival in riding. A long successful professional career, but always witnessing the man "who keeps fit". The busy doctor always insistent on relaxation and on healthful hobbies and always characterized by a youthful jauntiness and heartiness.

A generous, tolerant and most forceful man, radiating an easy confidence and always well-poised. An ideal temperament for the physician and surgeon and possessing the physical and mental equipment of an all-American half. Sickness meeting his contrasting health and cheer must be dispelled and routed.

Education, training, success, health, enterprise. There seems nothing lacking to bring happiness and contentment to him.

THE EVENING DISPATCH, APRIL 8, 1929

ELMER BLOMQUIST.

A big, complacent, smiling man. An exotic complexion that cosmetics would never give. Has literally painted and decorated an entire town and still at it. Prominently identified with the fraternal activities of Michigan City. He wouldn't know a mashie from a driver, but could tell you many batting averages and the standing of teams in either league. He is better at pinochle than at bridge.

Rather odd that he has never been in public office. He would certainly make a good man for commissioner.

Motoring and fishing know his perennial interests. He doesn't have to work as hard as he formerly did. Quickly adapts himself and organization to modernistic trends in decorating and will meet any competition. Knows every home in Michigan City, inside and outside.

As chairman of the Elks house committee, wish he would provide the 18 day diet menu for the members. So many of them need it badly.

THE EVENING DISPATCH, JULY 12, 1929

MIKE BODINE.

A classicist gone wrong, or better, diverted to commercial photography, revealing in the artistic heights of his profession the earlier educational background he enjoys. A flash of teeth, a gleaming eye, a swarthy arm and a vigorous walk indicate a virile health.

Once a real political factor in this locality, but surrendering the field to less worthy champions to devote his time to his profession. An able linguist reflecting in brilliant conversation a refreshing, if unorthodox philosophy.

Knows Epictetus, as well as the major, and enjoys either with equal gusto. Often wonder what he really thinks about these western people, so different in customs and manners from his own people. What hypocrites he must deem us, but he would only tell us in a laughing reference that would not sting.

THE EVENING DISPATCH, JULY 11, 1929

UP CLOSE AND PERSONAL

AL BOWEN.

Looks mad, but isn't. It is merely the result of intense concentration whether at work or at play. A demon at pool, but shooting in-and-out golf. Improving at bridge, but never should play pinochle. Salesman, auditor and loyal representative of great cash register company and a frequent winner of sales awards and bonuses.

Pounds a motor vigorously, but covers a big territory. Unable to walk leisurely, but must hurry. A resonant twang to his voice, a clear bright eye, a quick but controlled temper. An assertive chap and sure of himself. Watches basketball more closely and expertly than the rest of us, but, over-emphasizes the supremacy of his alma mater, Indiana in this sport. As an official will keep a team on its toes.

THE EVENING DISPATCH, AUGUST 6, 1929

———◆———

DR. WHITEFIELD BOWES

Author of a nation-wide slogan, "Hello-Al", derivable from the first letters of "American Legion. This same man induced the children of Belgium to gather poppies, for distribution by John Franklin Miller Post throughout America. He is a worthy representative of a family giving to our country a great general in the World War, and the doctor himself with a most laud-record as major in our medical forces overseas.

He is an idealist with the inevitable pipe. His office a home not for the vagrant train, but for the sick, weak and helpless and ever and always the welcome ex-soldier "to shoulder his crutch and show how fields are won."

A man enjoying a good fight, a well-balanced library, and all those second and fourth Friday nights when he will always be found at Legion headquarters. How that enthusiasm, love and interest in his cause overshadows and diverts our attention from so many other qualities of almost equal interests in this lovable personality. We do enjoy that office and that friendly doctor so ready to talk the night away.

His health is good, despite most serious accident that would have knocked out a man less rugged than the ex-major. His environment most favorable and, by the way, the only resident owner left on Franklin Street north of Tenth with a lot 85½ feet by 165 feet deep. There is also an enormous farm, out there in Coolspring Township which the doctor isn't at all anxious to sell.

THE EVENING DISPATCH, MAY 25, 1929

———◆———

A. A. BOYD

He came, saw and conquered. A street railway, a bank, a great subdivision in a swift panorama—revealing the vision, the organizing ability and the sure grasp of man. There is a touch of Midas in those gray eyes; there is determination and grimness in that strong jaw; there is efficiency and accuracy in that close clipped mustache and in that concise, accurate speech. Whether in dim cloistered private office or on Kentucky five-gaited stallion, or behind the wheel of luxurious motor, there is an impression of utilities, of coupon cutting, of syndicates, of success, happiness and wealth, and there is a smile in that twinkling eye. It is all so easy for "Thomme qui sait."

THE EVENING DISPATCH, MAY 8, 1929

———◆———

ALEX BRINCKMAN

Typical Moose, justly proud of one of the greatest humanitarian accomplishments of this century, Mooseheart—which will ever remain a great monument to the ideals and practical charity of his association in this proud organization.

Another railroad man, exemplifying in his life and habits the predominant dependability of service. Good habits, thrift, health, loyalty must be there in abundance or men will never get to be old in that exacting service. It is a loyalty and service which incidentally so often deprives Michigan City of excellent material for public office and trust.

Walking or driving he seems to he plunging forward in a hurried; determined manner but greeting a thousand and more friends and acquaintances throughout Michigan City. A life-long resident, freeholder, voter from a pioneer family of this city.

THE EVENING DISPATCH, MAY 18, 1929

———◆———

ALEX CARSTENS.

Senior member of oldest dry goods firm under same management on Franklin Street. Every day, at odd hours, leaving the store for that slow jaunt along the north end for a meditative smoke. There is a conservative, a reliable certain man, an even-tempered individual. There is calmness, suavity and poise in walk and talk, reflecting the certainty of a well-established firm as impregnable as old Lake Michigan.

We have known as a child, as a boy and as a man that same polite, courteous greeting for over a quarter of a century. May another quarter of a century find us meeting with that mutual welcome. There is easy walk to and fro every day to what must be a restful home.

Wonder how he votes and what he thinks of city manager government, high taxes, of business prospects and of the modern flapper. We would never dare ask him, but know his opinion and judgment would reveal careful reflection and tolerant judgment.

THE EVENING DISPATCH, MAY 4, 1929

––◆––

AL CHILDERS.

The heavy rhythm of the shop is suddenly shattered with a terrible crash, a shrill whistle, power shut off, a strange silence, in that great steel erecting shop where box cars are handled like match boxes. Then swinging down that enormous shop with huge strides may be seen Al Childers with his gang. He is a big-fisted, huge man in charge of the millwright gang. He is a trouble shooter, a mover of heavy equipment. How quickly he can get things moving again and how soon after he has been on the job we hear again that steady rhythm, and see Al Childers back to his shanty awaiting another call. He is ready and able with those fists and more ready to bring his enormous, trained strength and that of his gang to remove troubles in the shop. A thunderous voice, yet capable of most soft speech. A stern countenance so easily breaking into heavy gale-like laughter. A knack for ropes, levers and fulcrums that enables him to move enormous machinery with ridiculous ease. Fixed in his mind the location of every valve, in that complicated network of pipes, lines, conduits and wires, underground and overhead, in a helpless confusion to everyone but himself.

THE EVENING DISPATCH, APRIL 5, 1929

––◆––

"NEWT."

"Doctor Newton Clark, Dentist," may be seen on the door of a spick-span and modern office. He is the gentleman of serious studious mien and may be found at regular meetings of the Legion where he is zealously taking a prominent part in the activities of this organization.

Leadership and important committee appointments have been oftentimes confided to this tall veteran by other organizations also, and he is fast assuming a prominent place in our civic affairs. His loyalty is well marked, his sincerity unquestioned, his faith boundless and his energy unlimited. His professional advancement has been rapid. Prolific in ideas, broad visioned, easily enthused he is typical of a new spirit permeating one of our military organizations and fast molding it into the potent force it has lacked in the past.

THE EVENING DISPATCH, AUGUST 16, 1929

VICTOR COONROD

Organizing and developing one of our leading insurance and real estate businesses. Growing, building — ever planning, ever venturing—saving. Successful? Why, as inevitable as night following day, success must follow.

Grim-jawed, eyes far-off gazing, quiet spoken, seldom smiling, coldly serious, ever usual manner, but needs more and harder play that he might work harder. But our biographical briefs not embracing the work of the diagnostician, we digress no more. And even at that cautious and sure. Lions a needed and healthful recreation. Auto motoring in the intensity of work and be no handicap to success and happiness.

Loves politics more than political parties. Perhaps he sees ahead the breaking up of old party lines and re-alignment of different and new groups.

THE EVENING DISPATCH, JULY 25, 1929

AL COUDEN.

A steady, reliable, competent, easy-going man managing this $26,000,000 corporation called Michigan City. He is patient, calm and best of all courteous, and displaying always the gracious attributes that have ever been characteristic of the pioneer family whose name he carries. Let grand juries disturb others, commissioners quarrel, employees abscond, but the grit and patience of the man ever finds him with equanimity undisturbed.

THE EVENING DISPATCH, MAY 13, 1929

WALTER CRUM

A better fisher than Spyke or Kunkel, yet never bringing in the record breaker. Our most loyal sports fan, whether our high school football or club boxing. Have you ever missed him at the game?

Wiry, untiring in body or in words. From house wiring to everything electrical and now owning and operating one of our most successful electrical supply houses. His name seems to be his nickname because his friends all called him "Crum."

He advertised his wares more loudly than his fishing or hunting exploits. He likes blood in his games and protests loudly and vehemently from the sidelines at the quitter or grandstand player. Will argue to the bitter and dangerous end with a fan from Laporte who gets top noisy. Will cover quickly any careless betting offers made in the crowd. He's genuine. There is in him some of the sand and grit of Michigan City and insists on sitting there in the game.

THE EVENING DISPATCH, AUGUST 13, 1929

JUDGE HARRY L. CRUMPACKER.

It importance of office and dignity of same controlled the order in which these sketches appear, the Judge would have appeared first. If the manner in which official duties of a high order were discharged was a criterion, the Judge would have appeared first. If the degree of responsibility, of adaptability and temperament were controlling his appearance would have been first. But Beacon Lights is as haphazard as history.

For 15 years Harry L. Crumpacker has graced the bench of our Superior Court. A $15,000 or $20,000 judge on a $7,000 salary. Tall, broad shouldered, with the lines of a hurdler or racer. Calm, cool and a never failing poise. A kind, discerning eye, an excellent judicial mind and temperament, bring to the high duties of that office exhaustive knowledge and grasp of the law. Generally accepted by layman and lawyer alike as belonging in that office during his lifetime. Freed from the necessity of electioneering because offices do sometimes seek the man. Public life—our bench and bar—our legislative halls know this name so well. Our history traces the family back, through pioneer days of Indiana and through Colonial Virginia to Holland.

Honored tradition, high accomplishments so often following the name. We admire the Judge; we like the man; we enjoy the raconteur. He needs no gown nor white wig to "adorn that venerable place."

THE EVENING DISPATCH, MARCH 28, 1929

JIMMY CULLEN

Easily upholding reputation for wit, but not so easily his sense of humor. Easily one of the leaders in local real estate circles. Independent but will fight for his client. In his chosen field of anecdotes we rank him first in ability and interest. Boredom is impossible in his presence. A good judge of real estate values in Michigan City. Salesmanship comes easy to him.

A sharp tongue, a thick skin, a keen brain, a pipe, —always welcome and always dispelling the monotony and drabness in conversation. Can handle with the same sang-froid a million or a thousand dollar deal, and with unexcelled chances of success. Co-organizer of local Realtors—President of Manufacturer's Club.

THE EVENING DISPATCH, APRIL 10, 1929

RALPH DEAN

Bringing to Michigan City a needed championship of old Illinois, and an offset to the pervasive influence of Michigan University in our town. He is of piquant personality, laughing heartily and playing as heartily. Alert, quick and agile in mind and body.

Lumber and building supplies move quickly to the resulting benefit of the business he so ably operates.

A much better bridge player than golfer, a better motorist than equestrian. A good man to head a campaign or drive needing a real stimulus or organizing ability. Making intensive efforts to promote and foster development of our lake shore district.

An impatient fisherman or hunter and more interested in dogs and scenery than game or fish. Quickly captivates and holds the friendship of all. Hospitable, enthusiastic.

THE EVENING DISPATCH, APRIL 2, 1929

---◆---

WILLIAM DICKINSON

Shop production, factory supervision, turning out long lines of bright box cars which in their ponderous momentum seem to be still under the sure direction of this man of steel. A practical man typifying modern, industrial efficiency, keeping in a never ending moving harmony thousands of men and machines.

Raw iron and steel, timber, nail and rivets quickly and strongly molded into freight cars, moving the traffic of a nation, and solidly built under the calm mastery of this giant. Never hurried, always sure, calm, cool. A thousand details and a great plant under his control, his hand, his brain inspecting and keeping up production.

Men like him and work hard for him. A good fisherman but rather disdainful of a tiny golf ball, and why not with that background of moving freight trains.

THE EVENING DISPATCH, MAY 7, 1929

---◆---

FRANCIS H. DORAN

The youngest old man on the best working g committee in the Chamber of Commerce, the Good Roads Committee. Family traceable through pioneer days of Laporte County through Canada to both Scotland and Ireland.

Our first traveling salesman. Lumber, every civic affair, railroad work and politics long ago met his refreshing enthusiasm and ardent spirit. Postmaster, county auditor and frequent delegate to political conventions.

UP CLOSE AND PERSONAL

Still "carrying on" after half a century of ceaseless, tireless activity. Growing old gracefully and never losing his value to his community. Still in the harness of civic affairs, admired and respected by all. Our real Citizen Emeritus."

THE EVENING DISPATCH, MARCH 8, 1929

―――♦―――

BERNARD ECKSTEIN

As Ecky much better known. The haberdasher, of an irrepressible unique personality, bubbling over with enthusiasm. So glad to meet or see anyone, particularly in his store. So ready to do his bit in a civic cause, so quick in repartee. Of ready wit, pep at a table where men are often over eager fashion, winning more from Ecky's fancy than warranted by their originality. He dances, will sing at a stag, go to a fight or a fire. He will be golfing in 1930. He is courteous, ever pleasant, always friendly. He is salt in a dreary lodge meeting. He is pepp at a table where men are often over serious and dull.

THE EVENING DISPATCH, AUGUST 5, 1929

―――♦―――

JOHN ERICKSON

A blond Niles Aster, as clear, bright and sparkling with heath and energy as the jewelry he handles with such fond and discriminating care. An excellent salesman and a friendly companion building up a business on a sure foundation. Lithe, tall, and supple, splendid material for that easy golf swing, all rhythm and effortless.

Smiling through with his glamorous thirties with his own jewelry store or district superintendent of chain store as his sure goal. Politically minded with a cautious opinion on municipal affairs. Resigned from a commissioner race under a rather over-idealistic attitude towards the ethics of the situation, but he will always be a likely candidate for municipal office with his multitude of friends and acquaintances and a mighty clean record in his home town.

THE EVENING DISPATCH, AUGUST 12, 1929

―――♦―――

"HEMP" FEDDER

A troublesome force in a political campaign. There is a touch of David Harum in his rare ability, making the real estate business a successful vocation for him. Now our township

Arnold Bass

trustee. The care of roads and ditches, the relief of the poor, the duties of a school system fall to his present lot, and are discharged in that characteristic style. A man able to plan with long, cool deliberation in seeming idleness, but suddenly rising from an easy chair and selling our Starland Theatre. In his dancing days the best waltzer in La Porte County and one of our first dancing teachers. A popular barber. The father of our park bandstand. A lover of music, promoter and organizer. One of the immortal Crystal Trio that brought a needed punch to a recent city election. Just missed victory but at once landed a better and more responsible position, as township trustee. A certain candidate for next election and almost as certain of victory.

He is in the comfortable early fifties and always comfortably dressed. He is sill remembered as a well-known sprinter back of the early part of this century. Indirect in approach, whether business or politics, but invariably successful in either. Tolerant and liberal in thought and speech, enjoyable in a conversation, brightened with his droll expressions of false protest and ever provided with a humorous touch. Plays the leading part in the funniest incident ever told in Michigan City "a modern transfer of real estate by feudal livery of seisin.

Beware of him you candidate for public office. He is poison to a political opponent and therefore should be most assiduously cultivated. Line up his support and you will receive votes from strange sources unapproachable to you.

THE EVENING DISPATCH, APRIL 24, 1929

———◆———

BILL FINK.

Ideal secretary, filling a big chair and his penmanship resembling engraving. Never any juggled figures there. Proud of his work, faithful to his trust.

His laugh enormous, shaking, infectious in its wholesome, unrestrained hilarity. Democrats, Republicans, citizens tickets may come and go, forms of government may change, business men may succeed politician-- "Ole Bill" goes on forever because wise mayors, commissioners or city manager knowing the keeping of our financial records needs a man like Ole Bill.

Vacations, a walk to the lake front, a curbstone meeting on north Franklin Street, we have never seen him south of Eighth.

A magnificent head, a square and burly body, florid complexion, evidentially good liver, devoid of nerves due to a stolid temperament needed in the city treasurer's office of Michigan City.

THE EVENING DISPATCH, AUGUST 3, 1929

———◆———

BOB FLETCHER

Another man from Knox, scene of Moorman and Kramer   activities.   The man, Robert B. Fletcher, formerly a banking examiner, now teller and trust officer, and incidentally making us revive our bridge ratings in Michigan City. Another year will find him in the first ten.

He has that Knox flare for politics and is invaluable to his local party. He is a quick analyst of trial balance, financial statements or political campaign.

Favors gray clothes, soft hat, overcoat, in season, generally open. A heavy hard walker, five foot ten, 170 pounds and never varying much. A nasal twang, giving his voice a good carrying power. Shakes hands heartily and with a firm worm grasp.

Best election prophet on Franklin Street today. When Michigan City for the first time in her history elects a man like Pepple for governor, it will be because of men like Fletcher.

THE EVENING DISPATCH, AUGUST 15, 1929

JIM FOGARTY, OR—

Representative of a fast disappearing type in Michigan City—the railroad man. Man of brawn, endurance, bravery and intelligence. Through storm and sleet, summer and winter, night and day, driving their immense engines up and down the western division of the M. C.

What valuable men they have been and are, not only to their employers but to the communities within which they have lived. How loyal they have been to their employers and town and their friends. What good citizens they have been. Home builders, family men, democratic and independent.

There is Pepple, Doherty, Gaspar, McDonald, Mulqueen, all still seeing service. There is Faulhaber, Gilmore, Healion, of those who have finished their years of service in the cab and been deservedly retired. There are others, too, who will instantly occur to the reader as truly representative of the American citizen. Plain yet aristocratic in their free independence. Their lives and habits, customs and morals seem to reflect the undeviating, rigid and reliable schedules of their work. They are independent, safe, clean and certain.

The unfit man would never survive many years of railroad engineering. That engine cab is too small for the drunkard or the spendthrift. That Mogul can never be entrusted to the man of uncertain nerves or vision. The lives of passengers depend on the cool and brave intelligence of that man ever driving with clocklike precision along those steel rails. In you, Jim Fogarty, and all our railroad men of Michigan City, we find dependability, safety and in your brave and honest work and in your splendid citizenship and highest virtues there arises our own pride in you.

THE EVENING DISPATCH, APRIL 20, 1929

FRANK GARRETTSON.

A "Stone and Webster" man, which means a background of industrial and business efficiency. Now president of R. F. Garrettson & Company, underwriters investment bankers, with money to loan and bonds to sell and houses to build. He was a co-developer and organizer of a bank and of a great suburban developer. He is a survivor of the Florida boom.

He golfs and horsebacks for the exercise alone, but works and plans and builds for pleasure. Many civic enterprises have known his efficient cooperation and assistance. He is a plunger in Michigan City futures, investing and buying at home. His prosperity and success is ours. An invaluable man on our important committees, and always the careful, cautious man demanding exact and accurate information.

THE EVENING DISPATCH, APRIL 4, 1929

———◆———

ED GIBBONS

A barrel-chested man, fighting corpulency and at present winning back to his former fighting weight. A city-wide acquaintance reveals his many sided business and social acquaintanceship.

His brain and eye are far quicker than his hand or feet. A poor stroke at pool, yet playing an excellent game. Hunting and fishing evidently too slow for this man geared to quick, spurting speed.

Batting averages, the scores, the form sheet, boxing, baseball and a host of other activities find him equipped with expert knowledge. Bridge finds him among the first five, but well behind Kramer or Hahn. There is no quicker eye or brain in Michigan City.

His energy and omnipresence may be explained by his total abstinence from smoking, and we believe drinking. A good personification of the Elk and at his best in distributing Christmas baskets.

An all around man splendidly adapted for the insurance business. A good mixer who is never boresome. An outspoken man, but most loyal to his friends and welcoming a chance enemy. Of course, he is popular and well-known. In the ring or on the diamond he would be in good condition at 160 pounds.

THE EVENING DISPATCH, MAY 10, 1929

———◆———

JOHNNIE GLASSCOTT

Newsboy, coal retail and wholesale, general insurance, —occasional dab into politics and the Board of Tax Reviews where he seemed imbued with the theory that the people of Laporte County and their interests are paramount to the State Tax Board. An eager and keen observer of the passerby on Franklin Street. A sharp critic with a biting tongue. "Uncle John" to many nephews and nieces in Michigan City, including some of those inevitable Kruegers.

Knows and calls every old timer in Michigan City by his or her first name. Knows every Beacon Light in this town and would probably have a more interesting opinion concerning many of them than has the writer. A too keen and sharp observer of men and institutions to be a lover of books or interested in gardens, hardly having time for those relaxations. A leavening influence in our party politics and usually against the "in". An impressive head.

Our track team fails to win a point at the chip off the old block". Looks like a judge. (?)der if this expensive privilege isn't one of the most prominent realtors.

THE EVENING DISPATCH, MAY 25, 1929

THOMAS GLASSCOTT

Living philosophy, not talking, or studying it. Wit and humor illuminating a calm, cheerful countenance. The most wealthy man in Michigan City because he seems the most happy and peaceful man in our town. Of sports and athletics he knows nothing, of politics and civics he knows enough. But of men and women in Michigan City he possesses the most exhaustive knowledge. Their genealogy, their foibles, their fancies seeming to pour into that sympathetic soul and there find a security as safe as those valuables in huge steel vaults. The man in the bank, with the countenance of a benevolent cleric. The man on the street or restaurant that everyone seems to know. Has he found the fountain of youth? Have strange gods whispered the lore of ages to him? He has it— success, contentment, happiness and peace. May he ever wend his happy way meeting welcoming smile with sympathetic understanding.

THE EVENING DISPATCH, MARCH 30, 1929

JIM GLEASON

An attorney that looks like Landis and on a city court bench is somehow reminiscent of Anderson. A Webster head on a Randolph body. Ex-Justice of the peace, ex-police reporter and once a poultry fancier. A "way back whenner" to the days of Cunningham and Harriet Cobb.

Arnold Bass

An exceptional eye for news. Throwing a heavy mane of hair back or stroking his chin are characteristic gestures. An eloquent tobacco chewer, but speaks clearly and with conviction. Sums up a case quickly, whether on the bench or at the bar. Must know everybody. Should be a Democrat, but hard to determine under this managerial cloud. Responsible for precedent bringing police court news to our front page.

THE EVENING DISPATCH, APRIL 6, 1929

ORPHIE GOTTO

A Viking giant, master of his fate, captain of his soul. Super-power impressions always surrounding him—as a speedy pitcher in baseball—carrying a bale of hay under each arm—or a small tree. Building not a home but groups of homes in a city, opening up new streets, tearing down hills, holding back a lake. Dazzling speed, overwhelming punch, stupendous weight.

A visionary with power to realize dreams. A heavyweight champion with great brawn and brain eternally driving to those dreams.

There is great promise in a region that can produce his kind. A man of limitless capacity, untiring energy and unflagging brain—a great wave soaring to the crest and crashing over and across any barrier or reef. Rifle with him to far off shores. The father of Long Beach beautiful, an ultra modern and friendly community.

Farmer, feed and coal merchant, subdivider, developer, home and town builder and ahead of him—who knows the thoughts, who can see the dreams of that blond giant, gazing from aloft through the clouds into dim beautiful vistas.

THE EVENING DISPATCH, MARCH 16, 1929

FRED GRIEGER

A suavity of speech and well-groomed dress mark him well. An intense Elk, pounding cross-country to a national convention and typifying the local spirit placing his lodge so high in Elkdom. A successful retail business man operating smoothly two haberdashery stores. He doesn't plead "Buy at home," but by service, price and quality causes you to do so. His stores reflect his own love of neatness and order.

His speech is careful, his ideals are high, his friends are many. Courtesy, sympathy and enthusiasm are his principal attributes. Motoring, movies, musical comedies offer their seductive lures to this receptive man. Hardier amusements seem to fall in attracting him.

THE EVENING DISPATCH, AUGUST 28, 1929

D. A. GUTGSELL

"Andy" to a host of friends. A good liaison man between bank and depositor. Fraternal honors have come in abundance to him, including state office as treasurer in a prominent organization. A charter member who can give an eloquent, vivid history of an organization to the boys at anniversary banquet.

A baseball crank, but explainable in knowing that he is a cousin of Connie Mack. Not politically-minded. Why, in the name of civic efficiency should a community be deprived of the services of so many able men connected with banks? We presume they know their business, but we sometimes doubt it. Andy, being good-natured will pardon this intrusion. Being modest, he will welcome this conclusion.

THE EVENING DISPATCH, MAY 27, 1929

"JAKE" HAHN

An analogy in contrast. A slow heavy body, a complacent, simple countenance, camouflaging the most alert, quick brain and wit. Once was sheriff but at his best when a free lance and not in office.

A natural genius at bridge, possessing real card sense but not so good at games requiring physical prowess. A Democrat who will always be at the hub of political things if not the real hub. Has peculiar a genius for turning a quick deal in business and politics, but possessed of a temperament turning him from any business requiring long unbroken and monotonous attention.

The ideal man to see when in trouble. Always clean minded. Abilities appreciated by his real intimates. For a conservative bidder makes the best bridge partner in Michigan City. Easily interested in any civic drive and a generous contributor in time and money. Chief lodge is the Elks.

Lives on a beautiful farm at Waterford, but the last man in the world you would expect on a farm.

May be trusted by a friend, respected by an enemy and feared by a politician.

THE EVENING DISPATCH, APRIL 16, 1929

ED HEISE.

Out of the north----a sailing vessel landed the Heise family years and years ago on our lake front. In that vicinity they have lived through three generations. With them a young man facing an epic struggle and overcoming poverty and physical handicap. The life of Ed Heise seems a miracle of accomplishment, of pluck, grit and faith in the face of discouraging odds.

Clear, steady eyes, a strong race, masterful hands, well-marked features, quick brain, confident vision, optimistic spirit, saving, thrifty, years of public service. An ideal clerk. How much more successful he has been than many a man able to walk, but not knowing how to direct his walk. Our city records are a permanent memorial of his intelligent service, but only in the hearts and minds of children of ancestors who saw that old family land here with Ed so many years ago can there be that full appreciation of his brave and successful life.

THE EVENING DISPATCH, JULY 17, 1929

———◆———

"Guss" (August C. Heitschmidt.)

Do you know of a more infectious laugh, a heartier handgrasp or "hello" than Gus? Can you ever measure the benefits his entire glad life has sbrought to Michigan City?

Dispelling gloom, dispensing cheer and good fellowship in every assembly, still Gus can be gracious, dignified and mighty serious and efficient where the occasion demands.

How well Gus has combined business and pleasure is seen in the long-established business he has developed in Michigan City, and the hosts of friends he has made. Whether selling farm implements, coal or feed or engaged in some civic enterprise, the personality of the man breeds good will in abundance and assures to him an easy success.

We have always envied that healthy, whole-souled laugh and have always enjoyed it. His habits, his custokms, his manner may easily be understood and read in a happy, contented home, a healthy business, a live "club", all reflecting one of the most pleasant characters that has ever brought friendship into our life,---August C. Heitschmidt.

GEORGE R. HILL

One of our very few C.P.A., which means that the bearer may be entrusted with your financial statements, income tax, in fact all of your records, and he will obtain order out of chaos. Naturally he must have patience and exact knowledge and complete grasp of, all methods of bookkeeping and auditing.

May be called Major, a title fairly earned by many an arduous training course through many a hot summer. He is a calm, cool and deliberate man, but oddly enough putting some needed fire in Rotary, over whose luncheon meetings he now presides. He is frequently mentioned as a desirable man for city manager, but, his own business is so successful and exacting that he cannot sacrifice the necessary time. Just there we find a frequent source of trouble in our civic affairs. The man that, the job seeks so seldom can afford to take the job.

A springy, light walk, a precise careful speech, deliberate and logical thought, mark him well. Keeps in good condition; 150 pounds, five foot ten inches, light hair, blue eyes, wears glasses. Dresses neatly and conservatively. Drives car cautiously and plays bridge in same manner.

THE EVENING DISPATCH, MARCH 20, 1929

HERB HIRSCHMAN

True history is not confined to kings. Beacon Lights must welcome Herb for Beacon Lights are true stories.

He is an enormous man. A Falstaffian impression surrounds him. He has fished a thousands streams and lakes; hunted and trapped with unfailing success over Canada, our resort regions.

He is a generous host and a companion always holding up his end. An enthusiastic sportsman and particularly adept at trap shooting. How much he could add to Beacon Lights if such revelations were proper. How well he knows how to prepare a mesh of frog legs or perch. Of course, he is generous and friendly and always good for a loan. He must know many hypocrites, but he is tolerant, friendly and quick to forgive and forget. One can relax and rest out there on Willard Avenue with Herb, and incidentally hear some mighty good fishing stories, but one must eventually come back to Franklin Street and "carry on."

THE EVENING DISPATCH, MAY 23, 1929

HOPE, CHARLEY AND "PETE"

Hope always in the middle, walking rapidly down Franklin or to the park, always together and always engaged in vigorous, rapid conversation. Have we a like trio of friends in Michigan City, so inseparable seeming to enjoy so well each other's company and understanding so well the likes and dislikes of the others. Three friends loving a warm argument, philosophizing bravely and accurately as most philosophers. Three neatly, soberly dressed, dependable, healthy citizens.

Wonder what they thought when pajamas were worn on Franklin street recently. You may be sure the matter was discussed by them. Tell me their opinion, on a candidate, on waterworks proposition, on taxes, on dress, morals or beach concessions, and I'll tell you the opinion of the public, the voter, the taxpayer of Michigan City. No installment payments worry that inimitable trio, no labor troubles, no fads or fancies.

Arnold Bass

One of them would surprise the stranger with a most versatile curiosa of knowledge. Find out by listening to the three of them in the cigar store. Anyone on north Franklin Street will direct you to a convenient chair where they met in council regularly.

THE EVENING DISPATCH, AUGUST 31, 1929

———◆———

GEORGE HUNZIKER.

The mail man! Is there a more important Beacon Light? One more faithful to his trust, or loyal to his employer? Through all weather and in all seasons year in and year out, such men are so well exemplified by the ideals and traditions of their service. No better type can be found to illustrate the caliber of such men than George Hunziker. An enormous stride, covering countless miles in a tireless never-varying schedule. Long arms guarding a valuable mail and making the trip on an unvarying, clocklike schedule. How many people he can call by their first name and we all hear a welcome response. City governments may change, but Hunziker never. Families move in and out, chain stores squeeze out the small proprietor, but Hunziker still carries on with that mail. Upstairs, downstairs, in and out a thousand doors, a thousand times, with important mail, with unimportant mail, with greetings, advertisements, with enormous heavy magazines. What patience, endurance and loyalty Hunziker and all mail men must possess. What happiness they must witness with their coming, and what tragedies as well. The anonymous letter, the invitation, the dun, the letter of increased assessment, the foreign letter, the business or social envelope. Wonder if Hunziker and other mail men wonder what is in those letters.

THE EVENING DISPATCH, MAY 3, 1929

———◆———

WILLIAM HUTCHINSON, SR

ng man of 50 years. A builder of roads and bridges totaling millions in cost, throughout Indiana, Michigan, and else where and an artist in concrete. Disdainful of the asthete but master of things practical. A widely traveled man. He can be most impulsive and most generous, and will interest himself in a political campaign and fight hard for a friend. A nasal twang gives great carrying power to a forceful and confident speech. A quick and alert brain constantly driving an energetic and healthy body. A real Democrat always voting the Republican ticket but never running for office. There was always the golden spoon, but there was always the virile youth and man ready and willing to rough it.

Has spent many of his years outside Michigan City, but is a man we would like to see Make Michigan City his home permanently.

THE EVENING DISPATCH, APRIL 29, 1929

REV. PAUL IRION

"Unpracticed he to fawn or seek for power by doctrines fashioned to the varying hour."

No, no, better his holy, practical, well-founded and sturdy sermons. Much better his eloquent, true sermons in German and English, the dual mastery of which he enjoys, whether in formal sermon or warm friendly conversations.

No pandering there to sensationalism, to titles sounding of tin-pan alley. No lurid speech arresting the eye or ear in a shocked attention. He is an alert minister of virile, uncolored personality. A stamp collector, well entitled to be called a philatelist.

He is a man knowing men, a book lover knowing books, a theologian practicing it. He is truly a reverent leader of a revering congregation ever sensing the sound inspiration of his spiritual guidance.

THE EVENING DISPATCH, JULY 5, 1929

GEORGE JOHNSON

Shop, factory superintendent, real estate, insurance, bank director and president of our largest building and loan association. A lifetime in Michigan City and a life of self-education, progress and improvement, ripening into a cultured, poised product. A hard working man who has yet been able to take an active, if not a leading part, in many fraternal activities and various civic enterprises. Conservatism, caution and deliberation are striking characteristics.

Democratic politics have known his honorable association with a mutual benefit. A long life of good memories and still securely fixing and adapting himself to the future.

THE EVENING DISPATCH, MARCH 21, 1929

EDWARD KELLEHER.

Perfect symmetry of body working in perfect harmony with an alert brain. A model of enduring, untiring energy on a handball or tennis court. Another All-American in football or what have you but lost to the colegiate world because of economic necessity. Camp's daily dozens would never give that splendid animal a work out. How well he proves the necessity of health to complete enjoyment of life.

Arnold Bass

In the middle forties and yet as quick, active and agile as any man of twenty. An auditor who should have trained for the movies. Another insistance of splendid material for public office lost because of our rigid statutes limiting holders to residents within corporate boundaries. Good nature, tolerance and patience of the man so well exemplified in his willingness to play volley ball with men of forty who are fat.

THE EVENING DISPATCH, JULY 1, 1929

———◆———

DOCTOR KERRIGAN.

Way back in the horse and buggy age over there in Chicago a young physician and surgeon with a wife and five children is induced to locate in Michigan City. We know not the reason for his decision but believe our lives in Michigan City have been made a little more pleasant because of the gracious sympathy, the courteous kindness and the friendly contacts with the Kerrigan family.

The long professional career of the senior doctor has always been marked by his skillful, patient care and his keen, searching diagnosis at bedside or surgical, table. Despite the exacting demands of a busy profession he has found time to cultivates literature, science and the arts and in the particular field of history has acquired a unique and masterful grasp of this fascinating subject. Their ardent study is reflected in the tentative memory and brilliant conversation of the senior doctor.

May far-off twilight find him still adding luster to a great professional name and ever knowing the contentment and peace flowing from a useful life, cultivated mind and kind heart.

THE EVENING DISPATCH, APRIL 26, 1929

———◆———

WESLEY R. KIBBY

A man of action whose mannerisms sometimes remind us of the characters in the stories about the mounted police of the Northwest. Probably because he himself is a product of the north woods timber region. Practical, efficient, level-headed, a good judge of men.

Probably to his and the community's best interests that he, as chief of police, is not of the glad hand political type. The chief may thus unwittingly avoid entangling alliances. Is fearless, has plenty of nerve, possesses a powerful physique. Not a propagandist who can sell the idea of more and better equipment for his department, rather the type to make the best out of what he has and ready to give extended service when more equipment is provided.

Hobbies—Boy Scouts and the zoo.

UP CLOSE AND PERSONAL

THE EVENING DISPATCH, MAY 22, 1929

——◆——

"KING"

Newspaper reporter, co-partner in publication of newspaper. His nickname of mysterious origin. President of the Chamber of Commerce. Will never be stampeded by ballyhoo or by yells or flag waving.

Practical and successful, ever learning and observing. Most likable trait is a refusal to take himself too seriously combined with a refreshing sense of humor. Goes fishing without real enjoyment; a better traveler as witnessed by his surprising talk on "Keeping up with Evangeline," an inexplicable subject for a man who would have been expected to return with a treatise on paper making. But more understandable when we appreciate his evolution to philosophy.

Always a Republican but conversion to city manager form again reveals the gropings of a mind for a higher expression. A pleasant table companion and a better loser at any game than at politics. Will never lose in any business deal.

An interested and consistent reader and admirer of Dispatch editorials.

THE EVENING DISPATCH, MAY 1, 1929

——◆——

JOE KISTLER.

Clogged sewers, congested alleys, broken bridges, or any trouble meant a call on him as the head of our street and garbage departments. Lacking responsible guidance he still seems to possess qualities of leadership that well dispenses with the necessity of a boss. He is an omnipresent, untiring, hurrying man doing his work under disheartening conditions of disunity, dissention and irresponsibility among some of those officials and employes with whom he serves the public.

He will keep his word. He will not merely "Yes" you or put some figures in a notebook, but he will clean out that alley or sewer, fix that bridge or relieve that emergency as soon and as well as ways and means at his disposal permit. Of course, he is physically and mentally alert with no fat on brain or body, or he'd never be able to accomplish the work he does.

A fast walker with a short stride, he is pretty much "on the go" and is unafraid to tackle any job or accept any responsibility.

THE EVENING DISPATCH, JULY 8, 1929

——◆——

HARRY KRAMER

From Sloppy Joe's to local Elk's boxing bout and always that same trim, neat unruffled appearance. Sells groceries, but we never understood why. A good judge of men and markets. Through a long series will beat any man or woman in Michigan City at bridge. Once our county champion at pool; knows well such games as pinochle or poker. He never indulges in any form of physical exercise and flashing eye, perfect teeth, steady hand, nerve and brain are all that of a man in perfect physical condition. Will go to New York or Reno to attend a champion "set-up." will bet a reasonable sum on his judgment, be it football, boxing or stocks. Approaching the cynic in his keen insight of men and motives, but saved by a sense of humor. A boom ever hitting Michigan City would find him dropping his groceries and easily riding the wave.

THE EVENING DISPATCH, APRIL 30, 1929

———◆———

LEON KRAMER.

Keeping to the front one of the oldest established businesses in Laporte County. A typical product of families giving to the twentieth century our Frederick Wildes and Marcossens in journalism, as well as leaders in industry or business. About our first president of the Chamber of Commerce, and at one time or another the captain, head or chairman of most of our organized movements. He is generally credited with a leading part in the building of the Spaulding Hotel.

Shocked county politicians with his frankness and business ability as a member of the county council. Reputed to have receptive ear of banker and business. Can be devastating in argument, but one never doubts his stand, the sincerity of it or his ability to defend himself.

He and his brother, Harry, one of the most popular pair of brothers in Laporte County.

THE EVENING DISPATCH, APRIL 23, 1929

———◆———

FRANK OR JOE KREBS

The hopelessness of their separate identity prompts joint treatment of them, under their usual title "those Krebs brothers." Discreetly they have each refrained from marriage, tastefully they both dress alike, walk and talk alike, smoothly and successfully they conduct a partnership business. One of them, either Joe or Frank drives the car, demonstrating and selling, while either Joe or Frank watches the garage and radio business.

Both of them usher, sing, eat, play and work side by side through the years. What companionable brothers they have been.

Each can and will answer for the other. Fortunately they are never in trouble and imagine the difficulty of identifying either one of them with any certainty.

Heights identical, both smiling blonds and combing their hair alike, wearing the same clothes, shoes, socks—a baffling similarity in build, appearance, dress customs and manners. It may even be seen in their speech, reflected in their thoughts, observed in their actions. Both progressive, energetic and popular, demonstrating real aggressiveness in business and power of initiative and courage.

May they ever live together, in single blessedness, enjoying life in the pursuit of happiness?

THE EVENING DISPATCH, MARCH 27, 1929

ERNEST KROLL

Ex-restaurateur and buffet proprietor of Ernie's place, once our best known habitat of men about town. A pragmatic liberal, unafraid, enduring, blunt and direct. An ex-sheriff coming back for another try at it and never, never underestimate the vote getting possibilities of Ernie, because he can work hard and tirelessly and knows so many voters intimately. He is a generous spender and a vigorous, campaigner.

Hunting and fishing are his zealous, experienced pursuits. Valuable real estate and easily carried responsibility. He will go far for a friend and will not back up for an enemy. He has never refused to subscribe or donate to any local drive.

THE EVENING DISPATCH, AUGUST 7, 1929

"EMIL." (KRUEGER)

Still "Emil" to those of us who in far off days once struggled behind him on his black pony, and helped him drive a herd of cows from town to pasturage at Hanson's, who swam and played in Trail creek through a delightful summer day with him, and who Emil may have lifted onto that black pony for a ride with him--but Dr. Emil Krueger to most of us, welcoming his swift response to our bedsides and his quick efficient diagnosis and treatment. Dr. Krueger, honored in his profession and respected by all, and through many long days and nights meeting the great demands of his clientele. Driving himself fiercely and unrelentlessly and with only the occasional stolen hour in darkened "movie" for brief rest and relaxation, and that, so often broken, by that usher with his "Dr. Krueger wanted on the phone."

THE EVENING DISPATCH, MARCH 19, 1929

MARTIN T. KRUEGER

For over half a century Martin T. Krueger as mayor, lawyer and orator has loomed most prominently in our community affairs.

Practical efficiency, aggressive intelligence and exhaustive knowledge have always characterized his display of many versatile activities. His political and professional career did not exhaust the range of his surprising capacity. The gentler arts and sciences found in him an apt and sympathetic exponent. Horticulture, forestry, history and literature as well knew his practical mastery and we so well remember his seemingly inexhaustible fund of anecdotes and stories delivered in an inimitable style and force.

A review of his life, its wide scope and range would trace the career of a determined youth, deprived of all educational facilities but acquiring by observation, study, experience and naive intelligence, an exceptional education.

As his tremendous voice dominated any assembly, so his tremendous ability dominated for over half a century the political history of Michigan City. To his credit must we place our lake front park, saved by his vision and foresight for future generations. To him and his generosity we owe Memorial Park, a fitting memorial of this great citizen who so well understood woods. To him we owe a spirit of independence and freedom that never lost sight of the individual in his freedom and liberty.

No citizen of Michigan City has done more to save for perpetuation our lore of local history, and no one has done more to inculcate in us a keen appreciation and knowledge of our early customs and manners.

Pioneer, yet most modern; unschooled, yet most educated; gruff, aggressive yet most gentle and sympathetic. What an interesting, intense life he has led and how much he has influenced the mind and history of Michigan City.

THE EVENING DISPATCH, MARCH 5, 1929

MIKE KRUEGER

"The sleepless shoe man." What a slogan or nickname to live up to and yet how seriously and successfully he seems to be doing it. From nothing but a job to the owner and proprietor of a business located in his own corner building on Franklin Street. The usual and sure result of work, or better, "not sleeping on the job." Hurrying back and forth on Franklin Street, scurrying in a busy store, rushing to lunch, has he time for recreation or relaxation, for games, the theater or sports? Or does he usually sleep when his store is closed?

He is pleasant enough and will readily engage in a conversation but one feels his urge to trim that window, rush that copy to the press or re-arrange and therefore one proceeds to go

UP CLOSE AND PERSONAL

his lazy, slow way in a vague wonderment at the urge and drive forcing Mike to live up to that slogan "The sleepless shoeman."

THE EVENING DISPATCH, JULY 29, 1929

———◆———

PAUL A. KRUEGER

A poet lacking the ability, to rhyme. A lover of beauty, first editions, and old books. Has a varied and interesting background. See him now miles out in the breakers of Like Michigan, then as the "Red Grange" of Michigan City High School, a football star of real ability who disappointed many friends by not going out for the Michigan team. Next playing the zither in a Schutzenfetz park. Probably our only resident who ever attended national zither convention

Mexican border, World War. First commander of legion post in Michigan City. A good lawyer, with land titles his hobby. An ardent foe of prohibition, but made ardent and active as a supporter of law enforcement. Author of "Crime in Laporte County," first and oily editions of which are not yet in demand.

Terrible bridge—fair golf and good handball. An ideal candidate for our library board. Falsely accused of editorial propensities. Even tempered and calm all times. Probably the best educated man in Michigan City.

THE EVENING DISPATCH, MARCH 18, 1929

———◆———

LOUIS E. KUNKEL.

Grades, high school, Lewis Institute, Michigan university, Evanston and back to practice in his own town, a successful, experienced and capable lawyer approaching his prime. Generally wears glasses, but always ready to take them off. Handy with his fists, his rod or his dog. Forceful in measure as he warms to his subject. Can and will work hard but insistent on right to play hard. Analyzes a bridge hand better than anyone we know, but ranks only ninth or tenth in playing ability. Needs a partner of the Kramer type.

Ideal prosecutor and not to be stamped. Will go the limit for a friend; an undesirable foe. Takes Michigan "U" and its traditions rather too seriously for his own comfort in this day of Gip, Grange and the Four Horsemen.

Loyalty and friendship come easily to him. Can rise to heights of legal resourcefulness, eloquence and energy when and only when his sympathies are fully aroused.

THE EVENING DISPATCH, APRIL 15, 1929

JOHN LASS.

Insists on pronunciation as if spelled Lash with "a" soft as in "far". Military carriage, close clipped head of hair. Erect, trim, hurried walker, incessant smoker of Richmond Straights, that no one will ever borrow.

A suburbanite with five acres. Michigan City misses, however, that old horse and buggy.

Emphatic speech, rising to height of power and almost choking with the inspiration of volcanic zeal. The law finds him an able, well-rounded exponent, alive to best traditions. Many clients attest his loyalty to their interests. "Anything new?" is most characteristic.

Imagine, reader, you trying to go into foreign country like Russia or Poland, and not only mastering an alien language, but a profession. John Lass, (with two dots on the a) has done just that.

THE EVENING DISPATCH, APRIL 25, 1929

DR. LEDBETTER.

Franklin Street must mean a great deal to him, he owns so many buildings on it, from the heart of our business district south to another long series of neighborhood stores, and farther on to a wide stretch of residential property. His own beautiful home logically faces on the street in which he has invested heavily.

His honorable profession and business career in Michigan City has brought success to him and surcease from labor. But to rest or to relax he strangely roams from high mountain top to the big fishing grounds of America. To the keen eye and keener brain, to his gun and rod have fallen the elusive mountain goat, the unbelievable tarpon. There only remains untouched the Safari trail and the greatest of all game.

Golf and bridge have always found in him an adapt bringing to them the same pose, judgment and trained mind and body so efficient in everything he touches.

THE EVENING DISPATCH, MAY 16, 1929

CHARLES LEIST.

Presents the anachronism of a professed and an honorable, as well an honored, politician, as commissioner under city manager form of government.

UP CLOSE AND PERSONAL

He is a representative of a pioneer family in Michigan City. Woodworker cabinet maker, expert carpentry, installer of modern plate glass fronts, with an occasional surprising foray into the field of invention. The exactness, accuracy, fineness of eye and touch required of him in his work must reflect the qualities of his brain and nerve.

Being a practical politician, of course he makes a practical commissioner. Not swayed by fanaticism nor moved by the impractical or Utopian fancies of the visionary. Chews tobacco, and how many practical men and safe men do.

He has a distinct, clear voice, a cool brain, a wiry body, a grayish, wrinkled countenance characteristic of men whose work demands fine, accurate instruments and machines.

Could be re-elected to the city commission without effort on his part. Would make a mighty good city manager because he is on the square and practical.

THE EVENING DISPATCH, MARCH 29, 1929

———◆———

HERB LEVIN.

A wholesale distributor of newspapers and magazines. A long experience in the clothing and haberdashery business as well. A generous impulsive and loyal man, and a friendly man. Not a "yes" man, but sincere and honest.

Of solid build, curly hair, florid complexion, a heavy walker. A man quickly flashing a friendly smile or a hearty laugh. Easily imposed upon by drives and campaign solicitations. Will readily accept his share of civic responsibilities and will heartily discharge any assigned work.

Prominent in Rotary work and most sincere in observing all its proud ideals. A lover of music. A man always ready to help the young man to get a start. Democratic in temperament and by tradition.

THE EVENING DISPATCH, APRIL 22, 1929

———◆———

FRANK LINDNER.

The tall, romantic lover of out door sports, deliberately tying himself down to an old oaken desk filing cabinets, maps and office of an automobile insurance agency. Will a 300 yard drive or a hurtling auto drive calm its repressed urge? Will a made-to-measure suit, a home complete in Edgewood Beautiful hold him to membership campaigns? Evidently, if strangely, they do and he has succeeded well.

But if ever strange winds call, let him hire a horse, throw gayly colored coat o'er lithe shoulders, grab one of the major's swords, and even his Ko-Ko Bowl. Let him gallop wildly over dunes and dales. He will come back contented, to the mild marts of trade and to the auto game in the Peoples State Bank Building.

He sings his "Hello" with a gay, abandoned gesture, strides furiously when not driving so. His business seems rushing ahead with that same speed.

THE EVENING DISPATCH, AUGUST 30, 1929

———◆———

L. W. MACK.

About our only alumnus from Bucknell. Industrial chemist, always industriously smoking that inevitable pipe. A zealous worker in Boy Scout activities. His poise, appearance, sincerity and idealism make him a most excellent judge in a court of honor for Boy Scouts, awarding medals in degrees and in inspirational addresses.

He is an ex-member of our School Board, good vote-getting material for public office. Wholesale distribution of magazines a lucrative side line. Would rather be called a civic worker than a politician, but there shouldn't be any distinction.

He is wealthy in a most charming, talented and gracious family circle. His walk should be proud and contented. If eventually drafted for commissioner he will be disillusioned for future public service.

THE EVENING DISPATCH, JULY 24, 1929

———◆———

"STILL BILL" (W. B. MANNY)

He found this a tough lake port where wild Irishmen and wilder Germans were fighting for supremacy. He must have been hard fisted and tough skinned himself, so, looking for forier conquests, found a field of battle with untamed railroad men to his better liking.

Even now when the occasion permits, it is said by a shocked and admiring listener, that he can climb to the heights with most exquisite oaths, reminiscent of dock-wallopers, railroad man and sailor.

Any man capable of handling longshoremen and working his way up to high rank in railroad circles was naturally our choice for our first city manager.

Keenly, quickly and competently he ruled the roost and for a brief golden period Michigan City had business at the helm of things.

"W. B." roams far to all points of the compass and travels with characteristic benefits to himself and to his listeners, eagerly enjoying his travel topics.

Is he successful? There is not a man in Michigan City we would sooner entrust with our investments. His politics probably republican, although he talks like a democrat. His business—telegrapher, railroad commercial agents, real estate and easily drifting to capitalist, or syndicate. He will fit into any heights of business career.

Habits, customs and manner are most independent, self-sufficient, care free and generus—that's W. B. Manny.

THE EVENING DISPATCH, JULY 29, 1929

DOC MARR.

On executive committee appearing as precinct committeeman for the third precinct of the first ward. This marks the extent of his political activity. However, busy dentist with the inside tract on Saturday Evening Posts, always trying to get it before the release hour.

Light, fast walker, overflowing with stories. Witty and humorous, soft spoken, nervous laugh. Eats noon lunch at the Elks. Tried golf, but too impatient. Early radio enthusiast, once trying for distance, but now settled down to chain programs. Always knows latest song from latest musical comedy. Will attend any exhibition where action is furious, with preference for comedy.

Impossible at bridge, but one of our best pinochle players. Desirable in any company. Threatened with boredom by stilted steady conversation, Doc Marr will speed up the tempo.

A terror as chairman of the lapsation committee of the local lodge of Elks.

THE EVENING DISPATCH, MAY 21, 1929

CLARENCE MATHIAS.

Carrying On to completeness the dreams of Gotto. Master of the details of the organization and of the systematic plan so necessary to carrying out such dreams. An ideal partner and associate for that dreamer, slapping a canvas with a huge, broad brush. "Mat" completes the picture.

We have never seen him on Franklin street without that well-worn wallet. He is always scurrying and hurrying from office and bank and back to the community of beautiful homes. An invaluable man in any civic enterprise and active in Chamber of Commerce work, bringing to these activities that same driving power that has aided in building Long Beach.

There is little time for sports in the life of such a man, but he can play a good game of handball. How much men of his type may be responsible for the growth and development of a city.

The history of Long Beach and its transformation from a bleak sand dune region into a beautiful community center is so inextricably tied up with such men as Clarence L. Mathias. Their reward will not only be in a material gain, but in pleasing memories in that dim future when they, too, look back o'er the unfolding of that dune chrysalis into a flashing picture of glorious beauty.

THE EVENING DISPATCH, MAY 31, 1929

Arnold Bass

———◆———

EDWARD MCLUNDIE.

Bridge, golf, riding, boys' band, manufacturer. Passing at the first two, somewhat better at riding. Organized and maintained a boys' band in Michigan City as his proud contribution to our civil life. Successful at manufacturing, making and keeping friends.

Ideal build and poise for committees. Civic enterprises need his business acumen and judgment. Beach and town homes. Motoring in luxurious cars his hobby and real pleasure.

Thought the Scotch were mighty close, but wish Michigan City had more men of his stamp. Bank directorates find him desirable on their boards. Well-planned committees will seek his aid and co-operation.

Chuckles cheerfully and easily. Thinks and talks cleanly and clearly. Lives temperately and sanely.

THE EVENING DISPATCH, JULY 26, 1929

———◆———

VINCENT MILCAREK.

A hurrying, go-getting contractor able and ready to jump to the pit and work with any of his men. Sidewalks, sewers, paving—cement and universal application his particular field of work. Real estate and banking interest substantial. His business experience most ample. Pursuits and hobbies seem limited to the work he so joyously plunges into.

His voice rings with the good health and sturdy vigor he knows. Affable and friendly is he in his greeting to all. Braving all weather or hazards he always finishes his contracts within the allotted time. One of our few citizens who can boast a private fish pond, tennis courts and park. Active and energetic in any movement with which he becomes associated.

No one in Michigan City knows better the courses of our underground percolating water and no one more quickly or efficiently places them under control in order that construction may proceed.

THE EVENING DISPATCH, JULY 3, 1929

———◆———

FRED C. MILLER.

A well-known attorney, in explaining his statement that he preferred to be a city attorney under Fred C. Miller to any other man stated, "His long experience as mayor, councilman and knowledge of municipal matters has given him an unusual grasp of the subject. Working under him would be easy compared with being under most mayors. He is practical, conservative and above all possesses an exceptional gift for organization."

Fred C. Miller will readily admit the appellation of politician and his many friends will as readily prove that he was a good one and at the same time a good public official, rising high above the level of some present incumbents in public office who think they are business men.

Mr. Miller has known and fought fanaticism, hypocrisy and insincerity with an admirable calmness and patience. He has known the epic struggle of any man rising from poverty to a safe competency. As a dock walloper he was the man of strength and brawn, able to lift a barrel of sugar and soon rising from the ranks to leadership.

As councilman and mayor he always accepted responsibility. Many victories came to him and defeat as well, but all were met with that same calm, phlegmatic spirit that never has deserted him. An able foe of city manager form of government and how puzzled he must be at this Utopian form so permeated and broken out with politicians calling themselves business men and politics under the smug title of business.

Between public appearances Fred relaxes in the operation and control of substantial insurance and real estate business. He owns one of the few flagpoles maintained on private residences and each legal holiday will find the flag of our country proudly displayed thereon. Of many of our citizens, talking so much of their patriotism, this cannot be said.

THE EVENING DISPATCH, MARCH 25, 1929

---◆---

HENRY MILLER.

A Saturday's shopping tour sees Henry at his best. A fast walking man, ever ready to break in a run. Cutting and wrapping meat furiously and at the same time maintaining a running conversation with any or all of his customers.

Does he ever play or rest? There may be a rare motoring trip or an occasional evening at the Elks' club, of which he is a past exalted ruler. But mostly that man has been too busy, even for marriage

An inherited business has been by him modernized and energized to take care of a tremendous business from city and summer resort. A smile and a good laugh come easily from this cheerful man. He has taken fishing trips, but we believe in a rather hurried fashion, and always ready to cut them short so that he may return to his shop.

Work certainly his habit, his pleasure, and his most striking characteristic. His customers mostly call him Henry. His business is as tidy and clean as the man and as solid and certain.

THE EVENING DISPATCH, MARCH 15, 1929

JOHN D. MOORMAN.

There's gold in that determined jaw, heavy hand and level eye. There's fortune in that all-embracing and inclusive personality, and there is the ability to appreciate the things that gold brings in a cultured mind and healthy body. Politics, civics, financing, vocal quartets, volley ball, books, autos, suburban home, lobbying, bonds, oil—they all know him and obey him. Treasurer, executive, bass voice—what's down there in Knox that produces such men as Kramer, Fletcher and the Moormans? Such careful judgment, wise planning, certainty, confidence and success. Would one acquire such elements by being there a few months? But anyway, we vote with John, buy his bonds, enjoy that bass voice, ride with him and always marvel at the inevitability of him.

THE EVENING DISPATCH, JULY 2, 1929

ED MORAN.

Hurried, nervous, quick walking and talking. One of our leading druggists for many years. An attractive gay personality, a neat energetic man and with a most inimitable gift for mimicry. His conversations are enlivened by an empathic gesture and illustrated by that great fund of anecdotes.

We can't imagine him reading a book or playing a game of cards. That ready tongue and flashing brain are not to be so tied down. He is at his most likable best in a social group where stories are in order and where his story, illustrated by that flare for mimicry always satisfies and always pleases. In them and in such pleasant groups he finds his hobby and relaxation.

Never seen on a golf course or engaged in any athletic activity. He will however, go to a boxing bout or a musical comedy or to any attraction where the action is fast and furious. Always well-groomed from well-shod feet to the crown of his hat or derby. Cigarettes more to his liking than cigars.

In a corner drug store for many years and naturally knows everything that is going on.

THE EVENING DISPATCH, MAY 11, 1929

MOE MORITZ.

From 1865 to 1928 a name of great importance to the mercantile and commercial history of Michigan City. A name honored by Moe Moritz, a genial, quiet man of so much smooth efficiency.

His retirement from Franklin Street business gives us cumulative evidence of the change from home owned and controlled business to the great chain store systems. His retirement finds us vaguely regretful and puzzled at the effect of this trend. What is the real effect upon our community of the loss to our business world of such men as Moe Moritz? His soft voice, kindly smiling countenance, friendly eye and sympathetic interest are unforgettable, and Franklin Street will always have need of such attributes. We would like to see him in business again on that street that knew his name so well for more than 60 years. We need him on our important committees' on never-ending drives and in our many civic enterprises. We need his calm, cool judgment, his sound sure opinion, and his controlled and measured speech.

THE EVENING DISPATCH, MAY 9, 1929

---◆---

J. P. MORLEY.

Co-owner of one of Laporte's best factories, but loyally retaining his residence in Michigan City. Zealous yet gentle, successful yet unobtrusive, patriotic yet voting, industrious yet relaxing frequently in motor car behind liveried chauffeur on motor trips.

Most courteous and friendly and above all, loyal to his friends. His charities are considerable and yet so little known because of an innate reserve that seeks to conceal.

Knows well his Constitution, both of state and nation and discharges cheerfully his duties and appreciates his-rights as a citizen.

THE EVENING DISPATCH, JULY 23, 1929

---◆---

THOMAS C. MULLEN.

In his middle thirties and able to say through a successful legal career "ex-city attorney, ex-acting city manager, ex-school board, ex-chairman and ex-commander."

A big man with an easy voice and a valuable counsellor at law or business. With an acknowledged genius for organization and complete mastery of detail.

There is a good man with executive ability for chairmanship of a drive. So many of our civic enterprises, so many of our municipal offices have known his facile management and his keen sense of responsibility and efficiency. To him may be attributed the restoration of football

Arnold Bass

in high school athletics, the acquisition of Ames Field. For formal and ceremonial occasions Thomas C. Mullen is proper, but fifty percent know him as Carlon.

An experienced and able lawyer, a pleasing speaker. A convivial spirit but under good self-control.

A six-foot, 200 pounder in our golden age of city manager government responsible for the creation and origination of various departments impressing upon them the foundation principles of government on a business basis.

Relaxes at bridge and table. At one time, before the era of Boy Scouts, was considered Michigan City's best freight hopper. Has seen much of the country via "Blind Baggage." Not athletically minded. Enjoys a book on the Civil War period and brings it to the judgment and sympathy of a World War Veteran. A better zoologist, than horticulturist.

THE EVENING DISPATCH, APRIL 17, 1929

PETE OHMING.

Another man whose nickname reveals his popularity. A tall, thin man, never smokes or drinks. A druggist with that chain store trend. His right name Harry Ohming, but one doubts whether he would answer to the name of Harry or not.

Will be seen at the ringside of any important bout, either wrestling or boxing within many miles. Knows baseball very well and most other games, but just a fair bridge player, working too hard to give this game its required study.

Well-tailored and scrupulously neat at all times. A great capacity for detail, order and system.

On the payroll for many years as one of our most successful and efficient township trustees. A Democrat too, by the way, and always in the innercouncils of the party. The kind of a man that a defendant wants on his bond and can usually get, because Pete will go down the line for a friend.

Possesses business judgment and ability of a high order and the rare ability to work hard and long.

THE EVENING DISPATCH, MARCH 22, 1929

JAMES H. ORR.

Clean, bright eyed, pleasing smile, a well-groomed man, carrying on and building up for a third generation one of the oldest business firms in the country, J. H. Orr & Son. This man, easily qualified as an expert in many branches of insurance. Well established commercial law business and considerable probate practice also demand much of him. He a courteous man, needing no standards or guides in business or service. Beyond that, seemingly innate and instinctive with him, he is one of our persistent pedestrians, with no particular desire for athletics except as an enthusiastic onlooker. He possesses a genuine love of books and knowledge of literature inherited from a father who was our first real book collector. His judgment on a book is sound and reliable. Our Country club, School Board of Long Beach, and the Elks have known the gracious poise and helpful influence of this man so easily called a gentleman. No more likeable personality to be met on Franklin Street and few men more favorably and widely known in the business and professional life of the city.

THE EVENING DISPATCH, APRIL 3, 1929

"PEP" (WORTH PEPPLE)

Was ever nickname more spontaneous uttered and on a more fitting subject than Worth Pepple.

There has always been a dash and sparkle about this man. There has always hovered about him the expectancy of something spectacular, and he never disappoints.

A thrilling one-handed stop in baseball—rapid-firing devastating cross-examination, crushing a stubborn witness—the brilliant handling of a large assembly.

Honors have come easily to him and have been even more easily deserved. The vibrant, flashing eyed youth, singing a dazzling tenor, of course—then the spirited eloquent lawyer convincing and winning with ease—now the lawyer that "look like a lawyer,"—a striking mane of white hair and still those eyes of brilliance, reflecting sharp, alive brain.

A splendid physical specimen, a pulsating human dynamo, verily "Pep" is his right name.

Call it luck to win in a flash where we ordinary mortals must plod for years. Call it whatever you may, but best to call it "Pep". That best explains his charm, his success, his ability. But know him as resourceful, able lawyer, quick, competent and always interesting. Know him for the logical governor not only of a mere luncheon club, but of a state that, needs the color, the vibrancy and spirit of Worth Pepple.

THE EVENING DISPATCH, MARCH 6, 1929

HERBERT PETERSON.

Grit and perseverance overcoming lack of early technical training, enabling him to acquire engineering knowledge after his world war service, and fitting him for important engineering Work. A trained engineer, licensed now to practice his profession in Indiana, and by experience and training acquiring an exceptional knowledge of pavement and sewer construction. County and city engineering have both known his zealous and efficient service. He is a careful worker, his surveys are dependable and his contract estimates are most accurate.

His hobby is fishing in the streams and lakes of Laporte County. Caught 108 bass in the season of 1928, not in far off resorts but near his own home and entirely within this county. Fishing with such experts is still seen to be good even in our own county.

Tall and lean, well-fitted for the rigors of field surveying and engineering. Making progress because he has caught the necessity of never letting up but is always studying and learning.

THE EVENING DISPATCH, AUGUST 14, 1929

———◆———

JOHN POLSON.

To him has come the distinctive and rare honor of dining with the three
Presidents of these, the United States of America. Reason---his zeal and interest in waterways, inland or Canadian routes. His usual habit of thrift will break down when there is question of talking or promoting these waterways.

Of him may also be said that he has attended more meetings of our council and commission as a plain spectator than anyone else in Michigan City.

"Polsonville" recognizes his ownership of a group of 40 or 50 dwellings in the south end of town. Rather a good showing for a man who landed in Michigan City homeless, penniless and hungry years and years ago.

He is a keen shopper for bargains. He is his own carpenter, mason, plumber and builder and his homes shows that, he is an exceptional Jack-of-all-trades. John welcomes a fight in protection of his rights or interests and he is always ready to take up a campaign for waterways. His voice is usually rising to a high pitch as he warms up to his subject.

Complexion quite florid, a shrewd countenance, white hairs, a healthy old man, who may yet see his cherished dream of a deep sea water route with terminal at Michigan City, but under a Democratic administration.

THE EVENING DISPATCH, MARCH 23, 1929

———◆———

"THE MAJOR". (GEORGE REDPATH)

A looming personality, contact with which breeds a composite impression of Custer, Buffalo Bill and Pershing. An ideal military impression which for perfect harmony in life requires a setting on some tall bluff astride his brave charger, and surrounded by his staff, watching and directing a battle in the Valley far below.

Finding a livery stable or a farm with that same military directness and efficiency soon leaves them, an income producing property and George Redpath is free to conquer other worlds.

Extensive far-East travel and his colorful eloquent description makes available one of our best and most popular travelogues. Thoroughness and imagination help him form a collection of small arms, antique weapons, curios, that under his powers of exposition live again their dramatic associations.

The celebrities of the world have drunk from his Ko-Ko bowl, a typical symbol of the man and his picturesque imagination. Charm and graciousness, abide in his beautiful home and happy family.

There is sustained interest in his ripened years of experience. There is surging drama in his travels and there is authority in his speech.

THE EVENING DISPATCH, APRIL 11, 1929

GEORGE O. REED.

Can afford Tuxedo, but prefers high leather boots and reefer or sweater. A practical man, a business getter, "smooth guy". The construction of bridges and breakwaters or municipal projects between here and Florida his vocation. Casually leaves a crowd or lunch and starts for a trip to Florida, back next week.

Will place in first ten as raconteurs, but far below his brother Art in that accomplishment. A hard driver of himself and an easy boss, but getting the work from men.

Puts punch in a political campaign as organization man, but never runs for office himself. Would make a good city manager. He is a solid looking man with a complexion bronzed by long exposure to the elements. He is man of excellent habits, with an occasional Coca Cola his only dissipation. His tastes are simple. He likes to visit and talk with men of politics or stories, sports, or even bridge.

THE EVENING DISPATCH APRIL 2, 1929

HERMAN REGLIEN

Grips a cigar like Yost. Runs a laundry as if determined to make it pay. Walks hard and heavily with air of going some place. He must know everyone in Michigan City.

A son at Michigan caused him to become interested in football, but as a baseball fan with a leaning to the Cubs he is in his real element.

Carries well his poundage and enjoying vigorous health, a busy life and a contented philosophy.

Another one of the many good men mentioned in Beacon Lights as excellent material for public office, but they don't seem interested. We'd vote for Herman, though perish the thought, for the largest laundry in this vicinity is also a jealous mistress, requiring an undivided attention and care.

THE EVENING DISPATCH, JULY 18, 1929

———◆———

FRANK ROGERS.

In twenty years he can double for Lawyer Tut. Not as our local antiquarian, but he of Saturday Evening Post fame.

Tall, lean and lanky, dressing well and carefully. Has taken a successful fling at politics and discharged most competently and courteously the duties of Clerk of our Circuit Court. Has also sold many thousand pairs of shoes in a former period of retail merchandizing. Has hunted and fished through many woods and over many lakes and streams.

Now has drifted into law with characteristic suavity and assurance. Speaks with an appearance of selecting his words cautiously and expecting to find them in clouds, but effectively and carrying conviction.

Way back whenners will recognize in him the Weir resemblance. He knows the ropes, will cover a lot of ground and fight for a client and stick to him.

THE EVENING DISPATCH, JULY 24, 1929

———◆———

GEORGE P. ROGERS.

A cool, analytical mind, systematic, orderly and neat. Dress and habits in harmony. A cutting sardonic humor, conservative, strongly Republican by tradition but too intellectual to be too partisan.

Always furnishing a needed brake to over-enthusiasm and ballyhoo in gatherings, public assemblies or in business. Must be shown in black and white, but once convinced can demonstrate great determination and ability.

An efficiency and auditing expert with a bend for architecture approaching genius, if leaning, however, to the English type.

Able to fortify his tendencies by extensive argument and proof. Supporter of amateur athletics, golf enthusiast, pool and three cushion. Also bridge. An able exponent of any game requiring keenness of eye and neatness of mind and stroke. Can be caustic critic as well as a warm supporter. Reserved and aloof from the crowd, but an enjoyable companion, wearing well when once known.

Freed from financial worries, of course. Most excellent for trustee, bank director and the like. Gradually losing Cornell influence. Biographies will never accord him his real place of influence in our community affairs, but men associated with him, at once know his confident poise and sure grasp of any subject interesting his incisive, sharp intelligence.

THE EVENING DISPATCH, JULY 24, 1929

———◆———

DOCTOR (J. B.) ROGERS.

A civil engineer drifting successfully in to the medical profession. An English ancestry with name prominent in War of 1812 on American side. Graduate of Dartmouth '87. Engineering experience on railroads have proved of value to him as one of our first commissioners under city manager form of government.

Many lodge affiliations. An ardent civic worker willing to devote time worth $3.00 a call with unlimited callers to civic jobs paying $200 a year.

Professional looking, of course, with two professions at his command. A valuable and a solid man. Most common associate of "stock" in Michigan City. Co-organizer of the Clinic. Active in Boy Scout work and the inspiring director of drives for innumerable worthy causes; a cool, polished and sympathetic man.

THE EVENING DISPATCH, MARCH 11, 1929

———◆———

"NATE." (ROSENBERG)

Drifting in from the unknown and suddenly our great inspirational civic toxic. — stimulating drives, conciliating the angry, uniting the disunited or coordinating our energies. How come this comparative new comer is suddenly the entrepreneur of so many of our movements.

He is not so large physically, should not be so influential and necessary, yet Michigan City cheerfully and confidently accepts him as a peculiar, indispensable institution.

Chamber of Commerce work finds in his boiling energy the right man for the job and better. A small man with a big brain, cigar and brief case. Generally in a hurry but will relax at luncheon and meet all comers in story telling, business, repartee or what have you. An uncrushable, irrepressible man and our very best salesman.

THE EVENING DISPATCH, MAY 15, 1929

———◆———

GLEN B. ROSS.

Probably the only dentist in Indiana who ever worked the teeth of General John J. Pershing. Proud possessor of an autographed photograph of the General.

A quiet, conservative man. Avoids overweight and keeps trim by walking to and from his office. An ex-service man. A student of history and politics, possessing a mechanical genius which, fits in well with his professional work.

THE EVENING DISPATCH, JULY 30, 1929

BUNNY RYDZY.

Bicycles, roller skates, clocks, umbrellas, gas engines, dynamos or motors—he knows and understands them all. Mechanic, electrician, and assistant chief of the Michigan City fire department.

A familiar name, a well-known figure and face. Everyone—schoolboy to business man—all seem to know, at least claim an acquaintance with "Bunny."

Once blond, now slowly turning gray. Seemingly has a secret formula for keeping his youth and avoiding overweight, without trying the 18-day diet. A handy man for fixing that mechanism gone wrong, keeping our fire alarm system in repair, as well as performing in an efficient way the duties of assistant chief.

THE EVENING DISPATCH, JULY 9, 1929

FRED SADENWATER.

Collector of old coins, rare stamps and your tax titles with a uniform success. Confectioner and florist on the side. There's even a sidewalk popcorn stand. Rather enough for one man and probably explaining that hurried gait and quick movement.

Business credit and standing in the community prove his successful versatility and good grasp of variant activities, possessing an agile mind and body, an alert appearance and quick action.

Will express a sound and steady opinion of a public question or a political measure. Reflects accurately public opinion and particularly that of the Franklin street business man.

Temperate habits have preserved an athletic appearance even in the late forties.

THE EVENING DISPATCH, AUGUST 1, 1929

R. W. SCHOFIELD

Coming westward from English forbears to Ohio, and thence to Michigan City. The husky, wide-shouldered gray man behind the contracting firm ever growing in importance and reputation. A mighty man strict with himself, proud of America and her institutions and will to respect her laws without the necessity of a plea from a President.

Has convinced, Michigan City that we need not go outside to find a municipal contractor ready and able, and easily qualifying as the best bidder.

Once a justice of the peace and could also lead an undenominational religious service sincerely and earnestly.

Gradually unloading the business on to a capable son and now in a satisfied contentment facing an easy twilight far from cave-ins, quick-sand and contractor's many problems.

THE EVENING DISPATCH, AUGUST 2, 1929

---◆---

MIKE SHON.

Kid Shon they called him years and years ago when as a muscular featherweight he pounded Young Fox out of the ring. Now the proprietor of one of our largest furniture stores. Thrifty, saving, watchful business man, but always ready to plunge into a gamble offering big returns.

Disdainfully smiling and welcoming the aggression of chain stores—voicing cheerfully, the merits of establishment over which he presided—relaxing at beach home and club. He still has at least one good wallop in him, but time, exacting its certain toll, will make it a one-round affair.

Not only enjoys and tells a good story, but has inspired many of our best.

THE EVENING DISPATCH, AUGUST 10, 1929

---◆---

M. A. SCHUTT.

He found dentistry a guess and left it 40 years later an exact science, to devote his time to building, to the postmastership, to his family and his friends. A rare gift and faculty for Republican politics long ago entitled him to leadership and the postmaster job. Also best fitted by training, experience and intelligence for this position.

Dr. M. A. Schutt has always been an expressive proponent of the principle embodied in "A community is no bigger than its citizens." In other words, he stresses the freedom of the individual and the people, composed of these individuals, as the real source of power.

Arnold Bass

    Always frank and expressive in laying out the boundaries for a public servant who may have overstepped the same. A heavy real estate investor and a hard fighter against confiscatory taxes.

    A good companion who, will not object your smoking. A good citizen enjoying a statewide acquaintance. He can call our Congressman "Andy" and our Senator "Jim" and get by. That's M. A. Schutt. A characteristic walk, throwing his hands out to the side, a jutting jaw, a quick eye and ready tongue.

THE EVENING DISPATCH, MARCH 26, 1929

"SNOOK". (ALLEN J.)

    Allen J. Snook, democratic Justice of the Peace, real estate, marriage licenses, insurance, abstracts—disdainful of legal rigidity and technically—fully aware through some intuitive sense of justice in substance.

    Friendly comfort to the young lawyer and easily forgiving the old lawyer who has forgotten him; an easy prey to the helpless, friendless, needy and lonesome.

    Usually quasi-formal in dress and the like and no one will be more suitably apparelled at a wedding or funeral. A likeable individual and a storehouse of information for lawyers, courts, police and the common people.

    Somehow reminiscent of the village parson whose "house was known to all of the vagrant train," and to whom "fools came to scoff but remained to pray."

THE EVENING DISPATCH, MARCH 9, 1929

PHIL SPRAGUE.

    Climaxing the mastery of a manufacturing business with an astonishing display of versatility and originality in his varied activities. A resident of Michigan City for comparatively few years he has already grasped a unique command of our local history. As an amateur movie expert he as delighted hundreds. As an able, fluent writer demonstrating rich humor and ripened knowledge, he always interests and instructs. As a designer of a beach home of most novel and harmonious architecture, he has surprised everyone. Wide traveling here and abroad has enriched an observant brain and keen intelligence.

    Proudly participating in our civic enterprises, co-operating in every worthwhile movement, winning the confidence, trust and loyalty of all, his future is most bright and his ever-increasing influence in civic affairs has been of great benefit to Michigan City.

THE EVENING DISPATCH, JULY 6, 1929

SPIKE. (A. J. SPYCHALSKI)

City clerk during the memorable period of injunction, mandates, petitions and remonstrances. His campaign cards truthfully describe him as courteous and competent and correctly name him Alexander J. Spychalski. Now deputy clerk of the county and stationed in the Superior Court, in the same building that has known for so many years his presence and many triumphs. Active in politics, with a countywide following. Considered as a liberal with decided leaning to the Democrats.

A florid, tall blond, smiling or laughing quickly, keeping fit with many a successful fishing trip. Has the proud record of bringing in the largest small-mouthed black bass ever caught in Laporte County.

A stoic in defeat, but epicurean in habits and thought. Many years in public office have given him an exceptional acquaintance. Most enthusiastic in Red Cross work, political campaigns and fishing. An eligible bachelor, but too elusive. An invaluable man on a ticket, and one who has not yet fully appreciated and developed his political potentiality. Whenever he can select his own job in city or country.

THE EVENING DISPATCH, APRIL 18, 1929

CAPTAIN STARKE.

A giant hulk of a man, with an enviable military record overseas in actual battle and possessing a rare ability to "tell his story" and even better "telling it rarely."

Enormous strength and endurance fitting him for great physical exertion and an ardent spirit ready to drive that superb body. He is too big for a big chair. He belongs on a log jam, and makes a splendid man to break down doors in leading raids. An ideal police officer and worthy of any man's trust and confidence. We feel safe with men like him on the job. Generous to fault and easily beguiled by pleading charity. Around thirty years old and a loyal, zealous officer in a police corps of exceptional personnel. Is ready to help clean up Michigan City whenever you readers are ready to have it cleaned up.

THE EVENING DISPATCH, MAY 30, 1929

LOUIS J. STEIN.

Perhaps our most frequent visitor to New York, buying and replenishing the stock of his department store owned, controlled and operated by a home proprietor. A man torn between the conflicting demands of business and the love of recreation and home. Rushing in late to a volley ball or handball game and hurrying back to his store. Then rushing home, —also late.

His success in business in the face of the "chain avalanche" and of modern competition is a fitting proof of his stamina, courage and faith. He will open his pocket book for a civic cause. He will give his time to a drive. He will patiently attend a recital. He is too impatient for horseback riding, but finds his best outlet in a short, furious game of handball. He is a frequent attendant at baseball games, wrestling or boxing bouts.

A youthful man somewhere in the forties in good physical condition. A fast walker, hard worker and eager conversationalist.

THE EVENING DISPATCH, MAY 2, 1929

———◆———

FRED STERN.

"Watch him shoot for the ten ball" and know how he can put heart and soul into business and lift it to respectable proportions. Rather a good showing for that serious, cautious, cool chap we remember coming to America in his boyhood with a background of training and education in foreign customs and manners.

He is a husky, well-muscled, heavy walking chap. Politeness and courtesy come most easy to him. Sincere, striving and building. America has no limitations for him. There may be chain stores in him without surprising us. It is surely most possible in the product of mental ensemble this determined-looking gentleman possesses. Developing, growing, adapting— there is no end.

THE EVENING DISPATCH, JULY 31, 1929

———◆———

MARK STOREN.

Rather well-groomed, if extravagantly so. Always the silken handkerchief with tie to match, spats, expensive cigars. A quite successful lawyer with "money to loan." An exotic complexion—symmetrical build, five feet ten, 155 pounds when playing volley ball. A good voice and mind. A social, enjoyable companion on links or in club, but a dabbler at golf, bridge or pool.

Presiding at a lodge meeting with easy grace and poise. Came here from somewheres in southern Indiana following his graduation from Notre Dame. Can ride a horse, dances well, talks clearly, smokes incessantly.

Twice a candidate for public office and still a Democrat. Exalted ruler during every successful year. The youngest bank director in Michigan City.

THE EVENING DISPATCH, MAY 20, 1929

"TUT" (H. B. TUTHILL)

Behind his back, with a friendly familiarity, we speak of him as "Tut", but face to face we involuntarily call him Judge, title truly earned by a long, honorable career of eighteen years on our Superior Court bench. How well his welcome reminiscences fix his coming to Michigan City, way back in 1882, and how firmly the judge has taken root in the friendly soil of Michigan City.

As lawyer and judge his many labors have always been characterized by zealous study and great care. Alive to the great value of precedent in the law he was yet, in many far reaching decisions been able to blaze the trial and establish legal precedents now embodied in the law of the land.

No branch of the law was too obtruse or technical for the Judge. After 46 long hard years of professional activity he is still studying and working as hard as any lawyer in Indiana. The same ability and foresight that brought deserved honors to the Judge at bench or bar vindicated his heavy investments in the real estate and future of Michigan City. His researches into the sources of early English law and into American history have been vast and extensive. His grasp of the centuries-old history of Masonry have made him an able exponent of this fraternity.

An impressive poise and confident pose have always assured Judge H. B. Tuthill the respect of all, and yet a saving sense of humor never let him take himself too seriously.

His spirited enthusiasm and able leadership as Chairman of our Boy Scout program is only one more evidence of his entire useful career in Michigan City. After Forty six years he is yet the logical man to put pep in a drive. Can there be any better proof of the possession of great faculties entitling the man to an honorable place in these sketches?

THE EVENING DISPATCH, MARCH 7, 1929

JOHN TYRRELL

A spirited nature, unafraid, out-spoken and most sincere. Still possessing a driving energy after many years of unsparing hard work and now able to enjoy leisure, seemingly prefers a ceaseless activity.

Hotel proprietor, jobber, salesman, real estate, catering, are only a few of the many activities he has known. His voice is clear, his fists seem ready, his walk free and determined, his manner independent.

Arnold Bass

Politics would probably know him better in any other state but Indiana, because politics are sometimes queer in Indiana and rather restricted. If you really want public opinion talk to a man like Tyrrell and find out quickly enough. You may be sure that his opinion will be unbiased, impartial and above all, frank and sincere.

THE EVENING DISPATCH, JULY 16, 1929

---◆---

"TRUES" (G. T.) VAIL.

G. T. Vail, bank president, director, syndicate, bond issues, entrepreneur of any alert activities. And still in brisk and jaunty walk, dress and conversation there is a distinctive touch of the campus he left 25 years ago. Ranked high in bridge, low 90's in golf. Can carry a cane gracefully or wear spats or derby as well. A family history traceable and prominent through the mercantile and financial history of northern Indiana, and back through Colonial days to England. The type of man at whose feet waves of fanaticism break and under whose searching, analytical diagnosis, Utopian dreams are dispelled. A builder and a constructive, practical citizen. A careful voter and a wise financial counsellor. Has zealously discharged the usual range of civic duties of such a citizen with that inevitable jaunty and efficient dispatch. Country club, Chamber of Commerce, Rotary, as well as many others, are only a few of the many enterprises knowing his helpful association and direction.

THE EVENING DISPATCH, JULY 6, 1929

---◆---

WILL VAIL.

Adhering to strict code of professional and social ethics, derivable from an ancestry traceable through the pioneer days of Laporte County to colonial families in Connecticut, New Jersey and New York. A banker's son, a merchant's grandson and ideally equipped by tradition, heredity and training for conservative, sound and progressive banking. We have no more reliable type of citizenship. We have no more scrupulously careful and exact individual, always holding under strict control abundant reserve of energy and power.

Bank president and past president and chairman of many of our drives and campaigns. Instinctively chosen as trustee, treasurer or custodian. Courteous by instinct, a gentleman by birth and blood. Not the type of a man to be kidded or blarneyed.

THE EVENING DISPATCH, APRIL 27, 1929

UP CLOSE AND PERSONAL

ED VALENTINE.

Dependable, vacationless man on the job as co-owner of our first andstill our best taxi company. Always smiling, but a certain reserve preventing a hearty laugh. Diets, golf, politics, civics bother him not a bit, but the maintenance, operation and conduct of a taxi business find his consistent attention and care.

He is approaching the forties without an ounce of fat on him. Lean, tireless, hard-at-it in all weather and seasons.

His business has become as much of a public utility as our waterworks and entitled to almost an equal support and protection from our city.

THE EVENING DISPATCH, AUGUST 9, 1929

GARRIT S. VAN DEUSEN

Imagine a mayor in Michigan City with Knickerbocker stock in him. Yet he did it and continued to live here. A success in business, a man enjoying many friends, good name and with the usual European trip over twenty years ago.

Always has been in background of banking and industrial interest of Michigan City, a co-organizer of our telephone company, our Citizens Bank and associated with numerous factories. Now enjoys a walk down Franklin Street to the park. Must have many pleasant memories to mull over. A nice man to meet, with a pleasant smile and quick nod or wave of the hand for the passerby.

Affiliated by marriage with the Coudens and Hutchinsons, all Republicans. This man, by the way, was a member of the National Convention, nominating William McKinley. We would sooner have that recollection than all his factories or banks.

THE EVENING DISPATCH, APRIL 1, 1929

JIMMY VINE.

Most of us had long ago forgotten our very meager knowledge of Greek mythology, and the lives and teachings of our Grecian philosophers. Socrates, Diogenes, Plato had long ago become dim figures, fading out of our minds, but Jimmy, on Franklin Street, revives these old heroic figures of the past in a 1929 setting and brings them back to us in an unforgettable manner. They aid him constantly and instantly. He uses them in politics business and pleasure. They re-live in his characteristic speech, debate and argument.

Socratic in all his wisdom probably never dreamed that someday his methods would be promulgated from behind a soda fountain, or would be used in a Crystal Trio election. Plato would undoubtedly be surprised, even shocked, at Jim's Franklin Street demonstration of these immortal dialogues. We do not know the exact Grecian source of "tickling your enemy to death with a feather" but we have heard it advocated by an ardent disciple in this ultra-modern day on Franklin Street.

A proud son of greece is Jim and a heavy investor and gambler in Franklin Street real estate and business. He is a plunger in our Nordic futures. We have assimilated him but he has left his mark. His children and their children will give to us a needed touch of dramatic fire, of flashing eye and courageous zeal. How strange it is that Jimmy Vine should remind us that the right of petition is a sacred inheritance from English freemen. And how strange it is that a son of Wales should be the city attorney when this petition was denied, and how much stranger that the fight for the preservation of our right of petition should be led by this son of Greece, and yet that is the Commens case.

Jimmy Vine, proud father of Danny, you did defy the Klan, you did dare petition for election, you were and are loyal to our American institutions and you are a true American citizen. Even Grecian gods may proudly leave to you the exposition of their ideals and ethics.

THE EVENING DISPATCH, MAY 29, 1929

―――♦―――

JOHN R. WEAVER.

Do you remember his livery stable at 4th and Washington or farther back, when it was located on East Michigan near Franklin? Have you ever seen a more zealous enthusiastic interest in local Democratic politics? Have you ever heard more frank opinions of the ins when he was out or their defense when he was on the payroll, which was often because John was always eligible for public office and what is known as a repeater. Always discharged his public or private duties seriously and giving his best service, and now, attempting as bridge tender at Franklin Street, to satisfy at the same time boat traffic shrieking for the bridge and autos honking for the park.

He knows all the old timers and is the connecting link between our pre-auto days and the present era of twenty thousand autos jamming a park. If traffic is light stop and talk with him. You'll get some inside history on Michigan City that Tut overlooked at Rotary luncheon.

THE EVENING DISPATCH, JULY 19, 1929

―――♦―――

AL WEILER.

Bank cashier, locksmith, heavy real estate holdings, co-organizer of amusement enterprises, has seen America first and is now ready for European jaunt. A liberal(ist) and

UP CLOSE AND PERSONAL

pragmatist, with a legion of friends. Always voicing a philosophy pregnant with (tol)erance and friendship. Relaxes in an (?)used appreciation at the foibles, fancies and odd quirks of that philosopher in the opposite cage known as Mr. Glasscott. But ready smile does not disturb the keen business judgment and banking knowledge he so well exemplifies.

A descendent of one of Michigan City's pioneer families with relatives in every precinct and ward. Finds adequate exercise in a landscaped lawn and splendidly appointed homestead. Walks to work, goes home to lunch except on Saturdays. Motors on Sunday.

THE EVENING DISPATCH, MAY 14, 1929

———◆———

"DAD" WHEELER.

Co-organizer of orchestras years back in Michigan City, and during that same period a successful reporter and city editor. Our first modern syncopator. Also organized an abstract company now leading the field in Laporte county. Music and land titles are his surprising dual mastery and have won for him a good business success. Dancing eyes and business chin reveal his contrasting talents. Long bronze hair and neat, careful dress, again reveal that same duality of impression.

Offers an interesting study for psychoanalyst. A ready song leader accompanist for luncheon clubs and other occasions. Christian name is Louis but we have never heard anyone use it.

Politics, civics, sports, must be foreign and strange to a man deliberately plunging into music and land titles. There's no time left for much else.

THE EVENING DISPATCH, JULY 27, 1929

———◆———

BOBBY (ROBERT T. WILSON)

A jaunty, apt nickname for a supremely confident, likable Robert T. Wilson. There is a Buddha-like aspect in his inevitable smile, high forehead, oval-shaped head. He brings a refreshing enthusiasm to his business and social life. Let Moe saunter from club to continental travel. Cushman Mortgage Company is in good smiling hands with Bobby smiling through and so easily.

Does he drink, gamble, play pinochle, has he any bad habits? Let him answer, but know that clear head, steady hand, alert eye deny such vices. A likely candidate for political preferment, but let him graciously reject as he will all such possibilities for the better service he can render us in the all important business of general brokerage, investments, insurance and finance.

From Supreme Court to city court he is welcome. In bank, lodge or locker room he is at home.

Arnold Bass

Age, height, weight, all satisfactory, but for details, look in one of the many insurance policies he carries.

THE EVENING DISPATCH, AUGUST 29, 1929

———◆———

ART WOLFF.

Expert bicyclist, racing motorcyclist, and breaking into the auto game in its infancy. Piling up the mileage for over twenty years, including some rough driving on war trucks over shell-wrecked roads in France.

A punishing jaw, a fighting eye, a well-muscled and calmly poised man. A salesman deluxe. A son of an old Indian fighter. Persistent, untiring, possessing so many qualifications for success in business and in making and keeping friends.

Our choice in a hard drive over a long road in any kind of traffic or weather.

THE EVENING DISPATCH, MAY 28, 1929

———◆———

WILL WOLFF.

From hardware to the auto game in it's inception still one of the leaders as co-owner of a large garage, service station, and sales department. Shows a surprising proclivity for "muskie" fishing, when a love of books or gentler hobbies would be more expected. Is calm and quiet, careful and thrifty, understands well the necessities of modern business, of stock turnover, of accounting and of service above all. Also co-owner of sole beech grove left in this vicinity. Quietly courteous. Building well and permanently and proud of ownership of one of our real business institutions.

He'll take a good part in any civic enterprise, will bet on football or baseball.

Relaxes in beautiful beach home undisturbed by golf, bridge or the idle pursuit harassing the rest of mankind.

THE EVENING DISPATCH, AUGUST 8, 1929

———◆———

HERMAN ZEESE.

In dry goods before Tut came to Michigan City. A good cigar or meerschaum pipe have given him unlimited hours of solace. Nervous walker, dapper and neat in dress, a penetrating voice, friendly and courteous in greeting. Disdainful of shoddy merchandise and knowing and appreciating quality, he has through many years acquired and retained an excellent business clientele.

From clerk at 50c a week to proprietor of his own store on Franklin Street. His vacations few and far between, enjoying a real home, a walk to the club, a family picnic. Rather indifferent to politics, but will vote and generally the Democratic ticket.

One of our few surviving individual proprietors on Franklin Street and demonstrating that the individual can survive by service. The years have touched him lightly, as witness his jaunty manner, quick walk and spirited conversation.

THE EVENING DISPATCH, AUGUST 9, 1929

"What a shame someone couldn't have foreseen the coming of the horseless-carriage days and saved this wonderful relic from decay"
E. E. Coddington, April 6, 1937
HERALD-ARGUS

WHEN THE STAGECOACH RULED THE ROADWAY

Early commercial travel in and through La Porte County at the time when the cities of La Porte and Michigan City were first established was minimal. For the most part narrow dusty roads connected areas of population, winding through thick forests and grassy meadows. At times the elements made travel perilous.

Among the early written records of stagecoach travel in the county is the account of Harriett Martineau, when on June 19, 1836, she traveled through the county by stagecoach enroute from Detroit, Michigan to Fort Dearborn, now the site of Chicago. This intellectual and articulate English woman was born in Norwich, England, June 12, 1802. She died on June 27, 1876, at Ambleside England. A reporter for the EVENING DISPATCH said: "She was the first woman to provide the written history of Michigan City and the great expanse of territory flanking it on either side." A copy of her diary is on file at the La Porte County Historical Society Museum. Today millions of people travel nearly the same route. High performance automobiles ply Interstate Highway 94 at speeds in excess of 70 miles per hour. This ribbon of concrete and asphalt carries a great deal of the nation's commerce.

Today, what takes a day, took Martineau, depending on the weather, weeks. In her day the route taken by the coach took her through Niles, Michigan, to the city of La Porte and on to Michigan City. This description of her trip from La Porte to Michigan City was taken from her diary. The route described closely follows what is present day Johnson Road. The stagecoach entered La Porte on the edge of what was known as Door Prairie, on June 19, 1836. After changing horses they traveled on a "very bad road" that took them along the shore of a small lake. As they continued, the road passed through a wooded area. The rain had made the road difficult to navigate. The coach "...jolted and rocked from side to side, till, at last the carriage leaned three parts over, and stuck." All had to leave the coach, while the men "...literally put their shoulders to the wheel, and lifted it out of its hole." A short time later the same scenario was reenacted. About seven miles from Michigan City, the driver stopped to talk to someone at the summit. The information received indicated the bridge over a marshy area, in what is present day Waterford, had been swept away by a flash flood. The stranger was unable to say how much of the log road was left on either side of the wash.

The rain continued, making the road more dangerous, eliminating the option to return to La Porte for the night. A farm nearby seemed to be the only option. The log-built house consisted of three rooms; two under one roof and the third one appeared to have been added at another time. The family received their unexpected guests with open arms. Harriett's description of the family led her to surmise they were of the "Dunker sect of Baptists." Philip Sprague, who wrote the CIVIC COLUMN for the EVENING DISPATCH in 1925, concluded that the travelers were the guests of the Jacob Replogle family. The following year marked the ninetieth anniversary of Martineau's trip. The newspaper at that time identified the gracious hosts as the Joseph and Susan Foshier Pagin family. They were Quakers that were born in Lynchburg, Virginia.

The next morning they awoke to find it still raining. The new day seemed to lessen the intensity of the rain. After breakfast and cleaning up they were on their way to Michigan City. They "jolted" on through the woods for about two and a half miles, admiring the brilliant pink and white moccasin flowers and the scarlet lilies. Upon arriving at the site of the washed out bridge, they were obliged to wait for three hours in a house on a nearby hill while the neighbors, passengers and the drivers of the mail stage built a bridge.

The following excerpt describing the crossing of what is believed to be a branch of Trail Creek at Waterford was taken from Harriett's diary:

> "Slowly, anxiously, with a man at the head of each leader (horse), we entered the water, and saw it rise to the nave of the wheels. Instead of jolting, as usual, we mounted and rescended (sic) each log individually. The mail-wagon followed, with two or three horsemen. There was also a singularly benevolent personage, who jumped from the other wagon, and waded through all the doubtful places, to prove them. He leaped and splashed through the water, which was sometimes up to his waist, as if it was the most agreeable sport in the world. In one of these gullies, the fore part of our wagon sank and stuck, so as to throw us forward and make it doubtful in what mode we should emerge from the water. Then the rim of one of the wheels was found to be loose; and the whole cavalcade stopped till it was mended. I never could understand how wagons were made in the back-country; they seemed to be elastic, from the shocks and twisting they would bear without giving away."

With that ordeal behind them, they headed for Michigan City. As the stage reached the city, the driver announced their approach by sounding a "series of flourishes on one note of his common horn." They had arrived in a city that was begun just three years before. "It was cut out of the forest, and curiously interspersed with little swamps...." Several new houses stood, some only half finished. A few stores were scattered about connected by streets littered with tree stumps.

The morning of June 21, saw Martineau and the others board a wagon on their way to Chicago. Several miles east of the city, they turned toward the lakeshore, winding through the sand dunes, to travel on the packed sand along the shore of the lake.

Over the years numerous travelers followed the route described by Harriett Martineau. Little or no recorded information exists today of their adventures. However, a published report that appeared in the DAILY ARGUS on April 4, 1924 provides insight on another such trek. Fifteen months after Martineau's trip, September 12, 1837, there was another stagecoach trip through the northern part of the county. The coach belonged to the Chicago-Niles and Michigan Bus Line. It carried eight and one half passengers. The half fare probably represented a child. The names listed included: Fawler, Gurnsey, Clark, Hawkes, Hawkes (one half), Underhill, Doran and another whose name was illegible. Gurnsey was traveling from Chicago to a place seven miles west of Niles. His fare was $7. Another passenger was charged $1 for his trip from Wiley (possibly a long forgotten way station) to Michigan City. One of the passengers traveled from Chicago to Niles and paid a fare of $7.50. Four passengers left Michigan City on their way east. Doran, who was believed to be the father of F. H. Doran of Michigan City, traveled to Terre Coupe for $1. A total of $20 represented the fares collected for that trip by Mr. Tuttle.

The record of that trip came to light when an old three-story frame building, built in 1837, was being torn down. It was believed to be the largest building at that time between Chicago and Buffalo, N. Y. The building was thought to have been a hotel in that year. It was located on the west side of Franklin Street, across from the Vreeland Hotel. A musty waybill was found showing a picture of a "bus" drawn by four horses. Dick Mitchell, one of the men hired to raze the building in April 1924, turned it over to Fire Chief I. C. Bauman.

Figure 44 Fabian Matott married Amanda Ray in 1865. She was the daughter of James and Sarah Ray. Photo from the Westville Centennial Souvenir Booklet (1851-1951) La Porte County Historical Society collection.

Another stagecoach route connected La Porte and Valparaiso. A Mr. Windle and Til Hogan operated the line out of Valparaiso. A newspaper article in the files of the La Porte County Historical Society Museum indicates that the stage line carried passengers as early as 1851. The stage line's headquarters was the Captain Eli Hotel which preceeded the Teagarden Hotel at the corner of Lincoln Way and Monroe Streets. Fabian Matott, on the occasion of his 97th birthday, reminisced that passengers would write their names on a slate at the hotel. When the driver was ready to make the trip to Valparaiso he would drive around town and pickup the passengers.

Fabian was born on January 6, 1835, in New York State, near Lake Champlain. At the age of fourteen, the wanderlust bug bit him. The undeveloped country of the west held the promise of hope where a young lad could seek his fortune. He reached Buffalo, N. Y., by working his way along the Erie Canal. From there he traveled to Detroit and by train on to Michigan City. A new railroad was being built through Valparaiso. The possibility of employment caused him to head for Valpo. Odd jobs carried him through until he landed a job as a day laborer for the railroad. His enthusiasm and desire to stay in the area prompted him to take a job driving the stagecoach between La Porte and Valparaiso by way of Westville. Eventually he and Zip Smith bought the business from Windle and Hogan.

Figure 45 The stagecoach operated between La Porte, Westville and Valparaiso in the 1860's.
William Parkinson wearing the top hat. The photo was digitally repaired.
Courtesy of the La Porte County Historical Society.

Fabian, who later moved to Westville, Joe Drago of Valparaiso and Jay Parkinson of La Porte were among the drivers that gallantly drove the four-horse stage over the old Joliet Road. One of the earliest recollections of a "sit-down" strike was reported by the DAILY-ARGUS in April of 1937. Fabian's son J. C. Matott, a Westville merchant, remembered his father going to Michigan City to protest not receiving a raise in pay. He sat on a coach and remained there until they agreed to give him a pay raise. That accomplished, he returned to his job in La Porte. He drove the stage every day of the year and earned the magnificent sum of $16 a month, according to an article that appeared in June of 1930, in the NEWS.

The stage line had a $750 a year government contract to carry the United States mail. On a good trip the coach could carry as many as 19 passengers. Nine people could crowd into the coach, with another 10 on top, according to Matott. For many years the business prospered.

Fabian Matott was interview by the DAILY-ARGUS, May 1, 1923, on the occasion of the sixtieth anniversary of his marriage. Mrs. Matott was the daughter of James and Sarah Ray. She was born and educated in Westville. Fabian, during the interview, recalled the schedule and route the stage followed:

"The coach left La Porte at 6 a. m. passing through Door Village to Westville where horses were changed, and getting passengers and mail off a northbound Monon train due at 9 a.m.: the plank road (now Lincolnway) to Coburg, was followed into Valparaiso after which the return trip was begun. At Westville the stage waited for the southbound 9:30 p. m. train, and then continued to La Porte.... Connections were made at Valparaiso for Calumet, now Chesterton, the route being covered by hack line operated by Williams and Dalson."

The Civil War diverted Fabian Matott's attention from his business. President Lincoln had issued his second call for volunteers in 1861. For 16 years Fabian had driven the stage over roads and terrain too difficult for the modern mind to comprehend. Putting that behind him, he enlisted and served three years with the Indiana Volunteer infantry. William Parkinson of Westville purchased the line. His home was on Valparaiso Street, between what in 1915 were the homes of Pulaske Koontz and M. W. Lewis, according to the WESTVILLE INDICATOR. His daughter Charlena married E. E. Coddington. Their children Flossie, Arthur B., and Linton T. Coddington were living in La Porte in 1937.

The stage line continued carrying passengers and mail from La Porte and Valparaiso and points in between into the 1870's. The mode of transportation changed with the advent of the buggy, causing a decline in passenger traffic. Competition in securing the government contract to carry the mail created a bidding war that saw contracts awarded to the lowest bidder. Fewer passengers and reduced revenue from the government brought an end to the stage line.

In 1937 the ARGUS printed a reminiscence of the stage line recalled by several individuals. Mrs. Ben Henton of Westville remembered as a young girl "hitch-hiking out of Armitage corners, east of Westville, on the back to (sic) the stage, of (sic) get the cows." The most sobering yet amusing recollection was made by Billy Williams (a boy at the time), 307 Second street: "As the old stage coach went to decay back of (his father's) ...livery barn, (he) made it his play house."

Those journeying from Indianapolis to the relatively young city at the southern tip of Lake Michigan faced a strenuous trip. "Nodding back and forth with the motions of the uncomfortable stage coach, traveling over rough roads, through creeks and over almost impassable hills." This was the preferable means of travel back in the late 1830's. A man with little or no baggage might make the trip on horseback. That journey by stagecoach required two days of constant traveling. Today, the trip takes about 3 hours.

The Michigan City NEWS, November, 1929, provided an insight into the rigors of making that trip in the "Olden Days of 'Coach and Four'...." The stage route wound its way south over dusty trails and roads, through large forests, over meadows, and traversed its way around and through marshlands. About midway between Michigan City and Indianapolis was the village of Mexico, located on the Eel River in Miami County. The village became a trading center along the river for settlers. Mexico, in 1834, consisted of a few cabins connected by an Indian trail. The trail was supplanted by the stage route, and became the first road in Miami County. When the state legislature approved the construction of the Michigan road, the route included that section through Mexico.

In the late 1830's, a two-story building, constructed of hand-hewn logs, was built and used as a general store. A bar, a kitchen and a dining area filled the remaining ground level space. Upstairs were the bedrooms, one of them fitted with iron bars on the door and windows. More than likely the barred room was to accommodate prisoners destined for the state prison in Michigan City. This was what was to become the famous "Riverhouse Inn." It was the only inn on the road and as the NEWS surmised "...probably the first hostelry in the state of Indiana."

Numerous passengers stayed at the inn when the rain, wind and heavy snow made it impossible to travel. "Sometimes there were ladies in crinoline and gentlemen with beaver hats." Others were dressed in their homespun clothes. The NEWS stated that, on one occasion, Schuyler Colfax, a member of Congress and later Vice President, spent a night at the inn. Perhaps he was on his way to or returning from Michigan City, having visited with his cousin Harriet Colfax, the lighthouse keeper. By 1929 all that remained of the "Riverhouse Inn" was an abandoned "...old, tumbledown shack of a house," with cracked or broken out windows.

In the files of the La Porte County Historical Society Museum there appears a brief note that says another stagecoach line existed that operated out of South Bend that connected it with the cities of La Porte, Michigan City and New Buffalo, Michigan. Harvey Truesdell owned the line. Rollo B. Oglesbee's History of Michigan City, p. 205 ff., provides more information on the early stage lines that passed through the area.

A great deal of change has occurred in the way people travel since the establishment of Michigan City and La Porte. The Twenty-first century truly promises to bring further changes that the early pioneers of La Porte County would not or could not dare to dream.

*"Individuality may be the mark
of the genius but co-operation
is the tool by which ordinary
men get things done"*
The Michigan City NEWS
May 29, 1930

MICHIGAN CITY'S SPORTY GOLF COURSE

The game of golf attracts millions of people to the links every year. There is something about hitting a ball with a club that fascinates both men and women. Whether it is something psychological that motivates people, I can't say. The diehard golfer can be found on the course almost any time it's clear of snow and the temperature is above freezing. The true golfer enjoys walking over the gentle hills and valleys and around the obstacles a good golf course affords.

Scotland's Royal and Ancient Golf Club of St. Andrews had its beginnings in 1754.[14] The Chicago Golf Club opened at Wheaton, Ill., where Charles B. MacDonald had laid out the first 18-hole golf course in America in 1893.[15] Three years later, New York's Van Cortland Park was the site of the world's first public golf course. The popularity of golf in the United States spread rapidly. In its infancy the game attracted people of "status" and wealth. This was apparent in Michigan City in 1904 when the Michigan City Golf Club was formed. THE NEWS, during April of 1905, listed the following officers and directors: President, H. V. Ogden, Vice President, Mrs. John H. Barker, Secretary and Treasurer, G. T. Vail, S. W. Larsen, Judge H. B. Tuthill, and J. P. Cook. Although it was open to everyone over 16 years of age, it had few if any members from the general public.

The city of La Porte also boasted of an active golf club. As it is today, it was common to see Michigan City and La Porte compete in many arenas. The first golf tournament between the two cities was held on May 31, 1906, on the links of the La Porte Country Club. The La Porte team won 7 up. The ARGUS indicated that 22 golfers participated. La Porte's team consisted of F. T. Wilcox, Henry Bradley, H. A. Manning, J. B. Shick, J. H. Richter, J. V. Dorland, A. G. Tamlin, Ed Barnum, H. W. Richter, A. L. Osborn and L. A. Burt. No listing of Michigan City's team was found.

By 1928 it was apparent that wealth was not a prerequisite. Large numbers of men, women and children had taken up the game. The Michigan City NEWS estimated that as many as 75% of the golfers on municipal courses were of the "laboring class." The cost of clubs was in the reach of many, beginning as low as $1.00 each. A proposed municipal golf course appeared to become a certainty for the people of Michigan City in April of 1927.

The City Commission adopted an ordinance authorizing Albert Couden, City Manager and City Attorney Williams to negotiate the lease for an option to purchase 127.11 acres of land known as blocks 1 & 2 in Cushman Acres. The property was located approximately two to three miles east of the city on what was then known as State Highway No. 20. Today it is located within the city limits on what is now called Michigan Boulevard. The stated purpose of the purchase was for the establishment of a recreation center and public playground. Their ambitious vision was to include an 18-hole golf course, play fields, a swimming pool, tennis courts, handball courts, basketball courts, municipal campsites, as well as a community center. A second ordinance was adopted to create a five-member board to handle and oversee the development and management of the recreation center. Their term of offices was for four years. "Five resident freeholders" would make up the board, one of which must be a member of the Michigan City Board of School Trustees.

Like any major undertaking, there were individuals that opposed the expenditure of taxpayers' funds that seemed to be frivolous or not well thought out. The most prominent watchdog of the day when it came to unnecessary spending of tax dollars was Samuel J. Taylor. His opposition to the project appeared in the Michigan City NEWS,' "Voice Of The People" column on April 11, 1927. His position was that there wasn't a need to spend taxpayer money for swimming, etc., two or three miles outside of the city, and "enhance the value of surrounding farm lands...Who wants to walk three miles to play tennis or play golf." He detailed what he believed the cost of the project would ultimately be, painting a picture that reflected exorbitant costs that would lead to higher taxes. He also saw it as a scheme for some to get rich. Pipe city water to the swimming pool "...and then lots with city water connection will be sold all around the farm at fancy prices."

Debate over the issue continued for several months. The city was divided over the issue, causing the commission to rethink its position. The project was dropped when the Commission took stock of the many public improvements that were already in progress and realized that the city would be stretching its resources. A year later the issue of a municipal golf course was again raised. The directors of the Retail Board of the Chamber of Commerce revived the subject when they voted to ask the Chamber Board to include it in their Program of Progress for 1928. The resolution was forwarded to the City Commissioners with the Chamber's endorsement.

Over the next several months plans to construct the course went forward. The formation of the Michigan City Golf Association was in place by mid-May to promote and help facilitate the endeavor. Dale Merchant was its general chairman. Raymond Rademacher headed the membership and investigating committee. The decision was made to pursue the Cushman Acres site. Several experienced golf architects and engineers as well as "many prominent local business men" praised its qualities. The accessible location, topography and soil conditions made it their choice. A nine-hole course was laid out during the summer, with the likelihood that an additional nine would be added at a future date. Planning continued through the summer and into the fall.

The momentum continued with the organizing of the Michigan City Country Club. Their plan called for the purchase of the land and to build an 18-hole semi-public course if sufficient interest was apparent on the part of the general public. Membership would include a share of stock. The shares sold for $75.00 each. A three-payment plan was devised in order to attract a larger cross section of the population. Those inclined could put down $25.00 and over the next two months make payments of $25.00 a month.

This would provide the holder of a share of stock to a life membership in the country club with no annual payment and would entitle him to play golf for 50 cents a day. For nonmembers the weekday fee was $1.00 to $1.50 and $2.00 to $2.50 on Sunday and holidays

A membership drive to attract charter members was begun the last week of August 1928. A "coupon" was published in the NEWS in an attempt to reach "those whom the organization committee might not have on their list." A September 1st deadline was established in order to determine if there would be enough members to proceed with the construction of the first 9 holes that fall. It was their hope to start the work immediately in order to plant seed and have a playable course the following spring.

The following week at a dinner meeting held at the Spaulding Hotel for the subscribers to the semi-public golf course, golf architect, Leonard Macomber of Chicago, who had drawn the plan, lead a discussion of the possibilities for the course. Twenty-eight new members had been added by the 5th of September, bringing the total membership to well over 100. Inasmuch as the goal of 330 members by September 1st had not been reached, a decision to extend the sale of memberships for another week was approved.

At a September 11th, meeting at the Chamber's office in the Spaulding, Harry Northam along with the acting secretary, conducted the meeting that saw the subscribers unanimously elect a temporary controlling board. They included: Harry Northam, Leon Kramer, A. E. Simpson, Fred H. Burnham, Charles E. Arnt, Arthur Snyder, William Leverenz, Nate Rosenberg, and Louis A. Chinske. They were charged with continuing and heading up the membership drive as well as negotiating for the purchase of the land for the golf course.

Several members spoke at the meeting. Among them were Leonard Macomber and Burnham. Macomber reviewed the potential properties of the course, pointing out that the land had good natural hazards and a creek that would cross the course possibly at the fifth or sixth holes. Burnham offered a challenge that if nine other factories in the city would buy ten memberships, he would buy 10 shares.

During the second week of December the stockholders met and adopted new bylaws. Northam appointed a nominating committee at their December 28th meeting to nominate directors for the new corporation. Those elected at the meeting were Northam, Leverenz, Burnham, Rosenberg, Simpson, Kramer, T. Ziegler, Sam Boonstra, L. H. Krueger, and F. C. Bartels. The following Friday the directors elected their officers. Harry E. Northam was elected President of the Michigan City Semi-Public Country Club, Inc. Northam had been the acting President from the beginning of the project. Simpson was elected 1st Vice-president and Burnham became 2nd Vice-president. The post of recording secretary was bestowed upon Chinske. Bartels was elected financial secretary and Leverenz became treasurer.

Discussions and planning continued over the next few months. In April 1929, a series of dinner meetings were held in the ballroom of the Spaulding Hotel in preparation of what was hoped to be the final fund drive. Captains and teams were formed to canvass and solicit membership. Leaders of the community gave speeches in support of a municipal semi-public golf course, outlining the need and its benefits. Among the speakers were George T. Vail, President of the Michigan City Trust & Savings Bank and Charles E. Arnt, President of Citizens Bank. Both men were members of the private Pottawattomie Country Club. Vail was one of the original promoters of the private club. In fact, he was introduced by A. E. Simpson at one of the meetings as " the father of golf in Michigan City, who learned the game in the east and played it in pastures here where cows served as moving bunkers." Arnt was in charge of the greens and fairways of the Pottawattomie club.

It was during these April meetings that the corporation announced the purchase of the Wolff farm. The 131 acres was located one and one-half miles east of the city on what was then referred to as the "South Bend Road." Adding to its accessibility was that the South Shore railroad tracks were only a block away, "...enabling golfers to go to the links and return via the South Shore." A building committee was appointed to oversee the construction. They were: Chinski, Rant, Bootstrap, Simpson and Dr. W. A. Hall. The plan called for the construction of an 18-hole golf course. Construction of the first nine holes was to begin immediately with the expectation of completion by the middle of July. It was estimated that the improvements to the land would be about $50,000.

Appointed to head up the general membership campaign was A. E. Simpson. A. H. Snyder accepted the chairmanship of the committee to canvass and solicit membership from the businesses, factories and dealers. The campaign was scheduled to take place during the week of April 22 to 29. To stimulate and hasten the effort, the directors announced that club shares would be increased from $75.00 to $100.00 after the goal of 300 charter members was met. It was expected that between 75 and 100 workers would participate in the drive.

Carl Ziegler's Sporting Goods Store located at 620 Franklin Street was designated as the headquarters for the drive. A large sign was placed on the building to identify the headquarters. Irene Dittbrenner was given the task of directing the effort and to provide information and distribute literature regarding the drive.

The evening prior to the membership drive Catherine Barker Spaulding "... who is Michigan City's greatest benefactress," provided the campaign with a boost when she informed Harry Northam of her intention to purchase 30 shares in the new Michigan City Country Club. The EVENING DISPATCH pointed out that her purchase amounted to one tenth of the proposed charter membership. The next day Michigan City Trust & Savings Bank announced their purchase of 10 shares.

Leonard Macomber of Macomber, Inc., who had been providing consultation and design work for the new golf course, was given the contract to construct the 18-hole course. When completed, Macomber believed that it wouldn't be long before this section of the country recognized that the course was suitable for championship play. Macomber's plan called for:

> "...fairways sixty yards wide, cleared of all shrubbery, disced and planted with 150 pounds of special grass seed mixture to the acre of land. The   greens will contain...6,000 square feet, and each green will be surrounded by three or four bunker sand traps. The greens will be undulating in terrain, and all in all the course will be one of the sportiest in this section of the country.... When completed the course will be 6,470 yards long. The first nine will be just a little over half the length."

With the close of the drive on April 29, the numbers showed that the sales of shares fell a little short of the 300 quota. However, the drive was deemed a success. It was anticipated that when reports of those workers who had not submitted their final count were made, the goal would be achieved.

Although the construction of the course began on the first Friday in May, the formal ground breaking took place on Saturday, May 11. The ceremony began with a parade down Franklin Street. Eighteen automobiles filled with officials, directors and shareholders in the new country club lined up in front of the Chamber of Commerce office at the corner of Michigan and Franklin Streets. The combined Michigan City Boys Band and the high school band preceded the motorcade. At Detroit Street, the band members were taken by car to the club grounds.

A majority of the shareholders witnessed Fred Burnham turn the first spadeful of dirt on the new course and then listened to his brief talk. C. Matt Melville, Superintendent of Construction for Macomber, Inc., conducted a tour of the property explaining the layout of the course. The crowd was told that the first nine holes would be ready for play on the 4th of July.

By the first week in June six greens had been completed. Several of the fairways had been seeded. Ackerman and Sons began the task of drilling an artesian well. The water turned out to have a high content of sulfur, which was not suited for watering the greens. That coupled with a rainy June that washed out the newly seeded greens and caused a delay in their reseeding. The second green had to be temporarily relocated due to the delay of cutting down many large trees and the blasting of stumps in order to create the natural hazard for the hole at the original site.

As the end of June approached it became evident the course would not be ready to open on July 4th. A second six inch well was drilled to a depth of 100 feet but wasn't completed until July 1st. The pump and the iron piping that would provide water for the greens and tees was put in place over the next couple of weeks. While all of the fairways had been completed the greens weren't ready. They still needed to be seeded and fertilized. The opening of the course was rescheduled for August 15, barring unsuitable weather conditions and when the water was to be available at each green.

Work on the remaining three greens and fairways continued. By mid July the project began to take on the look of a golf course. The grass on three of the fairways had been cut. The grass on the remaining fairways was cut the following week. However, the delicate grass on the greens burned up due to the inadequacy of the water system and the drought like conditions during August. The decision to wait until the spring of 1931 to open the golf course was made in order to give the greens enough time to mature. In the meantime the greens were reseeded. An improved water system that would adequately meet the needs of the 1st nine holes that included a pump-house was designed and installed. It would also accommodate the 2nd nine when completed.

Harry Wagner, Superintendent of the country club grounds in an interview for the NEWS reported that the course would be ready for play in the spring. His experience over the previous nine years with the Grand Beach course helped to expedite the process. A garage and tool shed were built before winter set in. Bridges were in place, fairways were in excellent condition and several water hazards had been constructed. A stone road that would accommodate automobiles was built connecting Green no. 1 to Green no. 2, passing the proposed site of the clubhouse. Several paths on both sides of the road would allow for easy access through the grounds. Wagner also announced that the temporary greens at holes no. 1 and 9 had been replaced with permanent greens.

The annual meeting of the stockholders of the club was held shortly after Christmas. Northam, Zeigler and Rosenberg were reelected to serve as directors. Sam Boonstra a local architect, offered to draw up plans for a clubhouse. The directors, the following February, signed a contract with Taylor Lumber Company of South Bend to clear the trees from the area where the clubhouse and parking lot was to be located.

At their February meeting the board approved plans for the clubhouse. The plan called for a shower and locker room, a lounge and lunch stand. Signage was to be placed along the South Bend Road.

With the arrival of spring, the board of directors down to the greens keeper was all working to get the course ready to meet the Decoration Day opening deadline. Added to their toil were thirteen Tonn and Blank carpenters who spent a Saturday in early April erecting a temporary clubhouse. It was located close to the South Bend Road at the entrance to the course. The volunteers were: Fred Tonn, Charles Kuhn, William Kieffer, Ed Rieck, George Schrieber, Oscar Knoll, Clarence Rieck, Charles Pries, Willard Austin, Ray Schultz, Rudy Kunkel, Herman Wilke, and William Rieck. The material for the building was provided and donated by the Cash Hardware Company and the Central Coal and Lumber Company. The well-built 18 x 26 feet building would require several more weeks before its completion. The structure contained a refreshment stand, lounge and quarters for the instructor.

Although the goal of 300-chartered members had not been reached by mid May of 1930, plans to open the golf course on May 30th continued. Only 210 shares had been sold and paid for. Ten days before the opening of the golf course the board of directors announced the appointment of Pat Lahey as the golf pro for the first year of play. Lahey had been attending the University of Notre Dame. He was described as an excellent golfer and quite capable of giving lessons. His other duties were to manage the shelter, where a complete line of "up-to-date" golf equipment was available for purchase, and to be in charge of the course.

With only two weeks before opening day the fine details were being addressed. The temporary clubhouse was given a coat of paint, courtesy of Elmer Bloomquist. Sand boxes and benches were placed on the tees. Temporary sodding in spots on a few of the greens was done. Pat Lahey was kept busy with the furnishing of the clubhouse and getting supplies and equipment ready.

When the Michigan City Country Club was officially opened to the public on the morning of May 30, another historic day was added to the progress of Michigan City. The opening day ceremonies for the event were prepared by Loren W. Linard. Advertising Manager of THE NEWS. The honor of hitting the first ball was given to Mayor Harry B. Tuthill. "His honor teed a ball carefully, got the proper stance, and with a very official swing hit the ball straight down the fairway." Numerous rounds of golf were played that morning. One hundred and fifty boys "stormed" the course in anticipation of earning money serving as caddies. The dedication ceremony was held that afternoon with speeches and bows being taken.

Several prizes were awarded. First place prize of a golf bag from the Sporting Good store went to George Erickson for his score of 39. Clarence DeVeaux took second with a 41 and received a golf score register from Olsen and Ebann. John Erickson's 42 got him 3 golf balls donated by Walgreen's. A pair of silk hose from the Mike Krueger's Shoe Store went to Miss Helen Swanson for a score of 74.

The distinction of being the first casualty at the newly open course went to Frank Shadel, manager of the local Prudential Insurance Company branch. He was playing with John Blank and several of his family members. While playing the 7th hole, he was struck in the back of the head by a ball being driven by Richard Doherty. Fortunately he wasn't seriously injured.

"Golf…(has become) one of the most popular outdoor sports in the world. Millions of men, women, and children play golf as an individual or team sport, and in high school and college competition. Millions more enjoy golf as a form of recreation and exercise. Golf is also a popular spectator sport, attracting thousands of fans to tournaments. Millions more may watch tournaments on television.

More than 26 million Americans play golf every year. About a fourth of them are women. The United States has more than 16,000 golf courses. About 4,700 are private courses--country clubs and golf clubs available to members only. Another 11,300 are daily fee courses, which are privately owned facilities that admit the public for a fee. About 2,500 of these are publicly owned. The remainder is privately owned."[3]

"... another monument to the progress of the city."
Mayor Sallwasser

THE CENTRAL THEATRE: A VAUDEVILLE, PICTURE AND ROAD SHOW HOUSE

Unlike cities that succumbed to Urban Renewal in the 1960's, the city of La Porte has been able to preserve much of its rich architectural history. It remains one of the few cities in northern Indiana where a wide range of historic architecture can be viewed. A tour of the community provides a panoramic view of architecture from the mid 19th century to the present. These buildings stand as a testimonial to the farsighted residents that have preserved and restored these structures. One can still visualize what the downtown section of La Porte looked like during the first half of the 20th century. Many of the buildings exude the quaintness of that bygone era and bring back nostalgic memories. It is sad to say that despite the preservationists' efforts, the city of La Porte has lost some of its precious history to the wrecking ball. One of the most impressive downtown markers, however, is no longer there.

Once standing at the corner of Lincoln Way and Indiana Avenue was the beautiful Central Theatre. It opened its doors to the citizens of La Porte on March 29, l921. The theater was owned and managed by Orrin K. Redingote, a resident of the city since 1907, and George Rotes, a native of the county. The La Porte ARGUS quoted Mr. Redingote as saying, "the Central will be a vaudeville, picture and road show house. No production older than 20 days will be featured." He also pledged the best talent available would be presented on their vaudeville stage, "...while the road attractions will be those which play in the big cities."

The exterior of the building was of typical mission Italian design. There were four 22-foot marble columns at the front of the building, topped with the Corinthian caps overhung with Oriental spindle work. Stucco adorned much of the exterior walls. Two corner entrances as well as street exits at the head of every aisle made the building one of the safest in the state from the standpoint of exits.

Figure 46 Architect's drawing of the Central Theatre. The La Porte Argus, March 28, 1921, p. 1.

Upon entering the building, the public was mesmerized by a spectacular semi- circular lobby with a 46-foot dome. The lobby was decorated with green Vermont marble that circled the entire entrance. The flooring was of black and white tile design.

As one entered the auditorium, their eyes were drawn to the archway over the stage. The ARGUS reported that it was "...one of the most beautiful arches ever placed in any theater," measuring 32 feet wide and 20 feet high. The safety curtain was the only one of its kind in the state, made of asbestos, reinforced with metal. A four and one half foot wainscoting of green Vermont marble accented the auditorium walls. The main floor had a seating capacity of 800 seats and "...are so placed as to make every one a seat of the first class and giving an excellent view of the stage." A self-supporting balcony had a seating capacity of 400.

The formal opening of the theater occurred on March 28,1921, with three nights of notable events. Opening night was dedicated to Local 421, American Federation of Musicians. A 50-piece band representing the local organization under the direction of Professor Loose performed numerous selections. The La Porte Choral Society, directed by Reverend Clark R. Parker, also performed. A humorous monologue entitled, " When the boys Came Home," was read by May Beetles.

Numerous dignitaries were on hand and made speeches. They included Scott C. Defer, the architect, J. E. McCurdy, president of the musicians union, and Mayor Sallwasser. The mayor delivered an address of congratulations in which he praised Redingote and Rotes for the successful culmination of their work and declared "it to be another monument to the progress of the city." He went on to commend them for their part in "...bringing to the front the lighter and nobler side of life providing amusement, artistic and up lifting."

The second and third nights of the formal opening featured the Pathe Review, Pathe Topics of the Day and Pathe News that included "...up to the minute pictorial histories, and are filled with all the important current events." The double feature movies of "Get out and Get Under," starring Harold Lloyd and "Half a Chance," featuring Marlin Hamilton were also on the play bill. All of that entertainment for only 10 cents!

The La Porte ARGUS wrote, "In an atmosphere of melody and oratory the new Central Theater was opened to the public...with programs which will make the initial events a pleasing memory in the years to come."

How quickly we forget!

Upon the General Orders a camp of rendezvous for infantry forces was established in Michigan City

CAMP ANDERSON
& THE BOYS OF COMPANY A

The War Between the States caused a stampede to establish recruiting camps in Indiana in 1861. "Michigan City was on fire with patriotic fervor..." causing many men to enlist.[16] Captain William H. Blake organized and led the Michigan City Rifles, Company B. They were the first company to leave Michigan City, participating in the first campaign of West Virginia. First Lieutenant Asahel K. Bush and 2nd Lieutenant Alson Bailey were the other officers.[17]

The county board aware of the plight of the families left behind appropriated $2,000 for their relief. The county increased the amount to $10,000 as the number of volunteers increased. The county gave a $25 bounty to each man volunteering to serve in the military in 1862. The public-spirited citizens of Michigan City sought and raised $12,000 through pledges enabling them to provide a $300 bounty to each volunteer. The city's common council pledged the credit of the city and raised $4,000 by selling 10% interest bearing certificates, which allowed them to raise the bounty to $350.[18] Many men from Michigan City filled the ranks of succeeding regiments mustered in at other communities prior to the opening of Camp Anderson.

Upon the General Orders for Additional Volunteers issued September 1, 1863, by Adjutant General Lazarus Noble, a camp of rendezvous for infantry forces was established in Michigan City.[19] The camp was named for the Rev. Edward Anderson, Colonel Commanding, 12th Cavalry.[20] According to Martin Krueger, historian and former Mayor of Michigan City, Major Anderson was at Fort Sumter in the first battle of the war.[21] Camp Anderson was located about a mile and a half from the city just south of the Boyer farm.[22] It was situated on high ground near the creek having "sufficient water for all useful purposes." Hosler, Miles & Company constructed the buildings at a cost of around $100. An 18 by 25 feet officers' headquarters and an 18 by 100 feet barracks were the first constructed. The barracks was divided into five rooms and was capable of housing 124 men.[23]

The contractors were busy constructing several new buildings over the next few weeks. The sulter's building and the Colonel's headquarters were soon completed. Another barracks like the one first erected was also completed. The contractors were working faster than the supply of lumber could be delivered. Completion of the other necessary buildings was expected the next week.[24]

Camp Anderson became the temporary home for about 125 men early on. They were examined by Surgeon Dayton of the Enrolling Board of this District. All but one or two passed their physical. Capt. Alex Ewing recruited forty-two of these men from the Logansport area. Every one of Ewing's men passed. The Captain was expected to have a full company soon. Ewing enlisted when the war began. A newspaper reporter described him as an energetic and accomplished officer. Several squads, which included recruits for both infantry and cavalry made up the rest.[25]

The following is a description of the Camp's facilities found in the La Porte Herald:

"We made a brief visit to Camp Anderson last Tuesday. We only saw a few of the infantry, the most of them having gone out on recruiting furlough. There were eight companies of infantry represented, we learned and about seven hundred and fifty enlisted. The intention is to fill up this regiment within the next two weeks. They think this can be done. Eight companies of cavalry are full. It was not calculated that over four companies of cavalry would be raised in the District but the recruiting officers couldn't hold up: and now if permitted they could raise the other four companies in a week. They are not allowed, however, to do so, and the eight companies will be consolidated with the four raised in the Tenth District.

"The cavalry will probably go to Indianapolis next week. The infantry will remain in Camp Anderson until March.

"The camp is most splendidly arranged on high descending sandy land, where it is impossible to have mud. It was as dry and nice a pavement the day we were there. The barracks are of superior quality. Furnished with good stoves, floors, sleeping arrangements, and are closely battened, so that they are comfortable during the coldest weather.

"The Hospital is under the superintendence of Dr. Brown of Logansport, Surgeon, and Lysander Meeker of this city, Asst. do. Only ten patients were there, one of which was afflicted with a sore arm caused by vaccination. Only one was dangerously sick. Everything connected with the Hospital is in first best order, and all care and attention is given to the patients possible. Dr. Meeker seems to be just at home in the work and cannot fail in being a popular Surgeon. All the men in camp had just been vaccinated and there were a great many getting sore arms.

"We regretted very much that we were unable to meet Col. Anderson, who was at Indianapolis. We were under obligation to Capt. Peck, Capt. Ely, Surgeon Meeker, and Sergeant Frazier for kindness shown us.[26]

Nine buildings measuring 18 x 100 were constructed and in use as of February 1864.[27] Today the boundary of the camp is delineated by Michigan Boulevard, Woodland Avenue, the

Norfolk and Western railroad right of way on the north, and the alley behind the properties facing Edward Street.[28]

Michigan City must have been a fun and lively place with the camp nearby, according to Mrs. L. C. Palmer. Thirty-five years later in a talk before the Women's Study Club, she reflected on her memories of youth.

> "The town was quite gay with the uniforms of officers and soldiers. It was quite the thing to attend dress parade in the afternoon. I remember seeing two regiments as they marched away, quite a notable and impressive sight, with the sun shining and glistening on their bayonets. We were rather near the camp at our home on the hill, but were not molested in any way, only one night a party of intoxicated men tore down our large gate posts and front fence which presented a sorry sight the next morning. I believe these men were not allowed to go to town after that."[29]

Patriotism was evident in the hearts and minds of the residents of Michigan City. On occasion the commandant of Camp Anderson would march his regiment through the streets as bands played. The townspeople would cheer and while the ladies waved their handkerchiefs the men waved their hats high in the air. On designated days people from town would visit the troops in camp. Attending dress parades and witnessing the regiment taken through their drilling exercises was a popular thing to do.[30]

As is the case with many cities and towns that have military bases close by, a certain level of concern and discontent arises when the troops are allowed to go into town and unwind. Such was the case in Michigan City. The Common Council received numerous complaints from its citizens relating to the destruction of private property committed by the soldiers from Camp Anderson. It was reported that soldiers fired their weapons at townspeople when they tried to protect their property. Needless to say this prompted the City Council to approve a resolution to appoint the Mayor and Councilman Ames to meet the Camp's Commandant in order to put a stop to such proceeding.[31]

Letters from Camp Anderson dated from December 18, 1863, through February 4, 1864, preserved by the Indiana State Library would indicated that at least nine companies of the 12th Calvary were at Camp Anderson. Among the cavalry companies was one from La Porte County made up of 86 men under the command of Captain W. G. Peck. Besides the cavalry were numerous companies of infantry from throughout the state. Captain Levi Ely commanded the one from La Porte County.[32] The 127th regiment made up of Michigan City and Kendallville recruits under the command of Col. Anderson in April 1864, participated in the march through Alabama and Georgia.

The 128th recruited in the Tenth Congressional District was mustered at Michigan City on March 18, 1864. Five days later the regiment left camp and saw action with Sherman by participating in the march on Atlanta.[33] They numbered 891 fully equipped and armed men under the command of Lieut. Col. Jasper Packard. Although their time in camp was short they appeared ready to give a good account of themselves. They appeared confident, their maneuvers and drill elicited a warm expression of praise from the by-standers as they marched to the railway cars that would take them first to Indianapolis and then to the south. The 129th regiment also honored them by providing them an escort. The roster of the 128th included:

Arnold Bass

R. P. DeHart, Cass Co., Colonel
Major and Adjutant not appointed
Co. A, Capt. Bissel, raised in Newton
   and Benton Counties: 96 men
Co. B, Capt. Ewing, Cass Co.; 97 men
Co. C, Capt. Ely, La Porte Co.; 98 men
Co. D, Capt. Pierce, St Jo. Co., 97 men
Co. E, Capt. Sheffield, Porter Co.; 86 men
Co. K, Capt. Henton, Cass County; 80 men[34]

Jasper Packard, La Porte Co., Lieut. Colonel
I. Meeker, La Porte Co., Surgeon
Co. F, Capt. Staley, White Co., 81 men
Co. G, Capt. McAfee, Fulton and Cass
   Counties; 88 men
Co. H, Capt. Powell, Cass Co., 85 men
Co. I, Capt. Miller, La Porte, Benton and
   Pulaski Counties; 81 men

    They were assigned to General John Schofield's division and served in the Atlanta campaign.[35] They were active in fighting and "ridding the country of guerrillas and bushwhackers," in numerous skirmishes and battles.[36] The 129th Regiment recruits also came from the Tenth Congressional District and rendezvoused at Camp Anderson during the winter of 1863 and 1864.

    The LA PORTE HERALD of January 23, 1864, stated that through Colonel Anderson's energy and ability he "has been so active and vigilant in filling up the two regiments rendezvous at Michigan City, no district in the state has raised so many men as this...." With the conclusion of the war and "after a service brilliant in all its parts," Col. Edward Anderson retired from service in November 1865.[37]

    It was a sad day in the history of Michigan City when the last contingent of drafted men marched out of town to Camp Anderson on Michigan Street ankle deep in sand. Men women and children standing in the sand and sand burs watched and waved their farewells. "There were cheers from many and tears from some, from mothers, wives and children, from sisters and sweethearts...." As the drums marked the beat the fifes were playing that popular wartime tune, "The Girl I left Behind Me." The recruits were heading south to fill the thinning ranks of the Union Armies. After all President Abraham Lincoln had called them to arms to help save the Union.[38]

    A group of young men stood at the corner of Eighth and Michigan Streets and watched the procession go by. One of them said: "These are not the last men to go, all the men will have to go and if the war lasts long enough we will have to go too. When the rebels come here and take us all prisoners and take every thing away from us, then what are we going to do?" Another answered, "I'll tell you what we ought to do, we ought to get up a company and drill, and maybe when the rebels come we will...fight...."[39]

    They organized themselves into Company A, Home Guard, fearful that Morgan and his rebel raiders would invade Michigan City, "rob and burn it and perhaps kill many of its inhabitants."[40] Soon they numbered into the 20s, all living south of Eighth and east of Spring Streets. John C. Voss was elected Captain because he was the biggest in the bunch, which surely inspired respect. Harry Opperman was elected Lieutenant. One of the new recruits had a snare drum and was made official drummer. The fife was dispensed with since no one in the Company had a fife.[41] A later telling of this story has Martin Krueger, Lieutenant, William Holstein color-sergeant and Opperman the drummer.[42]

    Vacant land bounded by Tenth, Ninth, Lafayette and York Streets was selected for their drill grounds. The drills were held in the evenings. Captain Voss had a difficult time pounding "tactics in to the yellow heads of his soldiers." The cold winters in northern Indiana brought a halt to the drills. As the warm breezes of the spring of 1865 descended upon the land the war was over. The campfires of Company A were never again lighted.[43]

"The Boys of Company A put up their weapons and like all the citizens of Michigan City relished the peace that settled upon the nation. And after all summer would soon be upon them and their thoughts turned to summer vacation with all the activities schoolboys do. Oh! I may have forgotten to tell you these recruits of Company A, for the most part, were 'barefooted and bareheaded urchins' from 10 to 12 years old." Some of these boys, sons of German immigrants, had been in America for less than a year. The others too were sons of German immigrants. These boys talk of war and played war games as boys have done forever. They may not have understood what the war was about let alone the meaning of rebellion or secession.[44]

Sixty years later, almost to the day, the survivors of Company A came together to tell stories and reminisce. They met on the lawn of Martin Krueger's Springland Avenue home. Seated under the shade of the trees six members gathered to swap stories and recall the adventures of their childhood days. John Voss, Henry Opperman, William Meyer, Christian Kay, Fred C. Grischow and former Mayor Martin Krueger still lived in and called Michigan City home. Louis Lambka and John Luech were unable to attend. Some said that they were either too old or too far away. Frank Eggert died a few months prior to the reunion.[45]

As old soldiers do, they too enjoyed reliving and retelling the adventures of their soldier days. One recalled the help from a friendly Camp Anderson drill officer who drew a pattern of a musket on a piece of wallpaper. The pattern was used to saw "wooden dummy" rifles from old fence board. To add to the authenticity they added locks, triggers and bayonets made of scraps of tin. The scrap pile found behind Nagel's Tin Shop located opposite the St. John's building was a favorite place to scavenge untold treasures.[46]

Voss and Opperman learned and honed their skill by traveling out to the Camp to observe the rookies being put through their drills. It wasn't always an easy task for Captain Voss to "pound tactics in to the yellow heads of his soldiers." When his verbal orders were disobeyed or poorly executed the Captain "had the habit of emphasizing them with the toe of his boot and this always produced immediate results."[47]

They practiced fighting too, as one of the old veterans of Company A recalled with a "chuckle in his voice and glint in his eye." They all must have had a good laugh as the battle for hazel nuts was retold. Captain Voss marched his troops into Gould's woods in order to liberate the nuts. Standing guard was a large nest of hornets hanging from the lower branch of the tree. The troops spied the enemy on that Sunday afternoon and the battle began. The army fought with clubs and the hornets fought back with ferocity, showing no mercy. The assault lasted till dark with Company A victorious. The victory came with numerous casualties. The enemy had inflicted enormous pain with their stingers on the army. It was said that many a mother didn't recognize her son when he returned home from the battle with swollen face, hands and other body parts.[48]

The flag appeared to be their most prized possession. After all soldiers needed one to carry in to battle. In those days you couldn't go to the store and buy one, they were made. The honor of sewing the flag fell on Miss Minnie Holstein, later to become Mrs. Minnie Kay. She was Company A's Betsy Ross. She volunteered to sew the flag if the boys furnished the material. She produced a wonderful flag from some red, white and blue calico. Getting the money to buy the cloth was another story. A tax of 15 cents was levied on every boy in the Company and was to be paid in 30 days. Fifteen cents was hard to come by in 1864 one reminisced. These veterans sitting in the shade with a glass of refreshment in hand probably joked and laughed as they recalled how copper bottom wash boilers, old stove iron, brass, copper and pewter utensils disappeared in order to save the Union.[49]

Another amusing story evolved when the "young would-be soldiers" marched out to the camp shortly after he camp was closed. Their mission was to scavenge anything of value left behind that could be used to equip their ranks. Upon entering one of the abandoned barracks they found one of the compartments closed and barred. Needless to say that was the one they wanted most to enter. Above the door was a latched wooden transom. One of the boys was lifted on the shoulders of another, opened the transom and peered in. Much to his horror he spied "a dead man in there" and let out a yell and fell to the floor. "Every brave soldier" with his collection of junk ran from the camp as fast as he could.

As it turned out the closed compartment had been the office of the Camp Surgeon. Not having an immediate place to store his implements and equipment he left them behind until he could find a suitable place to store them. When the transom was opened a gust of air caused the human skeleton hanging from the ceiling by a cord to begin to move ever so slightly and thus the cause for the hasty retreat.[50]

They may have had tears in their eyes as they remembered returning after a drill to their clubhouse located in a deep "blow-hole" atop a high sand dune just north of what was Elston High School as they sang the popular war songs while sitting around their campfire. It was said that some of the boys at the time may not have understood the words to "The Battle Cry of Freedom," "When Johnnie Comes Marching Home," and "We'll Hang Jeff Davis on a Sour Apple Tree," but it didn't matter. It didn't even matter that their memories had faded and the stories retold were somewhat exaggerated.[51] What mattered was that their first reunion in sixty years brought several of them back together to reminisce, laugh, and raise a glass of cheer in honor of all the boys that were introduced to army life at Camp Anderson as well as themselves, THE BOYS OF COMPANY A.

UP CLOSE AND PERSONAL

PLATE OF BLOCKS 6,7,8 &9
CAMP ANDERSON ADDITION

Figure 47 This is a plat of Camp Anderson addition to Michigan City and treated as a part of the Addition recorded May 18, 1903, in Plat Book No. 3, on page 44 in the office of the Recorder of La Porte County and was north of the original plat. The lower drawing is a survey of Camp Anderson Addition to Michigan City filed December 2, 1902. It is located in the S. E. ¼ of the S. E. ¼ Sec. 28, T 38. It consists of Blocks Numbered 1 to 5 inclusive, which is divided into lots of the form, and dimensions as shown in plat. The Streets and allies are of the widths shown and were donated as public highways to remain as such forever. Copies of plats courtesy of Fern Eddy Schultz, County Historian

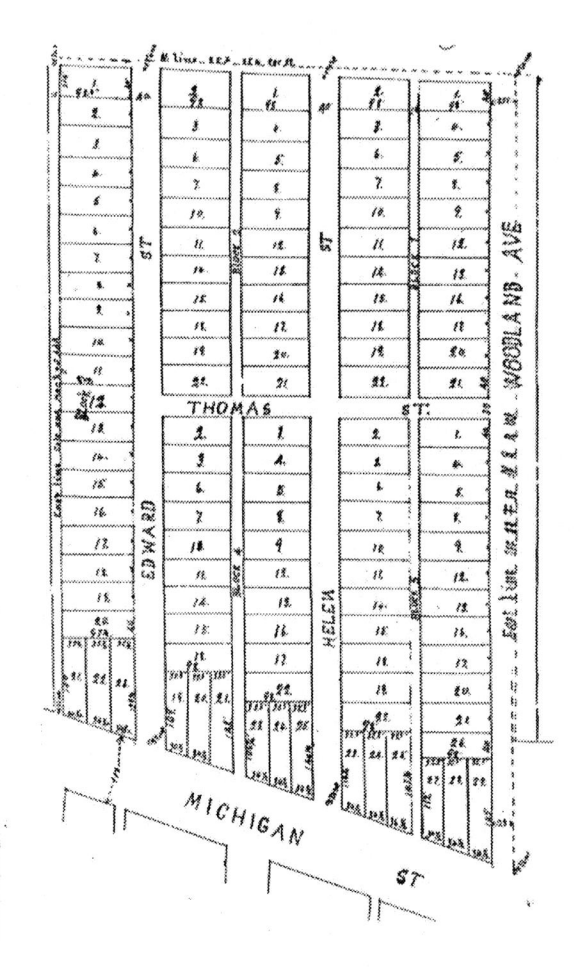

"The Protestants of La Porte County ...must at this time assume their proportionate share of caring for the sick, injured and unfit of the community,"
Management of Protestant Hospital Association
DAILY HERALD, *OCT. 30, 1925*

THE PROTESTANT HOSPITAL

Crowds gathered along the scheduled route in anticipation of the announced parade. At the appointed time the marching units from La Porte, Westville, Rolling Prairie and Michigan City stepped off to the sounds of the band. The marchers were carrying American Flags and other patriotic banners. Some of the participants were carrying crosses. The uniform of the day: a white smock that resembled a bed sheet and a pointed white conical hat with a flap and eyeholes that covered the face. Their message was that colored people, Jews and Catholics were inferior to the white Protestant population. The year was 1924. It was a time when The Ku Klux Klan dominated and controlled the government of Indiana. In fact the KKK of Michigan City, according to the headlines in the local newspapers indicated that the Klan controlled city government. The EVENING DISPATCH's headline on November 7, 1923, proclaimed, **"KLAN TICKET IS SUCCESSFUL."** The MICHIGAN CITY NEWS on the same day exclaimed, **"KLAN TICKET SWEEPS CITY."**

Against this backdrop of prejudice and dislike for foreigners, Catholics, and Jews, the "good" and prominent citizens of La Porte County decided that the people needed a Protestant hospital to tend to their serious health needs. The ARGUS reported on November 23, 1923, that it was rumored that the Ku Klux Klan was behind the move. Nearly a month later the DISPATCH reported the same rumor. The association, however, totally disavowed any ties to the Klan. John A. Parker, according to the DAILY HERALD, was the president of the association and the manager of the fund drive. At the onset the association had 20 members, five from Michigan City, five from La Porte, and ten from the rural areas of the county. These individuals of means and influence spearheaded the drive to build two hospitals, one, the larger, in Michigan City and the other in the city of La Porte.

Their initial effort came in the form of a letter that was to be sent to all county residents. A portion of the letter was reported in the March 22, 1924 issue of the DAILY HERALD:

"This assembly is composed of one member from more than 125 civic, fraternal and religious organizations, clubs, lodges and churches. There is only one requirement to be observed by each organization appointing a representative--that representative must be of the Protestant faith. The hospital, however, will know no creed or race."

Four months later the Reverend A. P. Meyer, pastor of St. Paul's Lutheran Church of Michigan City, reinforced the association's position by stating that these community hospitals were to serve the people of the county on a nonsectarian basis and were to be open to all regardless of race or religious creed, the DISPATCH reported in July of 1924.

Several days later the La Porte County Protestant Hospital Association released the results of a comprehensive survey of the county. They concluded that because of geography and the distribution of population there was a need for two additional hospitals. The city of La Porte provided a near central location in the county while Michigan City with the adjoining townships of Springfield and Coolspring had an estimated population of 28,000.

There were two long established hospitals already providing for the needs of county residents, Holy Family Hospital in La Porte and St. Anthony Hospital in Michigan City. Both were owned, operated and staffed with catholic sisters that supplemented the lay doctors and nurses. Reverend Meyer reasoned that a community should have 360 beds for every 150 people. Based upon that assumption, the county was in dire need of additional beds that two more hospitals could provide.

The La Porte County Protestant Hospital Association was organized in order to plan and develop a strategy that would culminate with the construction of two additional county hospitals. The names of the directors were made public for the first time in an article that appeared in the Michigan City NEWS on June 9, 1924. They were: John F. Lambka, Harvey O'Dell, George Felton, Charles Gale, George H. Wolfe, Henry Schaedt, Reverend Donald C. Ford and William J. Krause of Michigan City; Dr. Ira P. Norton, Ora Jackson, William W. King, A. M. Metzger, C. E. Wolfe and Edward Stern of La Porte; Roy McKellips of Westville; George Laramore, of Hanna; G. S. Jones, of LaCrosse; Marvin Freeman, of Union Mills; Hugh Tonagel, of Kingsbury; Bert McInterfer, of Stillwell; John Siddles, of Mill Creek and John M. Garwood, of Center township.

A meeting to outline plans for a $300,000 fund raising campaign to erect a hospital in La Porte was held at the Spaulding Hotel in Michigan City. Attending that meeting were Charles Gale and William Krause of Michigan City and A. M. Metzger and Ora Jackson of La Porte. The Collins property in La Porte, with a 260 feet frontage at 215 Pine Lake Avenue, was selected for the hospital. Two weeks later, on the 23rd of June, representatives of committees from throughout the county met in La Porte and voted to build the main unit of the new hospital in Michigan City. The property owned by M. A. Cushman, located on the corner of Fifth and Spring Streets was secured through an option to purchase. A few days later, in order to provide a larger base of support, a woman's division was organized with Mrs. Adolph Van Spanje as its head.

The machinery to facilitate the fund drive was in place the first week of July. A contest to involve the public was initiated. Ten dollars was offered for the best slogan for the Protestant fund drive and $5 for second best. Entries from throughout the county began pouring in. Among those received was one from a former nurse, Mrs. Anna E. Kuebel, R. R. 1, La Porte. Enclosed with her entry was a dollar, giving her the distinction of being the first to contribute to the cause.

The Michigan City's advance subscription committee met at the Y. M. C. A. A discussion of the issues and arrangements were made to move the drive forward. A few days later the EVENING DISPATCH carried an article that provided an elaborate description of the proposed Michigan City facility. The plan, prepared by Fred Ahlgrim, architect, called for red brick with limestone trim on the exterior of a three to four story, colonial style, fireproof building. As previously mentioned the hospital was to be built on the corner of Fifth and Spring Streets. A three story building already on the site was to be remodeled and used as a nurses' training school.

The plan for the "auxiliary hospital" in La Porte at the Dr. Samuel B. Collins property called for the remodeling of his sanitarium into a modern hospital. The two hospitals, when completed, would add one hundred beds to those already available.

Planning and organizational meetings in preparation of the fund raising campaign were held in Michigan City and La Porte on July 8th. The women's division met that morning at campaign headquarters in the Spaulding Hotel. The task of adding new committees and filling established ones was the order of business. Mrs. W. A. Underwood, Vel-Bert cottage, Long Beach and Mrs. Jesse K. Brennan of Michigan City were added to the Women's Advisory council. The La Porte division of the Business Men's Committee met at the Masonic Temple.

The Michigan City division of the Business Men's committee met at the Y. M. C. A for lunch. They too discussed various aspects of the campaign and their participation. Several new names were added to the committees' roster. The Reverend Donald Ford spoke, reviewing the purpose and plan for the benefit of the new members. The La Porte division of the Business Men's committee met for lunch at the Masonic Temple. They too reviewed the general plan of the campaign and gave an outline of the committee's task.

Three days later the La Porte Women met at the Rumely Hotel for tea. They elected Mrs. Eva Henry as their general chairman. The remainder of the meeting was devoted to organizing and planning their fundraising campaign.

During the last week of July 1924, the largest meeting of any division of the hospital organization up until that time was held in La Porte. Chairmen, committeemen and workers from Wanatah, Union Mills, Wellsboro, Westville, La Crosse, Stillwell, Center township, Hanna, Kingsbury, Rolling Prairie and Mill Creek were present. Following the supper that was served by Mrs. Henry Spitzer, Mrs. Roy Williams, Miss Myra Williams and Miss Dorothy James, Dr. Ira Norton presided over the meeting.

The last Sunday of July saw all of the Protestant churches in Michigan City focus on the Protestant Hospital campaign. The last major promotion aimed at the general public prior to the Tuesday kickoff was devoted to prayers and sermons that were intended to spiritually move the congregations to give generously to the drive. The next morning the All-Michigan City Men's Bible class held a large mass meeting at which Mrs. Mary Frances Kern, the campaign leader, spoke.

The stage had been set for the Tuesday kickoff luncheon meetings held at the Spaulding Hotel ballroom in Michigan City and the Christian Church in La Porte. The first day total reported was nearly $11,000, bringing the county total to $53, 694.40.

As the volunteers in Michigan City were about to take their places at the tables, the city's siren blew a "strong blast" to announce the opening event. Fire Chief Bowman and City Manager Couden had ordered the sounding of the siren. Added to the festivities and the excitement of the moment was the fire truck from station one that traveled up and down Franklin Street with its siren wailing. Among the reports given, one revealed that $43,694.40 was subscribed from the Michigan City area.

Both divisions held meetings everyday for the remainder of the week. At the following Wednesday's meeting the winners of the slogan contest were announced. Nearly 200 slogans were submitted. Mrs. J. Platt, Pine Lake received first place for her slogan, "Give It or Get It." The rationale given was that "...it seemed most helpful to the workers and would most express the spirit of the community that will put over the drive." The second prize went to Lillian Seeling, of Michigan City. Her entry was, "It Hurts No One to Help Everyone." It was the judges' feeling that it was "...a beautiful expression of the harmony of civic spirit and good will towards all that brings any movement of philanthropy and public welfare to a successful harvest." The judges, moved by the message, decided to issue a third place prize. It was awarded to Mrs. Ray E. Smith of La Porte. Her slogan was, " The dollars you give will Help Others to Live." The DISPATCH also announced that an additional $8,343 was subscribed in Michigan City and $3,000 in La Porte.

The issue of the Ku Klux Klan involvement and support of the hospital was called into question once again at Friday's luncheon gathering of volunteers. The Reverend Donald Ford, believed to be a member of the Klan by many, was an avid supporter of the Protestant Hospital. He addressed a question posed from the floor as to the Klan's support or management of the hospital. He responded that the Klan was sympathetic to the movement but had nothing to do with the hospital campaign. He assured the audience that the state would not allow a state chartered hospital to be taken over by the Klan. However, he did state that there were Klan members on the board of directors.

Besides the door-to-door and phone solicitation, two fundraising activities were conducted. The first, in early August, was the raffling of a quilt. Mrs. Henry Luecht made the quilt, donating the material and labor. The quilt was put on display in the show window of the Otto Aicher's furniture store in Michigan City. The raffle brought in $238. The other occurred in the latter part of September, when a pianist and a dramatic tenor from Chicago gave a recital at the Michigan City High School.

Looking ahead to the completion of the Protestant Hospital, the leaders of the fund drive proposed the formation of a permanent "inter-denominational board of directors," that would have control of the hospitals' construction and management. A plan was in place by early August. At a meeting in La Porte, provisions for a permanent governing board were approved. The new board would take control after the fund raising campaign concluded. The governing board would give representation to every Protestant church in both Michigan City and La Porte. The decision was made that all of the money raised in La Porte would stay in La Porte and all of the money raised in Michigan City would be used to build the Michigan City hospital.

The drive to raise funds took on another dimension in mid-August. Mrs. G. R. Turnbull, general chairman of the event, made a call for volunteers to sell tags in downtown Michigan City. Women were asked to meet at St. John's Hall, Franklin Street, on Saturday morning to receive instructions, canisters and tags cut in the shape of bricks. Women, only able to work in the afternoon, were to meet at the ticket office of the Sky Blue Arena. The tags sold for $1 each. The women also operated a refreshment stand at the arena, where items would "be sold very cheaply."

The end of September 1924 saw an announcement from the leadership of the La Porte Protestant Hospital Association, made public in the DAILY ARGUS, that due to some major objections to the Collins property, they had purchased the Charles F. Russell property at the corner of Michigan Avenue and Osborn Street. It would be more centrally located and not subjected to the delays associated with the N. Y. Central Railroad crossing. The large building could more readily be converted into a hospital facility. The property's 165 ft. frontage and 145 ft. depth would accommodate future expansion.

The Michigan City Protestant Hospital Association made their plans to transfer authority for the construction and operation of the hospital to a permanent board of directors. At a meeting held on February 3, 1925, over 500 contributors to the fund drive met in the assembly room of the Superior Courthouse to elect a permanent board. Among those speaking in support of the movement was the Rabbi Dr. Louis Kuppin. The following individuals were chosen to incorporate the organization: Walter G. Williams, M. A. Cushman, Adolph Van Spanje, Charles C. Gale, Otto Aicher, Donald C. Ford, Frank A. Rogers, George B. Johnson, A. R. Couden, Moses Moritz, Charles W. Tonn, Henry Koelin, E. G. Richter, W. W. Pepple and George J. Staiger. Nine more prominent men completed the board of directors. Although the Protestant Hospital movement may have had its origins with the Ku Klux Klan, it appears to have had little or no influence in the management of the proposed hospital. Rabbi Kuppin, and Moses Moritz, both of the Jewish faith, must have accepted that view. The need for an additional hospital in each of the two major cities of the county in their view was in the best interests of the people.

The location of the hospital on the Cushman property was reaffirmed at that meeting. The quarter of the block on the corner of Fifth and Sprint Streets had been purchased for $24,000, with a balance of $14,000 remaining.

Very little was accomplished over the winter months. The campaign appeared to lose momentum. Although $114,330.50 had been pledged, only $13,000 had been paid in by mid-August of 1924. Some of the Michigan City based doctors had decided to join forces and applied to the state to form the Clinic, Inc. with the thought that they might fill the void and build a new hospital. It became apparent to several of the doctors that the construction of the hospital at best would be delayed and at worst it would not be built. In their opinion, the need for additional hospital beds was immediate and could not be delayed.

By April of 1925, Dr. J. B. Rogers, president of the Clinic announced his group's intention to construct a private hospital at the corner of Fifth and Pine Streets, one block west of the proposed site of the Protestant Hospital. Dr. Rogers went on to say that it wasn't the Clinic's intention to supplant the Protestant hospital project, inasmuch as theirs would have a limited capacity of 25 beds and would be restricted to the practices of the doctors on staff. He added that his group still supports "... the Protestant General hospital...(and) will help raise additional funds and likely contribute more money toward its construction."

In spite of Dr. Rogers' announced intention to build the Clinic, the Protestant Hospital Association moved forward with their plan. They met on the 12th of June at their office in the Gregory building and elected their officers. Plans for further activities were developed in hopes of raising the funds necessary to complete the purchase of the property.

The early passion displayed for the fund drive to construct a Protestant Hospital was rekindled with the announcement that a carnival and circus was scheduled for the week of June

30th to July 4th. The report, which was carried in the HERALD-ARGUS, had a headline caption that read **"PICNIC AND CIRCUS TO RAISE MONEY FOR TWO KLAN HOSPITALS."** The La Porte County Klan No. 29 was to sponsor a "monster" picnic on the last day of the event in Michigan City. It was to attract several thousand Klansmen and women. Every Klansman and woman in the county was sent tickets with a request that they be sold.

Figure 48 Dr. Samuel B. Collins Sanitarium was located at 215 Pine Lake Avenue, which is now the location of the Round The Clock Restaurant. Photo courtesy of the La Porte County Historical Society

    Added to the festivities was a baby contest and a public wedding that saw two Klan couples, one from Gary and the other from Coal City, Ill. and McCool Ind. married. "The two couples were attended by twelve Klansmen in uniform," according to the EVENING DISPATCH. Reverend Donald Ford of the Christian Church performed the ceremony. In the meantime the doctors continued to move forward with their plan. Ahlgrim and Boonstra developed plans for an addition to the existing Clinic building. The remodeled structure called for the removal of the porch facing the Pine Street side, as well as the removal of the pointed roof so as to blend in with the flat roof of the new structure. Tonn and Blank was contracted to do the work. Dunlap and Son were given the sub-contract to excavate for the new basement. The brick veneer on the south and west sides of the building was removed and replaced with a yellow brick that harmonized with the new addition. Bedford limestone was used for the window and door trimmings. The new entrance was located on the Fifth Street side.
    The La Porte Hospital Association decided to revert back to their original location in 1925. The Collins property included an area of one and one-half acres with several large trees that bordered a natural growth of scrubs. The location was easily accessible. The Northern Indiana Interurban and bus line, the Jahn's Bus Line and the city bus serviced the area. The

Protestant Hospital Association had undertaken the task of remodeling the Collins property in La Porte. Progress on the work had been reported in the Michigan City NEWS in mid-October of 1925, with the expectation that the modernization would be completed by January 1, 1926.

An article in the La Porte TIMES, January 11, 1926, reported that several directors of the Michigan City division resigned while others were removed. There was no indication as to the reasons for the shakeup. Speculation would lead one to believe that there was discord among the leaders. The following day the vacancies were filled. William W. King was elected President a week later.

Efforts to raise the necessary funds to complete the La Porte hospital continued. Renewed efforts to raise the funds needed began in February. Workers were to canvass the residents throughout the county. Several luncheon meetings to coordinate and to receive progress reports were held in the basement of the Christian Church in La Porte during the campaign.

By mid-February the ARGUS reported that $21,500 had been pledged, at least half of that in cash already turned in. A small portion of the total came from a bazaar held at the La Porte hospital facility. The activity attracted many visitors, whose purchases were donated to the cause. It also provided them with the opportunity to tour the hospital.

Due to inclement weather, William King stated that the drive would be extended into the next week and would include sending workers to Knox in an effort to raise funds there. He also announced that work to complete the interior would be begun anew. Four days later King announced that enough money had been raised to complete the project. Nearly $2,000 had been collected.

The task of painting and finishing the interiors of the hospital and the nurses' buildings continued. An elevator had been installed. A "spacious convalescent porch" had been completed. Bathroom fixtures and lighting were in place. During the summer months the front and side lawns were seeded and growing well. Walks and driveways were roughed-in, to be completed just prior to the opening. However, due to the trickle of cash coming in, special composition flooring and the necessary hospital equipment had not been purchased. The project reverted to a state of suspended animation over the next four months.

In August the decision to float a $36,000 bond issue was made. The People's Trust & Savings Bank of La Porte handled the sale. The $50 gold bonds bore a 6% interest return, with various maturing dates that extended to August of 1936. The infusion of capital was used to purchase the equipment and pay the balance due contractors. The balance would be used to help pay the operating expenses during the first year of operations.

Another fundraising activity was held on the last Saturday of May of 1927. A benefit dance took place at the La Porte Casino. The Music Masters Orchestra performed the music.

Progress toward finishing the hospital moved at a snail's pace. Eleven months after the decision to float a bond issue, on July 1927, the public was invited to view the building. The facilities were nearly completed. All that remained was to complete the installation of equipment in the dining room, rest room, kitchen and storerooms, which were all located in the basement.

As the hospital was nearing completion the hospital directors conducted a search for a hospital administrator. Their search ultimately took them to Victoria Hospital in Prince Edward, Saskatchewan, Canada. Will W. King, president of the hospital board, announced that V. I. Sandt was hired and expected to be in La Porte on or before September 15th. The Sandts made their home at the Hoover Apartments, located on the corner of Harrison and Jackson Streets.

Sandt's credentials were impressive. The NEWS reported that he had transformed the Victoria Hospital from a losing institution to a profitable hospital. He possessed a wide range of experience in several phases of hospital work that included his "expert" skill as an X-ray technician. The fact that he was a native Hoosier and his two sons lived in Indiana made his decision to come to La Porte an easy one.

Upon his arrival, Sandt quickly went about the task of supervising the remaining details associated with the hospital's opening. Supplies arrived daily. The Ladies' Aid Society set about the task of preparing and making ready the linens. A Frigidaire and Chambers range as well as other kitchen equipment was installed. The board and Sandt were quoted as saying they would be, "...glad to receive any provisions, such as canned fruit etc."

He was also busy interviewing and hiring the staff of nurses, the housekeeping and ancillary help. Mrs. Ella Whitacre was hired to serve as superintendent of nurses. She was a native of Manistee, Michigan. She was a graduate of the Lutheran Hospital of Nursing at St. Louis, Mo., in 1907. Mrs. Lydia Decker Blake headed the obstetrical department. Hired to handle the task of general nursing were Miss Elizabeth Byers of Knox and Miss Elsie Holmes of South Bend. Two weeks later the newspapers in Michigan City reported that either in addition to or in place of

Figure 49 The Fairview Hospital renovations that completely encapsulated the Collins Sanitarium.

Byers and Blake, the hospital employed Misses Ruth Brown of Athens, Georgia, and Constance Ditland (the ARGUS spelled the name Eitland) of Chicago. Mrs. John Kaste was one of the maids. Richard Layman was employed as engineer. A few days prior to the opening Mrs. Walter Oswalt arrived from Lafayette to take charge of the kitchen. Her assistant was Mrs. Leslie Hatfield.

More than two years had passed since the remodeling of the property at 215 Pine Lake Avenue was begun. Officials of the hospital association proudly opened their doors to the community on Saturday, October 23, 1927, for two days of open house to be followed with a dedication ceremony on Sunday afternoon. The two-day event saw between 4000 and 5000 people from the county pass through their door. The crowd on Sunday afternoon became so large that it became necessary to allow a few at a time to pass through the front door.

The Reverend Alpha H. Kenna, pastor of La Porte's First Methodist Church, gave the dedicatory address, followed by a prayer. Superintendent Sandt and Mrs. Whitacre were introduced and briefly talked. William King, president of the board, elaborated on the physical facilities. The county's newest hospital would provide 23 beds for adults as well as a children's ward. Depending upon demand, the hospital could expand to 40 beds. He placed the value of the completed plant and grounds at $165,000. "This includes $30,000 for equipment, $125,000 for the hospital building and the nurses' quarters and $10,000 for the grounds."

The first patient to use the new facility was John Foster, 306 K Street, according to the ARGUS. He was a Teamster who worked for the Powell-Rose Saw Mill. He was there long enough to have 3 x-rays taken of his left foot, the result of which revealed a broken bone.

Although the Protestant Hospital found its birth in controversy, its contribution of meeting the health needs of the community was impeccable. It truly was a community hospital, which was demonstrated by the fact that no one was turned away due to color or race.

The La Porte County Protestant Hospital Association, nearly one year after the hospital was open, began deliberations of changing the hospital's name. William King stated that names for consideration included "The Maple City hospital," "Community hospital," "Pine Lake hospital," "Home hospital," and others. They finally agreed to change the name to Fairview Hospital. King announced in September 1928, that the La Porte Circuit was petitioned to begin the legal procedures. The new name was adopted soon after the court's approval.

INTIMATE SKETCHES OF BUSINESS MEN OF MICHIGAN CITY

CLOSE-UPS, INTIMATE SKETCHES OF BUSINESS MEN OF MICHIGAN CITY was the introduction for a number of biographies the Michigan City EVENING DISPATCH wrote to highlight the lives of individuals prominent in the business community. These in-depth articles described the passion, dreams and the motivation that propelled these men into the role of being the "Movers and Shakers of Michigan City." These INTIMATE PORTRAITS have been reproduced as they were written. Each biography included a line drawing likeness done by Herb Mason from photographs taken by the Bodine Studio.

FRED H. AHLGRIM

Scores of the finest buildings in Michigan City today stand as permanent monuments to the architectural skill of Fred H. Ahlgrim. He was one of the youngest men ever to be named to a seat on the city council and has always taken an active interest in movements which promised to make for a larger and more beautiful city. He was recently named as a member of the school board.

Born in a log cabin on a farm in La Porte county seven miles from Michigan City, he received his early education in the Hack School. Upon finishing the grades, he started laying brick at the age of 15, and for the next four years at that trade. He then entered the high school.

Through his work in building he had become interested in architecture and entered the University of Illinois where he specialized in this line. Following the completion of his studies he entered the employ of a Chicago firm of architects where he remained until 1912 when he returned to Michigan City and opened an office in the Gallagher building at Fifth and Franklin streets.

Business was slow at first and he soon realized the literal truth of the old adage that "a prophet is not without honor, save in his own country." However, the jobs which he managed to get were completed with a workmanlike touch and gradually business grew.

With the outbreak of the war in 1917 building stopped and he closed the office, going to LaPorte where he started to learn the business of tool designing. A few months later he went to Cincinnati and in less than a year was the highest paid man in the designing department.

Figure 50

FRED H. AHLGRIM

His political career started with his election to the common council in 1913, where he remained until 1917. The year after his election to the council he was named as chairman of the Republican Central Committee in Michigan City, and vice chairman of the LaPorte County Central Committee for the two succeeding years.

In 1920 he returned to Michigan City and entered the employ of the Pullman Car Co., in the designing department, gradually picking up his architectural business by working at night. He designed and acted as field superintendent on the First Methodist church, the Brinckman building, the community house at Memorial park, in addition to doing the work on numerous residences.

In February of 1923 he formed a partnership with Sam P. Boonstra. Plans for the recently completed Warren building, one of the most modern structures in the Middle West, were drawn by the firm. They are also handling the work on the new Elks club which is now under construction, and which will be a credit to the city when it is completed. Other buildings are the First Christian church, the Peoples State Bank, and The Clinic hospital, which are now under construction.

Mr. Ahlgrim is a member of the Masonic order, the Elks club and the Chi Psi fraternity. His hobby is fishing.

SEPTEMBER 9, 1925, p. 1.

UP CLOSE AND PERSONAL

JAMES C. BAINE

It was back in the days when the bicycle had just emerged from the risky "high wheel" cocoon, and the world was still admiring the "safety" wheel, the riding of which excited the admiration and envy of the populace and smacked strongly of a circus stunt, that James C. Baine first identified himself with the industry.

Today, as president and guiding spirit of the Excelsior Cycle Co. of Michigan City, employing more than 200 persons with an annual payroll of approximately a quarter of a million dollars, he is rated as one the largest bicycle manufacturers in the world.

The intermediate steps from that day when, as a 12-year-old boy he first entered the bicycle factory of the old Gormully-Jeffrey Co. of Chicago, to the present, are replete with the color, which fiction makers delight to borrow.

FIGURE 51

JAMES C. BAINE

It was young Jimmie, who at the age of 16 started the first bicycle store on North Clark Street in Chicago. Bicycling had become vogue in society circles, and realizing the opportunity, the lad set about giving free riding lessons to the exclusive set. As soon as they learned to ride he promptly sold them a machine from his store.

Racing came into its own. Manufacturers were selecting expert riders for teams and sending them about the country to compete at the various meets, which included everything from the county fairs to the national events. For several years he captured medals, cups and other honors in various sections of the country. Eventually opportunity offered itself and he got into the manufacturing end.

Born in Rochester, N. Y., he moved with his family to Chicago when he was seven years old, and it was there that he received his early education. There were nine brothers and sisters in the family, and at the age of 12 the lad started to work to support himself. In the assembling plant he worked 10 hours each day for $3.50 a week.

In a little over three years he had mastered the various processes in the manufacture of bicycles, and it was then that he saw the possibilities in the retail business. During the three years he had gradually accumulated a small savings account, which he invested in his new venture. Bicycles in those days were selling for from $125 to $150. Business prospered and he continued to operate the store while tending the various racing events. In 1899 he sold the retail business and entered the employ of the Excelsior Supply of Chicago. Nine years later this company, operated by a son of the founder, became involved in financial difficulties through a venture into the automobile motor manufacturing field, and Mr. Baine purchased the original bicycle end of the business, and changed the name to the Excelsior Cycle Co.

Viewed from one direction it seemed a poor time to start manufacture. Other concerns were engaging in a cutthroat battle of price shading. Mr. Baine and his associates decided to start on a policy of making a little better product and charging a little better price. Business began to come with increasing volume.

In 1916 with a view to obtaining more commodious manufacturing quarters, and better living conditions for the employees and their families, the plant was moved here to Michigan City, and with it came more than 50 families. As the plant got into operation more than 100 local people were given employment.

Today the plant is making between 60,000 and 70,000 machines each year, or an average of approximately 300 bicycles per day.

Mr. Baine is a 32nd degree Mason, a member of the Shrine and Consistory, the Manufacturer's club and the Chamber of Commerce. His home, on South Franklin Street is one of the show places of the city. He also has a summer home on the beach.

He is a boxing fan of the first order, and for years has attended practically every championship bout. Summer mornings find him hiking down the smooth sandy beach preparatory to a plunge in the lake.

JULY 22, 1925, P.1

B. H. BLOCKSOM

Michigan City today boasts of having one of the world's largest independent plants for the manufacture of curled hair, at the head of which stands B. H. Blocksom. The plant which gives steady employment to more than 135 persons, has an annual payroll of approximately $150,000, while the merchandise is not only shipped all over the United States and Canada but to the principal European countries as well.

Since he organized the company here in 1919 Mr. Blocksom has taken a keen interest in the development of the city, as well as in his plant which has enjoyed a steady growth.

When he was ten years old Mr. Blocksom's father died, and two years later he started battling the world on his own. Those were the days when there were no child labor laws and after his day's work in a toy factory was completed he spent the evenings in a shoe store, which on Saturday nights remained open until midnight, to augment the weekly paycheck.

Born at LaPorte, he moved with his people to Defiance, Ohio, at an early age and there started his education. Following the death of his father he went to Port Colborn, Canada where he lived on a farm with relatives for the next two years until his mother could make a home for him back in the States.

UP CLOSE AND PERSONAL

At the age of 18 he went to Chicago where he got a job as a coffee roaster XXXX coffee factory. He realized that education was essential to success and began saving his earnings. Later he entered Valparaiso University and by doing odd jobs, managed to complete several courses.

Upon the completion of his education he returned to Chicago where he entered the employ of Morris & Co., and in the following ten years mastered the various branches of the general packing industry. His work attracted the attention of Sulzberger & Sons Co., now Wilson & Co. and he accepted a position with this firm because it offered opportunity for greater advancement. To make the change it was necessary to begin on a salary of $16 a week, but in the course of a few years he was holding the position of manager of the byproducts department.

Here he specialized in the manufacture of curled hair and became recognized as an authority of the subject, bringing out and developing several new processes.

FIGURE 52

B. H. BLOCKSOM

It was in 1919 that the opportunity was presented to go into business for himself. He immediately began looking about for an ideal location for the new plant. Hearing of this, the chamber of commerce invited Mr. Blocksom to visit Michigan City, where he quickly saw the natural advantages offered in this section.

Through the perfection of a quick, sanitary and effective method of handling production the business started to grow rapidly, and is today recognized as one of the largest independent concerns of its kind in existence.

Mr. Blocksom is a 32nd degree Mason, a member of the South Shore Country Club of Chicago, the Pottawattomie Country club, the Long Beach Country club, the Michigan City Manufacturer's club, and the Rotary club.

Reading the old masters is his favorite form of diversion. He is particularly partial to Dickens, with whose entire works he is familiar.

AUGUST 6, 1925, P.1

ALBERT R. COUDEN

FIGURE 53

ALBERT R. COUDEN

Efficient service, productive of tangible results, has featured title administration of Albert R. Cowden as city manager, and today he is accorded a high place among the men who have the interests of Michigan City at heart.

Through the application of business methods to city government he was able to rapidly unsnarl situations that for years had been snarled. For more than 10 years attempts had been made to lay a main trunk line sewer, which would care for the south side of the city.

Although more work is actually being done today in the city, the tax rate has increased less than 20 per cent.

When Mr. Couden stepped into the office 18 months ago he found that a start on the work had been made but through a misunderstanding a deadlock had resulted and the work was at a standstill. One of his first moves was to call the men together, and thrash out the difficulty. As soon as the weather permitted the construction was resumed and completed in a few months.

For many years this sewer, which cares for about half of the city, had been an open ditch, menacing the health of the people. Not only was the job promptly completed, but also preparation was made for the future expansion, thus eliminating the necessity of going to the expense of relaying it in the course of a few years.

Three other sewer projects are now in the process of construction. These are the Wilshire Avenue, the South, Park and the Edwards and Holliday lines. With these finished the city will have a complete and modern disposal system.

Last year more than three miles of water mains were laid while this season work on another three miles is being carried on. In addition to these projects, several miles of streets have been paved and the necessary repair work taken care of.

One of Mr. Couden's first moves upon entering the office was to provide adequate fire protection on the west and east sides of the city. Arrangements were promptly made for the establishment of two new fire stations, which eliminated the necessity of crossing the railroad tracks, which might at any time be blocked for several minutes by freight trains.

Previous experience and training, prior to taking over the management of the city, admirably fitted him for his duties. He was born here of pioneer stock, his grandfather having moved to Michigan City 10 years after the founding of the village. Here he received his education, first in the grade schools, and later graduating from the high school course. While attending school he delivered papers to earn spending money.

Upon the completion of his education he entered the employ of the Haskell-Barker Company in the capacity of office boy, where he remained until he went to firing on the Michigan Central in 1903. The following year he went to Chicago with the Armour Company and entered the timekeeping department. Application to his work quickly won recognition and he gradually advanced until he was in charge of the department and responsible for the records of more than 15000 men.

Having completely familiarized himself with this work he was asked to return to Michigan City and install a modern system for the Haskell-Barker people. In 1913 he was made paymaster of the concern, and held this post until 1919, when be was placed in charge of the industrial relations department where he had charge of the welfare work for all of the employees and their families. In January of 1924 he was appointed to his present office.

Mr. Couden is past master of Acme lodge No. 83, F. & A. M., and a member of the Rotary club and the chamber of commerce. Motoring is his favorite form of relaxation.

JULY 8, 1925, P. 1.

J. R. CULLEN

Figure 54

One of the firm believers in the future of Michigan City is James R. Cullen. Any movement which tends toward the making of a bigger and better Michigan City finds in him a ready booster. Coming here seven years ago he immediately saw the advantages offered and today is one of the foremost developers of real estate in the city.

He is one of those men blessed with a spirit of adventure and a keen sense of humor. At the age of 21, equipped with his education from Clongowes College, Royal University, Dublin, he left the shores of his native Ireland and came to the States, which he believed offered greater opportunity for a man willing to work.

He landed with his determination and little else. The first job that presented itself was juggling ingots in a brass foundry ten hours a day. At the end of each ten hours he was awarded $1.35 for his efforts. A few months later he arrived in Cleveland where he took a job as a street car conductor, and shortly afterward went to work in a department store as a drygoods clerk.

It was in 1901 that he first entered the insurance game in the same city, and seven years later moved to Erie, Pa., to take charge of the company's interests there. In 1906 he went to South Bend where he affiliated with Vernon C. Hastings in the insurance and real estate business, and just after the close of the war came to Michigan City to act as manager of Laporte county for the Aetna Life Insurance Co.

Having been thoroughly sold on Michigan City in the two years that followed he opened a real estate office and began selling Michigan City to others. He also handled a general line of insurance and bonds specializing in contract bonds. Two years later the business had outgrown its first location, and in company with J. H. Orr he opened his present office.

Since that time he has taken an active interest in opening up several of the city's new subdivisions, including the Memorial Park, the Dune Highway Estates, Pleasant Ridge, in addition to considerable beach property. Mr. Cullen also is actively interested in the financing of small homes.

When the Real Estate board was organized here four years ago he became its first secretary and one of its most enthusiastic charter members. He is also a member of the Chamber of Commerce, the Rotary club, the Long Beach Country club, the University club, the Knights of Columbus, and the Y. M. C. A. He denies active membership in the Klan.

His pipes are his hobby. Whenever a good pipe is found around any of the banks, or offices where real estate deals are pending, Jim is always the first man called to identify it as a possible member of his stock of some 30 pipes, which he has been collecting for several years. He is also an inveterate "bridge" player.

Erin Vale, Mr. Cullen's Long Beach home which was recently completed is considered one of the show places of the city.

He was named as a delegate to the National Convention Of Real Estate Boards held at Detroit, and owing to the difficulty experienced in obtaining accommodations at Detroit, made reservations at Windsor, Canada.

SEPTEMBER 24, 1925, p. 1.

MARTIN KARPEN

Twenty years ago, Martin Karpen winging a lunch basket, entered the Chicago factory of S. Karpen & Bros., and worked through the various departments from errandboy to salesman, studying every branch of the business from the design of the furniture to the merchandising of the finished product.

From Karpen to Karpen for over five generations the family have been master furniture builders and, therefore, it was natural that in 1916 when S. Karpen & Bros. purchased the former Ford & Johnson plant in this city, that Martin was placed in charge of the Michigan City branch, which was to operate in conjunction with the factories of S. Karpen & Bros. in Chicago and New York.

The local factory started at that time with a force of 150 men, while today there are over 500 employees with an annual payroll of over $1,000,000, and it ranks as one of Michigan City's largest assets with Martin Karpen as its managing director.

Careful and conscientious, modest and unassuming, Martin Karpen goes about his work always having in mind a larger and better furniture industry for the city, and the carrying out of sound and practical ideals and policies which Mr. Martin S. Karpen's father established for the good of the furniture industry and for the benefit of Karpen's workmen.

It is no mere accident that this plant has been kept in steady operation since its reopening. Through a sound knowledge of furniture building, a vision with anticipation of what the public desires and a natural application to duty, Martin Karpen has been able to make the progressive improvements which have resulted in the steady and continuous operation of the plant.

Figure 55

MARTIN S. KARPEN

Workmen and associates intimately connected with Martin Karpen tell that, in his walks through the factory, especially when new samples are being made, at a glance, with a slight touch here and there, the toning down of a color, the selection of proper cover, and with out any commotion, or boastfulness, a new and delightful combination has been given to the public.

Style changes are not limited to clothes and motor cars, for the furniture industry, presents to the public, style changes and new designs four times a year, and all of this tedious, delicate painstaking work accomplished in this factory revolves around Martin Karpen's ideas and suggestions.

The Michigan City people probably do not know that the fiber furniture, now so popular in sun parlor and even living rooms, originated in this city, and when the Karpens took over the present plant with their genius and master touch, they brought this fiber furniture into universal use and approval.

The Karpen factory under Martin's direction and guidance is a human institution which is just as much interested in the welfare and upbuilding of its employees and their families, as they are in the development of the industry.

A gift to their employees when they are married, a gift at the birth of each child, and provision made for the payment of an insurance benefit upon the death of the head of their family, and in addition to all of this a bonus at Christmas time—all of which shows a steady and continual interest in their employees from the cradle to the grave.

We could continue to tell you of the accomplishments of Martin Karpen and the firm which he so faithfully represents. Even in civic affairs, in the organization and development of the Manufacturer's club, on the city planning commission, many memberships in the chamber of commerce in fact, everywhere you find Martin Karpen, you find the same activity and loyalty for better and greater accomplishments. Such is Martin Karpen, a citizen of the highest and soundest character.

JULY 15, 1925, P. 1.

MATT J. KENEFICK

FIGURE 56

MATT J. KENEFICK

No need to tell you who this is, just plain Matt J. Kenefick, a big and broad versioned fellow. We went in to talk to him and found him more interested in his friends and more willing and interested in talking about their success than about himself. We found that he and George Baker, when they were boys, carried papers together, and they had all kinds of fun seeing who could get the most subscriptions, and that today Baker was one of the leading bankers of this city, and had an excellent future ahead of him.

We found him enjoying the accomplishments of Herb Riley, and most particularly interested in Martin and Harry Karpen, and how these two young fellows had built up a furniture plant for Michigan City, that rivaled anything that the town thought of in the old days of The Ford & Johnson Company.

How the city was growing, changing, and no telling how far or how fast the city would grow, the fellows like Blocksom, McLundie, Angsten and Baine, at the head of manufacturing plants, are increasing their business and putting Michigan City on the map.

We learned that Matt went to St. Mary's School of this city and from there went to Notre Dame and came home and started in the law and insurance business and his business today is one of the best of its kind in this city.

We tried to talk to him about politics, but all we could get was a smile, and the answer that that was long ago, and was now only a memory. That his experience as city attorney was very valuable and gave him broader ideas of public relations.

To know Matt Kenefick is to like him and we came away with the impression that here is a fellow who would make sunshine out of the rain. You simply transfer your troubles to him and forget them.

SEPTEMBER 30, 1925, P. 1.

UP CLOSE AND PERSONAL

W. B. MANNY

Standing out against a colorful background of more than half a century of residence in Michigan City, William B. Manny looms prominently among the Men who pioneered the way and assisted in the up building of the town.

Discovery of the value of the dune sand for foundry work, the starting of that industry here and the removal of the seven-million-ton Hoosier slide; the serving of the city as its first City Manager under the new form of government; a record of 38 years of railroading on the Monon; the recognition of the beach possibilities, and the building of the first cottage there--these are among the high lights of his career.

Figure 57

W. B. MANNY

It was back in 1872, as a 10 year-old lad, that he first made his appearance on the streets of Michigan City-- "City" by courtesy, for in reality the town in those days was a small village of less than 3,000 inhabitants, with board sidewalks and rough corduroy roads. By night these streets were illuminated by smoky kerosene lamps, in which, owing to the fact that they were the latest thing in municipal improvement, the folk felt deep pride. It was to this village that he came with his parents from Waukegan, Illinois, where they had moved to shortly after his birth at St. Joseph Michigan.

Seven years later the fates started him on his railroading career. It seemed at first as though he was adapted for school teaching. A small country school five miles out of town was without a teacher and he took the job, walking both ways night and morning. At the end of the first month he was tricked out of his pay, and laboring under the belief that even a school teacher is entitled to eat, he quit. It was at this psychological moment that he was offered the job as roustabout for the local station of the New Albany and Salem Railroad, which is now the Monon.

This job paid real money. Those were the days before union hours had gained such a wide spread popularity, and a grind of 16 to 18 hours was not at all uncommon. The fact that he occasionally met himself "going back to work" when going home at night, attracted the attention of the officials of the road and in a few months he received his first promotion. In 1887 he was made traveling auditor of the entire system, and three years later returned to Michigan

City as general agent. His next step up came when he was promoted to division freight agent, and this position he held until he resigned from service in 1917.

Meanwhile he was on the alert for opportunity which was never forced to knock at his door. Shortly after he had started his railroad work, foundries began to spring up around the country, creating a demand for the purest of sand. Hoosier Slide towered nearly 200 feet in height, the biggest of the dunes, and year by year, driven by the off-lake winds, it was gradually creeping over toward the town.

Mr. Manny discovered a way to rid the town of this menace, and at the same time supply the foundries. Consequently a spur of track was laid and the shipment of the sand begun. Year after year the cars were filled and shipped until today nothing remains of the Slide but the memory. It is estimated that if all of the cars of sand which have been shipped were strung into one train the engine, in the state of Maine, would be pulling the caboose out of Michigan City.

During most of the time that Mr. Manny was with the Monon, Michigan City was one of the largest lumber markets in the United States; the lumber coming in by boat and being shipped out by rail. Large shipments of salt, pig iron and railroad ties came into its harbor, and he was kept in very close touch with marine matters when Michigan City's harbor was one of the greatest on the lake.

Years ago Mr. Manny realized that Michigan City's beach, formed of pure white sand, and recognized as one of the finest on the Great Lakes, would be a popular summer watering spot. It was with the late I. I. Spiro that he became interested in the development of the east beach as a summer resort, buying all of the land from Washington Park up to and including the Hermitage. Folks laughed, and he, blessed with a keen sense of humor and the ability to laugh at himself, laughed with the others, but nevertheless went ahead and built the Pioneer cottage, the first on the beach. Their pioneering — and it was pioneering because few had time to think of summer homes in those days—paved the way for the greater improvement that was to follow.

With the change of city government to the present system, the commission in casting about for someone who could take the tangled affairs and straighten them out, as well as work out a sound financial footing for the city, selected Mr. Manny. For nine months he worked at the job, and as soon as he could "see out of the woods" he resigned.

The attention Mr. Manny has given to his several endeavors may be well reflected by the following personal letter he received from the President of the Monon Railroad when he resigned from the service of that company: "It is with a keen sense of regret that I am brought to a realization of the fact that after thirty-eight years of faithful and effective service, you are no longer to be with us. I regret it particularly because it is brought about by your condition of health. I, am sure there has never been a time when you have failed to give the Monon the very best you had, and I am sure that the many both small and large matters which have been entrusted to your judgment have been handled to the satisfaction of your superior officers. I think it may truthfully be said, "in your years of service here, you have done your duty and have done it well."

Having watched the village develop from the oil lamp stage to an electrical city, and from the hand-organ to the radio, Mr. Manny smiles, and it is a smile that bespeakes faith in the future.

JULY 29, 1925, P. 1.

UP CLOSE AND PERSONAL

G. G. McLAUGHIN

For nearly three years G. G. McLaughlin has been in Michigan City. During that time thousands of visitors, have come within the radius of his friendly greeting. Carrying away with them a pleasant memory that lingers. Today the Vreeland hotel is known as a place where there is a lot of good fellowship, coupled with comfortable surroundings.

Born in San Pierre, Indiana, Mr. McLaughlin started his education there in a little district school which he attended for two years until his family moved to Chicago. Following the completion of the grades he attended the John Marshall high school, and later the Lewis Institute of Chicago where he prepared for Notre Dame. As a boy he started his career with a paper route.

His college days date back to the time before the press of the nation had begun devoting so much space to Notre Dame's football activities. In those days .50 cents admitted one to the games, and the majority of the time the elevens played to sparsely filled stands.

Those were the days that baseball was sitting on the sport throne of the university and it was on the diamond that "Mac" did his stuff out around first base. His tall frame made a fine target for his mates to throw to, and at the same time made it possible for him to keep one foot on the sack while reaching halfway across the diamond to garner in a wild one.

Figure 58

With the completion of his education he became a farmer of sorts. At the request of his mother he took over the management of the estate, which comprised approximately 2,000 acres near LaCrosse. In addition to the raising of corn, wheat, oats, and other crops, much of the acreage was in wild hay.

Those were the days before excelsior had come into its own and the eastern glass manufacturers were crying for wild hay to be used in packing their product. Late summer

G. G. McLaughlin

would hear the whine of the mowing machines as the hay was cut and stacked. In the early fall this would be baled for shipment. With an annual production of over 6,000 tons of hay, it was found expedient to run in a spur to the railroad to take care of the loading and shipping directly from the presses. It was in January of 1923 that Mr. McLaughlin, in company with Noel Cooke came to Michigan City and purchased the Vreeland hotel. The establishment immediately underwent repairs which were necessary to put it in first class condition. Together the men operated in partnership until last March, when Mr. McLaughlin took over the entire business.

Since his boyhood "Mac" has always been a lover of nature and outdoor life. His hobby is hunting, and he is particularly partial to ducks, grouse and other forms of wing shooting. His kennel of bird dogs has the reputation of being among the best trained in this section.

Recently he was able to put a pet theory of his to a test. He had long maintained that environment was what in reality made the wild animals wild. A farmer plowing near one of his farms routed out a gray timber wolf from a haystack. Later in the day he returned and shot the animal. Further investigation proved that the wolf had a nest of cubs in the stack, and the farmer rather than let them starve took them in to the barn.

One of the pups was presented to Mr. McLaughlin who raised it on a bottle. Today, the wolf, which is two years old and full grown, plays with the children and to all appearances is a high grade police dog. Never has the animal shown the least sign of treachery.

Mr. McLaughlin is a member of the Elks club and the Knights of Columbus.

SEPTEMBER 16, 1925, p. 1.

ROBERT H. MOORE

Figure 59

ROBERT H. MOORE

Michigan City needs no introduction to Robert H. Moore, for those who didn't know Bob personally will, and those who did can't forget him. He loves nothing better than being in the midst of a good scrap, settling someone else's scrap, for he is an attorney by vocation and an orator by avocation.

Immediately following the War he became county prosecutor, which office he held for the following three years. He has also had a frequent finger in flavoring the city's political pie.

Born in Dundee, Mich., of sturdy pioneer stock which had taken root in American soil for generations back, he started on the road to knowledge in the public schools of Michigan City where he had come with his parents when he was four years of age. Upon completion of the grades he entered the St. Mary's high school from which he graduated in 1904.

Since the days of William of Orange, of whom he is a direct descendent, his family tree had been liberally sprinkled with barristers, and in accordance with an old family tradition he was dedicated in the law at the baptismal fount. But in spite of the preordination it seemed for a time that it would be impossible for him to ever be admitted to the bar, for the problem of financing a university education seemed to bar the way.

Young Bob however, went to work and in a year had saved enough to enter Valparaiso university, where with the aid of a paring knife he met all of his expenses. Legend has it that as the champion "spud" peeler he hung up a record of a bushel an hour which has never been tied or beaten.

In two years time he had completed a four year course of study, comprised of a two year law course and an oratorical course of equal length. It was during his last year in school that he indulged his penchant for debating by challenging Arthur Marlowe of Chicago, and Reese of Toledo, in addition to other prominent socialists to oratorical tilts on deep subjects. He was admitted to the bar a week after he became of age, being at that time the youngest attorney in the state.

Upon his graduation, he immediately returned to Michigan City where he started practicing. In marked contrast to his present suit of offices in the new Warren building, his first office was in a little room furnished with a kitchen table and chair. But Bob hustled and business began to come. Clients found that Attorney Moore had a habit of winning his cases.

It was discovered that in the court room his oratorical ability, coupled with a knowledge of law and applied psychology, liberally sprinkled with quick repartee made it possible for him to present the facts in a clear-cut fashion which remained in the minds of jurors after they had retired to their deliberations.

In politics, in which he became totally indulged, he took a keen delight, and while his opponents might hurl other charges at him, it was never said that he lacked the courage of his convictions. If he believed a certain issue was right he went out preaching that doctrine with a liberal display of pyrotechnics. Others might sit on the fence if they choose, but it never took long to tell which side Bob was on, and he was inevitably found on one side or the other.

A tribute to his agility at painting word pictures came at the outbreak of the war when he was chosen as one of the original 40 Indiana Minute Men who toured the state in the interests of national defense. Again, just before the Harding election Attorney Moore was summoned by the party leaders to Chicago to make a speech at the national headquarters in behalf of the late president, and the following night he was given charge of the entire floor. It was at this time that he won the title of "the whirlwind orator of Indiana."

Early in 1918 he enlisted in the officer's training camp and was sent to service at Camp Taylor where the armistice found him. Following his discharge he returned to Michigan City where he became county attorney, resigning this post a few months later to take over the duties of the office of deputy county prosecutor. As prosecutor he established an enviable record for the rigid prosecution of crime.

He enjoys law as some men enjoy golf, taking a keen relish in matching wits and words in a court room. If he is scheduled to appear in a case spectators are insured of an hour by no way dull, for his quick and witty sallies break up the boredom with which the legal machine, sometimes grinds. He has the rare gift of wringing the music out of words, simultaneously setting forth the issues in a concise and vivid fashion.

In addition to reading the old masters of the English language, his hobbies are swimming and horseback riding, while the most strenuous exercise of which he is guilty is moving pictures. Fraternally he is connected with the Odd Fellows and the American Legion.

To the inspiration of two women he attributes whatever measure of success he has achieved, or as he aptly puts it: "My mother was an angel and she willed her wings to my wife."

SEPTEMBER 4, 1925, p. 1.

MOSES MORITZ

Figure 60

M. MORITZ

With a fixed determination to succeed, Moses Moritz began as a boy helping his father in his clothing store after school and during the evenings. Today he stands at the head of one of the city's leading clothing houses, which is backed by a record of more than 60 years of service to the community and is one of the finest equipped concern of its size in Indiana. He has always taken an active Interest in movements which would make Michigan City a better place in which to live.

For fifteen years he was a director in the Michigan City Charity Organization. His early education was received in the public schools, following which he entered the old Central high school and completed the commercial course. Upon finishing his education he entered the store with his father gradually mastering all of the various phases of the business, which had been founded immediately following the Civil war.

The first location was in the old Sherman block which in recent years has been used as the Elks' temple. The post office was in those days located in the rear of the store building. In 1879 the firm was moved to the Mozart Hall building where it remained for the next five years until another move was made to the Orr block which housed it for more than 40 years.

In 1913 Mr. Moritz's father died and he assumed full control of the business. Five years ago he purchased the lot where the present building now stands. The old store had outgrown its location and the new property was acquired with a view to expansion. In 1924 plans for the new two-story building were drawn and building operations started, with the result that today the new store is considered the finest for its size in the state.

That Mr. Moritz is a firm believer in the future of the city is attested to by the fact that foundations have been put in which will carry additional floors when this space is needed. The first floor of the building now carries the men's department while the second floor is devoted to children's stock.

Back in the days when electric lights were considered the seventh wonder of the world Mr. Moritz's store installed them, and was the first concern in town to take this step. He also brought the first airplane to Michigan City directly after the war. It was at first planned to land it near the prison, but it was found that the wire interfered with this, making the operation extremely hazardous. Consequently it was brought down on the Bull farm several miles south of the city where there was plenty of room to land and take off. Several thousand persons visited the spot to get their first view of the curious machine.

Mr. Moritz is a member of the Rotary club, the Masonic lodge, the Odd Fellows and the Elks. One of his hobbies is music, and the other is his orchard. As a young lad he took up the study of the violin, and until recent years when his daughter has outdistanced him, played occasionally for his own pleasure. His orchard is located on a ten acre beauty spot on the Waterford road, which is considered one of the few really primitive sections left. The orchard is on three acres which are cleared, while the remainder is in its natural wild state, through which runs the creek. Because of its dense foliage it a favorite spot for birds and other animal life. When not engaged in keeping Michigan City dressed up, Mr. Moritz can often be found out there taking a bit of relaxation.

SEPTEMBER 19, 1925. p. 1.

E. G. RICHTER

Twice president of the Chamber of commerce, former exalted ruler of all Chicago Elkdom, and twice head of the salvation Army drives—these are a few of the outstanding highlights in the career of E. G. Richter, one of Michigan City's leading boosters and a past master in the art of making friends. At 12 years of age he started to make his own way in the world and today stands at the head of one of the largest wholesale and retail cigar concerns in this section of the state.

Mr. Richter's regime as head of the chamber of commerce was a period of rapid advancement for the city. By preaching the doctrine of faith in one's self, faith in each other and faith in the country, he did much to weld the organization into a solid and powerful unit. It was during this period that the Sullivan Machinery Co. the Eastport Manufacturing Co. and the Universal Plating Co. were brought here; local postal facilities were increased, the contract for the south side sewer was let, the Center street bridge and the new Masonic temple constructed, new dock facilities obtained, the contract for the new Dunes highway put through, the Greenwood Cemetery taken out of politics and trustees appointed. A state appropriation obtained for Dunes Park, in addition to many other forward steps.

When the housing shortage became acute it was Mr. Richter who broke the ice by building a new home out on Springland avenue. Others followed his example and today this section of the city is rapidly developing.

Born in Michigan City, he received his early education here, and at the age of 12 was forced to leave school and get a job in the car factory, where he remained for the next four years

Figure 61

E. C. RICHTER

until the wanderlust seized him and carried him to Mississippi. There for the next two years he worked in a general store, before returning here to take up the business of furniture making at the old Ford & Johnson factory.

Seven years later, with a wife and two children he moved to Chicago and started as a porter in a wholesale liquor house at $10 a week. Realizing the need of' more education, he entered the night school of the Metropolitan Business college. His determination to succeed, coupled with his ready faculty for making friends, attracted the attention of the heads of the concern and he was offered a position traveling, on the road. There he remained for the next 26 years, gradually working his way to the top of the sales department.

With his headquarters in Chicago, he joined the Elks in 1898. It was in 1911 that his natural gift for leadership asserted itself, and he was named esquire. His rise was steady through the various chairs of officialdom until in 1916 he was elected exulted ruler of the Chicago lodge, which is one of the largest in the entire order, numbering between 1,600 and 1,700 members.

As exalted ruler of the lodge Mr. Richter was responsible for the organization of one of the first hospital units to be sent to the battlefields of France. Another outstanding achievement of his regime was the building of the new Elks' temple, which is not only one of the show places of Chicago but is among the finest buildings of its kind in the country.

He won the hearts of the organization. At the close of his term of office the lodge gave a banquet at the Sherman houses, attended by the highest officials of the city, at which he was presented with a life membership in the Elks, and a diamond ring. Three times he was elected to represent Chicago at national conventions held in Boston, Atlantic City and Los Angeles, the latter after his return to Michigan City. This is the only instance where a man who has moved from the city has ever been named to this honor.

After his return here a parade of cars was made up of prominent Elks of Chicago, including the leading city officials and jurist, and a Sunday run was made to Michigan City to pay him a visit.

With the coming of prohibition in 1919 he returned to the old home town and opened the wholesale and retail cigar business at the head of which he today stands.

UP CLOSE AND PERSONAL

In addition to being a life member of the Elks he is a member of the Masonic order, the Rotary club, the Manufacturers' club and the Long Beach Country club. He is a "high tension" baseball fan, and a lover of a close game of billiards.

SEPTEMBER 2, 1925, p. 1.

FRANK A. ROGERS

Frank A. Rogers, Deputy County prosecutor, is the Nemesis of the crime fraternity in Michigan City. They have a standing challenge to meet him at any time in either the justice, city or superior courts and records show that a high percentage of their members, who have shown a willingness to joust, have come to grief. Both as clerk of the circuit court and as deputy prosecutor, he has been ever ready to further movements which would make the city a cleaner and more progressive place in which to live.

Starting life on a farm five miles south of LaPorte, Attorney Rogers has had his own way to make in the world since he was 15 years old. His early education was received in the district schools, and upon completion of the grades it became necessary for him to finance himself if he wanted further education. He immediately went to LaPorte and obtained a position in a shoe store where he could work after schools and evenings while attending high school. Upon graduating in 1900 he came to Michigan City, where having thoroughly mastered the various phases of the business, he was connected with the Throckmorton and Niemer shoe store. Here he remained for the next 12 years.

Figure 62

FRANK A. ROGERS

In 1912 he was offered the Virginia and Maryland territory for the Mishawaka Woolen Manufacturing Co. where he spent the next four years in opening up the territory and building up the business, but as the work required his constant absence from his family he came back to Michigan City in 1916 and returned to his former position.

The legal profession had always held a strong attraction for him, and he determined to take up the study of law. He was elected clerk of the circuit court where in order to better fit himself for his duties, as well as to realize his ambition, he spent his evenings and other spare time in training for his future work, eventually passing the examinations with high honors and being made a member of the LaPorte county division of the state bar.

Michigan City knew him as a clear, level-headed thinker, a man conscientious in the discharge of the duties of public office, and when it needed, a deputy prosecutor to do battle with the lawless element, he was named to the post. The record which he has made in the office has justified their confidence.

As deputy prosecutor, Attorney Rogers has charge of all prosecution for the state in the justice, city and superior courts where he has established a record for convictions. Mr. Rogers has an elegant suite of offices at 407 Warren building.

He has established a reputation for his ability to present the evidence in criminal cases in a pointed, concise fashion which stands the acid test of the courts, as well as for his willingness to co-operate with the police and other departments.

Fishing and bird shooting are his favorite forms of diversion. He makes an annual trip to the lakes of northern Wisconsin to angle for the big muskies which lurk there, while his favorite bird hunting grounds are the marshes of the Kankakee River. He is a member of the Elks lodge.

OCTOBER 7, 1925, p. 3.

S. J. TAYLOR

Figure 63

Samuel J. Taylor

Having saved the taxpayers of Michigan City and LaPorte county several hundred thousands of dollars through his altruistic interest is good government, as former deputy chief of the Indiana Bureau of Statistics, and as a firm believer In the future of the city, Samuel J. Taylor takes his place among the men who have been prominently identified with the upbuilding of the community. For many years he he was auditor of the Haskell & Barker Car Works, and was a close friend of the founder of the concern.

He it was, who, in 1921 discovered the "mystery fund" of $30,000 of the county taxpayers' which was being applied on the completely discharged debt. As president of the Taxpayers Association, two years later, he succeeded, after a hearing before the state board, in obtaining a tax reduction for Michigan City amounting to approximately $50,000. Last year a smaller amount was saved. He also worked for a reduction of school taxes which amounted to about $10,000. He was a member of the first county council which effected another tax reduction of $105,000.

Born of a prominent Scotch family at Stranraer, Scotland, he received his early education at the local academy, following his graduation went to work for his grandfather, who operated a large timber and slate concern. Mr. Taylor, who is the fourth in direct line to bear the name of Samuel was in his younger days fond of athletics, being a member of the football, rowing and cricket clubs. Shortly after completing his education he joined Company C. of the Galloway Rifle Volunteers, an organization similar to the Militia, of which his father was major, serving under him for six years as sergeant. He arranged the first rifle match between Scotland and an Ulster team, he himself shooting second high score. He was a member of the guard of honor to receive the Prince of Wales when he visited Scotland.

It was in 1890 that Mr. Taylor first came to Michigan City in charge of the office of the Amazon Hosiery Co, a Prison manufacturing plant which employed more than 200 prisoners, in addition to outside help. With the removal of this plant to Muskegon, Mich., six years later, he accepted the situation of deputy state statistician. This position was obtained in competition with 57 other men who were handy with figures.

Later he was offered a position with the Haskell and Barker Company as actuary, and given charge of all disbursements with the exception of the payroll and timber bills. His efficient handling of his duties brought him to the attention of Mr. Barker and for many years a close friendship existed between the two. Upon the death of the head of the concern he was elected auditor, and in addition was responsible for the obtaining of three-fourths of all the great bulk of supplies. In 1915 his health failed and he retired.

The old craving for good government which ran in the family when, for generations there was a Taylor sitting at the council sessions in the old burgh in Scotland, now exerted itself. Several investigations, which resulted in political shakeups, were launched by Mr. Taylor, and two years ago he organized the local association, which is a unit of the statewide organization.

It was the reading of a life of Lincoln, The Pioneer Boy and How He Became President, which first stimulated young Taylor's interest in America as a land of opportunity. In 1888 he sailed for New York, which gave him a "cold reception." A terrific blizzard was raging which made it impossible for his ship to land until she was four days overdue.

With him he brought letters of introduction and his first stop was made at the grocery house of Park and Tilford, where the cashier, J. R. Agnew, another Scotchman, changed Mr. Taylor's $66 into United States money. Upon returning to New York 20 years later he looked up this cashier to find that the concern had become a gigantic business, and that the former clerk was at the head of it. From New York He came directly to Chicago, working first for the Spaulding sporting goods house, and then for Marshal Field and Co.

He has been a staunch Republican for many years. In 1896 he was named as a member of the city central committee and is at present precinct chairman and vice chairman of the county committee. For 30 years he has attended practically all of the state conventions, and here he formed friendships which grew stronger as the years went by. Today he numbers among his close personal friends, Harry S. New, postmaster general, Frank 0. Lowden, former Governor Winfield T. Durbin and former Governor James P. Goodrich.

His interest in politics is the larger one. He is not a seeker after tasty political plums and favor, but rather a public spirited citizen who is desirous of seeing that government of the people by the people shall be a success.

Having taken his first work in Masonry before leaving Scotland he has since joined the chapter, council, commandery and consistory, and is also a member of the Eastern Star, as well as the Elks, Foresters, the Indiana Association of Certified Public Accountants, the Real Estate board, the Indiana Real Estate Association, and the Traffic Club of Chicago. He was a member of the first board of directors of the Y. M. C. A, and president as well as first secretary of the Rotary club, and is now one of five honorary members.

Mr. Taylor is a firm believer in the scriptural doctrine which points out that bread cast on the waters will return, and that, even though this may not be in a form, yet the joy of giving is greater than the joy of receiving. Since his arrival here he has been a believer in the future of the city and today has all his investments in Michigan City real estate and bank stocks.

His hobbies are the scanning of a tax notice, books, history, radio, and the passage of a state law compelling treasurers to send tax bills to all tax payers. He has original letters signed by Sir Walter Scott, Daniel Webster, Livingston, and Harriet Martineau.

AUGUST 12, 1925, p. 1

DR. F. R. WARREN

Figure 65

DR. F. R. WARREN

Standing as permanent monument to what may be considered one of the most unique forms of diversion, are the Warren building, Michigan City's newest, largest and most modern business block, and Pottawattomie Park, its most beautiful residential section. Dr. Frank R. Warren, whose Life work is the practice of medicine and surgery, finds in these projects the same refreshing relaxation that others get from the golf links, a hunting or fishing trip. He was also one of the prime movers for the chamber of commerce.

Proof that he finds rest in following his hobby of community building is to be seen in the amount of work which he is able to accomplish in a day's time. After hours of office consultation or a difficult operation he finds a mental refreshing up by concentrating for an hour or so on the solution of a knotty business problem. Playing the game as he does for his own amusement his moves are made with a complete lack of pyrotechnics, and folks seldom know what is happening until they see the actual results. In this way he has worked out the dreams of his boyhood.

The fact that Dr. Warren has a vision of the future development of Michigan City is seen in the construction and efficient arrangement of the new building, which is said by state officials to be not only the most modern and best built structure of its kind in northern Indiana, but to contain the most attractive lobby.

The city needed more store space, a new and up to date office building, and additional hotel accommodations. By the erection of a six-story structure it became possible to fill these three requirements and at the same time place them on one lot, under one roof, with one elevator, and with one heating plant, in addition to reducing the operating cost approximately over one-third over what it would have been had three separate two-story buildings, been built. Thus the new building becomes a triumph for modern efficiency, making 24-hour service possible, a thing which has never before been attempted in Michigan City.

By placing the hotel accommodations on the fifth and sixth floors it became possible for guests to be above the mosquito, and fly line, and insomuch as all of the rooms are outside rooms, to be afforded a bird's-eye view of the city. In hot weather the rooms catch any breeze that may be stirring. The same advantages are offered by the club rooms on the sixth floor, and the Tokay Roof Garden on the seventh floor.

Further proof of Dr. Warren's confidence in the future of the city is found in the fact that all preparations have been made in foundations, construction and plumbing, to carry the building up four additional stories in the future. The building is built to last. So excellent is the material and workmanship that state building inspectors call it the "Best built building in the state." In the arrangement of the structure from the basement to the roof there is no waste space, it was pointed out.

Pottawattomie Park offers another example of the doctor's originality in the development of unique and constructive plans for community building. He, it was, who originated the plan upon which the development is based, and which has brought forth much favorable comments from big real estate concerns in various parts of the United States.

The 93 acres which go to make up the tract are located ideally for residence purposes, protected from future encroachment by the country club on the east, Memorial park on the west, Trail creek, and an 85-acre section of woods on the north extending to the Grand Beach road, owned by the doctor. The American Park Builders of Chicago, nationally known firm of landscape architects, laid out the tract, devoting one-third of the entire ground, or 31 acres, to parks, children's playgrounds, athletic fields, tennis courts, artificial lakes, and scenic drives, which makes it possible for a man of moderate means to enjoy all of the exclusive comforts to be found in the great private estates.

Each person owning a lot holds a deed which covers a blanket interest in this park space, thus making it impossible for it to ever be used for any other purpose. It is also one of the few places in the country where a person may choose his neighbors. Ownership automatically makes one a member of the Pottawattomie Park Association, Inc., without the sanction of which, it is impossible for the Michigan City Community Land Co., Inc, which handles the sale of the land, to issue a deed. With the final selling out, the land company automatically ceases to exist, while the association continues to carry on. It is also the only place in the United States where a home owner does not have to attend to his own grounds, for with the deed there is an endowment fund set aside, the income from which is ample to take care of the perpetual care of the parks as well as the private grounds. The restrictions which are placed upon the park are artistic rather than financial. The only requirement is that the type of architecture blend harmoniously with the general park scheme.

It is also impossible for anyone to have over two lots, each of which is a quarter of an acre, and in this way no one person can build a large private estate within the park itself. Thus the folks who live in Pottawattomie Park control their own destiny.

Dr. Warren was born at Otis, Ind. His father had won renown as a civil war surgeon and before he was 12 years old the boy was assisting in emergency cases. His grandfather before that had also been a physician, and consequently it was only natural that he carry on the family traditions when it came to the selection of a life work. Upon the completion of the grades he attended the West Division high school in Chicago, graduating in 1890. The following two years he spent taking his preparatory medical work at the Chicago University and in 1892 entered upon his medical course at Rush Medical college, from which he graduated four years later.

He immediately returned to his old home at Otis and began practicing, but in 1899 his health gave away from over-work and he was forced to take a vacation of several months. It was during this time that he learned the trick of concentrating upon a business problem for a few hours in order to rest and break the monotony.

In 1900 his practice in Michigan City had developed and he decided to move here. The following year he purchased the property upon which the Warren building today stands. Confident that the town had a future, he continued to invest in property, until today he is one of the heaviest individual real estate holders in the city.

AUGUST 26, 1925, p. 1.

> *"If not curbed it will usurp the functions of the state and be destructive of government itself."*
> Senator Culberson, Texas
> **THE EVENING NEWS**, *Michigan City, IN.,*
> *May 24, 1922, p. 4*

KNIGHTS OF THE KU KLUX KLAN

This paper on the Ku Klux Klan was evolved from a review of the primary newspapers published in the cities of La Porte and Michigan City between 1920 and 1930. The very nature of the Knights of the Ku Klux Klan, the Invisible Empire, dictated that it be founded on the premise of secrecy. For that reason it is difficult and nearly impossible to find documentation that explicitly verifies the contents of this paper. The names, places, and events described in this work are only as accurate as the news reporters' stories. It is not my intention to demean any individual or his/her family. Those named in this article were named in the county newspapers and are a part of newspaper-recorded history.

The Ku Klux Klan of post-Civil War days had died out by the 1880's. It wasn't until World War I when the Klan saw a resurgence. The War brought with it the seeds of suspicion and fear of foreigners. It stimulated anti-German hysteria and brought out feelings against "hyphenated Americans." A small group of intellectuals in the United States began writing and exaggerating the racial inferiority and weakness of certain ethnic groups. They promoted immigration restrictions as essential to preserving American racial purity. Their doctrine was eagerly accepted by a segment of the upper class that favored the interests of native-born inhabitants over immigrants. It was this kind of mentality that gave rise to the rebirth of the Knights of the Ku Klux Klan.

Colonel William Joseph Simmons and some thirty friends, on Thanksgiving night in 1915, gathered under a fiery cross on top of Stone Mountain near Atlanta, Georgia and swore allegiance to the "Invisible Empire." Thus was created a modern imitation of the secret order that played an important role in what some would say saved the South from the excesses of the carpetbaggers. This new order attempted to bring together under one banner all of the post-war hysteria and prejudice created by the First World War. The Klan, by all accounts, was fanatic in its fundamental doctrine on religion and politics. They took pride in being anti-Negro, anti-Semitic, anti-foreigner, and anti-Catholic. Simmons at first had little success with most of his following in the South. The decade of the 1920's saw a resurgence in its strength and prominence throughout the United States.[52]

The Klan left its mark as well on the moral and political direction of the state of Indiana and many of its communities. Michigan City in the 1920's seemed to possess the ingredients needed to nurture the seeds of discontent more than other communities in the county. The Klan did gain a foothold in the city of La Porte and other county communities later. However, the sparseness of newspaper articles relating Klan activity in the southern portion of the county seems to indicate that it wasn't as dominant as it was in Michigan City.

The Ku Klux Klan in August 1921 filed Articles of Incorporation with Indiana's Secretary of State. The Articles were approved, thereby legitimizing their organization in Indiana. The articles defined the Klan's role "as a patriotic, fraternal order designed to teach and inculcate among its membership respect for the stars and stripes and for the constitution."[53] Governor McCray had publicly gone on record against this organization. He stated his "opposition to any class of people undertaking to administer justice without going through the organized processes of law."[54]

An editorial in the Michigan City DISPATCH reported that several Klan workers had previously and again in August visited the city intent on exploring the possibility of organizing a branch.[55]

The first tangible evidence that the Klan intended to establish itself in the city occurred when twenty men wearing white robes and tall peaked white caps interrupted an Evangelist tent meeting conducted by Hamilton-Pollack on East Sixth Street on the evening of September 22, 1922. Rumors had been rampant in the community that the Klan was attempting to organize a branch in Michigan City. The audience had been led to the "heights of song under the leadership of Song Director Ralph Pollack" when the "Kluxers" entered the tent and marched down the aisle to the platform. Reports indicated the audience was "visibly excited, even intense", displaying a variety of emotions.

The leader of the group handed Mr. Hamilton a letter. Then the white-robed figures dropped to their knees, raised their right hands, and in silence remained in that position for a noticeable period of time. Then they suddenly rose and without speaking filed out of the tent. Hamilton handed the letter to Donald C. Ford. Mr. Ford read the letter to the audience.

"Mr. Hamilton:

this is to assure you that there is an organization composed of Hundreds of the best men of the city which believes in the following principles:

"The tenets of the Christian religion. White supremacy. Protection of pure womanhood. Just laws and liberty. Closer relationship of pure Americanism. The upholding of the constitution of the United States. The sovereignty of our state rights. The separation of church and state. Freedom of speech and press. Closer relationship between American capital and labor. Prevention of mob violence and lynchings. Preventing unwarranted strikes by foreign labor agitators. Prevention of fire and destruction of property by lawless elements. Limitation of foreign emigration. Much needed local reforms. Law and order."

"And this organization is behind you to a man in the great work you are doing here."

Sincerely yours, "Knights of the Ku Klux Klan,
Provisional Klan of Michigan city, Realm of Indiana" [56]

Mr. Hamilton was quoted by THE EVENING DISPATCH as saying, "Well, from some newspaper reports I had some impression that you were a gang of men who did nothing but tar and feather. But if you are for the Christian religion and for law and order, I'm for you."[57]

The following week the Klan petitioned the City commissioners and was granted the use of the bandstand in Washington Park. An estimated crowd as high as 8,000 spectators gathered to hear Dr. Lester A. Brown of Atlanta, Georgia. Dr. Brown was a Baptist minister and a member of the National Lecture Board of the Ku Klux Klan. Brown, looking out over the crowd from the bandstand, blamed the politicians and newspapers for the general misunderstanding of the principles of the Klan. He asked the audience to judge the Klan on common sense and fairness. He went on to say Martin Luther, John Wesley and Abraham Lincoln were criticized, condemned and attacked by many during their time but have since been held in high regard by millions. He pointed out that historically the Freemasons were considered to be a traitorous organization, but are a part of every city, town and hamlet in the nation. He outlined the work of the Klan by pointing out that it was American in nature, Christian, benevolent and helpful. "It puts its hands down in its pockets for the support of widows and orphans, and no deserving member is allowed to be out of a job any longer that it is possible to get work for him." [58]

The requirements for membership were explained. An individual must be Protestant, American born, and white. Dr. Brown elaborated by saying that Catholics were excluded for the same reason that they exclude Protestant from their organization. That the vast majority of foreign born have little regard for the flag or nation, who have come here, "with a bomb in one hand and a knife in the other, for the purpose of amassing money and taking it back home."[59]

The Klan wasted little time in establishing a visible presence in Michigan City. The women of the First M.E. Church had conducted a tag day sale for the purpose of raising funds for the new Methodist church under construction at Seventh and Pine Streets. That evening, during the first week of November, the ladies gathered at the Glidden and Heise Bakery Shop, 617 Franklin Street, to count the day's collection. Late that evening "about fifteen Knights of the Ku Klux Klan in full regalia" filed silently into the shop. Their leader placed a sealed envelope on the table. They then filed out and vanished as mysteriously as they entered. The women on opening the envelope found $100 in bills and a letter written on Ku Klux Klan, Realm of Indiana stationery. The letter stated that the contribution was to be added to the funds already collected.[60]

The November 1922 election in Michigan City provided the Klan with another opportunity to display their influence. Hundreds of ballots headed "Information Sheet" were distributed about the election polls. The ballot, like the form, listed the candidates with their religious affiliation, "Protestant", "Roman Catholic", or "Jew."[61]

In the same edition, the NEWS proclaimed that the "Klan moves for Moral Reform". Six men had been arrested for gambling at the Berghoff Poolhall. James Vine, the owner of the Berghoff, was arrested and charged as a keeper of a gambling house. The article went on to say that the Klan was suspected of calling in the complaint to the police. They had earlier announced their intention to clean up vice in Michigan City. The report anticipated that the state headquarters of the Klan would direct other moves at moral reform in the city.[62]

One week later the NEWS and the MICHIGAN CITY EVENING DISPATCH reported that the police has seized a large quantity of liquor. Robert H. Moore, Deputy Prosecuting Attorney, acting on information from an anonymous source of illegal booze alerted the police. The NEWS attributed the information coming from the Ku Klux Klan. The liquor was allegedly being transported from Detroit to St. Louis. The "machine" broke down at Michigan and Jackson streets. The next day it was towed to Wolff's garage. The owner of the car, Anthony Stevens, would not allow anyone to inspect the car or make repairs. Moore, Chief Arthur Sullivan, and Patrolman Pietrowski went to the garage, arrested the driver, Vassal Christoff of Detroit, and seized 168 bottles of Canadian Whiskey. Stevens had already left for Chicago to supposedly buy parts. He never returned.[63]

A meeting held in the Superior Courthouse Auditorium provided another forum that left little doubt of the Klan's conspicuous presence in the city. The public had been invited to hear Dr. Ridley of Atlanta, Georgia lecture on "The Knights of the Ku Klux Klan, its purpose and Place in American Life Today."[64] The DISPATCH indicated that Dr. Ridley was one hour late. He apologized and said that while in Kokomo he had received notice of the meeting at the last minute and had been on the road from 2 pm to 8:30 pm. He used the opportunity to denounce the "damned lies" told about the Klan. He divulged to the audience that the Klan had experienced a large increase in membership over the last few months.[65]

Some men of prominence and stature began to speak out about the evils disseminated by the Klan. Dr. Fredrick E. Hopkins was one of them. As pastor of the First Presbyterian Church in Michigan City, early in December, he publicly denounced the Klan. He announced from the pulpit on a Sunday evening "that he was opposed to the methods and principles" of the Klan. He declared the "in his opinion hiding behind a bed sheet and a pillow case did not figure in 100% Americanism". He asserted:

> "Prejudice never gets people anywhere and never will and that the division of the citizenship on religious lines will do more harm to the city than the Chamber of Commerce and the Rotary Club can repair."[66]

The DISPATCH reported that the overflowing audience was composed of people of all nationalities and creeds. He reminded them that a large segment of Michigan City's population consisted of foreigners that became citizens. They purchased property and had "given their best to make this country a better place to live in." Dr. Hopkins urged the audience to continue the peace and good will practiced for many years in Michigan City. He declared that he was opposed to secret societies that hide their identities. It was his belief that the Ku Klux Klan was un-American because it was founded on prejudice and whose principles attacked immigrants and the religion of the Jews and Catholics.[67]

Two weeks later, in the city of La Porte, Reverend Hopkins delivered a similar message to the Kiwanis at a luncheon meeting at the Rumely Hotel. He spoke "upon the need for a greater application of the Christmas spirit" and that the world owed much to the Catholics and Jews.[68]

A week later in Michigan City, at about 10 in the evening, a blazing cross illuminated Yankee Slide. Hundreds of people observed the cross and were spellbound. From the downtown area the DISPATCH said it gave the impression that the cross was suspended in the sky. Firemen climbed the hill to investigate. They found a fiery cross of 2 x 4's wrapped in kerosene soaked burlap as well as two partially filled cans of kerosene.

The end of nineteen twenty-two exploded upon the scene with the controversial firing by City Manager Horace Bowen of Arthur Sullivan, Chief of Police. This was followed by the resignation of Captain Thomas Gruntkowski. "Captain Grunt" felt that it would be in his best interest to quit while the "quitting was good." He believed that it was just a matter of time before "unseen interest" would have him removed.[69]

Sullivan filed his response to his firing with the city clerk, which was subsequently published in the EVENING DISPATCH. He began by reviewing his administration of the department stating, he had directed in person numerous raids on "soft drink parlors" for liquor violations, "the red light district was entirely banished and eliminated", and only one business was burglarized.

He related that he was receptive to suggestions for the improvement of the department and was willing at all times to cooperate with the city manager and the commissioner to improve his administration. However, neither the commissioner nor the city manager "laid down any policy for the department." In fact, Sullivan alleged that the department was running satisfactorily.

The remaining portions of the petition focused on the accusation that the Ku Klux Klan was responsible for his discharge. He stated that several months prior to his firing he "was approached by a city commissioner and solicited for membership in the Ku Klux Klan". He alleged that for "one solid week" the commissioner and one other man solicited and told him of the political advantages of the Klan. He observed that his refusal to join the Klan "started a dissension in the police department and moves to unseat me."[70]

Another related incident tells of two Ku Klux Klan organizers the past November, masquerading as "federal agents," entering the police station demanding that the police assist them on a raid of the Berghoff poolroom. At the trial the agents didn't appear. Sullivan and his officers refused to sign affidavits due to what they felt was weak evidence. They also took the position that it was the "federal agents" responsibility to make the charges since they initiated the action.

Sullivan also discounted reports that he had gone on a hunting trip with several bootleggers. He also stated he believed the city manager, at times, showed a lack of confidence in him, "although I was always faithful to the city manager and the citizens of Michigan City." Sullivan intimated there might have been ulterior forces that may have influenced Bowen's decisions. He also stated that in some cases the effectiveness in the enforcement of the law was reduced by " 'nolle prosses', continuances and failure to file proper charges..." leaks and other loopholes that allowed offenders to get off with light fines.

In regard to Ku Klux Klan parades, former chief Sullivan claimed to have consulted with manager Bowen who would not make decisions. It was left to the Chief to decide, "stating that as long as I was in charge... there would be no masked parades in Michigan City...."

He concluded his statement with a challenge. "I also defy any man to show where I have at any time accepted money, protected any persons in law violations, tipped off raids, or in any way willfully failed to performed my duties".

Sullivan's attorney R. N. Smith of La Porte, advised him to "file a demand for a public hearing on why he was ousted," in anticipation of having the city manager set out the reasons for dismissal. The commissioners, however, placed his request on file without a public reading.[71]

Public debate raged for months, with the DISPATCH leading the charge in support of Arthur Sullivan. The NEWS came to the defense of the city manager. Irwin Nieman, city editor of the NEWS, declared "... that Sullivan was ousted because the public didn't want him". He also said that under Chief Sullivan's administration his officers were ordered not to sign affidavits against those arrested for gambling and bootlegging, preventing them from being prosecuted. Other than Sullivan's claims, Mr. Nieman was not aware of any Klan influence being brought to bear for the chief's resignation.[72]

Nineteen Twenty-Three began with another turbulent upheaval for Michigan City. The commissioner of public works, R. H. Fedder, received notice just days before that his services were no longer needed. The DISPATCH referring to a note written by City Manager Horace Bowen to Fedder disclosed that in the interest of economy the office of the board of public works was being abolished.[73]

In the days, weeks and months that followed, the DISPATCH and the NEWS, in their editorial columns, continued the war of words. Each newspaper hurled charges and accusations against the other. The Michigan City EVENING DISPATCH pointed the finger at the Klan and its supporters within the city government for the firing of Arthur Sullivan. An editorial that appeared in the February 5th edition supporting their contention that Sullivan's firing was Klan backed quoted the official Klan publication as saying, "THE INFLUENCE OF THE KLAN HAS BEEN FELT, SULLIVAN IS GONE, a real chief is on the job...." The DISPATCH further admonished the NEWS for not having the courage of its convictions by not admitting the Klan's influence in the dismissal of Sullivan. A March editorial accused the NEWS of attempting to hide behind the commission form of government "...in condoning the activities of the Klan and its administration members." It accused the editor of the NEWS of adopting a "wolf in sheep's clothing, crawfish policy," in its denial of Klan influence. In another editorial they attack the city administration for ignoring the law in its dismissal of Sullivan and illegally abolishing the office of superintendent of public works.

The NEWS on the other hand, admonished the DISPATCH for using Sullivan's firing for what it contended was an attack on the commission form of city government. They claimed that The DISPATCH and the "bootleggers" opposed the commission form of government. They contended that the DISPATCH'S fight against the Klan was really a fight against the commission form of government.[74]

The firing of Chief Sullivan finally played itself out and disappeared from print. The growing presence and strength of the Klan in the county took center stage. Rumors abounded in the city of La Porte in mid-January that an organizer of the Ku Klux Klan had opened an office there and was gaining a foothold in the city. This view was further strengthened with the appearance of "The Fiery Cross" on the streets of La Porte on January 27, 1923. The agent for the paper was seen making the rounds of the downtown area. The paper was believed to be the official voice of the Ku Klux Klan. However, the agent denied the allegation saying the paper wasn't a part of the Klan organization but merely a sympathizer.[75]

Three days later several men descended on the office of the HERALD displaying invitations to a "closed" meeting of the Ku Klux Klan to be held in Richter Hall, over the La Porte Gas and Electric Company offices. The invitations bore a Michigan City postmark. The card in part read:

"As a red blooded, 100 per cent American (which your friends state you are) you will be given an opportunity to hear the REAL TRUTH about the GREATEST MOVEMENT of all time in the history of our Glorious country, at an Admission by THIS CARD ONLY. DISCUSS THIS WITH NO ONE."[76]

Slightly different versions of what transpired at that evening's meeting were reported in the La Porte DAILY HERALD and the Michigan City NEWS. The News carried a short article that stated the meeting "fizzled." According to their count only 13 people attended the meeting. Six of the 13 were potential members. Four were Klan organizers. The remaining attendees were "spies." Many others planning to attend had second thoughts when they approached the door to the hall and were confronted by a large crowd.[77] Two days later the DISPATCH reported Klan organizers had the phone removed from the office they were using and were about to leave La Porte, having little success in signing up members.[78]

The HERALD sent its new cub reporter, Ernie Pyle, to cover the recruiting meeting at Richter Hall. Ray E. Smith, city editor of the newspaper thought that since Ernie had been in town for just a few days his presence would not be detected. Smith was quoted, "Word got around that this stranger was there and he was followed to the YMCA (where he roomed) by several men, who questioned him…. He was warned not to publish anything but refused."[79] Ernie, not to be intimidated, wrote the story. He reported that a small number of local citizens were there. Observers reported that 22 local men went up the stairway, but eight were denied admittance. A carload of 5 men, members of the Klan, according to the DISPATCH, came from Michigan City. Four other cars reportedly came from Elkhart and South Bend, raising the total attendance to 30. Several cars had been parked in front of the hall with their headlights shining on the entrance to the hall. This appeared to be a deterrent that kept the attendance down. It was reported that at least one carload of "would-be" klanners seeing the entrance to the building lighted up by the car lights "…jumped back into their machine and drove away." [80]

The article continued saying that C. E. Weller of Kokomo, was an organizer for the Klan, and the leader of the meeting. Later reports were to the effect that he was using aliases while in La Porte. He provided a litany of the Klan's tenets to those in attendance, adding:

"We do not deny any Catholic to worship God in the manner he chooses, that is his inalienable right but we are going to prevent him from holding an office in which he is the dictator to hundreds of thousands of red-blooded American citizens….You know that it is fatal for America for the white and black to mix, therefore we propose to keep them separate…. We are also against the Hebrew as long as he continues his present attitude in American affairs. The Jews seem to think that the American dollar and the American women are their legitimate prey, and their greed and grasp is so strong that they will stop at no end to secure their desires."[81]

At the close of the meeting he invited those present to join the Klan.

It was also reported in that article that an organization had been formed in La Porte to fight the Klan. It had allegedly raised $1000 to fight the Klan and that more money could be obtained if necessary.

The Klan continued to make its presence in the county known. During the last week of February and the first week of March fiery crosses were ignited in several locations in Michigan City. Vail and Michigan Streets was the scene of a burning cross on two successive nights. Another cross burning occurred on south Franklin Street near Homer Street. The evening of March 1st, the police department received a call at 8:10 of a brightly burning fiery cross in a vacant lot at Michigan and Wabash Streets. The fire department was dispatched to the scene but did not extinguish the burning cross. A large crowd was on hand to watch the spectacle.[82]

The Klan in an effort to secure police powers in Indiana, established numerous Horse Thief Detective Associations throughout the state. The Klan attempted to use an obscure state law that had been enacted following the Civil War allowing ordinary citizens to form organizations with police power to arrest horse thieves and anyone who violated the laws of Indiana, according to the American Unity league.

That effort to gain a foothold in La Porte County occurred during the first half of March. Michigan City Auditor Thomas Crumpacker received the filing of articles of incorporation for the Michigan City Detective Association by trustees Gustave W. Krause, Charles H. Felton, and Charles H. Hodler. Gust W. Plubiak, William Hale, Lawrence A. Schumaker, Forest L. Richter, William H. Short, William J. Baist and Eugene J. Meloy signatures were also on the document. Their principal place of business in Michigan City was listed as 427½ E. 7th Street, the residence of Gustave Krause, according to the charter. Simultaneously the county commissioners received a petition "praying" that their association members be deputized.[83]

A similar organization, the La Porte Horse Thief Detective Association, was formed in the city of La Porte. Wilber C. Winkler, part owner of a cigar store on Lincoln Way was listed as one of its trustees according to the DAILY HERALD. He defended the association from accusations that it was a Klan agency pointing out that it was legal under state law and open to all regardless of religious beliefs.[84] However, the editorial staff of the Argus described the Association to be "as useful in a community as the well known fifth wheel on a wagon." The ARGUS challenged their existence saying it was outmoded because the "clever horse thief no longer plies his trade in La Porte."

Klan presence in the county was dramatized by a spectacular parade on the streets of Michigan City. A week before the planned event, an individual introduced himself to City Manager Bowen as the imperial representative of the Ku Klux Klan. His purpose was to acquire a permit to parade as well as permission to hold a public gathering to initiate new members. However, the law at the time did not require permits.

Hundreds of Klansmen in automobiles arrived from South Bend during the day of the parade, while others came by way of special interurban cars on the South Bend and Northern Indiana railroad. Another one hundred seventy five came from Chicago on a special Michigan Central train. All in all, between 1300-1500 members of the Ku Klux Klan were in Michigan City to march in the parade.[85]

The county's newspapers were there on a cool, rainy night in early April to report Michigan City's first parade of the Ku Klux Klan.[86] The uncooperative weather delayed the start of the parade. Thousands of curious spectators lined the parade route, some on the sidewalks and others in their parked automobiles. It was estimated that at least 500 La Porteans drove to City to watch the parade.

Prior to the eight o'clock starting time marchers began to assemble on the Valentine property at the corner of Coolspring Avenue and Franklin Street despite the frightful rain. Hundreds of Klansmen were dressed in their regalia while others without masks waited for the showers to stop. Just before the parade was to begin all the lights in the city suddenly went out. The streets and buildings were plunged "into inky darkness" for about 5 minutes. Just as the lights came on a sudden downpour of rain forced the watchers to seek shelter. "Even nature seemed conspiring to add to the mysterious atmosphere of the occasion," quipped the DAILY HERALD reporter. It wasn't until 9 P.M. that the "...white clad procession appeared."[87]

Police officers were stationed along the parade route to handle traffic and ensure the peace. Klansmen were observed at a number of principal intersections along Franklin Street. Off in the distance a blazing fiery cross was the first evidence the parade had begun. Leading the procession mounted on horseback were eight masked Klansmen in flowing white robes. Each was carrying an American flag and a cross illuminated by red electric lights. The mounted entourage was flanked on either side by a group of Klansmen dressed in ornate robes that may have signified their rank in the order. Behind them marching in a double file formation with folded arms were the other Klansmen. Some were wearing their white hooded robes while others were not. Dispersed along the procession were many carrying American flags. At least one other marcher carried a fiery cross.

Depending upon which newspaper account was read there were either one or two bands and one drum corps playing marches. The same was true regarding the number of women marchers in the Klan's auxiliary referred to as "Kamelias." The numbers marching ranged from 20 to 250. The procession marched north on Franklin Street. Varied accounts indicate the marchers turned west on either Michigan or Second Street and then south on Washington Street. At Tenth Street the parade returned to Franklin and then south back to Valentine Court. Again, depending upon the news report, an initiation ceremony was conducted in a field near the Second Street Bridge or back at the field where the parade began.

Rumors abound that the Klan would make an appearance in the village of Rolling Prairie in the days following the spectacular demonstration of the Klan's strength. About one week later, April 15, at the morning service of the Christian Church, the Reverend Ora Oxley announced that a delegation of Odd Fellows had planned to attend a special service at the church. The rumor quickly spread that in reality the Odd Fellows were really members of the Knights of the Ku Klux Klan.

That evening 104 members of the Klan arrived by special car over the Chicago, South Bend and Northern Indiana interurban line. Another 25 to 40 arrived by car.

> "Suddenly, about 8 o'clock, there was a stir at the door, and the Knights of the Invisible Empire came filing down the aisle of the church. A hush fell over the congregation, nothing being audible but the tread of the marching visitors."

Approximately 100 unmasked Klansmen filed into the church. Another 20 hooded Klansmen slowly passed by the rostrum to take a seat in the choir box to the rear of the pulpit, as Reverend Oxley watched. Oxley preached that a Christian organization was needed in America and that it didn't matter if it was known as the Ku Klux Klan or called by some other name. He added that if those foreigners that came to America were dissatisfied they should return to their "fatherland." It was announced that the Reverend Donald C. Ford pastor of the Michigan City Christian Church would speak on "Klanism" at the high school auditorium on Tuesday evening to those interested. Many believed that Reverend Ford was "an avowed member of the Klan." Those wearing masks removed them at the conclusion of the service. The HERALD reported that the members of the congregation recognized many of the Klansmen.

The Klan made its presence known in other parts of the county by the burning of fiery crosses during April and early May. The first reported in La Porte's newspapers took place in Fox Park near the Truesdell entrance at the foot of Detroit Street about two blocks from the Pere Marquette crossing. The cross was 6 to 7 feet high with 3 to 4 foot cross arms. It had been wired to an oak tree about 12 feet above ground. The blazing cross was first observed at 10 P.M. The HERALD said this act was the Klan's first public demonstration in La Porte. The ARGUS said it was undeniable evidence that the Klan had gained a footing in La Porte. To the large number of "colored persons" living just south of Clear Lake the burning cross was ominous.

A 12-foot high and four foot wide cross was set ablaze in Mid-April at about 10 P.M. when most of the residents of Wanatah were in bed. The fiery cross was located in the schoolyard. Two weeks later the Klan held an organizational meeting in Woodman Hall.

The city of La Porte experienced its second cross burning during the first week in May. Those attending the carnival at the fairgrounds observed the fiery emblem of the Ku Klux Klan about 9 P.M. Many drove to the small knoll just southwest of Dr. H. H. Martin's Cedar Lodge on Eleventh Street to get a better view. The seven foot high cross was held in place by wires attached to the cross arms and was staked to the ground. Like the other cross burnings, no one knew who was responsible. A carload of men was observed leaving the scene shortly after the cross began to burn.

Two weeks later activity at the fair grounds was observed when a number of men who appeared to be strangers to La Porte were erecting a tent. The gate with a flag draped over it was guarded in order to prevent access to the grounds. It was learned that the Ku Klux Klan intended to conduct a meeting and initiate a large number of candidates into the order. Word had spread throughout the community that the Klan would parade through the streets prior to their meeting and initiation service. The DAILY HERALD reported that 8,000 "curious persons lined the streets" in anticipation of the parade. The news article said that the crowd attracted to the parade was the largest ever in La Porte's history for such an event. Police officials were caught off guard and had to call in officers who were on patrol in residential areas in order to direct traffic and maintain order along the parade route.

As the crowds of people began filling the streets, hundreds of Klan members were entering the city. Three special interurban railcars, two from Michigan City and one from South Bend brought the white-robed Klansmen to La Porte. Others arrived by automobile. The HERALD assumed the visitors came from Knox, Valparaiso, South Bend and Michigan City. Thirty-three automobiles entered the fair grounds. It was estimated that 400 Kluxers attended the meeting.

Shortly before 9 P.M. those having the regulation regalia donned their masks. However, many of the marchers were unmasked. A large cross was set ablaze prior to the start of the parade. The procession left the fair grounds and proceeded to march to Lincoln Way. They traveled east on Lincoln Way to Detroit Street and then back on Lincoln Way to the fair grounds. The parade marked the first public appearance of the Ku Klux Klan in La Porte. Two hooded Klansmen on horseback carrying American flags led the parade. A large white cross illuminated with miniature lights was carried by one of the marchers. According to the HERALD 319 members of the Klan marched, ten to twelve were unmasked women. One of the ladies was recognized as a La Porte resident, but the newspaper did not identify her.

For the most part the parade proceeded without incident. A few curt remarks were directed at the marchers. There was also an occasional applause as they passed. An incident on the serious side occurred just as the parade was leaving Lincoln Way when someone sounded a false fire alarm from a box at Washington and Adams Streets. Cars and people began to move as the fire truck sped down the street endangering many lives.

The initiation service was conducted at the fair grounds at the conclusion of the parade. Absolute secrecy was maintained with the posting of hooded guards at strategic locations. No one was allowed to enter the grounds without giving the secret password.

Several days later La Porte's Board of Public Safety ordered the fire department to avoid using Lincoln Way when answering a fire alarm when the street was congested. They were especially concerned about Saturday afternoons and evenings, "on band concert nights" or any other time when Lincoln Way was busy with vehicles and people.

The two La Porte newspapers reported increased Klan activity within the county during the month of June. Two meetings were held at Union Mills. The second one occurred on the last Friday of June at the schoolyard. A large crowd gathered to witness the initiation of several of the community's men. At the schoolyard in Hanna, and in Wanatah the Klan also made its presence known. In fact there were two meetings held in Wanatah, the first on June 15th and the second on June 20. The ARGUS publicized the second meeting as being "one of the most orderly and well conducted meetings ever held in Wanatah." The Indianapolis based speaker provided the gathering with a comprehensive explanation of the Klan's organization and purpose. The report continued by saying the speaker took a conservative approach to the issues and "in no way was abusive or offensive to anyone."

The first public installation of candidates into the Ku Klux Klan ever held in La Porte occurred on Saturday, June 23, 1923. The public had been invited to witness the initiation of 150 candidates. The event took place south of La Porte on Monroe Street near the Yellow River. Between 300 and 400 cars filled the grove and lined the road. The crowd witnessed the induction of La Porte candidates into the order. Two gigantic fiery crosses, 35 feet high with 15 foot cross arms, cast an eerie glow that added a touch of mystery to the 45 minute ceremony. The one hundred or more robed and masked figures formed a circle about 60 feet in diameter around the candidates. The self-professed Klansman from Michigan City directed the ritual and administered the oath to the kneeling candidates. Adding a patriotic touch to the event, the Klansmen closed the ceremony with a display of fireworks.

The bandstand on La Porte's courthouse square provided the location. The last band concert in the month of June provided the forum for the Klan's propaganda. There was little advanced publicity announcing the occasion, however, a large number of hand bills were distributed during the concert. The majority of the 1,000 people in attendance were taken by surprise when twelve masked and robed figures escorted on to the bandstand the unmasked Reverend Blair. One of the individuals was carrying a large American flag. Another followed him carrying a wooden cross illuminated with red light bulbs. For more than an hour the Rev. Blair exalted the Klan's virtues and urged the audience to show greater devotion to the flag and country. According to the ARGUS he affirmed that the Ku Klux Kan was "not opposed to religious or racial freedom, but that the Klan is opposed to religious and racial domination." His remarks were well received, as was evidenced by the frequent applause given.

The Klan continued its crusade during July to persuade the public of their virtuous cause and to attract new members. They drew a large crowd in Westville earlier in the month. During the latter part of the month the Klan was back in the city of La Porte. The weekly Wednesday night band concert on the courthouse square provided the opportunity for a ready-made audience. Depending upon which newspaper one read the audience that remained after the concert numbered between 250 and 1000 to hear an Indianapolis speaker. As was the case of other presentations, the speaker outlined and defined the Klan's purpose. He also used the occasion to demean "foreigners" that took advantage America's institutions. Several members of the Klan dressed in full regalia complete with their usual accoutrements of an American flag and a cross outlined in red lights were seated on the platform.

An interesting letter was sent to the "Voice of the People" column and was published in the Michigan City DISPATCH in mid-July. It speaks to the rancor and infighting that appears to have existed within the local Ku Klux Klan. The letter, written by Gustave W. Krause, identified himself as a former chaplain of the Michigan City Klan. The FIERY CROSS that was purported to be the official Ku Klux Klan newspaper had reported that Krause "had been banished from the Klan because of political activities in connection with the attempt by Bob Moore (Michigan City attorney) to use the Klan as a vehicle to ride into the attorney general's office." Krause contested the statement by saying that he was suspended from the local Klan "for creating discrimination" within the rank and file members of the local Klan. The incident revolved around the purchase of an "electric washing machine for a certain Klansman." He alluded to other Klan charges against him such as having political connections with Bob Moore and George West, being affiliated with the communist party as well as not keeping his "solemn obligation" and betraying his fellow Klansmen.

In his letter he challenged Donald C. Ford, pastor of the First Christian Church, to a "public debate on the principles and practices of the Invisible Empire of the Knights of the Ku Klux Klan." He named Ford as the "exalted cyclops of the Michigan City Klan (elected at the May 18, 1923, meeting of the Klan at the Moose hall)." His open letter seemed to exude a feeling of anger for and betrayal of trust by Reverend Ford. After all, "That on this Sunday (May 5, 1923) I occupied the pulpit of the First Christian church during Mr. Ford's absence" so that he could attend a Klan meeting in Indianapolis. It would appear that Mr. Krause's challenge went unanswered. Nothing was written in the newspapers that gave any indication that a debate or for that matter a meeting between the two took place. (see appendix no. 2)

The Klan's physical presence during the month of August continued to be seen throughout the county. A midnight meeting held near the bathhouse on the Michigan City's east beach brought out several hundred people. It was said that the Klan had invited numerous guests that included quite a few women. It was reported that the meeting included a prayer by the Reverend Kramer, pastor of the Michigan City First Baptist Church as wells as Klan memorial service for the late president. A fiery cross that appeared to be a large fire caught the attention of the Coast Guard. The fire department was alerted but did not respond. The DISPATCH had learned that the fire department phoned the water works and was told that the blaze came from a fiery cross. The paper questioned the action and motives of the department for not responding in the usual manner.

The city of La Porte experienced its second Ku Klux Klan parade on the 11th of August. Again there was a discrepancy in the number of Klan members that participated. One newspaper estimated the Klan participation at about 184 while the other said 500 took part. The La Porte City band marched and played "Onward Christian Soldiers." Two special interurban cars brought members from Michigan City.

Figure 66 This image of the Ku Klux Klan was indelibly imprinted in the minds of
La Porte County citizens. Photo courtesy of the La Porte County Historical Society Museum.

The Klan continued in its efforts to strengthen its presence in Westville and Hanna by conducting meetings on the schoolyards of each of the respective towns during the month of September. Their parade in La Porte and gathering in Westville and Hanna prompted the Michigan City Commissioners to meet in special session to adapt unanimously a resolution that prohibited all organizations of masked persons gathering or parading in the city. The ordinance directed the police department to enforce the law "in order to preserve peace, prevent crime, suppress riots and prevent unlawful and dangerous assemblages in Michigan City."

The Knights of the Ku Klux Klan continued to maintain a visible presence in Michigan City and defied the City Commissioner's ban by seizing upon the opportunity afforded by the tent meeting of Evangelist Hamilton. During the latter part of the month 30 white robed and hooded figures startled the attendees of an Evangelist tent service that was being held at the rear of the Michigan City 1st Bank on Sixth and Franklin Streets. The Klansmen silently marched into the tent, handed Evangelist Hamilton a letter pledging their support of his work and accomplishments in Michigan City, and left as silently as they entered. According to the NEWS, the audience "sat fear-stricken as the mysterious figures came and went." Interestingly nothing appeared in the newspapers regarding police enforcement of the commissioner's earlier ordinance.

As the election of city offices drew near the DISPATCH and the NEWS chose sides. The DISPATCH indorsed Herman M. Kemp, Leon Kramer, John Ramion, Joseph N. Munning and William J. Feallock. This ticket included one Jew, two Catholics, and two Protestants.[88] They along with numerous prominent citizens "guarantees that these citizens and taxpayers are

243

in no wise contaminated with the kluxer virus." The paper went on to say that to clean out city hall and keep the Klan out voters must vote their anti-Klan ticket.

The NEWS on the other hand urged and argued that its endorsement of Roger M. Cox, William F. C. Dall, William J. Feallock, Louis Hauser, and Leon N. Kramer were best qualified. These candidates have the business training and ability as well as the reputation to insure the security and the progress of Michigan City. They argued that party or politics should not enter into the electorate's decision.

The Klan it was believed was circulating its own ticket. The NEWS' position was that part if not a majority of the candidates on the Klan ticket and the anti-Klan ticket were opposed to the commission manager form of government. The NEWS, however, believed that the present members of the commission were more qualified than some of the other candidate and therefore it would be in the best interest of the city to return them to office. Michigan City was the only city in the state governed by a Commission. Many of its citizens, with former Mayor Martin Krueger leading the charge, viewed the Commission as inefficient and corrupt. The NEWS' viewed the DISPATCH'S position supporting the anti-Klan ticket as camouflage of the real issue of eliminating the commission manager form of government. The DISPATCH on the other hand argued the issue was purely Klan and anti-Klan in nature.

The war of words raged on during the week prior to the election. The DISPATCH accused the NEWS of bringing religion into the fray when it allegedly printed " neither do they (the voters) want a government top-heavy with any particular religious faith. That would be bad of business." The DISPATCH saw this as a veiled insult to a large number of the citizens of the city. They continued to urge the voters to "rise in their might and swat this un-American organization which dares to try to subvert all things to its invisible will or whim."[89] To vote for members of the "city-hall News ticket" in essence would allow the Klan to take control.

Klan members diligently "littered" the city with their pink colored sample ballots hours before the polls opened urging the election of the Klan ticket. They also distributed the pink sample ballots into the hand of voters as they entered the voting places. The DISPATCH speculated that as the election day progressed, conflicts with un-authorized appointed Klan officials attempting to stop voters and asking them for their names and address and otherwise intimidating them with their advice could cause a disturbance at the polls.[90] That didn't materialize.

It was reported that a large crowd assembled at the NEWS' office and overflowed on to Michigan Street to await the results of the election. The election had generated much interest on the part of the voters causing a record turnout. The previous record of votes cast in a Michigan City election was bettered by 2,000 votes and stood at 7,703. It became evident that the Klan endorsed ticket would win a sweeping victory. With the smell of victory in their nostrils a Klan parade magically appeared before the bewitching hour of midnight and ended with a big celebration of Klansmen and their sympathizers. With the final tally of votes in, the headline of the Michigan City NEWS on November 7, 1923, blared out the results, **KLAN TICKET SWEEPS CITY.** The five top successful candidates, all backed by the Klan, were William F. C. Dall, Carl Ahlgrim, Christopher C. Wilber, William Lansberg, and Harvey L. Odell.

The town of Westville also elected the Klan supported People's ticket that saw James H. Allison and I. N. Plant elected to the town board and Charles P. Kalies to the clerk-treasurer office. A huge cross was burned on a vacant lot in the village to celebrate the Klan's victory.[91]

The EVENING DISPATCH in an editorial observed that the results of the election in La Porte County gave strong indication that the political allegiance to either the Democratic or Republican Parties was shifting to Klan and anti-Klan loyalties.[92]

Several days following the election, Gustave W. Krause, sent an announcement to the Michigan City Dispatch, which alleged he had been attacked and molested by George L. West a Klansman. He used this forum to notify Richard J. Kruse, Chief of Police of Michigan City, who he alleged was a member of the Ku Klux Klan, of his attack. It was his contention that this attack occurred because he had exposed the Klan and their treasonable acts. His letter denounced the Klan and warned the citizens of Michigan City that the Klan Commissioners recently elected to office owe their allegiance to the Invisible Empire and would serve and obey the constitution and laws of the Knights of the Ku Klux Klan at the expense of the community.[93]

A few days later the people of Michigan City were invited to on open meeting held at St. John Hall where a Reverend Shouse of Indianapolis explained the principals of the Klan. It was reported that a large crowd that included many from the county was on hand as he "explained in a very satisfactory manner" what the Klan stood for. The meeting included a short musical program that entertained the crowd.[94]

As the time honored axiom proclaimed, "To the victor go the spoils," the newly elected Commissioners gave notice to the community that they were taking charge. The week prior to Christmas, letters were sent notifying Horace Bowen, city-manger; Alexander Spychalski, city clerk; Robert H. Moth, city civil engineer; and R. J. Krueger, water collector that they would no longer be employed by the city after the first of the year. From the perspective of the Michigan City DISPATCH they were ousted because they were not members of the Ku Klux Klan or their sympathizers.[95]

The ARGUS reported on November 23, 1923, that it was rumored that the Ku Klux Klan was behind the move to establish a Protestant County Hospital in La Porte. Nearly a month later the DISPATCH reported the same rumor, saying that $1,000 paid for an option to buy the Interlaken School building just north of La Porte. Michigan City Police officers petitioned the Commission and was granted permission to hold a tag day in order to raise funds for the hospital.[96] Prominent La Porte County citizens, however, totally disavowed any ties to the Klan. A Protestant Hospital was eventually established in the city of La Porte.

The newly elected Commissioners at their first meeting of the year wasted little time in repealing an ordinance passed by the Commission on September 5. With the abstention by Mayor William Dall, the vote to repeal the prohibition on masked parades on the streets of Michigan City was unanimously approved. This action left little doubt in the mind of the NEWS that the newly instituted government of the city was in the hands of the Ku Klux Klan.[97] The Knights of the Ku Klux Klan held their regular meeting three days later. Approximately 150 La Porte members filled two interurban cars and traveled to Michigan City to attend the meeting.[98] Leading members of the Klan the next day announced that Michigan City would host the Klan's territorial meeting on Friday, February 22nd.[99]

Controversy over the actions of the Commission continued with the firing of Walter J. Behrens from the police department and James H. Mitchell from the fire department. Behrens, in a letter to the Voice of the People that appeared in the DISPATCH alleged that his dismissal was due to derogatory remarks he made and was denied a public hearing. The DISPATCH editorialized that "The police row is much of a tempest in a teapot and is confined exclusively to Klan members so let them settle it."[100] Mitchell also wrote a letter that appeared in the

DISPATCH. He admitted he had been a member to the Klan and ended his relationship when he discovered "their aims and practices were to promote religious and racial hatred and boycott to secure their political and business aspiration." He went on to say that he was asked to rejoin but refused. He had also warned his friends not to join the Klan. It wasn't long after two Klan members circulated a petition to have him and others on the fire department discharged. He alleged the city manger fired him for no other reason but "talking about the klan."[101]

Now that the Klan had completed its dominance and control of Michigan City government, they continued to exert their will on its population. The opportunity to establish and impose its tenet of the Christian Religion on the community was at hand. The Commissioners took up the issue of requiring the reading of the Bible and the reciting of the Lord's Prayer in the public schools. There appeared to be little opposition to the measure, at least publicly, until Armin Meyer, Pastor of St. Paul Lutheran Church spoke of his concerns and warned the community of the danger inherent in subverting the Constitution of the United States. He took a bold and dangerous path in light of the sentiment of support the Knights of the Ku Klux Klan was enjoying locally and nationally.

In his letter to the DISPATCH'S "Voice of the People" he eloquently expressed his thoughts as how this intrusion into the public school would undermine our American institutions "and particularly the destruction of that greatest of all gifts under our illustrious American flag—the religious freedom and the right to worship God according to the dictates of one's own conscience." He argued that the public schools were not the tools of the Christian religion to instill its religious creed or faith on the minorities of Michigan City. The public schools are not the place where religious convictions or beliefs are to be propagated, that's for the respective churches. The schools belong to the state and not the church.[102]

The two local newspapers took opposite positions of the issue. The NEWS opposed the intrusion while the DISPATCH "says that the reading of the bible in the public schools will do no harm."[103] The editorial pointed out that the school city is separate from the civil city. The only control the commissioners had was to elect school board members and to pass proposed bond issues. The school board "are the real bosses of what shall be taught...." Pastor Meyer said, that while some believe it to be a small matter, "so are all beginnings.... But the edge of the wedge need only be entered and the rest is easy.... Little influences of evil have undermined great institutions."[104]

Despite the passionate pleas to vote down the ordinance, the City Commissioners met and voted to adopt the ordinance. It was anticipated that a large crowd would be on hand. The meeting was moved to the assembly room of the courthouse. The issue was the last item on the agenda. The packed assembly room broke out into enthusiastic applause that lasted more than a minute when the final reading of the ordinance was approved. The only nay vote came from Mayor Dall.[105]

The Reverend Donald Ford also let his voice be heard on the issue and in support of the commissioners' action. His letter to the "Voice of the People" was also eloquently stated. He quoted noted American statesmen and renown literary giants in defense of the commissioners' vote. He used moral and religious examples to demonstrate why he was convinced that it would have a stabilizing influence on the morals of young people as well as "to pointing them to the right issues in life…"[106]

As the end of February approached the Michigan City branch of the Knights of the Ku Klux Klan and the city administration made plans to host the Thirteenth District meeting of the organization. Some ten thousand Klansmen and Kamelias, the ladies organization, were expected. The occasion was expected to be the largest in the history of Northern Indiana Klandom. Some of the advance guard of the Klan arrived in the city on February 21, the day before the event with the purpose of helping with the preparation of the meetings. A local committee of Klansmen was to check the restaurants.[107]

With the arrival of the big event came a heavy snowfall. The bad weather made the roads impassable. City employees were directed to clear the snow from the park where the parade was to form that night as well as the paths leading to the Casino. The inclement weather materially reduced the number of attendees to what was estimated at 2,000.[108] The Northern Indiana Rail line ran special cars for the event. One car brought 50 women of the Klan from La Porte; with four more expected that evening. Six other cars were expected to pass through La Porte from South Bend, Goshen and Elkhart on their way to the meeting that evening.[109] Drifting snow forced the delegations from Warsaw and Knox to turn back.[110]

The event was orderly and free from disturbance. Michigan City police and special officers "appointed for the occasion had little or nothing to do but to wear their robes and look pretty."[111] The "special officers" also acted as guides to provide the visitors with information and directions. The women were directed to St. John's Hall, which served as their headquarters whereas the men's gathering place was not reported. Local women of the Klan as well as fifty girls from La Porte conducted a tag day to raise funds to benefit the La Porte County Protestant Hospital.[112]

The courthouse auditorium accommodated meetings in the afternoon and evening and was open to the public. The DISPATCH reported that local Klansmen were disappointed because the woman state organizer scheduled to speak in the afternoon did not show up due to the bad weather. Harry Kern (aka. Kearn) of Indianapolis, instead, gave the address. Henry Smitter, (the alleged head of the Michigan City Klan[113]) and the Reverend Donald Ford from Michigan City substituted and gave short speeches in place of the National Kleages who didn't show up. The meetings were advertised as non-political and only district business of the Klan would be conducted.[114]

The evening events included a parade followed by a closed meeting held in Washington Park at the Lakeview Casino. The parade began in Washington Park. Illuminating the staging area was a large electric cross. The marchers started south on Franklin Street to Williams Street, north on Washington a few blocks and back to Franklin and back to Washington Park. Thousands of spectators lined the parade route. Klansmen in their regalia and approximately thirty ladies of the Klan proudly marched to the music of four bands. One of the bands composed entirely of Klansmen came from Elkhart. Another band was made of members of the La Porte City Band. Many of the marchers carried red lights. There were "nineteen horsemen, four floats and four automobiles" used to carry dignitaries. Every county in the 13th district was represented. The American flag was evident throughout the line of parade. Thousands of spectators were seen respectfully saluting the flag as it went by. Aerial rockets and displays fired off at intervals illuminated the parade route.[115]

A closed meeting was held at the Casino to induct a large number of new Klansmen at the conclusion of the parade. The delegates selected Warsaw as the site of the next district meeting. The city ordered extra police officers and firemen to guard the building while the meeting was in progress in order to assure its secrecy.[116] At the conclusion of the meeting a Michigan City Klansman thanked the city for its cooperation in making the district meeting a success.

Little if any Klan activity following the district meeting was apparent in the county during the remainder of February and much of March. The primary election coming up in May brought out the rumors that the Klan indorsed several persons that had filed their intention to seek office.[117] Forty candidates had filed to seek office one month before the primary. The election promised to be one of the hardest fought in the history of La Porte County. The heat of battle was expected to extend into both political parties. It was reported that 152 people filed for precinct committeemen. There were 61 precincts in the county with one person from each of the parties. Ninety-three Republicans were fighting over 61 positions and 59 Democrats to fill their respective seats. Rumors throughout the county indicated that members of the Ku Klux Klan had filed for Republican committeemen and nearly had a full slate of county candidates. Speculation was that if the Klan could elect a majority of committeemen they would be able to select the party chairman and other officers who in turn would choose Republican Delegates sympathetic to their cause.[118] Some politicians were saying that if this situation occurred statewide the Klan would be able to nominate Ed Jackson a Republican candidate for governor.[119] The same scenario was true for the Democrats. However, the Klan didn't appear to have as strong a grip.[120]

Samuel J. Taylor of Michigan City and Earl Rowley of La Porte on behalf of the Republican voter of the county, in a bold move to thwart the reported aspirations of the Klan to have its candidates listed on the primary ballot, filed a complaint of fraud and irregularity in the petitions filed by 10 alleged Klan delegates. Judge J. C. Richter issued a temporary restraining order and set a date after the primary to hear arguments before ruling on a permanent injunction.[121]

Several days later Peter Ewald of La Porte and Raymond M. Dunlap of Michigan City filed petitions to reinstate the deposed candidates.[122] It was reported that Joseph Hall, Michigan City, an alleged La Porte County KLAN official hired attorneys from Indianapolis and Knox to argue their side. Lawyers Alfred J. Link, Ben C. Rees and Lemuel Darrow representing Taylor and Rowley successful argued their clients' position before Judge Richter.[123]

Secretary of State Ed Jackson responded by sending an official from his office to investigate the legality of the county Republican Party organization in securing a restraining order that remove the names of the 10 alleged Klan members from the primary ballot. Also in question was Judge Richter's authority in matters of affecting election ballots.[124] Jackson, the Republican candidate for governor, followed up with speaking engagements in La Porte and Michigan City.[125]

The 1924 primary election was noteworthy in the political history of La Porte County due to the Klan vs. anti-Klan issue and its influence over the issues and policies as they affect of the November election according to the La Porte DAILY HERALD. The HERALD ran a full-page ad that listed Republican Party candidates that were not Ku Klux Klan members and urged the good citizens of the county to vote for those listed.[126] The results of the election indicated that 90% of the votes cast in the county were Republican. It was believed that the poor showing of Democrats voting was due to the small number Klansmen in the Democratic Party and few contested offices. It was also apparent that Klan opponents choose Republican ballots in hopes of sabotaging the aspirations of Klan candidates. Officials at the 61 county precincts reported that the voting was peaceful and orderly.[127]

Political observers said that the Klan backed Earl L. Alexander for surveyor, and Peter Ewald who acknowledged he was a Klan candidate for county recorder. Ewald's margin of victory in Michigan City was by 1000 more votes than his nearest rival. Andrew Hickey, Frank Fosdick,

UP CLOSE AND PERSONAL

```
KU KLUX KLAN
CHARITY CIRCUS
FIVE DAYS
AT THE   Arena Grounds
June 30 to July 4th
MICHIGAN CITY, IND.
SOMETHING SNAPPY EVERY EVENING!

Tuesday Night—A Real Klan Wedding.
Wednesday Night—The Fiddlers' Contest.
Thursday Night—Tacky Dressed Couple.
Friday Night—Handsomest and Homeliest Man
    Popularity Contest.
Saturday Afternoon—The Baby Show.
Saturday Night—Coronation of the "QUEEN OF
    THE CIRCUS."

MONSTER KLAN PICNIC ALL DAY SATUR-
DAY, FOURTH OF JULY.

A BIG GALA KLAN TIME!
Parking Space a Plenty!
```

Figure 67 The above advertisement appeared in
The Michigan City News, June 18, 1925

Frank A. Rogers, Justin Loomis and John Sweitzer secured places on the November ballot disappointing the Klan.[128]

The Klan's effort to nominate Ed Jackson for governor and gain control of the state Republican Party was a success in nearly every county of Indiana. The Herald's observation was that La Porte voters "do not intend to turn the management of the county affairs over to the wearers of the hooded masks." However, the election results showed that the Klan still controlled Michigan City.[129] The Klan was able to elect twelve of its seventeen precinct committeemen in Michigan City.[130] The same was not true for the city of La Porte. Only in one of its precincts did a Klan candidate receive a large majority.[131] The party faithful held a majority and re-elected Harry L. Marum as the party's chairman of the Central Committee. They also elected Sam Taylor as vice-chairman.[132]

Members of the Klan in May, July and August participated in events outside the county. South Bend hosted a rally that brought 4,000 Kluxers and anti-Klaners to their city. Four interurban railroad cars left Michigan City filled with Klan members. About 25 boarded the train when it stopped in La Porte.[133] A Fourth of July gathering at the Valparaiso fair grounds saw a large contingent that included residents from Hanna and Oakwood travel there.[134] The parade that night included about 50 boys of the Junior Klan that marched behind a banner proclaiming they were from La Porte.[135] A number of La Porte Klansmen took part in an Elkhart parade along with 10,000 other Klan members.[136]

Elaborate plans to host the annual Tri-State conclave of the Ku Klux Klan on August 16, was announced by the leaders of the Michigan City Klan. It was anticipated that 50 to 60 thousand Klansmen, members of the Kamelia and their families would attend. Bad weather, however, held down attendance to about 5,000.[137] Participants arrived by automobile and trains. Special trains were chartered that brought people from Michigan, Illinois, and Indiana and arrived throughout the day. Mrs. G. R. Turnbull recruited a large staff of women to man a booth as well as sell one-dollar tags on the street to benefit the Protestant Hospital fund.[138] Members of the Klan distributed handbills throughout the business district announcing the burning of a large fiery cross on the side of a sand dune adjacent to the arena.[139] The Morris and Castle Carnival setup east of the Sky Blue Arena on east 2nd Street and provided entertainment all week.

The Sky Blue Arena served as the headquarters for the event as well as the site for the meetings. Nearly 3,000 people attended the afternoon meeting to hear distinguished speakers and Klan leaders. Hiram W. Evans the Imperial Wizard of the Knights of the Ku Klux Klan made an appearance.[140]

The highlight of the day was a parade that began at the monument in the early evening at the entrance to Washington Park. More than 2,000 marched in the parade. Numerous members of the Junior Klan were among the participants.[141] Beside the marchers were horse mounted Klansmen, two bands and a number of floats. The Elkhart Klan drill team dazzled the spectators by forming a large cross during the progress of the parade. Thousands of red lights illuminated the parade as it travel south down Franklin Street through the business district returning by way of Washington Street and east on Second Street to the carnival.[142]

As the November national and local elections approached both political parties and the Klan began to make preparations. Former Indiana Republican Senator Albert J. Beverage, Democratic Senator Pat Harrison of Mississippi as well as the gubernatorial candidates came to La Porte.[143] Accusations or dirty politics were raised by the EVENING DISPATCH.

On the State level the voters endorsed Klan policies by electing a majority of Klan candidates. Ed Jackson the Klan candidate was elected governor. Locally the voters appeared to forget party affiliations and voted along Klan and anti-Klan lines. All but one Republican that lost was strongly opposed by the Klan. Victory rallies celebrating the election of Ed Jackson and the defeat of five anti-Klan county candidates were held in Michigan City and La Porte. Nearly 700 people took part in the Wednesday parade in the harbor city. Numerous banners boasted the election of Ed Jackson and county endorsed candidates. None of the celebrants wore robes.[144]

The rally in La Porte the next evening saw approximately 200 men, women and children gather at the court house and marched down Michigan Avenue to the home of Othie Jack the newly elected County Clerk. The La Porte City Band led the procession. A drum corps from Michigan City was also on hand. Jack received a hearty ovation and marched off with the celebrants to the home of Paul Summy the new state representative. Earl Alexander's, elected surveyor, was the next home on the route. The revelers returned to the courthouse, circled it and disbanded. Many of the same banners such as "Hurrah for Ed Jackson and the Kluxers" and "The Klan will Clean Up Politics" were displayed at Michigan City the previous night.[145]

Michigan City Klan leaders, as Christmas was approaching, requested all Klansmen to bring to Klan headquarters articles of food for Christmas baskets for needy families. Several hundred baskets were distributed to local families on Christmas Eve and morning.[146]

The La Porte County Klan appeared to be in a state of hibernation during the winter of 1924-25. As the spring of 1925 approached, events were revealed that would shake the very foundation of the Indiana Ku Klux Klan and marked the beginning of the end of its control over the politics of the state. David C. Stephenson, The Grand Dragon and leader of the state organization was arrested and charged with the murder of Madge Oberholtzer. She accused Stephenson, while on her deathbed, of kidnapping and taking her to Hammond by train. She alleged that while on the train Stephenson raped her. She related that while at a Hammond hotel she took the poison that ended her life. Testimony revealed "Stephenson took her back to Indianapolis, locked her in his garage, and refused to get medical aid." Stephenson was convicted and sent to the Indiana State Prison in Michigan City.[147]

With spring at hand the county Klan organization seemed to come to life. The Klan rally originally scheduled for Valparaiso would be held in the city of La Porte on May 10 in the Madison Theater. Some 3,000 Klan members and families from Porter, La Porte, and St. Joseph Counties were in attendance. The purpose of the gathering in the afternoon and evening ceremonies was to bestow upon a large class of candidates the K-Duo, or second degree of the order. The participants did not wear their usual garb of hoods and robes. Streets in the vicinity were lined with parked cars. The Madison Theater burst at the seams. Fourteen hundred jammed into a 900-seat theater with hundreds unable to get in. State officials in charge scheduled a second meeting in order to accommodate those that didn't get in. The remaining candidates had their degree conferred the following Saturday at the same location.[148]

Plans to bring the Rodgers and Harris Circus to Michigan City at the end of June and the first week of July were announced by Henry Smitter, chairman of the shows executive committee. Those wishing information regarding the circus or the scheduled events were informed to contact Al Smith at Michigan City headquarters.[149] Klan officials established a contest for the purpose of naming a Queen of the Circus. One young lady from La Porte, Miss Dorothy James, entered the competition. Thirteen young women from Michigan City registered:

Enid Billings	Elna Johnson	Thelma Sundeen	Mrs. Doretta Rogers
Lucille Crozier	Mildred Burnett	Mabel Lansberg	Mrs. Arthur Zeiske
Mary Wilson	Edith Ducey	Nelllie Denow	Mrs. Waunelia Heise
Polly Sights			

The lady with the largest vote was crowned on July 4th, the last evening of the charity event.[150] Enid Billings took the early lead with 29,000 votes followed by Elna Johnson with 22,500 and in third place was Mabel Lansberg with 16,500.[151]

The circus arrived over the Nickel Plate Railroad from Fort Wayne and proceeded to setup on the show grounds east of the Sky Blue Arena. On the opening night of the circus two weddings were performed. The bride and groom from Coal City and McCool were greeted by a delegation of Klansmen upon their arrival that afternoon and escorted to the Spaulding Hotel. A luncheon in their honor was catered as Mayor Dall's gift to the couple. He also played host during their stay in the city.[152]

The marriage of a Gary couple was included as a last minute addition. The joint weddings were performed in front of a large crowd in the main exhibition tent. The Klan supplied the license. Lee F. Dresser donated the wedding rings and Emma McCracken supplied the flowers. The Reverened Donald Ford of the Christian Church conducted both ceremonies. Several children from Michigan City acted as ring bearers and flower girls. Twelve Klansmen in traditional garb took part in the joyous occasion.[153] The circus band played the wedding march and the circus owner's wife sang. The general public was invited to attend the ceremony "and each person has the privilege of showering a gift on the newly weds just like they do at an old fashioned pound party." Members of the Klan passed the plate for a cash offering which was given to the newly weds. Klan officials collected numerous gifts from the business and financial community with nearly 40 establishments participating. The newly weds were driven to the Spaulding Hotel following the ceremony where they stayed in the bridal suites, compliments of the hotel.[154]

Other events scheduled in conjunction with the circus included a band concert along Franklin Street every afternoon at 4 P.M., and a Wednesday evening fiddlers' night and contest at the circus. A baby show contest was held on the four of July at the Klan's all-day picnic. Many proud parents went to Klan headquarters in the Schutt Building located at 424½ Franklin Street to register their babies:[155]

Dorothy Jane Skibinski	Betty Jane Keller	Marian Moore
John Edward Wenzel	Gene Daren Robert	Merna Keil
Mildred Snodgrass	Betty Jane Dron	Gene Cassidy
Mabel Evelyn Wilson	Edna L. Mahler	Raymond Fox
Robert Alton Elliott	Mary Jane Walters	John Scholl
Rodgers Eugene Moncell	Marie Carpenter	Albert Archer
Wanda Virginia Carpenter	Betty Ann Heise	Betty Valentine

The 4th of July picnic brought out a large crowd. The final results of the Queen of the Circus were announced. The three young ladies that held the early lead sustained their positions throughout the contest. Enid Billings was crowned Queen of the Klan Circus. Her prize was a diamond ring. Johnson finished 2nd with Lansberg holding on to third place.[156]

The national convention of the Knights of the Ku Klux Klan was scheduled the following weekend in Washington, D. C. The timing of the event caused local officials Mr. & Mrs. Henry Smitter, Mr. & Mrs. D. M. Hutton, Mr. & Mrs. Frank M. Wolfe, and Mr. & Mrs. A. D. Manley to leave on the morning of July third, thereby missing the big picnic.[157]

The women of La Porte County continued to play an important part in the Klan organization. Although they didn't appear to be as aggressive or political, they maintained visibility, participating in social and charitable activities. When one of their own or someone with strong Klan ties passed away as was the case of Mrs. Frank Fogleman, they were there. Thirty-five ladies of the Klan, dressed in full regalia attended her burial at Greenwood Cemetery. The Reverend Donald C. Ford officiated.[158]

The combined meeting of the 12th and 13th Klan districts met in Michigan City at St. John's Hall in the fall of 1925. Delegates from Elkhart, South Bend, Goshen, La Porte, Michigan City, Whiting, East Chicago, Gary, Hammond, Plymouth, Chesterton, Knox and Valparaiso descended upon the harbor city. The Past Excellent Commander of Michigan City greeted the delegates following registration.

Luncheon was served by the ladies of the Christian Church at the Peristyle building in Washington Park.[159] Following the meal the delegates returned to St. John's Hall to hear reports of the organization's activities throughout the districts. This was followed up with the initiation of a class of junior girl members. The state degree drill team dressed in full regalia provided entertainment that captured the attention of all in attendance.

Nearly 500 men and woman attended the evening session to hear an address from a State official. The Long Beach Orchestra opened the session followed by a comical presentation by the Tri-K Girls' Kitchen Orchestra from Elkhart. The drill team did a repeat performance of their afternoon's routine.[160]

Women of the La Porte Klan gathered at their headquarters in November at the calling of the Excellent Commander to a rehearsal. To her surprise the ladies staged an impromptu carry-in dinner. She was escorted to a white covered chair and presented with a bouquet of

UP CLOSE AND PERSONAL

Figure 68 Funeral procession at Pine Lake Cemetery.
Photo courtesy of the La Porte County Historical Society.

red roses and an envelope "containing a good size purse." The dinner was followed with an entertaining program.[161]

The November general election "marked the climax of a quiet campaign" throughout the county. The two major political parties conducted business as usual. The Klan seemed to stay in the background until the eve of the election. In La Porte the Klan reportedly endorsed John Line and other Republicans with the exception of Emmett Doolittle. Prominent members of the Klan vigorously denied the report asserting that their members were told to make their own choices.[162] Line was elected La Porte's mayor. The speculation, nonetheless, that his victory over his Democratic counterpart was due to Klan support prevailed.[163]

The commissioner's race in Michigan City drew little attention. Here to, on the eve of the election, some unexpected politicking went on. Circulars were distributed urging voters to elect Vern O'Dell and John Boss if they wanted a "square deal." The DISPATCH viewed this as a Klan endorsement. As the newspaper predicted O'Dell and Boss were elected giving the Klan "continued unanimous control in city affairs."[164]

The over all results of the election in La Porte County showed a Democratic landslide. The Klan, it appeared, played a minor role in this election. An ARGUS editorial succinctly summed up the tenor of the election and prophesied the future strength of the Knights of the Ku Klux Klan. "Although the Klan ideal is strong in the minds of many persons in the county, the actual workings of the political organization is getting weaker. It will probably not figure in the next county election"[165] Several months later Lee Smith, head of the Indiana Klan announced the organization would no longer act as a unit to endorse a set of candidates.[166]

Figure 69 The photo taken on the first occasion of the Klan's official participation in the funeral of a deceased member, Abraham J. Layton at Pine Lake Cemetery. Herald-Argus, July 15, 1925

Controversy between Klan and anti-Klan forces erupted shortly after the start of the New Year. The battle lines were drawn within Michigan City over the replacement of Judge James F. Gleason. The Ku Klux Klan dominated city commissioners appointed Fred Mitchell to be Judge of the Michigan City Court. It was reported that Mitchell was backed by the local Klan organization who in turn pressured the Commission to make the appointment. The majority of local attorneys opposed Mitchell's selection.[167]

Debate over Mitchell's appointment erupted. The commissioners had met in secret session prior to the regular meeting to review the candidates for City Judge. At that meeting they had agreed to appoint Robert S. Baker. At their regularly scheduled meeting, contrary to their earlier agreement, Fred Mitchell's name was placed in nomination. Commissioner O'dell, Mitchell's brother-in-law, moved quickly and called for the adoption of the resolution. Under protest from Wilbur and with the absence of Carl Ahlgrim the motion was passed. Adding to the debate was Mitchell's lack of legal training. He was after all a tradesman at the Haskell and Barker Car Shop and not an attorney.[168]

The slogan "The invisible Empire" seemed to take on a new meaning. The newspapers had little to nothing to report on the gatherings or activities of the Klan during the remainder of the winter of 1926. The ARGUS told of the La Porte ladies staging a potluck supper at their regular meeting. The program was a celebration of Lincoln and Washington's birthdays.[169]

The spring primary election saw the reemergence of Klan activity. Klan meetings in Michigan City and La Porte on the Friday evening prior to the election were well attended. Numerous candidates running for public office attended with the purpose of seeking their endorsement.[170] The Klan claimed they made none. However, the results indicated to the NEWS, Klan members overwhelmingly voted the Republican Ticket countywide and gained the nomination. The results of the election also showed that many crossed over to the Democratic ballot in order to select their favorites.[171]

The month of June saw published reports appearing in the Michigan City newspapers that the offices of the Akiah (Akia) Club, the official Ku Klux Klan organization, and located in the Schutt Building had been broken into. Membership and organization records were taken along with $70. Interestingly, the report of the details of the burglary that appeared in the rival local papers was contradictory. The NEWS reported that there were no visible signs of forced entry, no marks on the door or file cabinet. The only ones with keys were head Klan officials.[172] The DISPATCH account revealed that the door had marks on it where someone forced the lock and an attempt made to remove the hinges.[173] There was no indication the crime was ever solved.

The women's arm of the Klan met at the La Porte County Fairgrounds the first week of July and held a public installation of officers. Reportedly one thousand people attended from throughout La Porte County and South Bend. The silhouettes of white robed women with flaming red capes were lighted by a 30 foot tall burning cross and red burning torches as they marched, saluted the flag and then sang "The Old Rugged Cross" while kneeling to form a cross. Mrs. Earl McCurdy's Orchestra played during the installation and the performance of the drill team. A group that included eight men and women sang hymns.[174]

With another general election approaching in November rumors of Klan endorsements reappeared. Many candidates were quick to disavow any connection to the Klan. A high placed Klan official requesting anonymity attempted to put to rest the rumor that the La Porte Klan had endorsed the entire Republican county ticket and denied the report.[175] However, at voting centers, slates of candidates marked favorable, unfavorable, and neutral were distributed by a number of organizations attempting to persuade voters to elect individuals supportive of their cause. Among them was the Klan.[176]

Over the next 13 months the four major county newspapers either ignored the activities of the Ku Klux Klan or its members leaked nothing newsworthy. The activities of the Kamelias, the women's branch of the organization, were also not publicized for much of the year until the news broke that charges were leveled against two of its members for misuse of approximately $200 of the La Porte group's funds. The Realm Commander appointed a woman from Hammond as receiver. The two met with the La Porte group and after a heated meeting were unable to bring a satisfactory conclusion to the dispute. Unnamed sources stated that several women resigned following the meeting.[177]

The La Porte Klan moved from the Rainsberger Building in October of 1927 and opened its office in the old Guenther Building located at Lincoln Way and Madison Streets.[178] The women of the Klan met in the new hall several times during December. They hosted a countywide meeting and potluck with representatives from Michigan City, Hamlet, Whiting, Hammond, Gary and Chesterton as well as others from throughout the territory present.[179] The week before Christmas they met for a carry-in supper and a 10-cent gift exchange.[180]

Within days of the dawning of 1928 the Knights of the Ku Klux Klan in Indiana were under attack from Attorney General Arthur L. Gillom. He filed suit in the Marion County Circuit Court to revoke their charter and asked that the organization cease to operate in Indiana. He charged that the Klan received its charter under "false and fraudulent misrepresentation of its charter and of its business and activities."[181]

The Klan and its leaders were under investigation to determine its involvement in political corruption and financial misconduct. The former Klan Cyclops of South Bend, Hugh "Pat" Emmons decided to tell all. One of the schemes he related was the formation of a Klan affiliate for white, Protestant foreigners called the "Crusader." The membership fee was $10. He disclosed to the Attorney General that the "jack-pot" was split three ways. He received $2, the Reverend Donald C. Ford, pastor of the First Christian Church getting $2 and the national Klan receiving $6.[182] Ford denied the accusation.

Mid January the Ku Klux Klan of La Porte as an act of defiance or just a coincidence let all know that it was still alive and healthy. Between 75 & 100 La Porte Klansmen dressed in their Klan regalia stepped off to the sounds of drums as they paraded on Lincoln Way.[183]

In what appeared to be an effort to give the Klan the appearance of respectability and remove the veil of secrecy Hiram W. Evans, the Imperial Wizard of the national organization, ordered the unmasking of all Klansmen. Joseph Huffington, Grand Dragon of the Indiana Klan, in an effort to further legitimize the organization announced that the Klan would follow a format similar to the Masons and from time to time would confer three degrees of Klanhood.[184] The new organization would be called the Knights of the Green Forest. The new organization would confer three degrees: Klansmen, Knights of Kamelia and Knights of the Great Forest.[185]

Klansmen in 150 Indiana cities conducted ceremonies to unmask pursuant to the decree handed down by the Imperial Wizard. La Porte and Michigan City followed suit. Ceremonies to confer the Knights of the Great Forest degree were held in conjunction with the unmasking. Forty members of the La Porte County Klan traveled to Valparaiso to receive the third level degree. Over 70 men met at a late hour in La Porte the evening before to assume the obligations of the new organization and receive the new designation. It was reported that this totaled approximately one-half the membership of the La Porte Klavern. It was expected that the others would receive the third degree within a few weeks. It was revealed that the membership was larger than 1927 but much less than four years previous.[186]

In April 1929, the Klan took to the airways in an attempt to sway public opinion. The first broadcast over the La Porte radio station WRAF originated from Klan headquarters in the Guenther Building in the form of an address to local Klansmen by a noted Ku Klux Klan speaker.[187] Later in the month they rented WRAF. John A. Blake of Kentucky spoke about "Restricted Immigration." It was billed as non-partisan and non- political. The gist of his presentation was to point out the effect of unrestricted immigration on unemployment in America.[188]

The activities reported in the press the previous year and throughout 1928 would indicate their energy and purpose was redirected toward social events. Their regular April meeting centered on a potluck dinner.[189] The next reported meeting took place in September. Following a short business meeting the ladies partied and enjoyed a potluck dinner.[190]

The La Porte County Klan once again played host for the annual convention of the 13th District. Between 400 & 500 delegates representing both the men's and women's order from Knox, Warsaw, Goshen, Michigan City, Mishawaka, South Bend, Plymouth, Elkhart and other places were expected to attend. The Mishawaka delegation of 52 persons chartered an interurban train, making a dramatic entrance with an electric fiery cross lighted on the front end of the car. The joint meetings were held in the Guenther Building and included refreshments. Elaborate plans were developed for the entertainment of the visitors.

An imperial representative of the state, the Great Titans from the 10th and 13th districts along with officers of the local Klavern spoke. The La Porte women's drill team performed. They were also scheduled to compete at the Hobart, IN, convention and picnic on the 4th of July. The decision was made to conduct the district meeting every 2 months.[191] The Pottawattomie Park Lodge was the scene for the August 16th convention. Many if not all of the same activities conducted at the June convention were held. Special transportation was arranged from the train and interurban station to the park. Approximately 600 delegates attended.[192]

UP CLOSE AND PERSONAL

The La Porte Klan hosted still another district meeting on a Sunday in March of 1929. Two fiery crosses were burned in the eastern part of La Porte Saturday evening. Nearly 300 men representing their local Klaverns from La Porte, Porter, Lake, Starke, St. Joseph and Fulton Counties as well as a delegation from Indianapolis attended. The purpose of the meeting was to make an attempt to gain support for legislation for a farm relief bureau and lobby Indiana's senators. A prominent official for national Klan affairs spoke, urging those present to contribute to the 100,000 postal card campaign. This action was the first time the Klan officially supported relief for farmers.[193]

The 1929 annual district convention held in the city of La Porte appears to be the last reported announcement of the La Porte County Knights of the Ku Klux Klan, Klavern # 29 activities. The four major newspapers in the county were scrutinized for additional reported Klan activity following their convention. None was found. However, small obscure announcements could have been overlooked. There doesn't appear to be an explanation for the sudden disappearance of public information in the media. The entry in CARSONS MICHIGAN CITY DIRECTORY FOR 1929-30 identified Frank T. Henry as the Kleagle and would suggest the Klan met every Tuesday of the month in their headquarters at 304 ½ Franklin Street. The 1931 CITY DIRECTORY is void of any reference to the Klan. They disappeared from view as mysteriously as they appeared in La Porte County. The "invisible empire" in fact became the invisible empire.

There is no doubt that the Ku Klux Klan was a powerful force in Indiana and for this study specifically in La Porte County. They affected the political, social and moral fiber of our citizens. For a time they were purported as having control of local government units and police agencies. They walked among us at religious, business and social activities. Some of them were our fathers, mothers, brothers and sisters and depending upon your age our grand parents. Their activities in La Porte County seems to be an anomaly. We have read or been told of their divisiveness, their racial and religious discrimination, their use of violence toward African Americans and others who, as they perceived, violated moral and ethical rules.

Throughout the United States as well as much of Indiana the media regularly reported the incidences of violence perpetrated by the Ku Klux Klan. Violent acts resulting from clashes between Klan and anti-Klan factions were also reported. African-Americans today will tell of the discrimination and the intimidation they suffered in Michigan City at the hands of the Klan. There well might have been acts of violence committed by the Klan in the name of "moral and racial justice." If they in fact occurred in La Porte County they went undocumented. The only act of violence that received public attention and was aired in the newspaper was an incident of battery on a white protestant excommunicated Klansman. Gustave Krause was assaulted by a Klansman because he allegedly exposed some of the organization's inner-workings.

One might conclude that the Knights of the Ku Klux Klan in La Porte County did not mirror the ultraconservative point of view of its state and national organizations. Violence does not appear to be a tool used by the local organization. Their publicized activities centered around political, charitable and social events such as their financial contribution to a church building fund, a charity circus, card parties and potluck dinners. The Jewish community publicly if not privately supported klan activities. Whether that participation was to do intimidation and fear or charitable reason we will never know. The Pottawattomie Council of the Boy Scouts of America must have held the klan in high regard as evidenced in their invitation to the Ku Klux Klan along with churches, clubs and other community groups to organize a scout troop.[194]

Some would say that no matter what was or was not reported in the media Klavern # 29, the La Porte County arm of the Knights of the Ku Klux Klan was a plague on this earth that intimidated and/or terrorized Blacks, Jews, and Catholics. Their leaders spread the doctrine of hate and intolerance. Who they were or what they really stood for is left to the reader and history to decide.

APPENDIX NO. 1

Voice of the People
Michigan City Dispatch, July 16, 1923

Challenge to public Debate.

I, Gustave W. Krause, former chaplain of the Michigan City klan hereby challenge Donald C. Ford, pastor of the First Christian church and also exalted Cyclops of the Michigan City klan (elected at the May 18, 1923, meeting of the klan at Moose hall), to meet me in a joint public debate on the principles and practices of the Invisible Empire of the Knights of the Ku Klux Klan. I, herewith numerate the points at issue:

1st. That the Indivisible Empire of the Knights of the Ku Klux Klan does teach and practice deception, creates mutual mistrust, divides people into warring factions, alienates friends, creates suspicion.

2nd. That the invisible empire of the Knights of the Ku Klux Klan has become a far greater disturbing element and danger to our social and economic life than the danger of America ever becoming dominantly Roman Catholic politically.

3rd. That the Invisible Empire of the Knights of the Ku Klux Klan does teach and practice the boycott. That within the local klan a secret committee was appointed to investigate and spy on the members and report any who did not practice klannishness, or, in other words, report those who traded with Jews, Catholics and others.

4th. That the Invisible Empire of the Knights of the Ku Klux Klan does meddle in politics and is in fact itself a gigantic political organization. That Donald C. Ford attended a meeting of the klan in Indianapolis, Sunday, May 5, 1923, at which meeting the klan machine was discussed, and that he gave a report of the Indianapolis meeting at local klan headquarters. That on this Sunday (May 5, 1923) I occupied the pulpit of the First Christian church during Mr. Ford's absence.

5th. The Fiery Cross, issue of July 13, 1923, states, "that I was banished from the klan because of political activities in connection with the attempt by Bob Moore to use the klan as a vehicle to ride into the attorney-general's office." I desire to correct this statement that I was not banished but suspended from the local klan on the charge of "creating discrimination" as stated in the presence of Mr. Gustave W. Plubiak (auto radiator king), who was suspended at the same time and on the same charge by the assistant Kleagle, Mr. Flowers. When I requested Mr. Flowers to explain the charge or more clearly define the meaning of "creating discrimination" I was informed by Mr. Flowers that "creating discrimination" meant that Mr. Plubiak and myself had circulated a story to the effect that the local klan had purchased an electric washing machine for a certain klansman and this story had apparently caused dissension within the ranks of the local organization. This washing machine story I also brand as an untruth and when I take the platform I will give the people of Michigan City all the facts in the case. I defy Mr. Donald C. Ford to prove that I ever "tried to pervert the klan principles to the use of politicians" (if that were, possible). That I ever had any political connections with Bob Moore or Geo. West or that these former klansmen ever used the local klan for political purposes: they were banished because they would not support Ed Jackson, the klan candidate for governor of Indiana.

6th. I further defy Mr. Donald C. Ford to prove that I "was a ward chairman in Chicago and had to leave there when certain trouble arose in connection with what afterward developed into the communist trials which were held in Michigan and a number of persons convicted on "red" charges as reported in the Fiery Cross, issue of July 13, 1923. For the information of the public of Michigan City I will state that I was secretary of the 26th ward branch of the socialist party of Chicago for a short period prior to my service in the United States army. I connected with this organization for the same purpose and reason that I became connected with the Ku Klux Klan, to study the inner workings of these organizations and thus have first hand knowledge of a reliable kind. At no time have I been connected with the communist party. And at no time has the United States government brought charges against me. If Mr. Ford desires to acquaint himself as to my character prior to my coming to Michigan City, I will gladly furnish him with the names and addresses of my two former Chicago employers and numerous friends and enemies. And he can have my consent to request a report as to my character. I served in France for a period of one year with Battery A, 306th F. A., 77th Div. of New York. My honorable discharge from the United States army contains this statement as to my character and services rendered: "Excellent character, soldier's services honest and faithful. No A. W. O. L. or absence under G. O. 31-l2, or 45-14." If my character had been questionable Mr. Ford surely would not have requested me to occupy his pulpit during his absence at a klan meeting in Indianapolis May 5, 1923. And further, I surely would not have been appointed chaplain of the local klan or have been permitted to audit the books of the local klan two weeks prior, to my suspension.

7th. The Fiery Cross of July 13, lays stress on the fact that I "held as naught a solemn obligation and betrayed those with whom I would affiliate." I answer this charge with a counter-charge that The Invisible Empire of the Knights of the Ku Klux Klan taught me to hold naught this solemn obligation. Six weeks prior to the actual banishment of Bob Moore from the local klan the Fiery Cross heralded broadcast in an article that covered half of the front page of that publication the news of his banishment. The fact remains that Bob Moore was banished six week after this article appeared in the Fiery Cross. The Invisible Empire Of the Knights of the Ku Klux Klan violated a solemn obligation when it heralded this information to the general public through its mouthpiece, the Fiery Cross. Under these circumstances what right has the klan to speak about breaking solemn obligations? The oath was administered to me by a robed and masked person, and under such conditions I do not now or ever shall, consider such an oath binding.

8th. Will Mr. Donald C. Ford please inform the public of Michigan City as to the reasons why the present Kleagle left Columbus, Ind.?

If Mr. Donald C. Ford accepts my challenge to debate the questions involved, suggest that a committee of five persons be selected, two by either party interested and the fifth to be selected by the four thus named. This committee to arrange the details of the debate.

Awaiting Mr. Ford's decision in the premises, I herewith attach my signature.

Gustave W. Krause.

APPENDIX NO. 2

ANNOUNCEMENT
Michigan City News Dispatch, November 12, 1923

I Gustave W. Krause, hereby notify Richard J Kruse, Klansman and a citizen of the Invisible Empire of the Knights of the Ku Klux Klan and also Chief of Police of Michigan City, that I was attacked and molested by Klansman George L. West, Thursday evening, November 8th, at about 10 P. M. on Franklin Street of this city. Not knowing the full intent of this malicious attack or whether Mr. West is the hired agent of the Michigan City Klan, hired to do me bodily injury because of my exposure of the Klan and its treasonable practices, I have undertaken such steps as will insure me a degree of safety and any further molestation by Mr. West or any other Person will be dealt with according to the law. If Mr. West or any other persons has any charges to bring against me I request that such persons resort to the courts and not, take the law into their own hands.

Since the election of four Klan Commissioners last Tuesday a serious situation has arisen and one which vitally interests all the citizens of this city. Messrs. Carl Ahlgrim, Christopher O. Wilbur, William Lansberg and Harvey L. Odell are Klansmen and citizens, of the Invisible Empire of the Knights of the Ku Klux Klan. And as citizens of the Invisible Empire they are no longer citizens but "aliens" to 'the Commonwealth of the- United States of America. And according to the "Fiery Cross," the mouthpiece of the Invisible Empire, they cannot serve two masters, they are blood sealed oath bound to "faithfully obey —the constitution and laws—and willingly conform to—all regulations, usages and requirements of the Knights of the Ku Klux Klan—which do now exist—or which may be hereafter enacted—and will render at all times loyal respect and steadfast support— to the Imperial authority of same— and will heartily heed—all official instructions—of 'the Imperial mandates--decrees — edicts — rulings of the Wizard thereof—I will yield prompt response—to all summonses—I have knowledge of same—Providence alone preventing."

The foregoing are the exact words of the Klan oath which these gentlemen have Allegiance, not to the Government of the United States, but to an Invisible Empire. These men who have taken this oath have delivered themselves to the overlordship taken and please note this is an Oath of Kleagles, Cyclopses, Grand Dragons and Imperial Wizards. And as "aliens" to the Republic of the United States of America can these men represent the true citizens of the United States?

If these Commissioners desire it I will gladly furnish them with a complete copy of this treasonable oath which they have taken and after they have carefully studied its every provision I believe the citizens of Michigan City have a perfect right to request public statement from each of these gentlemen.

I hereby challenge the elected Commissioners to a public debate on the practices and principles of the Knights of the Ku Klux Klan. I hereby charge that the institution of which the four mentioned elected Commissioners are a part is un-American.

2. That it teaches deception,

3. That it teaches the boycott,

4. That it sacrifices to popularity and cheap publicity the sacred emblem of the "Cross" on which the solidity and also the sanctity of the whole Christian world rests,

5. That it misuses the sacred emblem of the United States of America "Old Glory." While It requests others to uncover their heads in respect to this sacred emblem, they, the Klansmen, are permitted to cover the heads with a dunce cap and mask and carry the flag unfurled at their midnight carnivals of hate and all this done contrary to the regulation prescribed by the Government of the United States.

6. That it is anti-Jew,

7. That it is anti-Catholic,

8. That it is anti-Negro,

9. That it is anti-foreigner.

If these four gentlemen cannot satisfactorily answer these charges I believe they ought to respect the Government of the United States and its true citizens sufficiently to resign from the positions to which they were elected by the citizens of a treasonable Invisible Empire, so called and such in practice, within this Republic.

Signed

Gustave W. Krause

APPENDIX NO. 3

(La Porte County Historical Society Museum file)

**KNIGHTS OF THE KU KLUX KLAN
LAPORTE COUNTY KLAN, NO.29
REALM OF INDIANA**

OFFICE HOURS

424 1/2 Franklin Street 10:00a.m to 12:00
Michigan City, Ind. 1:00p.m. to 5:00
816 1/2 Lincolnway 6:00p.m. to 8:00
LaPorte, Ind.

Phones-1698, LaPorte; 1120, Michigan City

Faithful and Esteemed Klansmen:

On May 10th, 1925 the K-Duo or 2nd Degree will be conferred on the eligible memebers of this order, somewhere in this County.

You have been selected as one worthy of this degree and it is important that you report at your respective office by 8:00p.m. May 8th, that you may learn furthur details concerning this matter.

You of course understand that this Degree is conferred on the chosen members without cost.

Faithfully yours,
In The Sacred Unfailing Bond:

Wm J. Baist

Kligrapp
LaPorte County Klan NO. 29

APPENDIX NO. 4

Queen of the Circus contestants:
Misses Enid Billings, Elna Johnson, Thelma Sundeen, Lucille Crozier, Mildred Burnett, Mabel Lansberg, Mary Wilson, Edith Ducey, Nellie Denow, Polly Sights, Mrs. Doretta Rogers, Mrs. Arthur Zeiske, Waunelia Heise of Michigan City and Miss Dorothy James of La Porte.[195]

APPENDIX NO. 5
(La Porte County Historical Society Museum file)

References: _____

Address: _____

Address: _____

Address: _____

Person securing application-MUST get this information.
Applicant's occupation is _____

Employed by: _____

His age is _____ years.

His weight is _____ lbs.

His height is _____ ft. _____ in.

This applicant was elected to membership in this Order by _____

Klan No. _____, Realm of _____, 192____

This applicant was duly naturalized by same, 192____

I certify the above to be correct.

Signed— _____

Klan No. _____ Realm of _____ Kligrapp.

Form K-115—50M—8-15-23

APPLICATION FOR CITIZENSHIP
IN THE
INVISIBLE EMPIRE
KNIGHTS OF THE KU KLUX KLAN
(INCORPORATED)

To His Majesty the Imperial Wizard, Emperor of the Invisible Empire, Knights of the Ku Klux Klan:

I, the undersigned, a native born, true and loyal citizen of the United States of America, being a white male Gentile person of temperate habits, sound in mind and a believer in the tenets of the Christian religion, the maintenance of White Supremacy and the principles of a "pure Americanism," do most respectfully apply for membership in the Knights of the Ku Klux Klan through

Klan No. _____, Realm of _____

I guarantee on my honor to conform strictly to all rules and requirements regulating my "naturalization" and the continuance of my membership, and at all times a strict and loyal obedience to your constitutional authority and the constitution and laws of the fraternity, not in conflict with the constitution and constitutional laws of the United States of America and the states thereof. If I prove untrue as a Klansman I will willingly accept as my portion whatever penalty your authority may impose.

The required "klectokon" accompanies this application.

Signed _____ Applicant

Endorsed by

Kl. _____   Residence Address _____

Kl. _____   Business Address _____

Date _____ 192____

The person securing this application must sign on top line above. NOTICE—Check the Address to which mail may be sent.

267

ENDNOTES

[1] See Mrs. Frank J. Sheehan, <u>The Northern Boundary of Indiana</u>, Indiana Historical Society Publication, 1928, research paper vol. 8 num. 6, p. 290

[2] La Porte ARGUS-BULLETIN, December 3, 1903

[3] <u>Op cit</u>, p.293

[4] See Russell Hickman, <u>Historical Society Tour of the Lakes</u>, August 26, 1961, Ordinance Line-"Old Indian"

[5] See Robert Day, <u>The Old Indiana Boundary Line, The First Hundred Years, 1932-1932</u>

[6] <u>Op cit</u>, Mrs. Frank J. Sheehan, p. 296

[7] <u>Op cit</u>, Mrs. Frank J. Sheehan, p. 311
The Music of Black Americans, A History, 2nd Ed. p. 280. Souther, Eileen, W. W. Norton & Co.

[8] *Ibid*

[9] Information received from Gene Mc Donald, March 1975, La Porte County Historical Society Museum.

[10] The La Porte Daily Herald-Argus, June 24, 1925, p. 5.

[11] *Op cit*, Music of Black Americans.

[12] *The Columbia Dictionary of Quotations* is licensed from Columbia University Press. 7Copyright © 1993, 1995 by Columbia University Press. All rights reserved.

[13] *The People's Chronology* is licensed from HenryHolt and Company, Inc. Copyright © 1995, 1996 by James Trager. All rights reserved.

[14] *ibid*

[3] *World Book, Millenium 2000, History of Golf*

[15] <u>History of LaPorte County</u>, Jasper Packard, 1876

[16] <u>History of Michigan City</u>, Oglesbee and Hale, 1906, p. 217

[17] *Ibid*, p. 218

[18] "Camp Anderson-Michigan City's Cornstalk Militia," Patricia Harris

[19] 128th Regiment correspondence, Indiana State Library

[20] Michigan City News Dispatch, January 3, 1929 p. 4

[21] Twentieth Century History of LaPorte County Indiana, Rev. E. D. Daniels 1904

[22] La Porte Herald, October 31, 1863, p. 2

[23] *Ibid*

[24] *Ibid*

[25] La Porte Herald, January 30, 1864, p.1

[26] Letter Charles Case, Commandant to Adjutant General Noble, February 5, 1864, Indiana State Library

[27] Plat of Camp Anderson Addition to Michigan City, December 1, 1902 and August 28, 1903

[28] Michigan Evening News, November 3, 1899

[29] History of La Porte County, Rev. Daniels, 1904, p. 876

[30] Michigan City Council Minutes, Clerks Office, A: 94, February 13, 1864

[31] La Porte Herald, January 2, 1864, p. 2

[32] *Op. cit.*, Terrell, pp. 280,281

[33] La Porte Weekly Union, March 30, 1864, p.3

[34] <u>*Op. cit.*</u>, Jasper Packard, 1876

[35] Report of W. H. H. Terrell, Vol. 3, p.266

36 *Op, cit.*, Packard, p.232
37 The Evening DISPATCH, Michigan City, IN, September 22, 1924
38 *Ibid*
39 Michigan City News Dispatch, January 3, 1939, p. 4
40 *Op. cit.*, Evening DISPATCH, September 22, 1924
41 Michigan City News Dispatch, January 9, 1939, p. 4
42 *Op. cit.*, Evening DISPATCH, September 22, 1924
43 *Ibid*
44 *Ibid*
45 *Ibid*
46 *Ibid*
47 *Ibid*
48 *Ibid*
49 *Op. cit.*, News Dispatch, January 9, 1939, p. 4
50 *Op. cit.*, Evening DISPATCH, September 22, 1924
51 THE AMERICAN NATION, Hicks, John D., Houghton Mifflin Co., p. 538
52 THE MICHIGAN CITY EVENING NEWS, August 13, 1921, p, 1
53 THE MICHIGAN CITY EVENING DISPATCH, August 9, 1922, p. 4
54 DISPATCH, *op cit.*, August 9, 1922, p. 4
55 DISPATCH, *op cit.*, September 23, 1922, p. 1
56 *Ibid*, September 23, 1922, p. 1
57 DISPATCH, *op cit.*, p. 1
58 NEWS, *op cit.*, September 28, 29, 1922, p. 1
59 NEWS, *op cit.*, November 8, 1922, p. 1
60 *Ibid*, November 7, 1922, p. 1
61 *Ibid*, p.1
62 *Ibid*. November 13, 14, 1922; DISPATCH, November 14, 1922, p.1
63 NEWS, *op cit.*, November 18, 1922.
64 DISPATCH, *op cit.*, November 20, 1922, p. 1
65 DISPATCH, *op cit.*, December 4, 1922, p.1
66 *Ibid.*, December 12, 1922, p. 1
67 THE LA PORTE ARGUS, December 18, 1922
68 DISPATCH, *op cit.*, p. 1, *op cit.*, NEWS, December 30, 1922, p. 1
69 DISPATCH, *op cit.*, January 2, 1923, p. 1
70 *Ibid*
71 THE LA PORTE DAILY HERALD, January 4, 1923
72 DISPATCH, *op cit.*, December 30, 1922, p. 1
73 *Ibid*, February 5, 1923, p. 4; February 7, 1923, p. 4; March 5, 1923, p. 4
74 HEARLD, *op cit.*, January 27, 1923, p. 1
75 *Ibid*, January 30, 1923, p. 1
76 NEWS, *op cit.*, January 31, 1923
77 DISPATCH, *op cit.*, February 2, 1923
78 The story of Ernie Pyle, p. 26, by Lee G. Miller, Viking Press, 1950
79 HERALD, *op cit.*, January 31, 1923, p. 1
80 *Ibid.*
81 NEWS, *op cit.*, March 1, 1923, p. 5; March 2, 1923, p. 1
82 Ibid, March 5, 1923, p. 2
83 Ibid, March 13, 1923, p. 6; Smith Directory of La Porte, 1923
84 ARGUS, op cit., April 9, 1923 p. 1

[85] NEWS, op cit., April 9, 1923, p. 1
[86] HERALD, *op cit.*, April 9, 1923, p. 1
[87] ARGUS, *op cit.*, November 5, 1923, p. 1
[88] DISPATCH, *op cit.,* November 5, 1923, p. 4
[89] *Ibid.*, November 6, 1923, p. 1.
[90] DAILY ARGUS, o*p cit.*, November 7, 1923, p.1
[91] DISPATCH, *op cit.,* November 14, 1923, p. 4
[92] DISPATCH, o*p cit.*, November 12, 1923, p.4
[93] NEWS, o*p cit.*, November 15, 1923, p.1
[94] DISPATCH, o*p cit.*, December 19, 1923, p.1
[95] *Ibid.*, December 18, 1923, p. 4.
[96] NEWS, o*p cit.*, January 8, 1924, pp. 1,8
[97] HERALD, *op cit.,* January 12, 1924, p. 2
[98] DISPATCH, *op cit.,* January 12, 1924
[99] *Ibid*, January 19,20, 1924, p. 4
[100] *Ibid*, February 18, 1924 p. 4
[101] *Ibid*, February 9, 1924. p. 4
[102] *Ibid*, February 1, 1924. p. 4
[103] *Ibid*, February 9, 1924. p. 4
[104] *Ibid*, February 12, 1924, p. 1
[105] *Ibid*, APRIL 11, 1924, p. 4
[106] NEWS, *op cit.,* February 21, 1924, p. 1
[107] DISPATCH, *op cit.,* February 22,23, 1924, p. 1
[108] HERALD, *op cit.,* February 22, 1924, p. 12
[109] DISPATCH, *op cit.,* February 23, 1924, p. 1
[110] *Ibid*, February 23, 1924, p. 1
[111] DISPATCH, NEWS *op cit.,* February 22, 1924, p. 1
[112] HERALD, *op cit.,* May 12,1924, p. 1
[113] NEWS, *op cit.,* February 21,23, 1924, p. 1
[114] NEWS, *op cit.,* February 21,23, 1924, p. 1
DISPATCH, *op cit.,* February 22,23, 1924, p. 1
[115] *Ibid*, February, 23, 1924, p. 1
[116] HERALD, *op cit.,* March 21,1924, p. 1
[117] *Ibid*, April 7,1924, p. 1
[118] *Ibid*, April 17,1924, p. 1
[119] *Ibid*, April 7,1924, p. 1
[120] Argus, *op cit.,* April 19,1924, p. 1
[121] HERALD, *op cit.,* April 24,1924, p. 1
[122] *Ibid*, April 25,1924, p. 1
[123] *Ibid*, April 19,1924, p. 17
[124] *Ibid*, April 24,25, 1924, p. 2
[125] *Ibid*, May 5, 1924, p. 5
[126] *Ibid*, May 6, 1924, p. 1
[127] *Ibid*, May 7, 1924, p. 1
[128] *Ibid*, May 8, 1924, p. 1
[129] NEWS, *op cit.,* May 9, 1924, p. 1
[130] HERALD, *op cit.,* May 7,1924, p. 1
[131] *Ibid*, May 12, 1924, p. 1
[132] *Ibid*, May 19, 1924, p. 2.

[133] Argus, *op cit.*, July 11, 12, 1924, p.9, 2
[134] HERALD, *op cit.*, July 5, 1924, p. 8
[135] *Ibid*, August 8, 1924, p.2
[136] NEWS, *op cit.*, August 18, 1924, p. 2
[137] HERALD, *op cit.*, August 15, 1924, p.2
[138] NEWS, *op cit.*, August 16, 1924, p. 2
[139] NEWS, *op cit.*, August 18, 1924, p. 2
[140] Herald, *op cit.*, August 18, 1924, p. 2
[141] NEWS, *op cit.*, August 16,18, 1924, p. 1,2
[142] Herald, *op cit.*, October 20, 1924, p. 1
[143] *Ibid*, November 5,6, 1924, p. 1
[144] *Ibid*, November 7, 1924, p. 1.
[145] NEWS, *op cit.*, December 22, 1924, p. 1
[146] *Ibid*, August 17, 1925, p. 3
[147] LA PORT HERALD ARGUS, May 11, 1925, p.1
[148] NEWS, *op cit.*, June 17, 1925, p.5
[149] LA PORT HERALD ARGUS, *op cit.*, June 25, 1925, p. 6
[150] NEWS, *op cit.*, June 29, 1925, p.5
[151] DISPATCH, *op cit.*, June 29, 1925, p. 4
[152] NEWS, *op cit.*, June 29, 1925, p. 4
[153] DISPATCH, *op cit.*, June 29, 1925, p. 4
[154] NEWS, *op cit.*, June 29, 1925, p. 5
[155] *Ibid*, July 6, 1925. p. 1
[156] DISPATCH, *op cit.*, July 3, 1925, p. 1
[157] DISPATCH, *op cit.*, September 9, 1925, p. 2
[158] *Ibid*, September 24, 1925. p. 4
[159] HERALD ARGUS, *op cit.*, September 25, 1925, p. 2
[160] *Ibid*, November 13, 1925, p. 8
[161] *Ibid*, November 4, 1925, p. 9
[162] DISPATCH, *op cit.*, November 4, 1925, p. 1
[163] DISPATCH, *op cit.*, November 3,4, 1925, p. 1
[164] HERALD ARGUS, *op cit.*, November 4,13, 1925, p. 1
[165] DISPATCH, *op cit.*, March 22, 1926, p. 4
[166] HERALD ARGUS, *op cit.*, January 5, 1926, p. 1
[167] NEWS, *op cit.*, January 5, 1926, p. 1
[168] HERALD ARGUS, *op cit.*, February 11, 1926, p. 10
[169] DISPATCH, *op cit.*, May 1, 1926, p. 2
[170] NEWS, *op cit.*, May 5, 1926, p. 1
[171] *Ibid*, June 1, 1926, p. 1
[172] DISPATCH, *op cit.*, June 1, 1926, p. 1
[173] HERALD ARGUS, *op cit.*, July 8, 1926, p. 10
[174] *Ibid*, October 25, 1926, p. 1
[175] DISPATCH, *op cit.*, November 2, 1926, p. 2
[176] HERALD ARGUS, *op cit.*, November 23, 1927, p. 1
[177] *Ibid.*, October 29, 1927, p. 2
[178] *Ibid.*, December 3, 1927, p. 8
[179] *Ibid.*, December 17, 1927, p. 8
[180] *Ibid.*, January 4, 1928, p. 1
[181] DISPATCH, February 21, 1928, p. 2

[182] *Ibid.,* January 14, 1928, p. 2
[183] *Ibid.,* February 22, 1928, p. 1
[184] NEWS, *op, cit.,* February 23, 1928, p. 8
[185] HERALD ARGUS, *op, cit.,* February 23, 1928, p. 1
[186] *Ibid,* February 2, 1928, p. 2
[187] *Ibid,* February 26, 1928, p. 1
[188] *Ibid,* February 28, 1928, p. 14
[189] *Ibid,* November 16, 1928, p. 10
[190] *Ibid,* June 15, 1928, p. 1
[191] NEWS, *op, cit.,* August 16, 1928, p. 1
[192] *Ibid,* March 18, 1929, p. 6
[193] NEWS, *op cit.,* September 4, 1926, p. 1
[194] HERALD ARGUS, June 25, 1925, p. 6.

INDEX

A

A. F. and A. M. 59
A. M. E. Church 51, 56
Abel, Virginia 101
Ackerman & Sons 181
Adams, Abigail 61
Adams, Laura 56, 57
Adams, Oscar 53, 55
Advance-Rumely 26, 55
Aero Agents Company 45
Aero Club 24, 27
Ahearn, Ray 36
Ahlgrim, Carl 102, 244, 254, 261
Ahlgrim, Fred H. 58, 199, 207
Aicher, Otto 118, 200–201
AKIAH (AKIA) Club 254
Albright, Helen 98–99
Alinsky, Diana L. 70
Allen, George W. 52, 54
Allen, William 57
Allison, Fran 114
Allison, James H. 244
All Men's Bible Class 3
Amazon Hosiery Company 227
American Federation of Musicians 186
American Kennel Club 64
American Legion 22, 39, 59, 91, 121, 222
Ames Field 152
Anderson, Edward 189, 192
Ankony, Assom 79
Ankony, Sam 79
Anthony, Susan B. 61
Appollo Male Chorus 59
Archer, Albert 252
Armitage Corners 175
Armour and Company 107
Arndt Brothers 91
Arnt, Charles E. 36, 39, 42, 97, 179, 180
Austin, Willard 182

B

B'nai B'rith 91
Baber, George Wilbur 52
Bader, June 101
Bagely, Mrs. S. A. 27
Bailey, Alson 189
Bailey, Henry V. 55
Bailey, James 55
Baileytown 106–107
Baine, James C. 43, 44, 209
Baist, Wiliam 238
Baker, George 216
Baker, Robert S. 254
Balaban, Barney 112
Balaban and Katz 112–113, 115
Banks, Berry 51
Bannwart, Fred 43
Baptist Church 53, 56, 242
Barber, Ira J. 21
Barker, Catherine 44, 102, 180. *See* Spaulding, Catherine
Barker, Howard 53
Barney, LeRoy 44
Barnum, Ed 177
Barrens, Williams 56
Bartels, Fred C. 39
Bartlett, Tommy 113
Bastian-Morley Company 102
Bauch, Irvin 29–30
Bauman, I. C. 173
Bayer, Thomas 93
Beal, Charles A. 2, 21, 22
Beal, Charles A. Jr 22
Beament Lake 90
Beatty, Earl D. 17
Beatty, Elmer D. 29
Beatty, Georgia 83
Beckner, Charles A. 25
Beech-nut Co. 30
Beetles, May 186
Behrens, Walter J. 245

Behrndt, Walter 33
Bell, Paul 53
Belle Island, Michigan 31
Beloit Air Lines 18
Bendix and Allison Company 115
Bentley, Floyd 5
Bergen, Ralph D. 44
Berger, Fred 3
Berghoff Pool Hall 233
Berry, Russell 86
Bethany Lutheran Church 53
Bever, John 55
Beverage, Albert J. 250
Biederstaedt, Bill 119
Billings, Enid 251–253
Bisbee, Joseph B. 92
Black, Vivian 101
Blair, Esther 86
Blair, Rev. 241
Blair Farm 32
Blake, John A. 256
Blake, Lydia Decker 204
Blake, William H. 189
Blank, John 45, 183
Blick, Robert E. 37
Blinks, E. G. 119
Blocksom, B. H. 210
Bloomquist, Elmer 182
Bob-White Cottage 85
Bodine, Mike 120
Bodine Studio 207
Boesch, William 24, 25
Bojewitz, Joseph 44–45
Bolka, Joseph 58
Bon Air Subdivision 38
Bon Ton Millinery Shop 62
Boonstra, Sam P. 208
Borgerd and Tritt Electrical 26
Boss, John 253
Bostick, W. F. 53
Bowen, Al 121
Bowen, Horace 235–236, 245
Bowers, Whitefield 39
Bowes, Whitefield 121
Bowman, Fire Chief 200

Bowman, Paul 4–5, 25
Boyd, A. A. 122
Boyd-Garrettson Arces 43
Bracy, C. 55
Bradley, Henry 177
Bradley, Robert 39
Bray, William A. 63
Brennan, Mrs. Jesse K. 199
Brewer, Arthur T. 102, 103
Brickhouse, Jack 115
Brinckman, Alex 122
Brinckman Building 208
Broaden, James 55
Brolly, Arch 112
Bronner, Thais Ann 70
Brooks, Henry 91
Brooks, Raymond 55
Brown, Andrew 55
Brown, Dr. 190, 233
Brown, Emanuel 51
Brown, F. W. 90
Brown, Geraldine 101
Brown, Lester A. 233
Brown, Mrs. T. 101
Brown, Ruth 204
Brown, Thomas 17
Brown, Walter B. 91
Browne, E. G. "Babe," 77
Brown Instrument 112
Brunson, Al. 55
Buck-House Company 91
Bull, George 33
Bull Farm 33, 223
Burlingame, Elmer 13, 14
Burnett, Martha 83
Burnett, Mildred 251, 265
Burnham, Fredric H. 44–45
Burt, L. A. 177
Bush, Asahel K. 189
Business & Professional Woman's Club 61, 70, 98
Byers, Elizabeth 204
Byksa, Alex 44

C

Cains, Walter E. 33
Calhoun, T. H. 51
Call, Harwood 17
Calvert, Gwalter "Dude," 78
Calvert, Walter 5
Campfire Girls 92–93
Camp Anderson 189–195, 269
Camp Taylor 221
Capone, Al 30
Carpenter, Marie 252
Carpenter, Wanda Virginia 252
Carr, Olive 101
Carstens, Alex 122
Carver, Marion 31
Carver's Carpentry Shop 31
Cash Hardware Company 182
Casper, Pink 55
Cassidy, Gene 252
CBS 112
Center Township 198–199
Central Cigar Store 98
Central Coal Company 91, 182
Central School 69
Central Theatre 185–186
Chamber of Commerce, La Porte 16, 18, 20
Chamber of Commerce, Michigan City 6, 37
Charity Organization Society 59
Charles Foster 74
Chicago-Niles & Michigan Bus Line 173
Childers, Al 123
Chinske, Louis A. 179
Chipman, C. D. 2
Chlebowski, Robert 8
Christian Church 53, 56, 199, 202–203, 239–240, 242, 251, 252, 255
Chunn, R. D. 53
Cichon, Stanley 26
Citizens Bank 70, 165, 180
Clark 39, 64, 123, 173, 186, 209
Clark, Flora 64
Clark, Newton E. 39
Clayton, Edwin 99, 100, 102
Clear Lake 48, 240

Clendenen Kenneth 22
Clifford, Mrs. L. 101
Clinic Hospital 98–99
Coast Guard 37–38, 42, 75, 78, 242
Cobb, Harriet 131
Coddington, Arthur B. 175
Coddington, E. E. 175
Coddington, Flossie 175
Coddington, Linton T. 175
Coffeen, Robert 19
Cole, James 53, 55–57
Collins, Dr 199, 202
Collins, Ona 101
Columbia Yacht Race 37
Condra, John B. 5, 23
Conn Holloway High Tension Orchestra 3
Construction Co. 30, 107
Continental Airways 29
Coody Flying Circus 36
Cook, County, IL 74
Cook, Dick 7
Cook, J. P. 177
Cook, Warren 2
Cooke, Noel 219
Coolspring township 121
Coonrod, Victor T. 44
Copeland, Frank 42
Cory, Fred 91
Couden, Albert R. 34
Cox, Herman 55
Cox, Roger M. 244
Craig and Moenkhouse 86
Crawford, Marie 101
Crocker National Bank 112
Crowe, Earl 2
Crowley, Francis 91
Crozier, Lucille 251, 265
Crum, Walter 124
Crumpacker, Harry L. 125
Cubbine, Evelyn 101
Cubbine, Mildred 101
Cullen, James R. 42
Cushman, M. A. 101, 198, 201
Cushman Acres 38, 178
Cushman Mortgage Co. 167

Cutler, Howard 25
Cutler, Louise, P. 25

D

Dall, William F. C. 58, 244–245
Daniels, Reverend 68
Daniel Guggenheim Fund 41
Danner, Marie Henry 5
Darrow, Lemuel 24, 248
David, E. W. 60
Davidson, Clifford 2
Davis, Captain 103
Davis, Jefferson 194
Davis, Laura 64
Dayton, Surgeon 190
Dean, James Arthur 60
Dean, John 55
Dean, L. 55
Dean, Ralph H. 43, 44
Decatur Airplane Company 18
Dedrick, Ray 19
Defer, Scott C. 186
Dehne, Gus 17
DeMass, Margaret 101
Denow, Nellie 265
Derrell, Edward 34
DeVeaux, Clarence 182
Dewitt, Al 29
DICK, CLEM 42
Dickson, William 126
Diggin's Flying School 33
Dignan, John 41
Dilworth, John B. 20, 53
Ditland, Constance (aka. Eitland) 204
Dittbrenner, Irene 180
Doherty, Richard 183
Donahue, Mrs. Dennis 99
Donnelly Sub-division 33
Doolittle, Emmett 253
Door Prairie 171
Door Village 174
Doran, Francis H. 126, 173
Dorland, J. Vere 18
Dorland, Mrs. J. Vere 18
Dorland and McGill 27

Drago, Joe 174
Dreamland Theater 69
Drescher, C. N. 65
Drescher, Marena L. (Bromberg) 65
Dreske, John 79
Dresner, Jack 2
Dresser, Lee F. 39, 251
Dron, Betty Jane 252
Ducey, Edith 251, 265
Dudeck, Andrew 90
Dudeck, Norman 94
Duffy, Captain 97, 103
Dumas, Jeff 55
Dumont 112
Dunes Highway 44, 58, 105–107
Dunes Highway Estates 214
Dunlap, Raymond M. 248
Dunlap & Son 202
Dunn, Charles 54
Dutton, Linia (Boeckling), (aka.) Mrs. Frank Boeckling 62

E

Earhart, Amelia 30
Early Birds Flying Club 18
Eastport Manufacturing Co. 223
Eastport School 85
Ebert, Irving 3
Eckstein, Bernard 127
Eddy, William C. 116
Eden, Walter J. 37
Edghill, J. W. 56
Eggert, Frank 193
Egly, E. J. 58
Eickstaedt, Rev. Paul 2
Elks Club 53
Elliott, Robert Alton 252
Elshout, G. 27
Elston School 82–83
Ely, Levi 191
Emmons, Hugh "Pat," 255
Erickson, George 182
Erickson, John 182
Erin Vale 214
Evans, Hiram W. 250, 256

Ewald, Peter 248–249
Ewing, Alex 190
Excelsior Cycle Co. 209–210

F

Fairview Hospital 48, 204–205
Fairway Shoe Store 7
Farnan, James J. 57
Farnsworth, Philo 111
Faulknor, J. B. 58
Faurote, David Leo 26, 30
Feallock, William J. 243, 244
Fedder, Hemp 127
Fedder, R. C. 58–59
Fedder, R. H. 236
Fedder, W. 26
Felton, Charles H. 238
Felton, George 198
Fiery Cross 236, 259–261
Fink, Bill 128
First Christian Church 56, 242, 255
First Congregational Church 59, 102
First Methodist Church 7, 52, 54, 58, 205
First National Bank 21
Fletcher, Robert B. 128
Flowers, George 92
Fogarty, Jim 129
Foglemen, Mrs. Frank 252
Folk, Joseph 30
Folk, Lawrence 30
Foot Warmers 7
Ford, Donald C. 58, 198, 201, 232, 239, 242, 252, 255, 259–260
Ford, Henry 18
Ford Airship Corporation 37
Ford and Johnson Co. 216
Fosdick, Frank 248
Foster, John 205
Foster, Lowell 94–95
Fox, Raymond 252
Fox Park 240
Fraley, F. O. 59
Franklin, Benjamin 12–13
Franklin, Oscar 12
Freeland, Elmer 5

Freeman, Marvin 198
French Aeronautic Federation 17
Frey, Harry 33
Freyer, Harvey 37
Froelich, William J. 30
Furst, D. A. 40

G

Garfield School 69
Garrettson, R. F. 43, 44, 91, 130
Garrily, Edward 41
Garrison Baggage Service 21
General Construction Co. 107
Gibbons, Ed 130
Gibson, Minnie 64
Gielow, Louis 42
Giesler, Arthur 26
Gill, Henry 55
Gillom, Arthur L. 255
Girl Scouts 92–93
Glasscott, John 131
Glasscott, Thomas 131
Gleason, James F. 254
Glidden and Hiese Bakery 233
Goede, Loretta 101
Gooden, William 15
Gordon, Mr. 97
Gordon, Ruth 101
Gorge, Matt 79
Gormully-Jeffrey Company 209
Gotto, Orphie 132
Gould's Woods 193
Grand Beach Road 12
Granger, Everett 41
Great Lakes Naval Training Station 30, 37
Grede, Hans 13–14
Green, Dwight E. 30
Green, Fred 29
Greenebaum, Walter 105
Greening, Elwin 109
Greenwood Cemetery 11–12, 31–32, 223, 252
Gregory, Donald 13, 31–32
Gregory, Rev. J. 51
Gregory Building 201

Grieger, Fred 132
Griffin, Ben 5
Griffith, Kenneth K. 45
Grischow, Fred C. 193
Gross Construction Co. 30
Grubbs, Frank I. 66
Gruenke, Otto 41
Gruntkowski, Thomas 235
Guenther Building 255–256
Guertine, C. 17
Guggenheim, Harry F. 41
Gutgsell, D. A. 133

H

Hack School 207
Hahn, Jacob 58
Hall, Joseph 248
Hall, Robert 58–59, 102
Hall, W. A. 180
Hamlet 255
Handforth, Russell 39
Hansen, Genevieve 101
Harmony Colored Quartet 53
Harrison, Hazel 53, 67–68
Harrison, Herom 52, 53
Harrison, Pat 250
Haskell and Barker Company 227
Hastings, Vernon C. 214
Hatchell, Genevieve 56
Hatfield, Leslie 204
Hauser, Louis 244
Haviland, Floyd 42
Haviland Storage Company 91
Headley, Marvin 17
Headley Luebker Specialty Co. 18
Hein, Maria 101
Heinbeck, Hazel 2
Heise, Betty Ann 252
Heise, Edward 70
Heise, Waunelia 251
Heise Bakery Shop 233
Heisman, Amalie (Ladd) 74
Heisman, Henry 74
Heisman, Herman "Ham," 79
Heisman, Hulda (Rehbein) 74

Heisman, Irene (Deneau) 74
Heisman, Lila (Stib) 74
Heisman, Madelon (Berry) 74
Heisman, Olga (Snyder) 74
Heisman, Wilhelmina (Niles) 74
Heitschmidt, A. C. 101–103
Helcide, V. 55
Helebrandt, G. C. 30
Henoch, Leonard 52
Henock, Frank 91
Henry, A. J. 44
Henry, Eva 199
Henry, Frank T. 257
Henry, John Sr. 43
Henton, Captain 192
Henton, Mrs. Ben 175
Hermitage 218
Hess, C. D. 65
Hess, Clara M. 65–66
Hickey, Andrew J. 6
Hickox, Charles 102
Higley, Lois 93
Hileman, Russell 115
Hill, George 98, 134
Hill, Thomas J. 43
Hinkle, Esther 101
Hirschman, Herb 135
Hoelocker, Harry 28, 30
Hogan, Til 173
Holloway, Conn R. 5
Holmes, Elsie 204
Holstein, Minnie (Kay) 193
Holstein, William 86, 192
Holy Family Hospital 30, 56, 198
Honeywell 112
Hoosier Slide 81, 218
Hoosier State Automobile Assoc. 107
Hoover Apartments 203
Hopkins, Anna A. 63
Hopkins, Elizabeth L. 63
Hopkins, Fredrick E. 234
Hopkins, Hazard 63
Hopkins Building 63
Horace A. Tuttle 74
Horsethief Detective Assoc. 238

Hosler, Miles & Company 189
Howard University 68
Huddleston, V. E. 29
Huddleston, Wesley 55
Huey, Ethan Franklin 3
Huffington, Joseph 256
Humphrey, Cecil F. 87
Hunt, Marvel 3
Hunt Brothers Drilling 90
Hunziker, George 136
Hutchings, Mrs. S. 101
Hutchinson, William Sr. 136
Hutton, Mr. & Mrs. D. M. 252
Hybner, Roger 3

I

Illsley, Rolf 86
Illsley, Walter 86
Indiana Real Estate Assoc. 38, 39, 228
Indiana State Prison 92, 101, 251
Indiana Stone & Supply Co. 100
Indian Boundary Line 47
Intercity Airline Company 34
Interlaken School 245
International Aeronautical Exposition 24
Irion, Paul 137
Izaak Walton League 91

J

Jack, Othie 250
Jackson, Champ 53, 54, 56
Jackson, Ed 248–249, 250, 259
Jackson, Louis 55
Jackson, Mrs. Champ 54
Jackson, Ora 198
Jahn's Bus Line 202
James, Dorothy 199, 251, 265
Jaske, Katherine 101
Jefferson, Thomas 47
Jenks, I. A. 24
Jenning, Samuel 55
Jentzen, Frank 37
Jewett, J. E. 22
Johnson, Arthur 55
Johnson, Captain E. 103

Johnson, Captain S. R. 37–38
Johnson, Elna 251, 265
Johnson, George B. 39, 201
Johnson, Orlando 39
Johnson, Victor 92
John Franklin Miller 39, 121
Joliet Road 174
Jones, Capt. 103
Jones, Dr. R. B. 27
Jones, G. S. 198
Jones, W. K. 41
Jones, William 42
Jones Garage 29
Josam Manufacturing Co. 102
Jurgensen, Charlotte 101
Jurgensen, Martha 101

K

Kabelin, Ed 53
Kaber Floral Company 54
Kalies, Charles, P. 244
Kamelias 239, 247, 255
Karney, Ralph, J. 59
Karpin, Harry 216
Karpin, Martin 214–215
Karpin, S. 214, 215
Karris, Joseph E. 78
Kaste, Mrs. John 204
Kay, Christian 193
Keel, Martha 64
Keeler, E. A. 7
Keene, Charles 86
Kegel, Arnold, H. 42
Keil, Merna 252
Keithley, Rudolph 39
Kelleher, Edward 137
Keller, Betty Jane 252
Keller, H. H. 55
Keller, Leslie 56–57
Keller, Mrs. Frank 51
Kelley, Berth 56
Kemena, Emil 58
Kemp, Frank 19
Kemp, Herman M. 243
Kenna, Alpha H. 205

Keppen, Hugo E. 101
Kern, Harry (aka. Kearn) 247
Kern Mary Frances 199
Kerrigan, Doctor 138
KFC Restaurant 49
Kibby, Wesley R. 138
Kincaid, Bradley 5
King, Martin Luther Jr. 51
King, Mattie B. 83
King, William W. 198, 203
Kingsbury 18, 198–199
Kingsbury Road 18
Kintzele Farm 39
Kistler, Joe 139
Kiwanis Club 53
KMOX 7
Knapp, Beryl 85, 87
Knapp, Merle L. 85
Knights of Columbus 58, 214, 220
Knights of the Green Forest 256
Koelin, Henry 201
Koontz, Pulaske 175
Kramer, Harry 140
Kramer, Leon 35, 179, 243
Kramer, Reverend 242
Kramer, Russell H. 98
Krause, Gustave W. 238, 242, 245, 259–262
Krause, Pamela S. 70
Krause, William J. 198
Krebs, Frank 140
Krebs, Joe 140
Kroening Coal Company 102
Kroll, Ernest 141
Krueger 11, 44–45, 86, 102, 141, 142, 179, 182, 189, 192–193, 244, 245
Krueger, Emil F. 44–45
Krueger, Evelyn 86
Krueger, L. H. 179
Krueger, Martin T. 102, 142
Krueger, Mike 182
Krueger, Paul 143
Krueger, R. J. 245
Kruse, Richard J. 39, 245
Kuebel, Anna E. 199
Kuhn, Charles 182

Kunkel, Louis E. 143
Kunkel, Rudy 182
Kuppin, Louis 201
Ku Kla, Fran and Ollie 114
Ku Klux Klan vii, 52, 68, 82, 197, 200–201, 231–244, 245–248, 249–250, 252, 254–261

L

Lacrosse 18, 198, 219
Ladies Aid Society 54, 204
Lahey, Pat 182
Lakeview Amusement Company 34, 36
Lakeview Casino 247
Lakeview Hotel 97
Lake Michigan Lodge 59
Lambka, John F. 198
Lambka, Louis 193
Lane, Amos 55
Lange, Dorothy 101
Lange, Henry 77, 109
Langford, Losey 41
Langford, R. O. 42
Lansberg, Mabel 251
Lansberg, William 244, 261
Laramore, George 198
LaResche, Paul 59
Larsen, S. W. 177
Lasalle Café 40
Lass, John 42, 144
Lawrence, Edgar H. 58
Lay, Harriet 59
Layman, Gertrude 101
Layman, Richard 204
Layton, Abraham J. 254
Lay Hall 68
La Porte Aero Club 24, 27
La Porte Airways 25, 31
La Porte Casino 203
La Porte Choral Society 186
La Porte City Council 31
La Porte County Bar Association 57, 91
La Porte County Fair Grounds 38
La Porte Gas & Light Co. 236
La Porte Hospital Association 202

La Porte Loan and Trust Co. 25
La Porte Municipal Airport 25
La Porte Supply Co. 38
La Porte Telephone Company 3
League of Women Voters 66
Ledbetter, Doctor 144
Leist, Charles 144
Leverenz, William 179
Levin, Herb 145
Lewis, Claude 24
Lewis, M. W. 175
Lewis Institute 143, 219
Liddell, Fred 25
Lilly Lake 48
Linard, Loren W. 182
Lindbergh, Charles 14
Line, John 22, 25–26, 56–57, 253
Link, Alfred J. 56, 248
Linnell, George 23–24
Lions Club, Michigan City 90
Little, H. C. 37
Littleton, Marjorie 93
Little Murphy, S. S. T. V. 79
Loetz, Mrs. Carl 93
Logan, E. S. 30
Long, Aden 5
Long, John Murr 5
Long Beach 5, 41–42, 45, 84–87, 132, 147, 153, 199, 211, 214, 225, 252
Long Beach Company 85
Long Beach Country Club 211, 214, 225
Long Beach School 84–85
Loomis, Justin 249
Loose, Professor 186
Love, John 75
Low, Milton H. 27
Ludlow, W. G. 5
Luebker, Clem 26
Luebker, W. C. 18
Luech, John 193
Luecht, Mrs. Henry 200
Luedtke, E. C. 3
Lutz, J. H. 43
Lyons, Murray 53, 56

M

MacCather, Douglas 11
Mack, L. W. 146
Mackenzie, William J. 41, 43
Macomber, Leonard 179–180
Madden, William 56
Madison Theater 251
Mahler, Edna L. 252
Mailey, Mildred 56
Mainland, Charles 24
Majestic radio 22
Majot, Emil 46
Majot's Mill 43
Majot Farm 42
Manley, Mr. & Mrs. A. D. 252
Manning, H. A. 177
Manny, W. B. 146, 217
Manufacturer's Club 125
Maple, G. B. 31
Maple City Four 3–4
Marr, Doctor 147
Marshall, R. 24
Marshall Fields 113
Martin, H. H. 240
Martineau, Harriett 171, 173
Marum, Harry L. 249
Mason, Herb 207
Masonic (order) Temple 223
Masons 256
Mason Dixon line 52
Mathias, Clarence 85
Mathias, Dorothy Jean 86
Mathias, Jimmy 86
Matott, Amanda (Ray) 173
Matott, Fabian 173–175
Matott, J. C. 174
May, Helen 45
Mayflower Nursery 22, 26
McCallister, Earl 55
McCastle, Audry 53
McCormick Farm 15
McCracken, Emma 251
McCray, Warren 107
McCurdy, J. E. 186

McCurdy, Mrs. Earl 255
McGinn, Louis 20
McGlinsey, Mrs. E. S. 62
McInterfer, Bert 198
McKellips, Roy 198
McLaughlin, G. G. 219
McLellan, Walter 16
McLundie, Edward M. 44–45, 98, 102, 148
McNeil, Jim 98
Meakins, Carl 39
Meeker, Lysander 190
Meier, Charles H. 2
Meinke, William 27
Melpar Inc. 116
Melville, C. Matt 181
Memorial Park 142, 208, 214, 229
Mensing, Robert 34
Mercer, Reverend 68
Merchant, Dale 178
Merchants National Bank 58
Meredith Publishing Company 115
Metcaff, Daisy 56
Metcaff, Joe 55
Metcaff, Warren 55
Methodist Church 6–8, 52, 54, 56, 58, 205
Methodist Fraternal Bible Class 2
Metzger, A. M. 198
Meyer, Armin P. 198, 246
Meyer, C. E. 33
Meyer, William 193
Meyers, William 53
Michaels, Everitt 42
Michigan Central Railroad 36
Michigan City Aeronautical Assoc. 42
Michigan City Bar Association 70
Michigan City Boys Band 181
Michigan City Country Club 42, 179, 180, 182
Michigan City Golf Assoc. 178
Michigan City Lumber Co. 91
Michigan City Trust & Savings Bank 180–181
Michigan City Yacht Club 75
Middleton, Charles 1, 3–4, 7–8, 23
Middleton, Leo 8

Milcarek, Vincent 44
Miles, Harry M. 105
Miller, Capt. 192
Miller, Fred C. 149
Miller, Henry 149
Miller, Lena 99
Miller, Mayor 29
Miller, Theron F. 39, 43, 44
Miller, Town of 106
Ministerial Association 56, 58
Misener, H. R. 43, 44
Mitchell, Caroy 55
Mitchell, Carry 53
Mitchell, Dick 173
Mitchell, Fred 254
Mitchell, James H. 245
Moe, Ingwald 107
Moffatt, John W. 56
Moncell, Rodgers Eugene 252
Monon Railroad 218
Moore, Kenneth 17–18
Moore, Marian 252
Moore, Robert H. 220, 234
Moorman, John D. 150
Moose 122, 242, 259
Moose Hall 242, 259
Moran, Ed 150
Moritz, Moses 32–33, 35, 38, 201, 222
Morley, J. P. 102
Morrison, Francis 15
Morris & Castle Carnival 250
Morris & Company 211
Morrow, Della 5
Moser, Ernest 34
Moss, G. Earl 2
Moss, Manual 55
Moss, Ralph 53
Moss, William 55
Moth, Robert H. 245
Motor Discount Corporation 35
Mozart Hall 222
Mrs. Haug 101
Mullen, Thomas C. 151
Munger, Elizabeth 31
Munning, Joesh N. 243

Murray, M. C. 42
Murray, Marjorie 101
Music Masters Orchestra 203

N

Nafa, Cora Mae 59
Nagel's Tin Shop 193
National Air Transport Co. 24
Naval Armory 76
NBC 112, 114
Neilson, John 2, 3
Nelson, Carl Edwin "Eddy," 17
Nelson, S. T. 36
Neulieb, Eleanor 101
New Buffalo, Mich. 37, 176
New Durham Township 65–66
New York Central Railroad 106
Nicewarner, Gladys (Bull) 33
Nickel Plate Railroad 18–19, 251
Nieman, Irwin 236
NIPSCO 81
Noble, Lazarus 189
Nolan, "Peg Leg," 75
Northam, Harry 179–180
Northern Indiana Brick Co. 91
Northwest Ordinance 47–48
Northwest Territory 47
Norton, Ira P. 198
Norton, Mary P. 64
Notre Dame 115, 162, 182, 216, 219
Nunnally, William (Tex) 115

O

O'dell, Harvey L. 244, 261
O'dell, Vern 253
Oaks, D. G. 51
Oakwood 249
Oasis Ballroom 39
Oberholtzer, Madge 250
Odd Fellows 3, 7–8, 222–223, 239
Ogden, H. V. 177
Ohming, Lizzie E. 68
Ohming, Pete (aka.) Harry 152
Olsen, Harry 23
Olsen & Ebann 182

Opperman, Charles H. 87
Opperman, Harry 192
Opperman, Henry 193
Opperman, Mary Louise 87
Orr, James H. 152
Osborn, A. L. 177
Osborn, K. D. 91, 93
Osborne, Hattie 64
Osborne, Joe 57
Oswalt, Mrs. Walter 204
Otis 230
Ox, Mattie 56
Oxley, Ora 239

P

Packard, Jasper 191, 192, 269
Pagin, J. Roy 5
Pagin, Susan Foshier 172
Palmer, Mrs. L. C. 191
Paramount Pictures 112–113
Parker, Clark R. 186
Parker, Cy 53
Parker, G. R. 5
Parker, John A. 197
Parkinson, Charlena (Coddington) 175
Parkinson, William 174–175
Payne, Emma M. 25
Pearson, A. G. 19
Peck, W. G. 191
Peglon, George 42
Penn Henry 55
People's Trust Savings Bank 55
People State Bank 60
Pepple, W. W. "Pep," 35, 58, 201
Perkins, Marlin 113
Petering, Fred 2
Petering, George 2
Peterson, Herbert 153
Peterson's Florida Crackers 3
Phi Delta Phi fraternity 91
Pine Lake 30, 32, 48–49, 198, 200, 202, 205–206, 253–254
Pine Lake Hospital 205
Piotrowski, Roy 39
Piotrowski, Tony 40

285

Plant, I. N. 244
Platt, Mrs. J. 200
Pleasant Ridge 214
Ploner, "Dutch," 41
Ploner, E. 42
Polk College 7
Pollack, Ralph 232
Polson, John 154
Polsonville 154
Pottawattomie Boy Scout Camp 89
Pottawattomie Council of Boy Scouts 90
Pottawattomie Country Club 180
Pottawattomie Lake 89, 91, 92
Pottawattomie Park 228–229, 256
Pottawattomie Park Lodge 256
Powell-Rose Lumber Co. 27
Presbyterian Church 53, 55–56, 82, 234
Pries, Charles 182
Protestant Hospital 100, 198–202, 205, 245, 247, 249
Protestant Hospital Assoc. 100, 198, 201–203, 205
Pullman 67, 208
Purdy, S. E. 41, 42
Purdy Sparrow 41, 42
Purple, Edwin 38
Putman, A. R. 91
Pyle, Ernie 237, 270

Q

Quale, C. C. 90

R

Raasche, Ortie 26
Radio Club 1–4, 6–7, 22–23
Rainsberger Building 255
Ramion, John 243
Rand, Sally 113
Ray, James & Sarah 173, 174
RCA 112–114
Reading and Boss 91
Redingote, Orrin K. 185
Redpath, George O. 35, 39
Red Apple Hotel 38
Red Cross 91, 161

Reed, George O. 155
Rees, Ben C. 248
Reese Solo Sextet 59
Reglien, Herman 155
Reick, Clarence 182
Reid-Murdoch Company 24
Replogle, Jacob 172
Republican Central Committee 208
Reynolds, George 5
Richter, E. G. 58, 98, 100, 101, 102, 201, 223
Richter, Forest L. 238
Richter, H. W. 177
Richter, J. H. 177
Richter, John C. 90
Richter Hall 236, 237
Ricks, Florence 101
Ridgeway Farm 16
Rieck, William 182
Riggs, Maurice 55
Riggs, Norris 57
Riley, Herb 216
Riverhouse Inn 175, 176
Robb, Charles 98, 102
Robert, Gene Darin 252
Robertson, W. L. 85
Robinson, Arthur R. 6
Robinson, James 55
Robinson, Mrs. William 56
Robinson, William 56
Rockford, IL 18
Roderback, Emma 99
Rogers, Doretta 251, 265
Rogers, Frank A. 201, 225, 249
Rogers, George P. 156
Rogers, Harvey 44
Rogers, J. B. 75, 92, 98, 102, 201
Rogers, Joe 55
Rogers & Harris Circus 251
Rolling Prairie 17–18, 28–29, 89–90, 92, 197, 199, 239
Roman Plunge 85
Root, H. A. 75
Root, James 92
Root Lumber Company 75

Roper, Evan 44
Rose, Earl 43
Rosenbaum, Iva 64
Rosenberg, Nate 43, 44, 46, 179
Rosenthal, Hascall 27
Ross, Glen 158
Rotary Club, La Porte 91
Rotary Club, Michigan City 211
Rotary Club, Valparaiso 91
Rotes, George 185
Rowley, Earl 55, 248
Royal and Ancient Golf Club 177
Royal Metal Manufacturing Co. 87
Royal Theater 53, 67
Royal Typewriter Company 38
Royal University, Dublin 213
Rudolph, Junior 86
Ruess, Mrs. Everette 93
Rumley Flats 52
Rumley Hotel 2, 30, 53, 55, 199, 234
Rupel, Mrs. J. B. 51
Russell, Charles F. 201
Rustic Hickory Furniture Co. 90
Rutledge, James L. 22
Rydzy, Bunny 158

S

Sacred Heart Catholic Church 26
Sadenwater, Fred 158
Sadenwater, Russell 92
Sallwasser, M. L. 185–186
Salvation Army 223
Sampson, Robert 52
Saturday Evening Post 111, 156
Saunders, J. W. 56
Schaedt, Henry 198
Schaeffer, Dick 86
Schaeffer, Freddie 86
Scharfenburg, George 66
Scharfenburg, Laura B. 67
Schnick, Henry 37
Schnick, Rudolph 37
Schnick Brothers Me at Market 37
Schoff, William 28
Schofield, John 192

Schofield, R. W. 159
Scholl, John 252
Scholl, William 45
Schrieber, George 182
Schultz, Fern Eddy 12, 195
Schultz, Ray 182
Schultz, Wilhelmina 41
Schumm, L. G. 20
Schutt, M. A. 39, 41, 58, 159, 160
Schutt Building 252, 254
Scipio Township 27
Screen, Henry M. 91
Sea Scouts 79
Seebirt, Eli 35
Seeling, Lillian 200
Seeling and Schumacker 91
Seibert, George 75
Seitz, Dale 5
Sensow, Don 26
Shadel, Frank 183
Shafer, William L. 39
Shaw, R. D. 42
Sheldon, Arthur C. 30
Shelton, Siegonous Flying Circus 36
Shelton, William 36
Shepherd, Florence 101
Sheridan, Lawrence V. 36
Sheridan Beach 40, 41
Shick, J. B. 177
Shields, C. V. 53, 91, 92–93
Shindell, Ruth 101
Shipley, Bill 86
Shivers, Joe 55
Shockey Flying Service 25
Shon, Mike 159
Siddles, John 198
Siegel, Dr. J. M. 20
Sights, Polly 251, 265
Signitz, George 5
Siljestrom, M. E. 53
Simmerman, Ella 66
Simmons, William Joseph 231
Simpson, A. E. 179, 180
Simpson and Adamson Plumbling 44, 86
Sinkus, John 86

Sinkus, Milda 86
Skibinski, Dorothy Jane 252
Sky Blue Arena 58, 200, 250, 251
Smale, John 41
Small, P. O. 22
Smiley, A. S. 20
Smith, Al 251
Smith, Alban 31
Smith, Ben 92
Smith, Captain 103
Smith, Earl 90–91
Smith, Earl J. 13
Smith, Elizabeth 52
Smith, Joe 74
Smith, Joseph C. 7–8
Smith, Lee 253
Smith, Marjorie 5
Smith, Mayor 31
Smith, Mrs. Ray E. 200
Smith, Myron H. 2
Smith, R. N. 2, 235
Smith, Ralph H. 19
Smith, Ray E. 200, 237
Smith, Russell 53–54
Smith, Zip 174
Smith Bros. Cough Drop Co. 91
Smith Music Shop 7–8
Smitter, Henry 247, 251–252
Snarltown 82
Snodgrass, Mildred 252
Snook, Allen J. 160
Snyder, Arthur H. 179
Society Brand Cloths 32, 38
Society Synconaders 3
Sod Busters 3
Soldier's Park 48
South Shore Country Club 211
South Shore Power Boar Club 77
South Shore Railroad 40, 95
Spaulding, Catherine Barker 44, 180
Spaulding Hotel 42, 57, 58, 81, 105, 140, 179, 198–199, 251
Spaulding Sporting Goods 227
Spitzer, Mrs. Henry 199
Sprague, Frank 86–87

Sprague, Phillip T. 34, 43
Springfield Township 198
Spychalski, Alexander J. 161
Spychalski, Clem 31
St.. Mary's High School 220
St. Anthony Hospital 44, 198
St. Joe Valley Aviation Club 22
St. John's Hall 200, 247, 252
St. John's Lutheran Church 2, 8
St. Paul Lutheran Church 74, 246
Staiger, George J. 201
Standard Oil Building 26
Stanley, L. 56
Stanton, Elizabeth Caddie 61
Starke, George 44
Starland Theater 128
Starrs, Melvin 53, 57
Steffenhagen, R. C. 27
Stein, Louis J. 162
Stephenson, David C. 250
Stephenson, Norman 55
Stephenson, Roscoe 40
Stern, Edward 198
Stern, Fred 162
Stevens, Anthony 234
Stevens, Clarence 55
Stevens, Lucille P. 25, 28
Stevens Hotel 6
Stewart, J. H. 17
Stewart, Marie 54, 57
Stewart, Rev. S. A. 56
Stewart, Sylvanious 52
Stick, August 41
Stillwell 198–199
Stinson Aircraft Corp. 13
Stockwell, W. R. 102
Stokes, R. B. 56
Stone Lake 30, 68
Storen, Mark 162
Storm and Sloan Music Shop 87
Stover, E. B. 101
Street Department, M. C. 91
Strong, Ken 111
Sullivan, Arthur 234–236
Sullivan Machinery Company 36, 223

Sulzberger & Sons Company 211
Summers, C. H. 39
Summy, Paul 250
Sundeen, Thelma 251, 265
Superior Courthouse 201, 234
Swanson, Helen 182
Swastick, W. W. 77
Sweitzer, John 249
Swift Brothers 5
Swihart, Dorothy 64

T

Talos Missile 115
Tamlin, A. G. 177
Tanger, Paul 2
Tarzan 85
Tasker, Hazel 98
Taylor, Clyde L. 58, 98, 102
Taylor, Joseph E. 39
Taylor, Samuel J. 59, 178, 226, 248
Taylor Lumber Company 182
Television Associates 115–116
Terrey, Libbie 64
Terry, J. W. 55
Terry, Mrs. James A. 18
Terry, Van Dien 53
Teverbaugh, R. E. 2, 16
Texaco Petroleum Prod. 22
Thomas, Danny 113
Thomas, Elbert 55
Thomas, Frances 83
Thomas, Gordon R. 83
Thomas, Gus 53
Thomas, Isabelle 56
Thomas, S. A. 55
Thomas, W. E. 55
Thomas, William T. 56
Thompson, B. T. 55
Thompson, Delores 57
Thompson, Enos 57
Thompson, Mrs. Enos 57
Thompson Aeronautical Corp. 21, 29
Three Oaks 19, 90, 93
Three Oaks Museum 93
Throckmorton & Niemer Shoe Store 225

Tillstrom, Burr 114
Tilt, E. W. 98
Timm, Walter 39
ToKay Roof Garden 229
Tomlinson 34
Tonagel, Hugh 198
Tonn, Charles W. 201
Tonn, Fred 182
Tonn and Blank Construction Co. 86, 90–91, 100, 182, 202
Trail Creek 141, 229
Trinity Lutheran Church 6, 90
Truesdell 66, 176, 240
Truesdell, Harvey 176
Tugboat Moore 79
Turnbull, Mrs. G. R. 200, 249
Turnpike Pacer 116
Tuskegee Institute 68
Tuthill, Harry B. 98, 182
Tuthill, Ralph 90
Tyrell, John 41, 42

U

U. S. Life Saving Station 76
U. S. Slicing Machine Co. 26
Ulrich, Anna 101
Underwood, Mrs. William H. 199
Underwood, William H. 43
Unemployment Relief Org. 28, 30
Union Hotel 74
Union Mills 16, 198–199, 241
United Airways 20–21
United Business Men's Protective Assoc. 39
United States iv, 2, 13, 14, 15, 24, 26–27, 30, 37–38, 40–41, 47, 61, 62, 67, 74–75, 77–79, 102–103, 110, 116, 154, 174, 177, 183, 210, 218, 227, 229–230, 231, 232–233, 246, 257, 260–262
Universal Plating Company 223
Updyke, Ralph 30

V

Vail, George T. 85, 98, 180
Vail, Mrs. W. W. 91

Vail, W. W. 98
Valentine, Betty 252
Valentine, Ed 165
Valentine, Kate 69
Van Deusen, Garrits 165
Van Giesen, Ted 78
Van Gisen, Charles 5
Van Kirk, Joseph 37
Van Ouse, Elizabeth 99
Van Spanje, Mrs. Adolph 198
Vel-bert Cottage 199
Vernon, W. T. 56
Vincent, Evelyn 101
Vincent Hotel 41
Vine, James 233
Voss, John C. 192
Vreeland Hotel 219–220

W

Wagner, Harry 181
Wales 7, 8, 55, 166, 227
Wales, Prince of 227
Wales, Taylor 55
Wales, Williams 7
Walgreen's Drugstore 182
Walker, Caryl 91
Walker, William J. 24
Walls, Malay 12
Walters, Mary Jane 252
Wanatah 26, 199, 240–241
Ward, I. I. 42
Warkentine, Henry 59
Warnecke Field 19
Warner, R. W. 57
Warnke, George 43
Warnke Farm 43
Warren, Frank R. 91, 228
Warren, Mrs. Frank R. 91
Warren Building 81, 208, 221, 226, 228–229
Warren Hotel 8
Washington, Samuel 53
Washington Park 34–35, 67, 116, 233, 247, 250, 252
Washington Park Marina 116

Waterford 133, 172, 223
Waterhouse, H. M. 17
Waterhouse, William J. 14
Watson, James E. 6
Watts, Verne 3
Watts Women's Auxiliary 113
Waybright, Alta Peters 70
WBBM 4
WBKB 113–115
Weaver, John R. 166
Webb, Mr. and Mrs. C. D. 19
Wedow, Helen 101
Wehrlely, William 29
Weidergott, Sisters 3
Weiler, Al 166
Weiler, Rudolph 64
Weir, Mrs. E. E. 27
Weir, Nettie 28
Weissmuller, Johnny 85
Welch, Charles 55
Weller, C. E. 237
Wellers Grove 68
Welles, Orson 113
Wells, Lillian 64
Wellsboro 199
Wenzel, John Edward 252
West, George L. 245, 261
Westinghouse Air Brake 116
Westville 65, 173–175, 197–199, 241–242, 244
WFLD 116
Wheeler, Louis "Dad," 167
WHEN TV 115
Whitacre, Ella 204
White, Edwin 98
White, Ina 93
White, Richard 91
White Fleet 76
Wilbur, Christopher C. 244
Wilcox, F. T. 177
Wilk, John 21
Wilke, Herman 182
Will, Virginia 101
Williams 55, 57, 68, 175, 178, 199, 201, 247

290

Williams, A. C. 55
Williams, Billy 175
Williams, Mrs. Roy 199
Williams, Myra 199
Williams, Obie 55
Williams, Walter C. 68
Wilmeth, Martin 8
Wilson, Eloise 101
Wilson, Joe 115
Wilson, Mabel Evelyn 252
Wilson, Mary 251, 265
Wilson, Robert, T. 167
Wilson & Company 211
Winkler, Wilber C. 238
Winn, J. E. 91
Wiseman, T. H. 59
Witt, W. W. 102
WLS 3–5
Wolfe, Arthur 39, 41
Wolfe, C. E. 198
Wolfe, Frank M. 252
Wolfe, George H. 198
Wolfe, Thomas Jr. 39
Wolff, Betty 86
Wolff, Will 168
Wolff Farm 180
Woman's Relief Corps. 65
Wood, F. Glenn 53, 56
Woodman Hall 240
Woolridge, Christine (Eddy) 110
Worley, John 51
Wright, Eugene 3
Wright, John Lloyd 85
Wright Brothers 13
Wright Junior College 113
WSBT 8
WTTW 116
WWAE 6–7

Y

Y. M. C. A. 2, 23, 99, 199
Yankee Slide 234
Yarbo, Albert 55

Z

Zale, Tony 115
Zeese, Herman 169
Zeiske, Mrs. Arthur 251
Zener, D. E. 24
Zerber, Floyd 4
Ziegler, Carl 180
Ziegler, H. I. 90
Ziegler, T. 179
Ziemer, Henry 33
Ziemer, Lewis 33
Zorn Farm 39